Barcelona, Under The Influence...

Barcelona, Under The Influence...

Jack Vickland

Sound Bytes Publishing

S
BP

Copyright © 2019, Jack Vickland

All rights reserved.

Published by Sound Bytes Publishing
Honolulu, HI 96815
USA
www.SoundBytesPublishing.com

ISBN 13: 9781079869514 paperback
ISBN 13: 9781079869514 ebook

Book Design and Cover by The Scott Jordan Group
www.TheScottJordanGroup.com

Jacques Derge, Editor
Steve Marcotte, Managing Editor
Cover Image by Jacques Derge

Printed in USA

5   4   3   2   1

Dedication

This book is dedicated to the memory of Frank Box

FRANK'S SONG

I love Happiness,
I love Spring,
I love Flowers
And Birds that Sing!

But I hate Winter,
I hate Ice,
I hate Snow
And Weather Not Nice!

(*Written, composed, and sung idiotically by Billy and Tarn*)

Quotes/Reviews

"I think a good name for this book would be 'The Last European Writings of Charlie Manson'."
— *Jacques, Barcelona, 1985*

"I liked the part about tits." — *Buxom Jeanne, 1986, Barcelona*

"Give me money so that I can live, You Motherfuckers!"
— *Pirate Steve's busking dialogue between songs. Barcelona, 1985*

"I feel like an oil-trapper's; wife!" — *Hannah, Ireland, 1985*

"I just jerked the suck right out!"
— *Frank, at the bar, holding his tooth in pliers. 1983, Barcelona*

"That was just a little wink in a frying pan."
— *Hannah, describing a trip to Limerick, 1985, Ireland*

"People are always saying to me, 'Who's gone off with the butter!'"
— *Hannah, in the cottage, Ireland, 1986*

"I wouldn't be able to make these sandals very water-proof, would I?
— *Billy, France, 1986*

"I've only got three pipes left — *Billy, Ireland, 1985*

"Jack, look, my sleeping bag is waterproof on the inside!"
— *Joe, after sleeping in the rain, Barna, 1987*

"Tell them to take their fucking purple heart an stick it up their ass!"
— *Crazy Alan, discussing Vietnam, Barcelona, 1985*

"I've had an octopus in my purse all night!" — *Suzanne, Barcelona, 1984*

We had to stay in the car all night! I wasn't going to get out and wade around in those bodies!"
— *Frank, discussing a flood in Pasadena, near a graveyard. Barna, 84*

"The beggar who did the best ever on the Ramblas was the one who had a sign saying he was in a Coma." — *Frank, 1984, Barcelona*

"You Stupid Motherfucking Shit American Twit! It's my Motherfucking Life you're talking about! You're too fucking Stupid to do it!"
— *Steve, answering Ellen's question about busking. 1984, Barna*

"Joe, you've got the fucking thing inside-out!" — *me, 1987, Barna*

"Tell me the truth, Jack, Is Ramon cheating on me?"
— *Fat Sally, asked of me while drinking with her and Ramon. Barcelona, 1984*

"You know Ramon better than that, Sally!" — *my answer*

"Tenk yoo berrymuch, my fren." — *Ramon, to me. Same bar.*

"I got my Period during the Six-Day-War."
— *Hadass, on Coming of Age in Modern Israel. Barna, 1984*

"What means 'Stroking a Throbbing Member'?" — *Hadass, 1984, Tapas*

"I'm not interested in Frank's Love-life! Girrme an OUelette!"
— *Harry, 1984, Tapas*

"No, I want to pursue more spiritual things, seek peace, I don't want to spend my whole life in my lower Chakras."
— *Hannah, discussing our love affair, 1987, Montjuich*

"Isn't it dangerous for us to just walk around in our bare feet? Mightn't we step on a scorpion?" — *Billy, Pyrenees, France, 1986*

What the critics say about "Barcelona, Under the Influence…"

"Great stuff, but I don't believe he drinks that much? Do you have a photograph of the guy?" — *Charles Bukowski*

"I liked the part about 'tits' tOO!" — *Madonna*

"Behind closed doors we loved it, but we could never print such shit!" — *Rolling stone Magazine*

"They should serialize it in Rolling Stone Magazine." — *Mick Jagger*

"One of my dead band members knew that guy?" — *Jerry Garcia*

"I would like to meet him, but that's Off the Record, OK?" — *Princess Diana*

"Everything he writes is correct about how Barcelona is, but how could a guy like that forget to mention that we also print graphic shots of nude women?" — *Interviu Magazine*

"The police finally kicked him out. I've begun an inquiry into why it took so long." — *Pasqual Maragall, Alcalde of Barcelona*

"I have nothing to add to what Mr. Bukowski said." — *Hunter Thompson*

"Alcohol and LSD don't mix, I've always said that. Read this book and you'll see why!" — *Timothy Leary*

"It's not printed in braille yet." — *Stevie Wonder*

"What book is that?" — *Lawrence Ferlingetti*

"I like everything about it except the title."
— *Frank Box, from his collection of essays entitled 'Posthumous humor*

"Don't forget, I paid him to write it!" — *Jacques, a protagonist in the book*

"It is not original." — *Rosa Jaws*

"My father had a much better self-image than this plagiaristic phoney." one of Henry Miller's bastard kids who offered this comment on the condition that they would remain anonymous
"He tells it like it is about Catalan History."
— *Leader of 'Terra Lliure', a catalan Terrorist Group*

"A sheep gone astray." — *Pastor Karnes*

"I've read it." — *the Author's Father*

"It's OK." — *Rebecca, the author's ex-wife*

"Why didn't he write more about the cars in his life?" — *Mechanic~ World*

"Don't ask me?" — *Jack Kerouac's widow*

"I think Neal would have liked it." — *Neal Cassady's widow*

"I'll read it later." — *John Lennon's widow*

"Barcelona will never live it down." — *Jordi Pujol*

"I'll boycott any bookstore that sells it." — *Jacques' Mother*

"Jacky's always had his problems, but we love him and we're proud he's a writer now." — *the author's Mother*

"What a load of crap!"
— *Pirate Steve, protagonist in the book and ex-songwriter for Pink Floyd*

"Home boy does well, we've heard." — *Palo Alto Times*

"He must be a pervert, but I like that." — *David Bowie*

"David's right-on!" — *Elton John*

"Let's just say it's the most profoundly ridiculous piece of literature printed in the History of the English Language." — *Allen Ginsburg*

What the critics say about "Barcelona, Under the Influence..."   xi

"I plan to sue him."   — *Howdy Doody's creator*

"My Come-Back is on the drawing tables thanks to this book."
     — *Andy Devine*

"Yaaaahhhhh!!!!"   — *Montana branch of the Denton Gang*

".. **It** will **be** sold in the USA, simple as that!"
     — *American Censor Department Spokesperson*

"Why isn't there a price on His head?"   — *salmon Rushdie*

"I would never have been watching dirty movies if I had known I could have been reading this book!"   — *Pee Wee Herman*

"He's a Punk posing as a heavy."   — *Charles Manson*

"Gary had literary ambitions too, did you know that?"
     — *Gary Gilmore's little sister*

"If this is what 'Free Speech' is all about, then my time has come!"
     — *Jean-Marie LePen, French Fascist Politician*

"You might notice it isn't 'Madrid, Under The Influence'~'
     — *King of Espanya*

"Four Stars! No, FIVE!!!!"   — *Penthouse*

"Tits!"   — *Playboy*

"So crude that we've decided to investigate the possibilities of serializing it."
     — *Hustler*

"Makes the Marquis de Sade sean like Hans Christian Andersen."   — *Time*

"Don't read it!"   — *Literary Times*

"You have to be a pervert to like this book, I guess. Isn't that what we're supposed to think?"
     — *Kathy Larson, Stanford junior, psychology student, Escondido village*

"I read the whole fucking thing." — *Author's brother*

"I can't wait until he's finished with it." — *Billy, author's son*

"But the worst 'vision' of all is related to your fucking book, it's actual! y become my worst Nightmare!" — *Jacques, the 'Editor'*

"Its well written! Extremely well-Crafted! Juvenile! Scata-logical! Imminently Read-able!" — *Morty Dibble*

Contents

PREFACE	xxiii
A Letter from Jacques to me in San Francisco	xxiii
How I Got to Barcelona, 1984	xxv

PART ONE: CECILE

CECILE	39
THE PARTY OF THE YEAR	43
How Frank Went Blind	43

PART TWO: HADASS

HADASS THE ISRAELITA	48
THE TAPAS, SANTI'S BAR	52
ROSA JAWS	55
RAMBLASFISH, FRANK	59
TITS	61
GOOSES, TITS, ROSA-JAWS, AND GARLICK	62
HADASS' BEE-OGRAPHY	64
JACQUES AND TAPIES, SOCIAL RETARD	67
Peter and Camels	67
CLINK, A DURO	71
DINNER AT THE TAPAS	75
El Loco painting	75
LA SAGRADA FAMILIA, MALLORCA	77
Carole Doesn't Slit my Throat in Sitges	77
HADASS AND THE TOWER OF DAVID	80
PHIL AND RENE'S PARTY	82
PATENTED PENGUINS	87
HADASS' PAD/THE PAD	89
WOODY ALLEN SIESTA	91

PIRATE STEVE'S RECIPE FOR ALI-OLI	93
Homing Jews	93
THE COWBOY SONG	100
EL MONSTRO	102

PART THREE: FRANK AND BILLY

I TAKE MY FIRST DRINK IN THIS BOOK	109
TRACY'S PARTY, PETER'S SHOES	111
Crow, Vivian	111
A FISH IS DANCING, DARK	114
A LIGHT CASE OF DT'S	115
Candy Turds	115
Barcelona Diarrhea	115
STORES IN SPAIN	117
HOWDY DONNA, DOODY'S SISTER	119
LORI, THE WHITE DONKEY	121
LORI'S TRIP TO FINLAND	123
FUCKING ISRAEL	126
NEW YEAR'S EVE, 1984	127
THE THREE KINGS	128
FRANK, DAVID BOWIE, HOWDY DOODY	131
SUE, WHY I HIT HER	132
ON THE STREET AGAIN	134
Frank, Peter; Norma and Rebecca in La Sardana	134
ON THE STREET AGAIN, AGAIN	137
Six Die in Barcelona	137
McDONALD'S SUICIDE, MICHAELANGELO, SNOT	140
NORMA'S GOING-AWAY PARTY, THE HAPPINESS OF STONES	143
SANTI'S, THE OPERA CAFE, UNCONDITIONAL LOVE	147
ANOTHER NIGHT AT THE OPERA CAFÉ	155

VISIONS FROM 'THE HOWDY DOODY SHOW'	159
Voices in My Head from another Dimension	159
THE ISRAELI GUARDS AND THE TOWER OF DAVID	161
THE ANDALUCIAN NATIONAL ANTHEM	166
The Catalan National Anthem	166
The Street-Beggars National Anthem	166
The Andalucian National Anthem	166
AMANI IS EVEN A WORSE FUCKER THAN I THOUGHT	168
GANDALF, BILLY, PETER, FRANK, JACQUES, VIVIAN	171
ON THE STREET. VIV. MICK. SUZANNE. THE MEADCM	175
I FALL IN LOVE WITH A CLOWN	177
Crazy Alan	177
AN EVENING WITH MY FRIENDS, AT THE OPERA CAFE	180
Suzanne and Gumming, Tolstoy	180
ELLEN PATRONIZES ME	189
EL MONSTRO, MY BLOODY NEIGHBOR, AGAIN	192
THE SHIT PAGE, BILLY, REBECCA, AND JACK	193
THE OPERA CAFE AGAIN	195
My Grandmother Appears	195
Frank and Materialism	195
Peter Explains Reincarnation to Ellen	195
The Problem with Ordering	195
SANTI'S AGAIN	200
Frank Patronizes and Insults Peter	200
Yet Another Night at The Opera Cafe	203
Frank explains auras to Ellen	203
ON THE STREET AGAIN, ONCE MORE	208
Lingering With No Visible Means of Survival	208
HOWDY DOODY, ARNOLD PALMER, MUGGINGS	211
Hit with a Stick, It Hurts to Write	
"Give me Money so that I can Live, you Motherfuckers!"	211
THE NIGHTLY MUGGING AND HOW IT CAME ABOUT	217
Rabbit, The Painter And Poet	217
Another Mugging	218

SITGES, SITGES, WHO'S GOING TO SITGES?	220
ON THE STREET, AS USUAL	225
Rabbit, Tracy and Crow	225
Meson Hadass	225
The Daily Ladrone Report:	227
Catalan Bread	229
Billy and The Brown Pigs, Again I Patronize Ellen, Again	230
Frank and Ellen Play Tennis in The Santa Clara Cafe	232
Cold Stone Streets (Yayy! 1)	233
Museum Hadass	234
European Babies. Maria-Jose and Logical Sadness. Chopped Liver	236
FRANK'S CARNIVAL REPORT	238
A LETTER FROM HADASS IN ISRAEL	240

PART FOUR: HANNAH

THE CLOWNS ARE BACK!	244
In Bed with Clowns	246
ON THE STREET ONCE MORE	248
The Sardana	248
The Peanut Gallery	248
ON THE STREET AGAIN, AS ALWAYS	251
Why do All The Secretaries Dress Like Whores?	251
FRANK'S TRIP TO MOROCCO	252
Why Billy Likes Puppies	252
Peter's Brown Fat	252
HANNAH, HANNAH, HANNAH	254
RABBIT	258
WAITING FOR HANNAH	260
MORE HANNAH	264
"Why do you do this?"	268
HOW I CAME TO LOVE CLOWNING, AID CLOWNS	273
THE 'FALLAS' IN VALENCIA	276
BARCELONA NEWS/PAD NEWS	283

SNUFFLING WITH HANNAH	284
AN ISLAND OF DRUNKEN CALM IN A FROTHING SEA OF CIVIC PRIDE	287
IDIOT WIND; THE WIND BLEW' MY BOOK IN THE STREET	290
Hannah Gets Pregnant	291
Frank's Teepee	292
"Why is There A Yankee Begging?!"	293
Lunch on The Patio with The Gals El Monstro Again	294
THE PEANUT GALLERY AGAIN	297
Atomic Bomb Dream	297
BUSKING	301
Love, Babies, Sailing Boats, and Mush	301
Opera Cafe Wake	301
Another Ladrone Report	301
Daisy, Amber, and Rose-Petal	301
DAISY IS DEAD	307
"Let's See The Baby"	307
Bleedi Hannah	307
Blow-Job And Brown Rice	307
EASTER WITH CLOWNS	310
THE BROWN PIGS AND BILLY, AGAIN	312
TRACY	314

PART FIVE: ON THE ROAD

THE MEADOW, A PARADISE	316
SHOESTRING CIRCUS IN SITGES	319
THE TRIP TO IRELAND, 1985	324
Pamplona, Boredeaux, La Rochelle, Brittany	324
AN UN-KNOWING POSTHUMOUS LETTER TO FRANK	330
A LETTER TO JACQUES, FRANK IS DEAD	332
TAKING A SHIT IN IRELAND	334
THE WEIRD TRIP TO MLREPOIX FRANCE	336
Jack and Billy and Ubiquitous Ladrones	336

PART SIX: MONTJUICH

BORED, SCARED, AND UGLY	350
PORTION OF A LETTER TO HANNAH IN ENGLAND. HANNAH'S 600 ORGASMS	352
BILLY'S BIRTHDAY PARTY	354
My Birthday Blowout	354
1/2-BRICK AND SECOND-HAND CARS	358
CHRISTMAS PICNIC IN BADALONA	360
THREE WORD PLAY	364
"Stick it In!"…Hannah, that first night	364
MONTJUICH AGAIN, 1987	367
The Truck Fire	367
Hannah's Fat Lip	367
The End?	367
THREE YEARS LATER	370
THE SWALLOWS OF MONTJUICH	373
THE BREEZE IS BLOWING GENTLY	376
MONTJUICH, IN THE APARTMENT, WITH A BROKEN LEG	377
A Frightening Experience: Rabbit and Joe on Coke	377
It's Pretty Hopeless	378
Alfie's Stapler	379
The Little Things	379
The Lizard in My Cast	380
Hard- Hearted Hannah	381
ALFIE'S HERNIA	382
THE LAST THING I WROTE IN BARCELONA	384
(A Letter to Jacques in Italy)	384
Overlooking The Picasso Museum with A Broken Leg	384
Hotel California, Low Rapes	384
The Next Day, Saturday	388
AFTERWORD…	396
BARCELONARIO DIARO GLOSARIO	397

APPENDIX

A LETTER TO BILLY IN GREECE	406
A LETTER FROM MY SON BILLY IN GREECE	408
A LETTER FROM JACQUES (MY EDITOR?)	412
ANOTHER LETTER FROM JACQUES (MY EDITOR?)	415
A THIRD LETTER FROM JACQUES IN SPAIN	418
A FOURTH LETTER FROM JACQUES	421
LETTER FROM HANNAH	424
THE ABU-DHABI NATIONAL ANTHEM (TUNE OF 'GOODNIGHT, IRENE)	425
"THE VERY BIT OF IT"	427
JACK NICHOLSON IS MY FAVORITE ACTOR	428
ARRREST RECORD	430
THE MENU, MESON HADASS	433
DRAWING OF BILL AND JACK	434

The Gothic Barrio Guide Barcelona

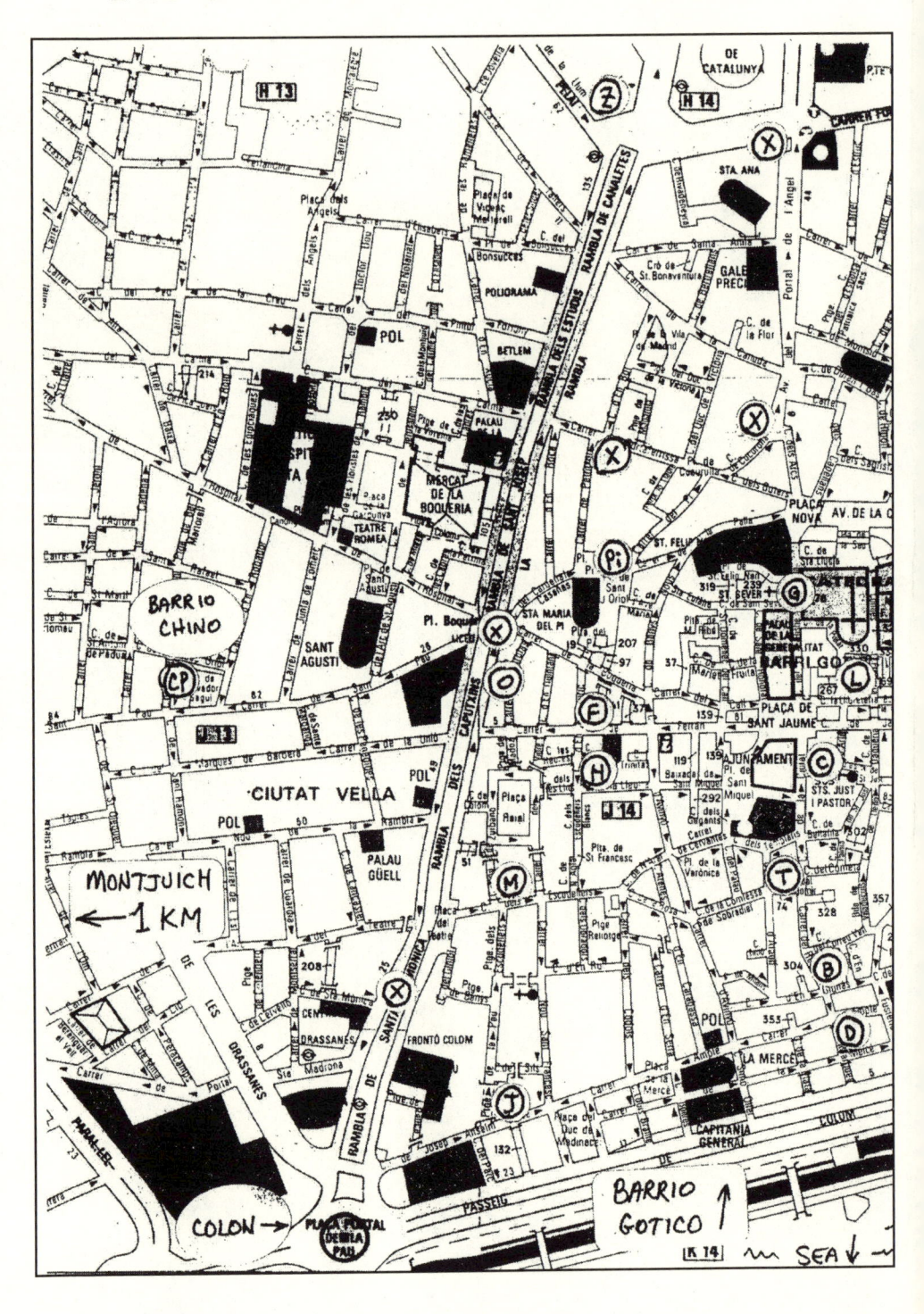

The Gothic Barrio Guide — Barcelona

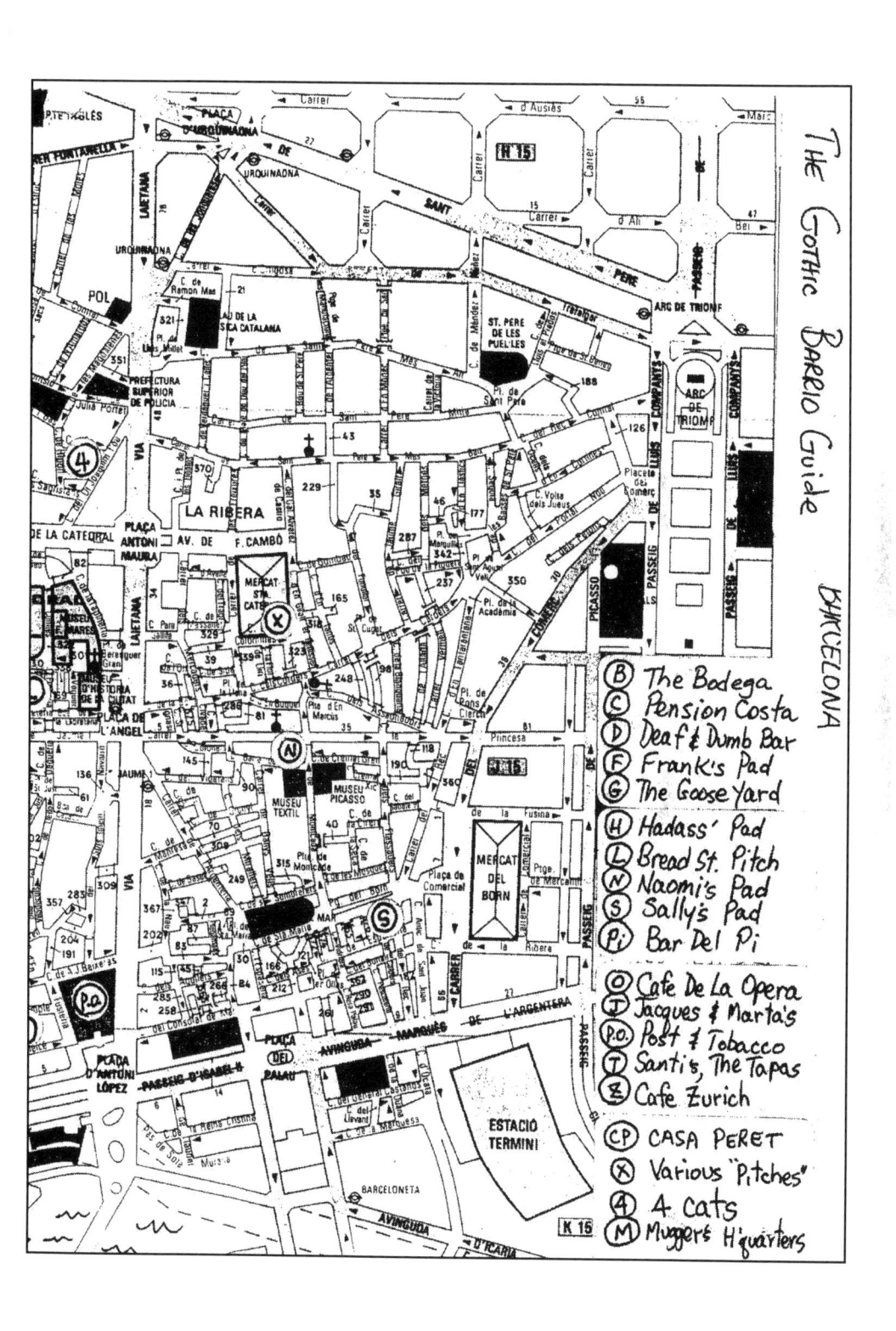

B The Bodega
C Pension Costa
D Deaf & Dumb Bar
F Frank's Pad
G The Goose Yard
H Hadass' Pad
L Bread St. Pitch
N Naomi's Pad
S Sally's Pad
Pi Bar Del Pi

O Cafe De La Opera
J Jacques & Marta's
P.O. Post & Tobacco
T Santi's, The Tapas
Z Cafe Zurich

CP CASA PERET
X Various "Pitches"
4 4 cats
M Muggers H'quarters

Preface

A LETTER FROM JACQUES TO ME IN SAN FRANCISCO
"24 May 1984 Barcelonaaaaaaaaaaa !!!

Dear Scandalizor,

Lately I've been spreading your Legend about, telling people about you, explaining your demise as sympathetically as I can. It's an old role of mine, but it's been resurrected these days. People always ask me about you, why even today I shared your Ed Sullivan message with Norma who had come over to reclaim her books. Once again I miss you, but for a couple of months (I'll admit it), I didn't. It was sufficient to recall your Cocaine-pocked face upon arrival for your (?) Holiday in Spain, and then the final visual of you in your Hats upon departure. Everything (almost) in between, it seemed better to block out, but now, yes, I miss you. Barcelona is still here, but there are a few new bars and a few new weirdos. Everything else is the same, more or less. Frank is still away, and Carol disappeared about the same time. Tapas is still there, but some of the regulars aren't, some of the Spanish regulars I mean. (For instance the Dunce who used to punch Manolo). I don't live at Pension Costa anymore. Now I live close to that Plaza I used to paint all the time, in an apartment with a girl named Marta that I met about three days after you left. She remembers you from seeing you one day when you were lingering with me in front of the Picasso. You don't remember her, but I think you might have almost hassled her when she walked by one day. I was almost going to get married but I chickened out; instead I'm just 'in love', a new concept for me. Marta doesn't speak any English and so now I speak Spanish, better than you probably. I stopped smoking hash, but otherwise I am your same old boy.

    I don't have to worry about money too much anymore because of Marta, but I still pose as a 'painter'. These days I am working on a commission, a painting of Santa Maria Del Mar, that big church over by Sally's neighborhood. Today some LaDrones stole my knapsack with all of my paintbrushes inside while I was in a cafe having a Con Leche. I thought I was keeping an eye on my stuff, but obviously now I realize I must not have been. The weather here has been bad, stupid, terrible, rainy, depressing, too cold, grey, ridiculous, horrible. It's no place for a painter, and if I didn't have a girlfriend

I would seriously consider becoming a bum burn again. I get to spend whole fragments (segments) of time doing nothing, or writing letters, or thinking about the Time. I eat good and listen to records, or I take hot showers; or I go out to see what's happening in the chalker's section on Ramblas. It's a new life for me, in a way, the Bohemian's Dream come true. The only problem is that, in a way, it can be boring. It's the first time in my hippie life I've seen things in this way.

Maria "Jose had a baby girl, named it Cenia. Ramon was happy, Leonardo not as much. Sally has a black eye because she took a radio away from some Gypsies who were blasting the music next to her classroom, and she paid the price because now she has a big black eye. (She wears a black patch over it, so her Punk act is together.) Phil is still here, lingering as ever. He decided not to go back to the States, a wise decision I've been long awaiting. Doug (Ricky) left eons ago, on his bike. Peter left too, went to Italy, and his last letter was from Yugoslavia where he was 'on vacation' after making 34,000 pesetas in a week in Italy (chalking). There is a vacuum where once there was frivolity, but things will come around. I'm sure of it.

I got a letter from Rebecca on the same day that your letter came, so I already know she'll be here shortly. (and Billy) I'll take care of them, you know. Already pension Costa is prepared. Sue writes to me, twice now, says she'll be back in Barcelona ASAP. I also know that I have more contact with her than you, which I understand in part (but only in part?)

The next time you write try and write. Like I say, I miss you again now, and so any news is Good News. Even if you tell me that you really will return to Barcelonaaaaaaaa.... Seriously, please write, tu amigo, Jacques."

(Author's note, 1992: so, as soon as I could, I sold my boat business and headed for Barcelona again, burning all bitches behind me.)

More Preface

HOW I GOT TO BARCELONA, 1984

Why it took me a week and a thousand dollars to get from San Francisco to here:

Jesse and Diane, two very good friends, He: for fifteen years, She: his 20-year-old girlfriend, daughter of my old girlfriend Sue, drop me off at the SF airport (it was difficult to get them out of the motel room where they have been living for a year snorting coke) and I get on the plane for England right according to Schedule. All goes well until we are over Cleveland, where I decide, "Well, I've made it, I'm practically in Barcelona already. I'll just have ONE BEER before we land in Boston." Famous Last Words.

There is a mere three hour layover in Boston and then it's Directly On To London. I am booked straight through on a Discount Ticket. No Problem. I mosey on down to the Airport Bar and order a Heineken. During my second beer I strike up a conversation with a young girl who is waiting for her old man to fly in. He won't be in for a few hours. We talk. She likes me. I make her laugh. I make her eyes get big with stories of weird people and places. We are having a grand time of it there in the airport bar. Another beer, I'll buy. "Oh, I hope my boyfriend gets to meet you, he's interested in the same things you are and would Love to hear your stories." I'll Bet.

Another beer. Fifteen minutes til plane-to-London-time. No problem. The bartender warns me that it is getting late. No Problem. I saunter out of the bar (five beers gone forever), head for the luggage lockers, retrieve my luggage, and head for the boarding area. I round the corner in time to see the nose of the 747 pulling away from the ramp, "Can't you stop it?, I plead. "Heh , heh, no, it can't be stopped.", from behind the ticket counter. Smiles all around. Everyone is having a Great Time, at my Expense. No REAL Problem. My ticket is good for tomorrow also. So, This could be Fun: A whole day to kill in Boston. I've never seen it before. Oh Boy! An Adventure, for FREE.

I head for the subway after stashing my bags and arrive in downtown Boston about dark. I inquire if there might be an Irish Bar in the neighborhood. Indeed there is. In Boston there are Irish Bars. I'm Home! My Grandfather and his Father both ran Irish Bars in San Francisco and Oakland before they died of alcohol.

That night I made many friends. I don't think I slept. At least, if I did sleep, I don't remember where it was.

In the morning I get on a boat which I think is a harbor-tour boat. It takes me for two hours up the River Charles to some small town where there isn't even an Irishman, let alone a bar. I get back on for the return trip to Boston. They sell beer on the boat, so, to kill time on the way back I get a little high on Indira Ghandi's Death. I am almost crying by the time we get back. I mean, she was an old lady, why kill an old lady? That's what I'm asking all the other passengers on the boat. "Why Kill An old Lady? 1", I ask, holding up the headlines.

Upon docking, I head for: An Irish Bar. I hit a couple more Irish Bars, wherein I am known as Jack Mulcahy, and then take the city-tour on a cable-car-type bus. I bring along a couple of Heinekens just in case. I am drinking only Heinekens at this point: two dollars a pop. I get to see Boston.

"Why kill an old lady?", out the open window of the bus, holding up the paper. Everyone seems to agree with me. Why? What the fuck are Seeks.

Well, it's mid-afternoon now and time to head for: An Irish Bar. There seems to be some kind of festival going on over there: "Think I'll head over that way and see if there's any good bars.", thinks I. I sit down next to a pretty woman and order a beer. She and I begin talking. I tell her that she is Beautiful. She says, "You have just made an old lady very happy!" "How old are you?" "Fifty." "That's not old!" Moving in now, can smell it, "I find you very attractive." (I actually do). She's Jewish, from Connecticut. Came down for a couple of days to meet her daughter's fiancee. This has made her feel old. Her daughter is going to get married. She doesn't like the guy. She's divorced. Lonely. Probably hasn't had a good fuck for quite a while. She senses that I may have some potential in this area. She's right. Both of us are grinning like maniacs, eyes glowing. We can both picture us writhing in ecstasy. We have agreed to hit another bar or two and then head for her hotel. The bartender refuses to serve me another beer. I have been describing passersby to my new friend in a loud voice and basically cracking-up the customers. I demand to speak to the manager because I will NOT be cut-off by some idiot in a rabbit costume. (there is some Bostonian Festival going on and the bartender is dressed like a rabbit, ears and all). The manager comes and asks what the problem is. I tell him that "this idiot rabbit refuses to give me another beer just because I'm talking loud, but I'm not drunk, I'm from San Francisco and I'm Irish and talking loud shouldn't be against the rules cuz there's a festival going on anyway, so gimme another beer, I mean, big deal, loud talk, (to the whole bar): you hear that folks, they're going to cut me off, the bunny is, because I laugh and talk loud!"

My new friend is laughing with me at this point and the rabbit takes his mask off to prove that he is not a COMPLETE IDIOT. He wants to fight, but I don't have my .22 with me. We leave that bar and right outside, in the middle of the carnival, I somehow gather a crowd by yelling how happy I am, This Lady and I are in Love, it's a Wonderful Life etc.

My friend and I head for another bar, I lose her in a crowd. No Problem. I head for the bar where we were heading before I lost her. Well, it's an Irish Bar, underground, mellow, I have a few beers, mellow now, waiting for my New Lover, (I'm going to live at her house in Connecticut for a month and fuck her a lot and make her feel young. In return, I get to drive the Porsche and watch the video-machine and otherwise indulge my upper-middle-class fantasies. plus, women over 40 give Excellent Blow-Jobs, she tells me.) Well, She doesn't show. Don't know if I scared her, or we got lost. I prefer to think it was the latter, but Jacques is pretty sure that she "ditched" me.

A couple more: Irish Bars, then back to the airport. Somehow I gather a crowd in the airport. They are laughing. The airport police are not. "What are you doing?" "Singing and Dancing and making these people laugh." "Why are you here?" "I'm heading for Spain."

The Airport Police and I head for the TWA counter. They want to make sure I don't gather any more crowds, they tell me. The guy at TWA remembers me and says that I CANNOT get on the plane to London. I promise, PROMISE, that I will just fall asleep. Tough shit, he says.

Now, this is a Problem!

Somehow, it's midnight, airport bar, I have to wait til morning to try to get a refund on my ticket. It expired at midnight. I hang around til morning trying to sleep on a bench, and talk to the ticket people. Their Attitude: Tough Shit, kid. So, I'll just buy another ticket (money is no problem?), BUT, first I have to fly to Newark New Jersey in order to catch a People's Express (cheap) to London. I fly into Newark and have twenty-four hours to kill. What to do? What to do? Let's see: how about a Library? naaaaah. Well, how about finding a nice park and sitting in the grass? Naaaaah. I know: I'll go into New York City and find: AN IRISH BAR!

I take a bus into NY, Manhattan, and walk to O'Grady's (I think) and have a couple of beers there and fall in love with the chinese waitress who is unbelievably bubbling and happy. I check my bags, I forget where, and just start walking around going into bars. At one point I'm sitting in a bar where I realize that I am the only one present who is not obviously of African Descent. A guy about my age chats with me for a while and we explain who we are and what we're doing and Become Friends. He says he will hang out with me til tomorrow to make sure that I don't accidentally get killed in the early morning in New York because I don't know enough to be able to tell who is actually dangerous and who (everyone else) just Seems Dangerous.

We go bar-hopping and he shows me around Manhattan until the next morning. It's a big city. A couple of times we ducked into hotels or alleys because he would see a gang coming down the street. I probably would have wanted to make friends with them and they might have killed me because they thought I was rich just because there were buttons on my shirt and my socks matched. He turned out to be a great guy and we have promised to stay in touch, but forgot to exchange addresses.

By this time I had been living in bars and airports for about three days. I had completely lost track of time but was beginning to realize that I would have to CONCENTRATE to get myself to London. Some of my bags were already there, waiting for me at Heathrow. Or Gatwick. I still had this typewriter and a red valise that belonged to my grandmother, Ruth Mulcahy.

Somehow I got on the plane to London. I had a few beers on the flight over, but couldn't sleep. I can never sleep on trains and planes. I met an English Woman in the airport in Newark. I fell in love with her, but I'm not sure how she felt, because she had three kids and a farmer-husband and three dogs. But, o my, she had the cutest little classic English features, and the cutest little accent, and she was forty-five but looked thirty (from being a farmer's wife) and she was on the verge of looking for some excitement in her life. It was probably a close call for her: We agreed, maybe, to go to a bar in London when the plane landed. (I got a letter from her a few months later in Barcelona; She'd waited for me in the cafe, I'd gone to the bar.) She had been worried about me the first night in Newark and was on the bus I took into Manhattan. She would have been a good Mother to me and I could have gradually snuck in the sex part later.

I landed at Gatwick. My bags were at Heathrow, waiting impatiently.

It was the middle of the afternoon. I met a young (30) English fellow on the train from Gatwick to Victoria Station. He said he knew some pretty nice bars around London and would be glad to show then to me. We became friends. The English pubs were all that you could ask for in a bar. There were all sorts of people hanging about. There were some wonderful arguments going on and my new friend and I joined into a couple of them. We met a couple of American Chicks who were on their way to Hong Kong via some extravagant route. They acted like lesbians, in that they always smiled knowingly at each other, and I was determined to get to the bottom of it, for sure. Maybe they were librarians, I don't know. Well, we all hung out and argued and generally carried on (the beer is strong there). At dark I left with the librarians so they could help me find a cheap "bed and breakfast hotel". I rented a bed in a room for ten pounds and headed back out into London. I went to a couple of pubs in the area but they were a little too subdued for my tastes. I found a restaurant and had begun to think that English food was pretty weird when I realized it was a Greek restaurant. I went back to the hotel after another pub and tried to sleep. I'd been awake for four or five days at this point. I just sort-of dozed fitfully until dawn. There was a lonely, catatonic Irishman in the same room who LIVED there and was on the dole and had almost no spark in him even though he was my age and looked like one of my tribe.

I headed out to Heathrow on a double-decker bus (That was fun) and retrieved my big bag. Bought the London Times and had a beer. Found out that I could catch a train to Barcelona in half an hour so I boogied back to the hotel by cab, got my shit and took the train to Dover.

Saw the white cliffs thereof, got on a big boat and sat down as near to the bar as possible and waited for it to open. A blonde girl sat down opposite me and we chatted til the bar opened whereupon I purchased four cans of beer. It looked like we were going to have an interesting crossing. She was young and lived in Reims. Her mother was English and her father was Lithuanian and she was studying in Reims (they thought). Actually she was living with a junkie (well, her boyfriend was a junkie and she spent a lot of time at his place). She Liked to Have Fun. We had a couple more beers. She decided to bypass her change of trains for Reims and go into Paris with me to make sure I found the right Irish Bar.

While riding the train into Paris, The Girl and I began Fondling and Real French Kissing. It was Wonderfully Erotick. I continued drinking those cute little bottles of red wine that you can get in the Bar-car. I vaguely remember getting off the train in Paris, and my friend taking me to 'An Irish Bar', where I had a bottle of wine. The next thing I know I am on a Train, the wrong one, headed for Northern Spain. I had to get off in some town and change again so that I would get on the correct one, but I left my bags on the one I was on. Or something. I got The Girl's address, but I don't know her name because it just says "The Kiss" on the piece of paper. (She also wrote to me a few months later. We corresponded and I've since lost her address) (fool).

Well, I finally made it to Perpignan, where I was supposed to change trains again. I had by this time retrieved my bags somewhere. The train that I was supposed to get on (Spanish?) did not sell wine. I had ten minutes before it left, so I stashed my bags and went back to the one I'd just gotten off of, which had a Bar Car. It left the station as I was ordering a bottle of wine, and I wasn't able to get off until Toulouse, where I spent about 8 hours in a couple of bars, and was finally able to catch a train for Gerona. When I got to Gerona they phoned around for me and found that my bags had been sent back to Perpignan. No Problem. I just caught the next train for Perpignan, four hours later, and found my baggage there. I went over to a bar that I'd been to the year before and had a bottle of wine, before catching the next Barcelona-bound train which brought me to Jacques' Front Yard (Plaza St. Juame) early in the evening, after having been awake and drinking for a week. He was glad to see me and took me to the Bar-Bar where we had a couple of beers and I acted out my trip for him.

I decided that after all this travelling I was entitled to have a couple of drinks and let off a little steam, so I went on a Minor Rampage for a couple of days, to everyone's Joy.

Barcelona, under the Influence...

BARCELONA

November 20, 1984

I sit here and stink.
I am the Novelist of the Ramblas. I can prove it: I am sitting on the sidewalk writing my first novel: I have my typewriter sitting on an old orange crate on the sidewalk of the Ramblas, which is the heart of Catalonia. I just set up the crate (table) and the typewriter down the street but was run off by the local police, a blue cop. He asked me what I was doing and I told him I was writing a novel. He couldn't comprehend it and told me to move on. There was a crowd of about twenty gathered before I had typed three lines.

It seems that this writing-of-a-novel-in-the-street may be my new source of funds. I have a sign nailed to the front of the crate which reads "Novelista de las Ramblas", and another underneath it which reads "Poquito de Ayuda, Gracias". The idea is that I am a starving artist, living a poor life dedicated to My Art. There are Street-Chalkers, Street-Musicians, Street-Magicians, and just plain down-and-out Beggars. Why not a Street-Writer? Well, there is one now. I even have a visor on, which reads "ESCRITOR" (writer).

I left California about three weeks ago with about $1200 in my pocket. I am down to my last 100 pesetas (60 cents). I'm not sure if this is Art, or Begging, but since I must, I must.

I am living in a pension with a young French girl, Cecile, who speaks practically no English or Spanish. Our communication is extremely labored: the only words I have been able to speak to her in French so far are, "Je te amor", I love you, I thought. It turns out that I told her, "I want to bite you." I believe this is corning true. I bit her last night in the midst of our first REAL attempt.

Cecile sells jewelry on the streets and has been doing so for about three years in Italy, Greece, Turkey, and Spain. She is 23 and beautiful. Blonde. Blue eyes. A Hippy Dream, for sure. So Tight. MY, MY. She is standing here now looking over my shoulder and wondering what I am saying about her. This could turn out to be Wonderful. She will certainly believe that I am a Writer.

Until I teach her English she will not be able to judge the Artistic Content of the Novel. She can, in good faith, write home that she is living with a writer. We met three days ago on the train from Almeria to Barcelona. I was there to visit my son, Billy, and his mother, my ex-wife, Rebecca. They are living there in virtual Poverty and Bliss, with a fifty-year-old American Wacko-Socialist named John. John was born on Malta but lived in the U.S. for about twenty years. He hates America, and Americans. They've been travelling with him for about three months. He is indoctrinating them with his version of world politics. They smoke a lot of Hashish and eat cheaply and well. Their apartment is about a block from the Mediterranean. Billy spends his days reading and making things out of junk which he finds on his twice-weekly scourings of the local dump. He has learned from John how to Survive with practically nothing. He has grown up incredibly in just six months in Espana. He taught me how to make hash pipes out of bamboo, which grows near the dump. They work! He also instructed me on how to smoke hash.

I asked him, "Do you know how old you were when I started smoking hash?"

"No."

"Well, Amy wasn't born yet."

Amy is his oldest sister, 19, living in Oregon. She's raising Sally, 13, the Punk Rocker of the family. They tried living with me in San Francisco recently, but found my drug-induced states difficult to relate to. They took my car and $100 and headed back for Oregon. The only trouble was that when they got there, their mother was deep in Spain. They will probably be joining us here in Spain in June. If they can save their money.

I quit drinking alcohol a few days ago because my choices and options were diminishing: Either become a writer (finally) in Barcelona, or buy some wine and die in Almeria. I chose the former. Here I am. (It looks like I've made about a hundred pesetas, so far. Good, I've doubled my money already).

The Ramblas, in most guide-books, is described as either the Most Beautiful Street in Europe, or Almost the Most etc. etc. It's True. There is always something happening here, It Never Closes. It's like a jungle in more ways than one.

Barcelona is "The City" in Spain, as far as I'm concerned. Wait here long enough and every True Weirdo is sure to wander by. Just now Frank (the Yank) and Amani (the Negro-American) have stopped by to groove on the beginnings of my Literary Career. They couldn't help but criticize my Office. The cardboard which covers the front of the crate says "leche esterilizada" on it. Frank suggested that people will think that I am selling Milk, and in his role as "Head Artist" he has advised me to repair my scene during my break. It's Siesta right now, which has caused the pedestrian traffic to slow down. Frank has just told me that Ahmed (pronounced Awkmedd) butted a friend's teeth out with his head last night. Ahmed is the Dueno (manager?)

of Pension Costa, where various artistic Americans have taken over. Pension Costa is where I prefer to live in Barcelona. It's where Billy and Rebecca also lived when they were here. My old friend, Jacques, the painter, lives there also.

Jacques has been here for about a year. He began with chalking on the street and gradually worked up to Canvasses, which he now produces on commission. He is surviving through his Art and provides critical light for my experiences. He also loaned me the nails for attaching the cardboard to the crate.

A black-man (African?) just came up to me with a 100pta coin and handed it to me saying, "Money, money."

I said, "For me? For me?"

He said "No, no."

I handed it back to him (I could already taste the soup I was going to buy with it tonight). He wandered off mumbling something that sounded like "telephone".

What I really must get is a pair of those gloves with the ends of the fingers cut off. I've looked, but so far all I can find is the regular kind. It's Cold and Windy. Cecile has just returned with some whole wheat bread and some cheese. We live on it.

I've moved down the Ramblas about a hundred feet, so that the sun is shining on me. I knew it would some day if I was patient.

I had a printing press when I was eight years old and published a neighborhood newsletter for a few months with stories about puppies and who has a new bike. I retired at nine so that I could go out into the world and gather some experience. I got it. I was arrested eleven times by the time I was thirteen. (NO sex crimes, yet, though). My arrests have passed fifty, at this time, and I have yet to Rob, Murder, or even Punch someone. My crimes have always had something to do with tail-lights, noise, beer, girls, or plant substances (see appendix); I am innocent. Now, I'm forty, and am taking up publishing where I left off. This is the Ramblas Newsletter, coming to you LIVE from the Heart-of-Spain! (Jacques got a new foul-weather coat).

Catalonia. Is it a part of Spain, or not? Madrid says it is. The Catalonians say it shouldn't be. It's been independent of Spain ten times longer than it's been a part thereof.

Ferdinand married Isabella one time, and they decided to share their possessions. Well, he owned Catalonia, she owned Castille, and the two together were the beginnings of "Espanya".

Of course, there's more to it than that: She was frigid and into Bondage. He was quasi-impotent. For kicks they would send weird or troublesome subjects out in boats to see what they could find. They got a big kick out of it when 'Cristolbol Colon' wanted to sail west. They said, "Why not, what harm can the asshole do?"

Everyone was in great spirits on the day of departure. They had given him three of the crappiest boats they had; one was so small and leaky that it had been retired from the harbor trade years before.

Ferdinand and Isabella held an Official Goodbye Party for him, and half the people in attendance were in complete ecstasy just being near such a weird guy as 'Colon'. Not to mention that he was planning to sail West. West!

Nobody would say anything directly to Colon for fear of discouraging him, but whenever he wasn't around the Mirth was Unbridled. Courtiers could be found rolling on the ground, drooling, and holding onto their stomachs and gasping for air because they had just seen the boats he was taking. For months after he left all you had to do to cause a fit of laughing was say, "Ninya, Pinta, Santa Maria".

Madness was the Court Style all over Europe at that time, but Ferd and Izzy, as they were affectionately called behind their backs, had raised it to a High Art. The Ceremony went off with only a few hitches: a couple of heart attacks from over-laughing. Colon was the only one present who didn't realize the true source of the Joy at the Ceremony. No one was about to ruin it all by pointing out to him that sailing West was a Sure Sign of Madness.

The Crescendo of Hilarity reached it's peak as the crew of Mental-deficients attempted to untie the sinking barges with which Colon was going to commit suicide. Izzy was so elated that she could hardly wait until the three boats had cleared the harbor before dragging Ferd down to the cellar for their daily session of 'Whips and Empire'; "Ninya, unh, Pinta, unh, Santa Maria! Unh! Unh! Colon! I'm Cominnngg!!". As far as they were concerned, the tons of gold which came in later from South America meant little compared to what Colon had done for The Royal Sex Life. If Izzy could have had orgasms from Regular Sex, Americans might be speaking Polish, or French, to this day. But not Spanish.

To promenade the Ramblas, one must be jaded. The Citizens of Barcelona have seen it all. They have only to walk on their main street for a few blocks and they will encounter every form of Foreign and Home-Grown Madness which exists on the planet outside of Iran. Directly across the street from me is the entrance to a street, "Carrer Nou de la Rambla", a home for transvestite whores who can't make it in their regular world. A half a block to my right is the Barcelona Opera House, reputed to be one of the most beautiful in Europe.

There is a Race of Small People. Some of them are here in Barcelona. No one warned me about them. No one ever said, "In Europe there is a race of people who only grow to be four to four and a half feet tall. They are formed as are other human beings, but they are small.", I had no idea they existed til I got here. It seems that they must come originally from a country where berets are made; I rarely see a full-grown male without a beret. They don't appear dangerous in any way (unlike the Gypsys), and seem also to be very busy. They are always going somewhere and you can rarely find them just 'standing about' (unlike some Spanish, and the majority of English and Americans that I know). It seems that it would be unwise to treat them the way midgets are treated in America. The Regular-sized Spanish seem to take no special notice of them, and I think that if you began laughing and pointing at one it could lead to Trouble. I don't know, but I'm taking no chances until I see a group of Adult Spaniards laughing at the Small People.

Speaking of Midgets: I had a very, very short girlfriend in Oregon a few years ago, Larson Porridge, and let me tell you, small people, as lovers, have been highly under-estimated. Have you ever seen mice or rats fuck? It's a study in Speed. The foreplay lasts three seconds and the consummation takes another two. And they claim that they both came, and in no way could it be construed as Premature Ejaculation. Have you seen the little cigarettes that they smoke after making love: about one centimeter long and they burn up in two puffs. Cecile is less than five feet tall.

I'm supposed to be writing a Novel Of The Ramblas and I've begun to think about the fucking rats again. It's a recurring curse I picked up in Humboldt County in California in the late 1960's. I was given this one rat. A very Pretty rat. I kept her in a box, no problem. What I Didn't Know: She was Pregnant. No Problem, bigger box so she and the kids would be comfortable, even built them a little swing set. Well; she had about seven kids, (I forget her name now, it's been so long), and after a couple of months they were all as big as her. No problem, bigger box, more swings on the swing set. Well, something weird must have been going on when I wasn't watching (which was most of the time), because the next thing I new she was pregnant again. Now I had about fifteen rats. These were not the ugly grey kind, no, these were black and white (the mother), brown and white, and light brown and white (sortof cream-colored). They were actually Very pretty and not at all the kind of thing that pops into your mind when someone offers you a 'rat'.

Well, the next thing I knew, some of the daughters were pregnant also. I knocked out some of the walls in the cabin/house we were renting and converted part of it into a rat-a- torium, and covered it with mesh and old windows. You could view the rat-village from three sides. It was 4ft by 4ft by 8ft tall. There were walkways and places where they would have to go through long tubes and then Leap through the air and then climb a ladder then ride a small elevator down, then dangle from a string: all in order to get their food. I had the rats for about six or eight months and spent most of my time drinking beer and watching them. The exercises they had to go through to get their food became more complicated and (for me) hilarious as time went on. At it's height my rat village contained about a hundred residents enjoying about fifteen nesting spots, (bird-cages, cigar boxes, etc), five feeding spots, and six generations descended from the first rat.

Rebecca, myself, and our child Amy decided to head south for Santa Cruz for a while. I couldn't leave the rats. I tried for a couple of weeks to find a decent Overseer for them (even offering 100lbs of rice), but was unsuccessful.

"Could you keep my rats for me for about six months. We're heading for Santa Cruz and New Mexico, and all you have to do is give them some grain, a few vegetables, and some water. You just clean the bottom of the cage about once a week. They're really amazing little guys, you can spend hours just watching them toddling around." It didn't work, no one wanted them, we had to take them with us, along with the dog and two cats.

(Finish Rat Story here, tell about rats getting loose in car, making nests in trunk and under seats, having babies, running under brake pedal, getting used to having rats running around in car while travelling, car breaking, selling car with rats to un-suspecting buyer in Berkeley, buying another car, again rats getting loose and having babies under car seats, Getting Loose at Sarah's house and hiding in kiln, exploding rat ruins Pottery; Sarah gets mad at us, has rats for years, They take over Boulder Creek, We go to New Mexico without rats)...

PART ONE

CECILE

Cecile

The Next Day. The Cathedral, The Cloister Plaza

Well, today I am sitting in the alley (street) which runs alongside the main cathedral in Barcelona. I had no sooner removed my typewriter from it's case today down on the Ramblas than a Blue City Cop came along and asked me if I had "Permiso". It was clear that he didn't want me there. So, I've moved in with a group of people selling jewelry and other beautiful things. It's sort of like a hippy convention. Cecile is setting up her ear-ring shop right next to me. It consists of a little cardboard box and a little blanket.

CECILE

We've been together for about three days. She was sitting in the train compartment next to mine when we left Almeria. I passed by a couple of times (like a shark?) and saw her curled (CURLED!) up into a ball on a seat by herself. Could be American, I thought. Finally, I went into her compartment and asked if she spoke English.

"Yayss, a leetle.", she shyly replied.

"It's OK if I move into this compartment?", I asked, using sign language also, just in case.

"Yayss, OK.", she said, smiling.

I wasted no time gathering my bags and kalumping on over there. We sat and talked and both soon realized that we could barely understand each other. It was a true test of my reformation from alcohol the day before. Just one bottle of wine, or maybe two, and it seemed I could look forward to an erotic train-ride through Spain. I resisted and tried getting closer to her without Any Drugs At All! It was easy. We are both friendly humans. We talked (?) for a few hours. I brought the conversation around to "What do you do for fun?", one of my favorite subjects. She told me. I told her how much I Love Life, and Copulation, for about an hour. She seemed to agree with me, but when I suggested that we draw the blinds, take off our clothes, and see what happens, she emphasized that she was really enjoying "hablar" with me. I retreated in slight embarrassment and pretended to sleep while fantasizing about How Erotic This Trip Could Be.

At some station about midnight a Herd of Short Fat Spanish filled our compartment. They turned the lights on brightly and began Carousing and Laughing. The trip was theirs, for sure.

To avoid having to sit next to one of the fat cackling sisters, I moved into the seat next to Cecile. The Night Wore On and all the Spanish began snoring, in spite of having drunk over a gallon of coffee. I had been feigning sleep and indulging in erotic fantasy for hours while Cecile rested her head in my lap as I massaged her neck, and other teenaged activities. I was throbbing, and moaning under my breath for hours. Somehow, I managed to get Cecile stroking my throbbing member under my casually placed shirt, as I fondled her round little rubber tits. We were both still pretending that noting sexual was occurring. Definitely Teen-age Visions.

I was having Erroll Flynn Fantasies by the time we de-trained in Barcelona. To the Pension: At last I climb into bed, naked, we have both bathed, I am ready to Fulfill the Fantasy, She is not. Again she tells me how much she enjoys "hablar" with me. She has a boyfriend.

He'll be here in a week, then they plan to head for Brittany where they'll have Christmas with their families and sell plastic birds at the Fair. For her, this is Co-habitation of convenience and short duration. I, on the other hand, can see us fucking in a villa ten years from now. I have seen her body; it's One Of Those! The kind we see in magazines. Oh My! Evidently she doesn't understand the RULES: We're in bed together naked, We're young, (well, she is), I'm EXPERIENCED. (How old is her boyfriend, I don't know). Life is Short. Love is Grand. Let's Fuck. Let's Fuck! But, NO! She will make love to Me (touch and caress me), but I cannot fondle Her! TORTURE! AGONY! My worst nightmare is coming true: I'm stuck in bed with a deluxe, young, firm, French, wandering young lady, WHO IS FAITHFUL TO SOME GUY I DON'T EVEN KNOW! AGGGGGHHHHHH!

I am writhing in erotic expectation as she kisses my neck and chest and otherwise manipulates me to Orgasm. Slight relief. THE POTENTIAL!

We spent the next day together: I am Falling In Love. She evidently thinks it is just another normal day. I don't think she knows who or what she really is: She told me that "mans are always trying to make love to me". I gave her lecture #13, "Why Mans Like Womans". None of the usual lectures seem to be working. She doesn't seem to realize that she is ABSOLUTELY DELUXE AND DRIVING ME MAD! It's a test, I can take it, I'm Older, I'm not driven by my reproductive lusts, I'm An Artist, I'm expressing my creativeness with a typewriter, not my cock.

THE SECOND NIGHT: I fail the test: I rape her. Well it seems like rape to me, but I can vaguely remember the earlier years when Womans and Girls HAD to be Seduced. It's a Seduction, that's what it is. Sure.

I try my best to make IT good for her, but I am up against the physical sensation of being SQUEEZED. Years of practice, years of training: all down the tube. I come in about five minutes. No Problem, the second time is usually better, only THERE IS TO BE NO SECOND TIME TONIGHT!

She says, "I sleep".

I say, "What? You're Crazy! Next Time: Longer, Better. Please!" It's Over. We're Friends.

The Villa: I can see it clearly now. She'll still be Absolutely Beautiful for ten years more, at the least. I haven't even begun to dress her in stockings and heels yet, even in my mind.

The next night is the same as the first, even though we have smoked some great Hash am I HAVE SEEN ALL WOMEN IN HER EYES. Does she think this happens all the time? Does it? Maybe it does to her, but it only happens to me about once a month, even when I'm on a cosmic-sex run.

Yah, She will DO fine; She Can Be My Gal. The Potential! I'm Burninging! Ahhhhhh! She's sitting on the steps next to me right now, Making Jewelry. I told her last night that when she's twenty-five all she will want to do is fuck all the time and that she should remember that "Jack is Available". I am secretly hoping that her boyfriend doesn't show. Gets lost? Train Wreck? I really don't care. Something!

THE NEXT DAY, SAME PLACE

I had to go to the Banco with Cecile this morning to cash her Francs that she was saving for her Christmas in Brittany. I think she must really love me now, she is risking her home-coming this winter for the sake of our pension rent.

Last night in bed with her was Pretty Good. We have worked out a routine for love-making that satisfies me, and leaves her still Faithful to the Missing Boyfriend, in her eyes. I have been having serious difficulty relating to the fact that Cecile pulls away from me whenever I try to 'French Kiss' her, with the exception of moments of Extreme Passion, but will nevertheless kiss and caress my body parts to help me to orgasm. I'm slightly confused, but not complaining, much.

We smoked some hash with Jacques last night and then headed for the pension about 1 A.M. where we bungled around in Franco/Anglo/Espanol conversation for a couple of hours. Peter had given us some 'Lavender Tea' which was supposed to put us all to sleep, but I suspect that he Accidentally put some Peyote in it, because Sleep was nowhere in sight.

Sometimes, when Cecile wishes to say something to me in Spanish, she must first look in her French/Spanish dictionary and then give me the Spanish word or phrase. If I don't know it, I must look in my English/Spanish dictionary. This is a Slow Method, but fun when stoned. We get carried away with laughing and trying to say the most common things and she just lays there with her perfect young tits, completely unaware that every few minutes the covers on my side of the bed make a little tent.

But, we Do Have Some Laughs. Last night I taught her to say, "O.K. you guys, get sick." This was because she wondered what I meant when I said, "I hope your Boyfriend gets sick." She didn't understand "get sick", so we had to spend about half an hour on That, then we had to spend another half hour teaching me the French words for "eye" and "eyes", the sounds of which are almost impossible for my Yankee Palette to form.

After we had said good night: Me, "Je Te Amor", I had almost fallen asleep (I have a Job in the Manana), when Cecile began chortling, and said, "I don't want that you bite me!"

"Well, OK.", I answered.

"Cigarette?", she asked.

"I hope your boyfriend gets sick.", I answered. In the middle of this language lesson she jumped out of bed with her unbelievable body to get her dictionary and I was off again in the Villa.

We spent two or three hours learning to sing a duet of "Summertime". We're pretty good, too, except that instead of "Hush little baby, don't you cry", Cecile sings, "Hutch Leetell Baeybee, donn yoo cryee."

I am getting suspicious: Everything is so GREAT, I FEEL GOOD, People like what I'm writing. I mean, Cecile alone would normally be enough to send me into Terminal Ecstasy, but Santi has even given me credit for Cafe con Leche.

The Party of the Year

HOW FRANK WENT BLIND

According to Frank, it was The Party of the Year. Cecile and I arrived at Rosa's early last night, eleven P.M.. The other eighty guests didn't finish arriving until about two. The house is almost a Villa. The Music, from the tape-deck upstairs, was Amazingly Loud. The whole Downstairs seemed like a Barcelona Disco, or a Sock-Hop from the 50's. The house felt like an Arab Palace: arches, curving stairways, beautiful gardens, polished furniture, and The Tower. Yes, The Tower: it's 40ft above the ground, with open arches all around, pillows, chairs, and a beautiful view of the stars and surrounding countryside. The perfect place for a Seduction on a warm summer's night. I felt like making a turban out of one of the blankets after sitting there for an hour.

We sat in the Tower, smoking hash, and laughing til our bellies couldn't take it, listening to Frank tell about the time he fell in Love with a Giant Mollusk in a Roadhouse in Nevada. He rented a room in town for six months just so he could be close to it/her. It was during this time that he developed his "Mating Call of the Giant Pre-Dawn Mollusk", which he performed for us. She is now working as a stenographer for IBM in Kansas City, but they write.

Downstairs, The Middle-Class Catalans were consuming about fifty bottles of liquor while dancing to the Disco-Beat. Peter was flitting from flower to flower in his attempt to repopulate the planet with Kiwis. I'm not sure whether he was able to effect pollination or not, but I saw him leave at about five with an incredible double-jointed fucking machine. Phil was also out on the dance floor scaring the shit out of his partners with his Walt Disney Dancing· and his imitations of Peter Lorre having a fit. It was a well-dressed crowd, seemingly educated and aware, which spent the morning Throbbing to the Base-line and otherwise squirming back to it's Ancient Iberian Roots. Had that much booze been consumed at a Party Back Home, there would have been fights (at least arguments) and wholesale regurgitation in the Yard. Evidently Catalans can hold their liquor.

The Hostess, Rosa, is a Full-Grown Catalan Female with Delusions of Bi-Linguality. Phil went to a similar party there last year and ended up staying as Rosa's Lover for four months. He gave her a little money for food, but otherwise had No Obligations. He spent some time explaining to me why he left, but I still couldn't understand it. Peter was also one of Rosa's Lovers, along with the man who lives there now.

Cecile was a Hashish Wallflower for a couple of hours until she began dancing: Transformation! She turned into Star*Girl, spinning like an Elf (and looking like one); her dancing reminds me of the Hippy Girls and the way they danced at the Gatherings of the Sixties in America. It was beautiful; I fell in Love again with her.

Frank found the room with the red light and took it over. He lay back on the large cushions, with his pipe at the ready, and entrapped any females who wandered within his web of Psycho-Babble.

I encountered Peter a couple of times returning from the garden mumbling something about, "She didn't Go."

Norma was there; Norma with her Shirley MacLaine face. She was obviously Happy, and having a Great Time in Spain. At one point she was the center of five guys dancing in a blatant Sexual Manner around her. She was eating it up. (forgive me). Between watching Norma and dancing with Cecile, and fantasizing about the two, my time was completely taken up. I Was Able to obtain Norma's phone number and have tentatively scheduled an appointment (some Starry Night, perhaps?) with her to show her my Writings.

By four-thirty the party was down to the one Obvious Drunk and the Hard-Core Dancers, one being Rosa. It was my first exposure to the Catalan Middle Class, and I will say that they seem extremely civilized. One thing which was Noticeable at the party was the way in which they would stop to talk, or gather in groups, with absolutely no thought for whether they were blocking the stairway or denying others access to the bar. Where they met, they chatted. I tried to point out that someone was Completely Blocking The Stairs, at one point, and the person in question made a gentle gesture that I should calm down. I felt Rowdy. I waited until the tide changed and was eventually able to make it upstairs.

Frank caused further stomach aches in the tower with an explanation of how he blinded himself: He was living in L.A. about twenty years ago and a good tan was considered A Basic. He went to the beach, smoked a few joints, and stared at the sun for a while. Well, he could tell that he was being damaged, so he closed his eyes and fell asleep until dark. When he awoke he was blind. He considered it A positive Experience and was having a blast Digging It and finding his way home. At home he got some white shoe polish and painted a stick and put a sign on the toy poodle which read, "I Am A Seeing-Eye Dog", and went for a walk. He was having a Blast. He found, that afternoon, that he could navigate around his house like a bat. He walked through the house hooting and listening for the echoes coming off the walls and furniture. He says he was enjoying it tremendously.

When his wife (a nurse) came home, she found Frank yelling at the walls and tapping things with a white stick. She took him to a doctor who asked Frank, "What do you do?"

"I'm an Artist.", said Frank.

"You're a Blind Artist now, and always will be.", said the Doctor.

Frank says he accepted this with Joy and continued to be a Blind Artist for the next three months. He got tired of it so he sat himself in a room which he knew inside out and began to imagine that he could actually see the room. He did this for a couple of weeks and pretty soon he actually could see the room. It was in this way that he cured his Blindness. To this day Frank is as pale as a ghost because he thinks Tans are Unimportant and they may be dangerous to your health. He claims that in the near future his skin will become translucent. He may be right; I've rarely seen him out in direct sunlight.

Maria, an American girl who is studying here, who I met yesterday and invited to the party, ended up having a "Terrible Time". She mentioned to Frank early in the evening (two oclock?) that she needed a ride back to Barcelona. I don't think he knew what to do with this information. Around four-thirty or five she came to me In Distress asking where "Frank and Everybody" had gone. I told her "They Left"; she got mad at me! She said, "I told Frank I needed a ride home!"

I told her, "Maybe he didn't know what to do with that information." This didn't seem to mollify her, and she became disgusted with the "Whole Disco-Hashish Scene!". I think she was expecting something more beatnik at the party. I connected her with Rosa, who got her a ride home with some friends. Cecile and I caught the train at six A.M. and got back here at six-thirty, exhausted, high, and horny.

Somehow Peter made it home this morning and got on the train to Gerona, where he will paint on the street today, trying make money for his pending trip to Italy.

It all worked out well, and "Party of the Year" will have to stand until Phil and Rene have their Open-House-Warming next Saturday Night.

PART TWO

HADASS

Hadass The Israelita

Hadass, the Israelita, just stopped by and we went to her neighborhood for a Cafe con Leche. Her whole neighborhood smells like piss. Really. We went into one cafe which even the locals must realize is BAD. We were going to stick it out but my eyes began to water so we moved on down the street. Hadass is from Israel. She's been chalking on the street for a couple of years and is always, "I leaving Barcelona." It's not for me to judge her.: she made 3,000ptas today chalking a picture of a "Santa" on the street. I would retire at 500, at this point in my street career.

To reach Hadass' neighborhood, we had to run the gamut of hash-dealers in plaza Real. (Plassa Ray-all). On the way in, a Turkish-looking guy asked us, "psst, psst, hashish, chocolatty, chocolatty, mooey good for you, pssss." I replied, "No, no, no queremos, tenemos, no, no." He followed us for about thirty feet babbling his retailers litany. We lost him. Then, it was on to a Cafe for a cafe. Then, later, on the way back through Plaza Real the same guy tried to sell us hash again. What a memory. It says something for his product. He's one of the Together ones.

There are some Moroccans here who make their livings selling fake hash to each other and then robbing each other. They're probably from the same neighborhood back home. There's a rapid turnover in their line of work. If I fail at Writing, I suppose I can ask them for a job.

I am fueled by cafe-con-leche. I've had three so far today, 50ptas each. I'm barely staying ahead of my fuel consumption. If my typewriter box doesn't clink a bit more regularly I may have to pretend to be disconsolate and slightly stupid so that Cecile will pay the Pension again tonight.

I have always had a vision of myself seated at a typewriter banging out my first novel. This is not exactly what it looked like.

Hadass wandered off into the alleys they call streets here. She won't have any trouble, of that you can be sure. She is about 6 feet tall and is wrapped in various-colored scarves, sweaters, pants, legwarmers, and boots. She has a perpetual scowl on her face (is Israel a happy place?) which, you learn after knowing her for a while, is actually her Amused Expression. If anyone were to try some mild form of harassment, she could destroy them with a smile. It is impossible to scare or rob someone who is laughing at you. Plus, if she spoke to them, her accent would confuse them completely.

Evidently, she is Fearless. She lives and hangs out in one of the Most Dangerous parts of town: Escudillers, Plaza Real, Barrio Gotico. I used to hang around there last year on Really Drunken Nights and only kept from being robbed by being weirder than the robbers. She just glides right through it like a zombie no one wants to know.

A WEEK LATER: WE GET TO KNOW EACH OTHER

THE CATHEDRAL ALLEY, THE CLOISTER (THE GOOSE-YARD)

I can see directly into the goose-courtyard, but cannot see the gooses.

    I had dinner at Santi's last night, as usual. Diane Showed up again. Hadass, Peter, Emma (his Catalan girlfriend), Frank, Helen (Tracy's friend, with unbelievably rosy cheeks) and The Editor were all in attendance. I had smoked some grass with Frank, Peter, and Helen earlier at Pension Costa and had barely been able to wobble back to my pension and collapse on the bed in a paisley swoon. I stayed there for a couple of hours until I heard Jacques calling me in his Hells-Angels Voice from Plaza Regomir below. I went down and joined the frivolity already in progress in the cavern.

    I asked Frank what the main topic of conversation for the night was.

    "As you might expect, All Tongues are Wagging Over Peter's Latest Costume.", he told me, grinning hugely.

    Jacques was so Taken with some of the passages from yesterday that he bought me a 'trifle', a jello, cream, and custard concoction of Barbara/Santi's design. It was delicious. I went into a Hippy-Trifle-dance upon the news of Free Dessert (made sweeter because I earned it with the sweat of my fingers), and finished it off in about three minutes, with Hadass' Help. It was a Sweet Evening.

    I walked Diane to her room in her pension and lingered for a couple of minutes looking out the balcony, waiting for her to attack me. None came. We parted with a European Kiss, I would like to see her again. I'LL attack next time.

    I headed up Calle Fernando and ran into Hadass, who was strolling/gliding deeper into the Barrio towards her apartment. I asked her if she would like me to walk Her home also. She replied in the affirmative. I invited myself up to her house for coffee and sex.

    She responded, "I don't know, Maybe.", to the latter.

    We climbed the 96 stairs (I counted) and entered her roof-top cave. She brewed coffee while I talked about how Lonely I Was Since The French Girl Left and Diane Kissed Me Good-night. We agreed that Sleeping Alone is No Fun. I pressed her for an answer to our sleeping arrangements, as my one oclock curfew at Rosa's Pension was fast approaching. We decided to smoke some Hash and discuss it from a Different Point of View. It worked, we liked each other a lot and began to talk of Where We Have Been and What We

Have Seen. She: Born in a Kibbutz and Raised in the Israeli Desert. Me: Born in Berkeley and Raised in the American Cultural Desert. She: Worked in a fish-factory in Norway. Me: Worked on a Ranch in Humboldt. She: Attended Art School in Jerusalem for five years and lived off her work for five more. Me: Been writing for a week.

Hadass is the first person I've met who recommends Stockholm. It's enough for me. I'm going. Got to meet my 8th cousins and find out what's been happening since my Great-Grandfather left.

She told me about the Israeli Army, and her two-year stint. I told her about the Navy and Vietnam. She told me about marionetting around Europe and I told her about Hippy-Caravanning around California. We both wanted to go where the other has been.

We ran out of Hash, so we descended into the Disco Night of Raurich Alley. She tried the 'Piss-Bar' first, but she said the chunk was too small for 500ptas. We headed over to Cafe De La Opera where She also found something wrong with the deal. Over to Plaza Real where she bargained a Street-dealer down to 400ptas for what I would call a Decent Sized Chunk of Dreams. Then it was back to the penthouse, smoke it up and continue "The Stories of Our Travels".

Dire Straits rocking on the Box, she will leave me the tape. Dim the lights, practice juggling (she can juggle four balls, I barely know what to do with the Two I've Got). More Hash, More Talk, Dimmer Lights; if we are ever to fall in love, this is a good shot. Shall We Kiss? Almost. We Don't. We were Having Fun. We Talked and Laughed til Four. No Lights, In Bed, Talking, Laughing: I touch her, she laughs. It's pitch black, except for the vague shape of the window. We fell asleep. Beautiful Night!

"How wheel I reemember deez teengs yoo haff tole me dees night?"

"You'll Remember. You'll Remember." It was good hash.

The next morning is Beautiful. We have a breakfast of Coffee, Whole wheat bread, Garlic, Tomatoes, Peppers, Garlick, and Eggs. We eat it sitting out on the patio: You can see the tops of all the Old Churches in Barcelona. It's sunny. The dog next door is Barking. What a Life! Hadass and I are both savoring the experience of Having A New Friend. It IS good. Hadass claims that I am Like an Israeli. I explain to her that that is probably because I've read the Old Testament about twenty times and have been intensely interested in the Jews since I first read "The Rise and Fall of the Third Reich".

We parted late in the morning with another European Kiss, with Hadass heading for a telephone to call Israel because she was picking up Weird Sister Vibrations from the Cosmic Web last night.

She said, "I may have to take the aeroplane to Israel right away!"

Hadass and I agreed in our feelings about War. While High, I went into about an hour Rap about Distribution of Food, Computers, police, Nationalism, Birth, Beauty, Outlaws, Dope, Tail-lights, Sex, politics, and My Own Personal Vision. She Received it. I apologized when I realized that I had been Ranting, but she said it was "goot".

Her Penthouse is even more beautiful during the day: White, Bright, and Light. The balcony is superb and I can already see myself hard at work out there. On a table, or a mattress. She asked me to tell her fortune last night. I explained that I didn't have my cards with me but that I could use an Alternative Method: Her Naked Human Body. She declined, but I told as much of her fortune as I could through her clothes. I gave her eight years until she begins to want to begin to start settling down, something like that. She has Travelling in her Atoms, Bad.

The Tapas, Santi's bar

Today is Santi's Birthday. His real name is Santiago. He's 34 today. He met Barbara, his English wife, while he was a cook and she was a waitress, in a London Hotel where he was a cook. They met while he was cooking. He is from Barcelona, and is still a cook. He was a cook in Barcelona before he went to London to be a cook. He married Barbara, and they came back to Barcelona and opened a combo Restaurant-Bar: "Taberne Les Tapes", ("Snack Bar", in Catalan), "english spoken here". She waits on the customers while Santi Cooks. He's a very good cook. (He's had a lot of experience cooking.) He must love to cook.

Some of his regular customers are obviously his childhood friends and most of the rest are English-speakers like me. (as am I? as I am?) .

The food is great. You can order it any way you wish, in English. Pork chops. Steaks. Fish Soup. Fried Potatoes. Excellent Salads. Broiled Chicken. Liver. Pork Steaks. Lamb. Sausages (3 kinds). Cafe. Fruit. Liquor. Beer. Lemonade. Lime-ade. Fish Steaks. Lentils. Steamed Vegetables. and more. (Oh yah, and Wine) .

Such a Small Cavern of a place. White stucco walls with glitter. Down a few steps to tables made in the old days for The Small People. What a Place! The first bar I went into when I got here last year. Frank still eats there every night because, even though he's lived here for about ten years, he still can't speak Spanish. Every evening at nine the place fills up with Estranjeros (Spanish: strangers, foreigners, us). It's located in plaza Regomir, two blocks from the state capitol and city hall, both in plaza St. Juame (Saint Hymie) .

You walk in, past the ten stools for those who wish to eat and drink at the bar, and then descend three steps into the Cavern. It's guarded by 'Manilow' the stupid yellow dog. (He has been punched in the head too often by one of Santi's old friends). There are weird old pieces of wood and strange posters on the walls. There is a light fixture that Barbara must have stolen from a circus, with three different coloured bulbs in it, hanging directly above the first two tables, Where the gringoes usually sit. If those two tables are full, you walk towards the closet-sized kitchen and turn right (duck, the roof is lower here) where you will find about four Small people tables. If someone has to use the 'servicios' (piss or shit) it necessitates about five people scraping their chairs around and leaning over their tables in order to stand up and let them pass; This again, when the Pisser returns. It's quite a Circus sometimes.

The Back Tables also seem to double as a 'tonguing-spot' for various types of sexual deviates. There are a couple of butch lezbians who use it on a regular basis and have caused several nearby philosophical and artistick conversations to whil off into a cacophony of mindless verbiage. I have seen one young Catalana almost choked to death in a butch tongue attack. Frank will testify.

Santi's black-clad mother has a difficult time suppressing giggles whenever she glances at the writhing couples on her trips to the kitchen and back.

With these few exceptions, (a fight every month or so), Santi's is a Family Bar. Barbara is the tit-mother. Frank is the first-born child. Jacques is a Relative Who Is Always Welcome, and I am a Third cousin who drops in once in a while, invited or not. Hadass is the Resident Ghost.

Both Barbara and Santi love to play practical jokes: Barbara can scarcely refrain from seeming to drop a glass whenever she hands one to me; Santi has given me sweet syrup on the pretense of it being 'very hot sauce'. He asked Billy if he wanted mustard. Billy said yes. Santi pointed the bottle of mustard at him and squeezed out the long yellow string onto Billy's shirt. It really was just a yellow string. He did it to me too. It seems real. ha ha, That Santi!

They work in the bar from ten to ten every day except Mondays, when, according to Frank, you can find them down at MacDonalds "getting some good food". Frank claims that Barbara can hardly wait each night to finish work so she can scurry down there.

They extend credit. I don't know the criteria they use to decide, but I ran up two hundred dollars last year while 'waiting for money from America'. I've written a Poem for Santi for his birthday:

You've got a Splendid Tavern,
And Barbra's great for Sure,
Although It's like a Cavern,
You can always Count on Her.

The Fish-head Soup is great,
The Bomba's are Sublime,
I guess it's just our Fate,
to Belch Time after Time.

Happy Birthday, Santiago,
We Know that You'll go Far,
Because you spent this Special Day,
At work behind the bar.

I hope to get a discount meal for this. At least a free Bomba. (fried mashed potatoes with hot sauce). I've asked Peter to do an illustration for the card but he said, "I can't."

"Why not? I've seen you draw, you're good.", I said.

"I have to be in the mood for it." , he said.

"Oh bullshit! ". I replied.

"It's a bit short notice. You could have told me earlier."

"Look, peter, I made that poem up on the spot."

"Yah, that's different, it's writing."

"Why is it different?", I asked.

"It's a different creative urge, writing, the words are already there in your head. All you have to do is sling them together.", he explained.

"Right.", I said. I guess I will get no illustration for Santi's Card.

Rosa Jaws

Peter and I were sitting in Santi's. Hadass joined us for a beer. "I have no problems. That's my Main Problem. I have to be on the road.", she said, trying to convince herself that leaving was Right.

Peter seemed to be in good spirits. I think he received some money from Australia. He had recently bought some New Black Pants to go with his Black Shoes and Black Animal Overcoat. We got to talking about women. Peter said, "I don't think I've made love to a Canadian Girl. I DON'T THINK I'VE MADE LOVE TO AN ENGLISH GIRL! WHO HAVE I MADE LOVE TO?!" We looked at him, amazed.

A moment later he continued, "I made love to a Thailand Girl. She was a prostitute though." From what I can tell, Peter has been lovers with most of the local female crowd. I may follow him around to learn his methods, now that I am free of Cecile. (sob).

Rosa the Catalana, who some call "Jaws", joined us. She putted in at full speed and made the conversation her own. She wanted to know what Peter had accomplished since she last saw him. She pressed him for details. She thinks she is an investigator for the Catalan Self-Betterment Society. I showed her what I had written, sixty pages so far. She immediately said, "It is not Original!", after reading only the first line of the first page and handing it right back to me. She instantly forgot it and was off talking about How Busy She Has Been Lately.

She teaches English to Catalan children, but is only a couple of notches above Ramon in English Murder. She, also, has been one of Peter's lovers. Rosa-jaws cannot stop talking: her mind just Churns it out in a constant stream, and she is compelled to open her mouth and spew it all over us.

In honor of Santi's Birthday, he gave us a bottle of Champagne, which served to loosen Rosa's jaw even further. She was friends with Rebecca and Billy while they were here. She had them out to her 'house in the country', as she calls it. She couldn't get over how much I look like Billy. I assured her that it was Quite the Opposite. When I told her that I had visited them in Almeria, but had gone nowhere else in Southern Spain, she scolded me, "I thought you were very poor in mind. I thought you would visit pretty places if you visit Almeria!" She was obviously very disappointed in me. She began to offer me advice concerning my Life, Writing, and Future. All this on practically No Information At All. It was our first-ever 'talk'. She is a wonder to behold.

Hadass claimed that she could not hold a conversation with Rosa-jaws; Rosa will not listen to her. I asked her to try: She was right. Rosa completely ignored what Hadass said and took off on a tangent of her own:

Hadass said to Rosa, "I think I leave next week."

Rosa answered, "You cannot find a policeman born in Catalonia, they are all from the south."

On and On it went, Rosa ranting, and the crowd chipping in whenever possible.

Lori the Finn made an appearance with a friend who looked like an escapee from Lynard Skynard. Lori began a Guitar Attack in counterpoint to Rosa's Babbling. He pointed it at us and strummed obnoxious, horrible blues chords, putting his friend into some kind of weird grinning trance. It was getting Eerie. They had come by to see if they could go in on a hash-deal with us. It was up to Jacques, he's the editor.

Peter contributed to Rosa's soliloquy, "Even the Catalan police speak Spanish!" Rosa explained the Police of Catalonia to us for another fifteen minutes.

Peter told Rosa, "New Zealand is God's Own Country."

Rosa answered, "But, it's very depressing, a country without people: you don't meet anyone!" She was warming for an argument.

Peter countered, "There are Sheep!"

"I cannot talk to Sheep!", she lunged.

Peter won, "YOU DON'T HAVE TO TALK TO SHEEP!" Rosa became quiet.

Peter continued, in the Glow of Victory, "New Zealand has more fucking sheep than any other country in the world!"

Rosa's silence gave Jacques his first chance to talk, he asked, "What about Auckland?"

"Auckland's a City!", Peter triumphantly told him. Jacques was in deep water and knew it, but he tried again anyway, "NO! Those islands down by Argentina: Where they had the War!" Jacques sensed that Something was wrong. Peter Had him, he readied for the Kill. He pounced, "THAT'S THE FALKLANDS, YOU IDIOT! !" Peter had won. He had lifted Jacques' Veil of Stupidity. He sat back smugly and waited for Rosa to begin again. She did.

She chastised all of us for our lack of accomplishments. She's very good at it. She's going places. She works hard.

Lori was deep into his interpretation of a retarded flamenco guitar player when Santi sent down one of his helpers to ask him to stop because his playing was interfering with the bar-crowd's TV-watching. What is Spanish Culture coming to? TV over Flamenco!

We decided to buy some hash and then Hadass would show me her apartment, since I would possibly be moving there soon. We headed out for her neighborhood, plaza Real's toilet. Jacques, Hadass, Peter, Rosa-jaws, me, and Lori and his zombie friend. We were trying to ditch Lori and friend, but they could smell a Score, and were impossible to lose. Lori kept attacking passersby with what he called "Walking Blues". We wound up waiting for Hadass outside of the piss Bar, where her connection hangs out. I was skeptical about the Deal, considering the location, but it turned out alright. Jacques had to "bargain" with Lori about the amount Lori would receive for his 100ptas (60cents). I couldn't believe it. Lori was acting like it was a deal for a pound. Jacques finally had to tell him, "Look, Lori, take it or leave it!" Lori took it, with a smile.

We filed into Hadass' building (right across the alley) and she slammed the gate in Lori's face. She explained to me that he couldn't come in because they were lovers last year and he owes her 200ptas and she was keeping an old table of his until he pays. Lori is a strange experience to be around sometimes; it's like he's in Finland and is finding it amusing to be freezing to death in a blizzard. His Chinese Eyes seem to be scouring the horizon for Something.

We walked up six flights of incredibly narrow stairs, to the top floor. A very funky old building. Hadass' place was a beautiful one-room apartment with a large window looking out onto and into the rooftops of Barcelona's Gothic Barrio. Out in the hall were the incredibly complicated toilet and shower mechanisms, behind a locked If door. She proudly told me that it's a private toilet, which is 'rare'. Across the hall is the door to the patio. An incredible view of the sky and the church spires nearby. There is a ladder leaning on the edge of another, even smaller, higher, patio. All private for Hadass. What a Fucking View! The place is worth its weight in olive oil. It would possibly be mine soon, with the stipulation that Jacques could come and paint on the patios any time he felt like it. No Problem. I was ready, I could sit up there and smoke hash and write. What a place! Jacques said that if I lived there and wasn't able to Create, that Kerouac's corpse would turn over in its grave. He was right. I couldn't wait, but I didn't really want Hadass to leave: I was getting to know her.

I made a hash-pipe out of a toilet-roll and some tin-foil, what we used to call a 'carburetor', and we proceeded to smoke up half the hash.

Rosa's mouth took off, out on the patio. She had Zeroed in on me, while the rest were trying to dig the cosmic night. She was telling me that I should plant some grass on the patio and move right in. I shouldn't even wait for Hadass to leave: the patio is public property and I have a Right to pitch my tent there. I told her to just keep the tent in her Garage until I needed it; I'd call her. She wouldn't stop. She sensed something about the value of conversational victory which the rest of us couldn't perceive. She was Merciless. It was becoming Combative Psycho-Drama. She was Yelling.

I was Yelling, "Tell me, Rosa, How Many lovers have you driven insane? How many men are out in the streets Babbling and Frothing, Screaming 'Rosa, shut up! Rosa! It was Rosa! She Wouldn't Shut Up! Help me! Help me! I can Still Hear Herrrrr!!!' How many have killed themselves, Rosa?!" I was screaming at Full Volume, six inches from her face.

She was undaunted: she was still telling me how to pitch the Tent on the patio, but paused to answer, "Three killed themselves."

I said, "I Believe it!"

It was a Draw. She was undefeated; I had used some of my most persuasive language to try to slow her, but had failed. I think she wanted me to come home with her on her motor-scooter and make love. I thought, 'maybe some other time, I might strangle her tonight'.

We all headed down the 96 stairs to Calle Raurich. Hadass walked Rosa to her motor-scooter on the Ramblas, and Peter, Jacques and I walked to pension Costa where I bid them goodnight. I walked down to Plaza Regomir where Cecile had rented me a single room in the Pension above the Tapas. She had kept the double room so that she and her 'amigo' could be together. I had seen them in the morning when I went in to get some of my things. She was radiant. The little French had been in there all night fucking. It reeked of fuck perfume. I was saddened but survived. I was missing her already, but I suppose I'll run into her again. Maybe we'll get that villa yet.

Plastic Birds, Indeed!

Ramblasfish, Frank

"Rumblefish", the movie, was emotionally draining last night. It took us on a roller-coaster ride of love and fear. Afterwards, as we were waiting under the marquee of the theatre (it was pouring), I was knocked from behind by a man as he fell face-first into the ledge on the wall beside me. I thought immediately that he had been stabbed. I reached down and turned him over, expecting to see a peckinpah wound in his stomach. There wasn't one, though his face was bleeding from three places. I decided that he had fainted or was an epileptic. I put my hand under his head to stop it from banging on the stone floor. I stayed like this for a few minutes until his friend was able to snag a taxi. He came to, looked about, and tried to bang the back of his head on the ground again. He got in the cab and was gone, leaving us there wondering when the Movie Really Was Going To End. I had bloody hands. Hadass asked me later what I thought of "Ramblasfish".

I heard Helen (Cheeky Helen) ask peter, "What does Frank do in Art now?"

"He's a Conceptual Minimalist.", he replied. Helen laughed, not knowing that Peter was telling the truth, hit the nail on the head.

Frank's Art is in his head, in his Life. He's been living in L.A., Paris, Rome, Florence, and finally Barcelona ever since The Big Killing, when I suppose he must have sold a Lot Of His Work. No one around here has ever seen him sweat. He lives as they did in Paris in the twenties. He admits it. He's proud of his degeneracy. He hypnotizes small groups of fledgling artists with his stories of weirdness-in-the-world, and his knowledge of Art and Art History. Jacques told me that Frank used to teach at the UCLA Art School in California. Frank told me that Dennis Hopper (the Father in Rumblefish) was his buddy and room-mate in Art School.

Frank is usually stoned on Marijuana or Hash, as he probably has been for twenty years. He is usually smiling and suggesting outrageous excursions or ideas. He loves to be the center of attention and usually deserves to be. People tend to either Love or Despise him. He is difficult to ignore. He has a vast storehouse of gossip which sometimes overlaps with his storehouse of Art History. He is familiar with the sex-lives of Most Great Artists. First-hand, he sometimes claims. He fucked a girl on Jim Morrison's Grave in Paris. For Frank, It's a Shrine. He says he never goes to Paris without getting high at the Grave.

Frank has taught me all that I know about Art, and Architecture, in the last two months. He is a Guru and Critic for Jacques because his criticisms have

Some Depth, whereas mine usually deal with stupid concepts like, "Wouldn't the dog look better over there?", Shit like that.

Frank has a third-floor room with a balcony which he rents year-round. It overlooks Calle Fernando about two blocks up from the Ramblas, in the Heart of the Gothic Barrio. He rents it from an old man who owns the house and treats Frank like a Father. It's a Perfect observation post for the comings and goings on the main barrio artery.

Every wall in Frank's room is covered with reproductions of the Best Art. Frank lays on his bed, smokes his dope, and flies off into the Art World on a daily basis. He can bend your ear, and mind, for hours about any one painting. He "loves to have fun, and hates to have a bad time", and tells everyone so, at every opportunity, on a daily basis. To sum up Frank in one word: Savoir Faire.

TITS

Black, Black, Black: Stockings, shoes, eyes, hair, dresses. Where are the paisley patterns of yesterday? When all my troubles seemed so far away. Why are they all wearing black? Can you make love to a woman dressed in black at a picnic? No. Do you seduce women at Funerals? (I don't, but I'm sure Frank Must have a story along this line.)

It's getting chilly. I want to be sitting in a Bathtub, but there's no Spanish word for it: they've never seen one here. I'm gonna have to stick this out, but I'm Faltering Rapidly. Jacques thinks I write some great stuff when I'm Miserable. It's not true: he's a Sadist.

I MISS the Peanut Gallery. Am I no longer a Novelty to the Estranjeroes? Have they abandoned me to my Stoney Fate? Where is the Encouragement I received so freely when I began this experiment with Life and Death? Where are Jacques' Criticisms? Frank's Insane Observations? I would even settle for a dose of Phil's Condescension! o that Peter would just stop by and offer some Idiotic plan for Instant Riches!

Fuck 'em! I'm going to write about something that EYE am interested in, for a change. Editors be damned! I got my ten pages!

TITS. Yes. Tits. I love tits. I love to squeeze them. I love to suck them. I want at least two other tits in my life from now on. I want to grab them through sweaters, I want to grab them through silk, I want to rub them and slobber on them and pinch the little things on the end with my fingers and teeth. TITS. Tits are the tits. When they asked Ringo what he thought of Playboy Magazine, during the playboy Interview, he answered: "TITS". I couldn't agree more: tits! Little firm ones! Big Firm Ones! Big Dangly Ones. (the kind you can fuck). I want to fuck: Tits. I want her to get on top and beat me with her: TITS! I want to rip open her shirt and rub: Tits! I want to go out to the farm and look at the cow's: TITS. I want to hang around the dog pound and watch the puppies suck: TITS! That's what we're talking about here: tits! Not Mammary Glands. No! TITS! Knockers? NO! TITS! Not "her big jugs". Fuck NO! We Want TITS TITS TITS!!

I don't want "Melons". NO! TITS! clink. ah, a "tit" man, evidently. Yes, Tits. tits. rub rub rub. My favorite words: "rub my tits more, Jack." Yah, that's what I want to hear, "Pleeeese Rub my TITS, Jack!" (I haven't even talked about "Pussy" yet).

Well, I got that off my chest. Now: On with The Novel! There are increasing numbers of strollers, now. There are humans of every description passing. Men in suits. Women with …aghhhh, TITS! Oh, no, I better say something about Rats. It's one of the only cures for Excessive Tit-Consciousness.

Gooses, Tits, Rosa-Jaws, and Garlick

The goose-courtyard, The Cloister, The Cathedral.

I believe Frank has put a curse on me: last night he suggested that the next section of the book be called, "Memoirs of a Celibate", due to My Handling (not enough?) of Cecile. I don't care; there is more energy in my writing today due to my celibacy. What a trade-off!

Last night Jacques warned me not to show the part about tits to Amani, "He talks just like that sometimes." It's true: I showed the part about tits to Amani and he has been standing here for a while going into ecstasy watching the bouncing mammaries pass.

"You can see hers even underneath her coat! What Knockers!", he ejaculates.

He said, "It took me three weeks to get kissed here. In Stockholm you just ask them to go home with you, and they do if they want to, No Problem."

"Sounds Great!", I said.

"Look at Those! Look at Those!", he told me.

I just returned from my coffee break with Phil at the Santa Clara cafe, where Hadass happened by and joined us am we had a couple of coffees and a re-union.

Phil told me, "Making Love to Rosa-Jaws was like making love to a cactus: She's Bristly!" I asked him if he thought I would be happy living at Rosa's.

He said, "Living at Rosa's would be Great if she was at work all the time." I asked him if she will be pissed when she reads this.

"She loves it if you pay Any Attention to Her at all, she even loves to be yelled at. She Craves Attention. She knows it, we've told her all this before."

Peter strolled up and joined us, read what I've been writing, and said, "When I knew her she was quite well-pruned."

"Peter, where did you get that sweater?", Phil asked.

"From the cactus.", Peter told him.

Phil was having a lengthy conversation with Hadass; he was trying to explain to her that Garlic Smells, a concept which she has never encountered before. She was sniffing in her purse because Phil told her, "Garlic is coming out of your skin!"

Last night She asked me, "You want me to go brush my teeth?", when I was considering kissing her; the garlic was overwhelming and I'd reeled back, instantly overcome. "Don't bother, it's in your blood.", I told her.

The guy at the stand next to me just pulled a bunch of Garlic out of his pocket. Phil is completely surrounded by Garlic-Eaters.

The sun is shining today, everywhere in Barcelona except this little Plaza. It only shines in this Plaza during the summer. It's a Beautiful Day, if a bit cold. They've closed the doors to the Gooses, for siesta: Even Gooses take siesta here. It's quiet from in there; they're resting up for the Evening's Performance; Their necks get awfully tired from all that bobbing around, not to mention hoarse voices from all that squawking they have to do to earn their living.

Hadass' Bee-Ography

Yesterday evening Hadass took me to a Bodega about a block from Santi's that I'd never noticed before. There were no other customers. She had something on her mind; she ordered a Jug of Wine for herself and a bottle of gas-water for me and Began, "I want better bee-ography. My bee-ography no good. You write what you want: It's your book. You no write I come from very poor family, in the country, eight kids always screaming, you write that. My parents have no money for art school, I pay for myself. I leave home at fifteen. I start drugs thirteen, drawing on street thirteen. You write that. My parents from Morocco, My father from Morocco, mother from Poland: I'm Second Generation in Israel." I was writing as fast as I could in my tablet as she kept demanding a better bee-ography.

"I come to Spain looking for roots. Five Hundred years ago my family in Spain. They leave inquisition in fifteenth, then one hundred years Catalonia, then to Morocco, then they move in late forties to Israel and they live in - how you call it - a Camp, until they find work. I am the third children born in the Kibbutz. So, my father left home only fourteen: it doesn't matter for anybody: It's Me! It's Me have problem with my beeography. You Don't want sometimes change your beeography? You can do it easy. You are Writer. It's True! It's Big Truth Behind!"

We sat there for a while, eating peanuts, discussing War, while Hadass loosened up with Red Wine. My pen was poised, for I knew there was another Rush coming.

"In Kibbutz is good Food, good Work, and good Sex. That's what they allways doing in Kibbutz: Fucking, Working, and Eating: It's very good in Kibbutz Life.", she told me. I was envious of her Up-bringing and told her so. She was well taken care of, had an excellent education, and had a hundred adults she could turn to in times of trouble. She spent all her time with eight other children her own age. She can Always Go Back.

She poured another glass of wine and began to tell me more, "All my family, they always: "I am leaving." My brother always going to India, back to Japan, and I am always going back to Barcelona, and my sister always going back to America. My mother she doesn't know what is going on. And now my father, he saving money to buy a Van and travelling all over America. At first it is a secret but now my mother, she going with him."

We laughed about her family and then began to talk about War again, "My grandfather in first war, he didn't die, he in Russia, he tell me story of war, many story. My Uncle was here, in the civil war for Spain, to help, you know, the fight."

Hadass is proud of her family. I've seen photos of them, dressed just like Californians: Palm trees, grass, shrubs, shorts, flowered shirts, sandals, lawns, it Looks like an easy life.

We began talking about Male-Female relations, Hadass told me, "In Israel women are looking for men who are very Smart and Ugly. If you go Israel, I will set you up with my friend. She like to fuck. Once I send her my most ugly friend in Israel. It doesn't work. He is too beautiful. I set it up. Nothing work. For you it is funny nothing works. She is nice."

I told her, "Hey, don't try to get me turned on by some girl in Israel!" She sat there grinning and laughing quietly about my pending trip to Israel and what she has planned for me.

"I think I leave tomorrow.", she continued, "What you think of Margo? Emotional Problem. California problem.", she answered her own question.

"She give me the idea I have to move, I have to go somewhere, but it's in Her mind, actually."

Margo was a crazy red-headed California Gal who followed Frank to Barcelona because she fell in love with him last summer in L.A. but he ignored her when she was here because she was Dangerously Crazy, so she stayed a couple of weeks and split.

We headed out into Barcelona and wandered around for a while trying to find a place for me to get a CafeconLeche. We ended up on Hadass' street, Calle Raurich. We stood outside the entrance to her building.

She said, talking about Children, "I know I'm Living Forever, so I don't need children."

"Just In Case, then.", I was suggesting Pregnancy.

"I Know I'm living forever.", she said.

"What if you're Wrong?", I insisted.

"I know I'm not wrong: I used to think like that, It's terrible, sometimes I have doubt about it.", she answered.

I tried to comfort her, "I think maybe we all do: You better have kids."

We headed up to her apartment to smoke some hash and then strolled through town, like hip-zombies, to Casa Peret, where we met up with Frank and Peter for the evening meal. Frank was Gone, Flying High. I hadn't seen him without his pipe at the ready for about a week. He was grinning Insanely, with his face about four inches from Hadass' face, chanting, "HaaaaDas, HaDaaaaasssss, HaaaaDaaaaasssss,

HAAAAAAAAAADAAAAAAAADSSSS!! I" Hadass entered some kind of Defensive Ecstasy, she didn't know what to make of the drug-crazed

American who was Psychically Drooling All Over Her Soul. It was Absolutely Hilarious! I was bending over from stomach-hurt laughing. He finished by collapsing into her lap. "Ahhh, La Lapp!", he exclaimed, as he pretended to die on top of her.

We were joined by Phil and Rene for dinner. Rene was trying to read the book but Phil kept interrupting her because he didn't want her to read what he said about her father and taxis earlier that day.

Frank was expounding on the scene in the restaurant, "RETRO is exactly the place to be, and we are There!" The place was full of the poorest restaurant-goers to be found in the Barrio Chino.

We had an 'excellent meal'. I paid 120ptas for Soup and Salad and Bread. Hadass helped me pay.

Jacques and Tapies, Social Retard

PETER AND CAMELS

Evening, Cathedral Alley, Gooseyard.

Jacques pulled up to the office and lingered for a while. He had just returned from Antoni Tapies' house, where he took one of his latest paintings, titled 'Homage to Tapies', to show to Tapies. He is Spain's Second Most Famous Artist, after Picasso, (if you don't count Maro or Dali) and Jacques has done a series of paintings of his sculpture 'Homage to Picasso', which sits on the Promenade near the Art Museum in the City Park. The sculpture itself is Surrealistic and Gross. (Frank cracked up while trying to describe it to me last year.)

Jacques' paintings of the sculpture have these added elements: Tapies himself standing examining the sculpture (as a young man, and as he is now), and Picasso naked, crucified on the Cross in the middle of the sculpture. 'El Loco' is standing there, crazy, in the pond surrounding the Sculpture.

Jacques knocked on Tapies' door, which was answered by a Maid, who invited him into the hall. He explained what he wanted, she liked the painting and disappeared with it up the stairs. She came back with Tapies' Wife, who seemed also to like the painting and informed Jacques that Tapies wouldn't be home til next week at the earliest. She asked Jacques what he wanted Tapies to do with the painting: Buy it? What? After some discussion, Jacques finally mentioned 30,000ptas but said that he would be Fulfilled if Tapies would only Look At It. She agreed to keep it at the house and show it to Tapies upon his return. Jacques needs the money, so I hope the Great Artist has a Sense of Humor. Otherwise, it could come back to Jacques slashed into small pieces.

He completed another painting, of the Ramblas, a couple of days ago, but has been unable to sell it to his Regular Patrons, "Jacques, I can't afford to buy a painting from you every month." It's a beautiful painting, Bright Colors for a change. No bricks or buildings (his specialty). Frank thinks it is the Beginning of a New stage in Jacques' Art. It IS Beautiful, but I think the dog would look better a little farther in the background.

He may have to set it up on an easel down on the Ramblas in order to sell it. This would be a Dangerous Move back towards the street, after he worked so long to escape the Chalk-World. He wandered off a while ago mumbling something about 'money from San Francisco', and I fear that he may be slipping down and back into one of his many Bum states of Mind. He was Flying High only yesterday. The twists and turns of Fate can Lay even the Mighty Low. Look at Napoleon. Look at Jacques.

I fear for my Hash Supply and my 100ptas/day. When he was lingering here he asked me, "Jack, I understand that Hadass is keeping you in Hash, now, isn't that true?" I said nothing, just laughed. He looked in my box and told me, "your days are numbered here, man."

I first suspected that Jacques was beginning to slip when he put Indira Ghandi in the Ramblas Painting. She is in the far-foreground, bending down talking with her nephew. What is Indira Ghandi doing ON THE RAMBLAS? Is this the work of a Sane Man? I may have to become HIS editor! He also has a Hooker in the painting, talking to two cops while a little old lady is having her purse snatched a few feet away.

What's weird is that sometimes he says the hooker is a transvestite and sometimes he says it's a woman, depending on what the observer thinks.

The Writing is easy, the money part is what's difficult. I'm getting about as much action as if I had a table out here with just a Dead Frog for sale. Maybe it's because I haven't eaten and my eyes are not exactly Friendly and Sparkling. I want to eat something and in a while I'm going to try to catch a goose; I'm sure I can do it.

Jacques told me, "Your Job is to write, not to worry about money. At times like this you gotta have faith. At least you're close to the light, so that if you have to be here til midnight, people will still be able to see you."

"Thanks.", I said.

"Well, Jack, I'm gonna go sit in a warm cafe and have a big meal, see you later.", he told me as he hunched off down the alley

It's been about two hours and Hadass has still not returned with some bread. Has she fallen in love in some dark bodega? Is she standing hypnotized in front of some street musician, letting the music bathe the desert in her soul? Has she stubbed her toe, and is right now limping towards me with the bacon? What?

Ah! here she is, right in Novel Time. She said she got delayed because she ran into Jacques and he had to explain to her how hungry I was, and what Bad Shape I'm in.

Ah! Bread, Cheese! TOMATO! I'm going to eat! YAH!

TWO WEEKS LATER

Puerta del Angel.

Yesterday was Jacques' Big Break Day. Tapies had probably looked at his painting by now, and Jacques was supposed to go out there and Reap His Reward.

There were two schools of thought:

1. Franks version: Jacques would show up at Tapies' House, the maid would answer the door, at first not recognizing him at all. Then, she would tell Jacques that Tapies saw the painting, didn't really like it very much, and appreciated the gift: He would probably keep it in the basement. With this, she would shut the door on Jacques, Brooking No Further Conversation, and leave Jacques standing there trying to find some Self-Respect. He's lost the painting for sure, because if he tries to make a scene and get it back, the Maid is in a mood to call the Cops.

2. Jacques' version: He shows up at the door, the Maid greets him like an old friend, invites him in for a cafe, and runs upstairs to fetch Tapies. The Master is Glad to meet Jacques, discusses The painting with him for a few minutes, pays him 40,000ptas, then takes him to the Studio where he shows him what he's been doing lately, Some Work Similar to Jacques', and tells him, "You're just the apprentice I've been looking for! You can help me around the Studio when I'm here, but I travel a lot, and when I'm gone you can use the studio, but keep it clean, and you can live here in return for tending the small flower garden out back."

What Really Happened: (regrettably, closer to Frank's version than Jacques'): Jacques knocked on the door, the Maid answered and said, "He looked at it.", and handed The painting to Jacques.

"Did he have any comment?", he asked.

"No.", she replied.

"Well, didn't he say Anything'?", he pressed.

"No.", she repeated, and shut the door.

Jacques Owns The Painting, again, and is going to take it with him today to plaza del pi where he is finishing up the Cathedral painting, and put a For Sale sign on it. His conclusion about the whole Tapies matter is, "Tapies may be an Artistic Genius, but he is a Social Retard!"

Frank told us, "Art is born in poverty, and dies in Wealth." Such a commitment is required to actualize this saying that I don't think it's worth it: I want Big Bucks.

Frank's Corollary: "The Aristocracy is always grinding the faces of the poor (he Loves that Phrase) just because there might be an Artist there!" He also informed us, "Devine is making a movie with Kris Kristofferson, and has the Number One Music Hit in the States!"

PETER AND CAMELS

Last night Peter surfaced to charge his batteries and sent us this message, "The Best Camels come from Australia. It's True! It's True! They're so good that they export them to. Africa." He continued, "Camels hold a Grudge: I knew this Berber in Morocco who was extremely cruel to his camel. Well, one night everybody went to sleep, with their camels; they sleep with their camels, and they lay their head right on the camel's belly, cuz that's where it's warmest. Well, he fell asleep, and the camel carefully raised itself up, being careful not to wake him, and crouched over his sleeping body and then lowered itself down on him. The camp was awakened by horrible screams and the guy was squished by his camel. Yup, camels hold a grudge." His batteries were charged now, so he submerged, raised his periscope, and cruised the rest of the evening just below the surface.

Clink, A Duro

Nov 28. The Cathedral Alley

Amani tells me that he is writing a script for a movie, his own creation, about something that takes place in Portugal. He said, "Well, it's not About Portugal, he just happens to be In Portugal." I asked him, "Have you been to Portugal?"

"No.", he answered. I suggested that he write a story about Catalonia instead, since he knows what the people are like here. He got irritated with me for not Grasping the Concept. He told me he is also writing a script for a 'contemporary movie', to be filmed here in Barcelona.

I said, "I'd like to see the script sometime."

He said, "She Had Some Bonkers!", watching a girl walk by.

Hadass is standing in the street, staring at the wall, as though she were related to the Grinning Gargoyle Hippy. Who Knows what's going on in her mind? She is Considering Something Very Weighty: maybe it's whether she should have agreed so readily to let me sleep at her place tonight. She has just taken off and we have agreed to meet at the Tapas later tonight.

It's gotten dark. Few people. The flute music has stopped but there's still a feeble stream of candle-lighters filing into the goose-yard. Still no 'clink'. I like the stuff I'm writing, though. At least it will make a good letter home: "What do you suppose Jackie has been doing in Spain? Oh, look, here's a letter from him now. My, look how big it is. Let's open it." (They begin to read). "Oh, my God, he's broke, and he's lonely! Let's send him a lot of money, right away!" It will be something like that, I suppose. Sure.

"Dear Jack: The book is great (the letter was great) but please leave out all the dirty parts from now on because we would like your sisters to be able to read it, too. Here's a couple of hundred dollars to tide you over. pay us when you can (along with the 13,000 you already owe us), and we'll be sending you a round-trip ticket in the next letter so that you can be home for Christmas and we can show you how much we all love you, in person, by giving you gifts."

Nov 29

I feel Great today. Had breakfast on the Patio with Hadass again this morning. No Garlic today, though. We stayed up til four again talking about who we were etc. That Hash! Hanging out with Hadass so much makes me wish I were a Jew. She read me some of Genesis in Hebrew last night, and it Was beautiful, just as she said it would be. I argued a few theological points with her, but was unsuccessful in convincing her that the New Testament should be a part of the Bible. My life, now, is so filled with New Things that I almost can't stand it. All the years of hard work are finally paying off.

Last night at Santi's was Rich with Strange Conversation.

Out of Nowhere Hadass piped up, "I've never sat with so many cowboys before!" She was referring to the Americans: me, Frank, Jacques, and Phil.

I explained to the others, "She thinks anyone without goat-shit on their shoes is a Cowboy.", which was a Cruel Reference to her Kibbutz up-bringing.

Canadian Steve was engrossed in a story that Frank was telling about being caught in a flood in Pasadena. Frank said, "We had to stay in the car all night: I wasn't going to get out and wade around in those bodies!" I reached for my pad and pen.

Commenting on my latest writings, Frank told me, "The beggar who did the best ever, on the Ramblas, was the one who had a sign saying he was in a Coma."

I said, "No Shit?"

"Surely.", he said.

Jacques told Frank that Peter had been feeling down the other day so Jacques had given him 'Hotel New Hampshire' to read, and he had felt much better.

Frank was Outraged, "It's Disgusting that I know people who can come out of a Suicidal Depression just by getting a New Book to read! Where are the Real people?!"

The conversation eventually turned to Art and Frank wrapped it up, "There's very little that Dali has done on canvas that I can forgive him for."

'Hadass said, "But he got better when he has more money!"

"Yah! When he got more money it gave him the freedom to do more SHIT!" I didn't get it: I've been to the Dali Museum and I think some of his stuff is pretty neat.

The talk turned to travelling and the differences between nationalities.

Frank said, "I had a Corsican girlfriend once, a descendant of Napoleon. She wanted to assemble an army and march on Paris. Her whole backyard was full of cannons. She wanted me to shoot a Cannon!" "Really, Frank?", I said.

Peter had a Date with his Catalan Girlfriend, Emma, last night, and decided to accompany The Gang to see 'Pink Flamingos', starring Devine, a Completely Gross Transvestite. I suppose that Peter was trying to Impress her by 'taking her someplace nice'. The movie ends with Devine eating dog-shit. I guess the movie made a Good Impression, I saw them coming arm-in-arm out of Pension Costa this morning. "We had a mouse last night!. Peter told me. The movie made me feel like barfing for a couple of hours. Don't go see it. Especially with a date you're trying to impress. Unless it's Emma.

Harry, the retired, one-eyed, Welsh, London Bookmaker, stopped by for dinner last night, as he has been doing off and on for ten years.

"Barbara, I'll have an omelette.", he ordered, after greeting Manilow, who was hanging over the balcony, rattling his chains and staring at people's food.

Barbara said, "Frank had four eggs."

Harry growled, "I'm not interested in Frank's Love Life, Gimme an Omelette!"

Jacques was telling me about what had happened in Pension Costa the night before. He needed a candle late at night, so he went over to Ahmed's room to borrow one.

Ahmed told him, "Shock, Pedro ees een heez room wiff a bombeeno. Ees Beeg trubble for me. Ees a Bambeeno, Shock!"

Jacques had to spend a few minutes assuring him, "It's OK, Ahmed, She's. 19, She's Peter's girlfriend, She's 19, She's Big. It's his Girlfriend, she's not a Bambino."

"Oh, good, Shock, You have save me big trouble if the police have come. I am in big trouble if Pedro is in his room with a bambino, thankyou, Shock, thankyou, thankyou." He had evidently been sitting in his room, next to peter's, listening to them fuck all night. And worrying about it.

I don't think she looks That Young. But, I guess compared to Peter, who is a rapidly aging Australian, she might look like a Bambino to Ahmed.

Ahmed, it is rumored, was born in Morocco, but has spent most of his life in Spain. He's in charge at Pension Costa: The Dueno. He is almost always the most Polite and Submissive person you will ever meet. He is friendly and unbelievably co-operative. But, he has a Secret personality: Raving Maniac. I have seen it only once: Sue and I were having a Yelling and Shouting Argument one time in the pension and Ahmed came charging into the room like he was about to kill me, when he realized that it was only Noise, and that no one was being hurt.

Jacques says that he has seen Ahmed in a State of Mind which he called "Absolutely Terrifying": Ahmed came home and found his wife/girlfriend in his best friend's room. He was drunk. He began beating up his friend, screaming, throwing and breaking furniture, punching his girlfriend, kicking and cursing in Arabic. Jacques says he watched from his doorway as Ahmed attempted killing the girl, who luckily was being protected behind Amani, but Ahmed got in a few punches anyway. Jacques says that. it was the Most Electrifying Example of Violence that he has ever seen, including My Rampages.

Eventually, the police were called, and somehow Ahmed convinced them that it was 'a family affair'. The girl was black and blue, and crying. The friend was bleeding and nearly crippled. The girl's (and Ahmed's) infant daughter had been locked in her room the whole time, screaming. The girl was unable to find her roomkey because she was in shock. The police left after giving Ahmed some advice about his temper.

A little while later, Jacques was drawn out into the hall again to witness Ahmed trying to kick down the door to the girl's room so that he could kill her. Jacques says that he started to go out into the hall to try to calm down Ahmed, but got part way out and realized it might be a mistake. He went back into his room and shut the door and tried to paint. Ahmed is a friend to all of us, almost.

Canadian Steve paid my way into pink Flamingos last night. He is amazingly clean-cut and wholesome-looking and seems to have as many girls as he wants. He's about twenty-five and has been travelling in Europe on his savings for about six months. Last night, during a discussion of his "tweeky-clean" appearance, it emerged that he is in 'disguise'. I asked him if he didn't look like that just to appear helpless and adoptable. He admitted that this was so. In his heart, he confirmed, he is just as much a dirty-old-man as the rest of us.

What a Smile! What Perfect Teeth! Jacques told me that Steve grooms himself in the Pension Bathroom for hours each day. It shows. I get in about two hours per year. It also shows.

Dinner at the Tapas

EL LOCO PAINTING

Nov 30, 1984

I'm back at the University. It's about 2:30, though I can't be sure because I sold my watch to Rene yesterday.

I told Jacques, "Man, it's gonna be so great when I forget I ever even had the fucking thing."

We finished up here about 5:30 last night, 300ptas richer, and headed back to the Gothic Barrio, looking for a hardware store where we could buy some legs for my table. Hadass and I split from Jacques because we were tired from lack of sleep the last few nights, and headed over to the Penthouse and smoked some more hash and tried to take a nap, which proved impossible because we were laughing.

We have Nearly decided to become Lovers. There's only one hurdle to overcome: She is taller than me. We are working on it and I have assured her that I am tall when Horizontal.

About nine oclock we headed over to Santi's for dinner. Only the Hardcore were present: Frank, Peter, Jacques, Canadian Steve. Frank was in the middle of a discussion proving that Steve's incredibly straight appearance was not a disguise after all, one of my Theories.

He told Steve, "You have a high threshold of excitement. You're like this: If you jumped off a roof, you'd spend your time on the way down folding your coat." Steve offered No Objection to Frank's Analysis.

Peter just sat there most of the evening looking like a U-boat commander with Grave Responsibilities and Psychological Problems.

The Book was read by all, and Criticisms and Scorn followed. Jacques said, "As long as he remains poverty-stricken, As Editor I can do whatever I want to. I realize that, after the first book, I'm Fired anyway." He has threatened to Edit Out Anything that is Not About Barcelona.

Jacques made fun of how long it was taking Frank to eat his stew while reading my book.

Frank defended himself, "I have nothing but Scorn for people who read and eat at the same time. I've even stopped my car and gone into restaurants and told people, 'Do you know what you're doing to your Emotional Health?

You know neither what you're reading, nor what you're eating!' I Despise it!" Jacques let 'Frank's food' drop.

My attention turned to Hadass for a minute; she was finishing her chicken dinner by eating the bones. When I turned back to the others, Frank was accusing Jacques of becoming a Jesus Freak just because it was a Fad.

The talk turned to the bible; Jacques was trying to convince Frank, "I'm sure there's something about a Kangaroo in there somewhere!" I worry about him sometimes.

Jacques admitted that he had Finally Gone Commercial, "Mass Production and Mass Sales! That's my New Way." He's Catholick.

It was a relatively boring night for Santi's. Frank needed new blood in order to get going. He Needled and egged us on, but we'd all learned to harden our hearts and try to ignore the barrage of barbed arrows which followed each of his tokes. There wasn't enough Ego at the table for Frank to get a solid bite. He Snapped and Drooled alright, but We Other Dogs knew that he was a Member of the pack, so no Really Vicious Interplay occurred.

Hadass packed it in early and Frank bid her goodnight, "What? Leaving So Early? On your way home to masturbate, Dear? Have a Good Night!" Hadass thanked him, smiled, and lurked on out into the night. When I left later, Frank asked me if it wasn't a bit early, and did I think Hadass had had enough time to finish the job. I told him I hoped not and bid all a good night. I was high on caffeine, and gripped my cane tightly as I slunk through the Barrio, waiting and hoping to be mugged.

Jacques' painting of me sitting here in the University 'Quad' is coming along fast. He says he'll probably have it finished by tonight. My main criticism is that my sunglasses look like the ones the bag-lady wears: pink, heart-shaped.

He told me, "That's the way I see it.", when I complained. Picasso's 'El Loco', my favorite, is in the background dancing through a doorway, and, according to Jacques, represents my Immediate Past; a good touch.

"Not a molecule of your Strangeness is escaping my brush!", he told me. I was pleased to hear it, it's my Main personality-Saving Trait.

I am making No Dinero today. The American Students gather around occasionally, but seem unaware that there is a Fee. They wish me good luck and wander off to classes. Most seem to think it's a good idea: they laugh when they read what I'm writing. But very few Clinks.

La Sagrada Familia, Mallorca

CAROLE DOESN'T SLIT MY THROAT IN SITGES

November 30, Plaza Universidad

Ahmed has informed me that there may be a room opening up at Pension Costa on Monday or Tuesday. If Hadass and I haven't solidified our relationship by that time (in other words: having a lusty and lurid love affair), I will gladly move over there. I don't think I'm going to work (?) tomorrow: I don't have to, I'm Rich, I sold my watch to Rene for 1200ptas. Instead, I think I'll spend the day looking for table-legs and maybe English classes. Or, maybe, I'll go to Guadi's Church: La Sagrada Familia, the Weirdest Building in the World.

    I haven't been there yet this year. I went there last year a few times. Carole (the Scar-faced, thirty-year-old, English, Lezbian, Killer), Sue, and I made a day of it: We took the elevator to near the top of one of the 300ft spires, climbed the rest of the way, and Sue and I fucked at the highest point. "I'm Coming! I'm Coming, I can see Mallorca!"

    Meanwhile, Carole was about fifty feet below us, on the narrow spiral staircase, Wailing and Blubbering. It turns out she has Vertigo, and Height-phobia. She was Utterly Paralyzed, unable to move an Inch, up or down. I tried to talk to her but was unable to get her to speak. Liquid was oozing from all of her Facial Apertures with each Blubber. At first, I thought it was a very Good Act, as Carole is usually the Most Fearless of People. (She has taken on Whole Gangs of Arabs, emerging Victorious amid pools of blood and body parts. She is a Street-fighting Bitch. She's BAD!) Nevertheless, There She Was, unable to move, Bawling like a baby. I got her to move her butt to the next lowest step, but she took one look out the opening in the wall (you COULD jump out of one easily. FALL OUT, even), and let out a series of high-pitched Wet Shreiks. It took a few more minutes to get her to move to the next step down. She could not stand. It took Sue and me about an hour to descend to ground level with her.

    Once on the ground for a few minutes, she became her Old Self, and we began scouting around for a bar where Sue could rest her feet, I could have a 'few beers', and Carole could try to seduce a young bird or get in a fist-fight. All was well again in Expatriate Barcelona.

I once spent the day in Sites with Carole. We had scheduled to meet at Santi's that day and Form Up for a Caravan by train to Sites, a beautiful Resort Town about twenty miles south. I had spent the previous night at Disco Celeste with Alexander, Ramon, and Sally, so overslept my appointment.

Frank, Carole (they're Best of Friends), Ricky Nelson, and a Crazy Welshman drove down without me. I followed by train a couple of hours later, decked out in my Top-hat, cane, full-length camels-hair coat, Hawaiian shirt, and Rampage Attitude. I found them at a beachfront cafe sitting at a table in the Warm Mediterranean Sun, and we spent the afternoon drinking and laughing and falling down and dancing and insulting the more 'normal' tourists. Carole and I had become drinking-buddies over the previous couple of weeks, and I didn't have even a suspicion as to how the evening would end. (Though Frank claims that he saw it coming from Birth). As it became darker, we wobbled our way up to the English Bar in Town: 'The Dublin Bar', where we drank some more and listened to sixties Rock and Roll. I began dancing and yelling: just generally having a good time.

Well, Ricky, the young American weight-lifter health-nut, became embarrassed by my antics, (the bartender had already politely asked me to keep it down) and threatened to take me outside and "beat the shit out of you". Well, I told him that there wasn't going to be any "beating the shit out of anybody, tonight", that if he wanted to stop me, he had better kill me because if he beat the shit out of me I would kill him if I ever came to. I yelled, "Fuck You, you little muscle-bound punk! I'll Fucking Kill You! You got it?", and like that.

The bartender came over again, this time with a great big club for us to look at, and told us to keep it down. Ricky wouldn't shut up and I got loud again when he threatened me. The bartender rushed over and grabbed me and made a Fairly Spectacular Scene out of ejecting me from the bar. It took a couple of minutes. I wasn't fighting back: he was sort of hitting me and actually just sort of pushing me out, while I Was Reasoning with Him. I'd been through the scene many times and thought little of it.

Evidently, it was a Big Deal for the people in the bar: every few minutes, someone else would come out to me in the street where I was sitting on the hood of a car with a bottle of wine I'd bought across the street, and warn me that "So-and-so is going to come out here and kill you!". This went on for about an hour, when I decided to go up and poke my head in the door to inquire of my friends when we might be leaving for Barcelona. (The Welshman had the car and I had negligently run out of money: I was stuck with them. Frank claims that Carole had been keeping me alive: Various English were planning to come out and kill me but Carole would talk them out of it. Frank thinks that it was about this time that I became "Hers", to do with as she pleased. Most of the people in the bar were Bar-owners from Sites and they were angered by my Ugly American yelling, like: "I can buy this whole fucking Town! I'm so fucking Rich I can't stand It!", and other such Psycho-dramatick bullshit which I find so amusing when drunk.)

When I stuck my head in the bar, Pandemonium Broke. The Crowd, almost all of them, wanted a Piece of the Action. Me. It was a Replay. On film it would have looked Extremely Violent, but I was Completely Unhurt. There was Something At Work Here, of which I was merely the Un-suspecting Focus. I ended up outside on the street again with my bottle of wine. I thought All Was Well.

About an hour later Carole, Frank, The Welsher, and Ricky joined me and we headed for the car, all drunk, except for Frank. His pipe had grown into his face. I was explaining to Someone that I didn't understand what was going on at the bar to cause all the commotion, when I was attacked by Ricky, then by the Welshman, and finally by Carole. The Welshman had my hands behind my back and Carole had my head held down on a car by my hair. She broke a bottle and was about to slit my throat, when Ricky grabbed her hand, cutting himself, and Saving my Life. Frank watched the whole thing from a short distance away, smoking his pipe, and probably wondering how he had gotten mixed up with such Violent People. I was wondering the same.

I spent that night sleeping in a field north of Sites, overlooking the Sea, because the Welshman, in his drunken stupor, put diesel in his gasoline-powered car and we broke down half way back to Barcelona.

Carole and I later became very good friends, but I never got drunk with her again. In fact, that was the last time I got drunk in Barcelona on that trip. It was a Very Close call. I hadn't seen it coming.

Frank claims that to this day he is not welcome at any bar in Sites, just for having been with me on that day. He tells the story often, and it has travelled ahead of me, so that people often ask me when we meet, "Are you the Jack from Sites?".

Carole disappeared from Barcelona about the same time I did last year, off to Portugal with a 'bird', and no one, including Frank, has heard a peep out of her since. When she does come back, you can bet the fun will begin again.

Hadass and the Tower of David

Hadass and I were sitting in her apartment smoking hash.

I told her, "You Are Your Life! Your life wasn't something that was Given to you and then you get to use it for a while and discard it when you want to, and then continue merrily on your way. NO! There is no difference between You and Your Life."

She said, "You are a drummer. Maybe this writing is just an excuse for you to drum. It is the same action. This is why you write!"

"Maybe so, maybe so.", I answered.

She continued, "It's True! This is why I'm living my life the way I am! "

"Why is that?", I asked.

"Because what I am doing now IS My Life!", she told me, making me wonder what I had been trying to explain to her. She had obviously assimilated the Concept long ago, in Whole, and was reaping its rewards at that very moment.

She continued, "I repeat myself, to myself anyway. I am always saying the same thing. But it is only One Idea."

A whole new world opened to me: she was generating Symbols that had me spinning. She is always expressing the Same Idea.

I finally asked, "What is the Same Idea that you're always repeating?"

"In my head.", she answered, "I am thinking and I don't want to stop."

She began making clicking noises and I answered with Thokking noises.

"Maybe I'll call Margo tomorrow and she'll come and you'll have a love affair.", she told me.

I told her, in my best Bogie Voice, "Listen, Sweetheart, you don't have to be a Jew to be one of the Chosen Few. That's the only part they got wrong."

She laughed, and it was obvious to me that Our Conversation had no rules.

"When you write, it looks like you are seeing sideways.", she told me as I sat at the typewriter and she practiced juggling her devil sticks.

"I've done it all my life.", I told her.

"Ahhh.", she said. One of us had just realized that you can only see yourself from the side.

We ate a meal of grapes, bread (great food), cheese, chocolate, and hashish. In that order. Hey Jude was playing on the little box. It was about one oclock. She was laying on the bed under a Navajo Blanket while I was typing.

It only snows about twice a year in Jerusalem.

"One time, when it was snowing in Jerusalem, It was very beautiful, I have climb to the top of the Tower of David. You can see the Desert on one side and you can see the hills. I meet a soldier in the museum there, he is on pass from the army, and we walk up to the tower together. It is very small there. It is SO beautiful! The Sky, and the Desert, and the Snow All Around! And he says to me, 'Is there Anything you could wish for now?' f And I tell him 'A Bottle of Whiskey.', And he pulls out a bottle of Whiskey and we are drinking it and We Make Love in the Tower of David and when we go down the steps we find that we are locked in the Museum. It was so Beautiful! This is a Memory I want everybody to know! And later we unlock the Museum and go out and throw the keys back in and He go back to the army and I go back to the old part of town, where the students, my friends, live, and I go to my friend's house and get in the bed and he makes me toast and we make love again. It is a beautiful time, for me."

I asked, "Did you know the soldier before?"

"NO, No, He is not a soldier: He is a 'Reserve'. It's Important!"

"There is people making Love Everywhere. I think it is because of The War-Time, the people get so horny after a war. The Atmosphere is something! They are all Fucking for two months after the War."

I said, "It's Life and Death, that's what it is." "Don't you think Barcelona is a Sexy City?", she asked. "Yah, but not so much for me, though.", I answered, hanging my head.

Hadass is trying out a New Concept: She's trying to see if she can sleep with a Man and Not Make Love. My timing must be off, Why Me? Why? She also told me that I am too much like an Israeli.

She continued talking about Sex and Lovers, "When I look back, I see that most of my lovers have look something like Marlon Brando."

"Well," I said, "That kind of lets me out: I look like Mickey Rooney."

"Maybe that is the solution for my love life: stop hanging around with Marlboro Faces!", she continued. I offered to carry her off to the desert and provide her with blond, blue-eyed children; she could always dye their hair black.

I told her about my evening the night before with Ramon and Sally in the uptown bars. She said, "Sally is good for you. I think you and Sally is a good one."

I told her, "you're Crazy! Ramon will Kill me! Kill me dead!! Sally is My Friend, It's Just Fine this way: I'm Alive."

She has calculated her Menstrual Cycle and told me that I must move out on Monday because she is sure to be Extremely Horny.

Phil and Rene's Party

Hadass and I arrived at Santi's around eight, after smoking some hash and practicing juggling for a while. Frank and Peter were already there, deep into the Psycho-preparations for the Party. Frank was sharpening his barbs on some of The Lesser Ones in the rapidly-growing waiting-cavern. By the time Jacques arrived, there were about fifteen people waiting to leave. Tracy and Helen, Judy, Amani, Canadian Steve and Valerie, Jive the German (looking like Peter), Frank, Peter, Me, Hadass, and a few other people I still don't know.

It was 930. Jacques ordered his usual chicken dinner, and ate a Leisurely Meal, while the rest of us Waited in Anticipation for The Finish of His Meal, and the Beginning of the Party.

After he finally finished, and Barbara had cleared his dishes, Jacques ordered a Cafe con Leche. A Groan went up from the Crowd .. Barbara brought his Cafe and he took a sip of it, "Oh! it's too hot, I'll just let it cool off a little." A few Moaned. Jacques was Positively Revelling in the Social Power he had acquired.

As we finally departed the Tapas we heard Barbara's high-pitched voice ring out, "Poor Phil!" She wasn't far from the Mark on that.

As I was the only one who knew the way to Phil's, I led the circus out of plaza Regomir, but by the time we reached Plaza St. Juame, the Midgets had gotten separated, and the Acrobats were setting much to fast a pace for the Clowns.

We invaded the Metro with our Cacophony of Foreign Babble, and finally managed to arrive at phil and Rene's, after a serious attempt by Hadass to head us in exactly the wrong direction when we came up out of the Metro.

We filed into the closet that Phil and Rene call their apartment and arranged ourselves according to Activity Preferences, and began drinking, smoking dope, and eating what Phil called "The Chili". I called it "Tomatoes and Beans".

Norma was already there, along with a few people I hadn't met before. I found 'Phil's Book', an attempt to compete with this Tome, and seated myself on the sewing-roam floor to read his version of the Barcelona Experience. It's good, especially the parts about me.

Hadass told me, "He write better than you but you are funnier." I was flattered and told Phil what she had said. He was flattered. I wandered out into the Living Room to watch Norma for a while. She was Lucille Ball tonight, in a bright red cloth coat that her mother had made for her, but you could still see Shirley MacLaine if you looked closely. I tried winking at her a couple of times but I think she missed them. I'm Terrible at picking up girls, especially if they know me.

Frank's pipe was surgically implanted on his lips and he was keeping Norma in Minor Convulsions.

I overheard Frank explaining Peter's Wardrobe for the night to Jacques, "Peter's got himself so Cosmeticized that Regular Girls are sitting there talking to him as though he were Normal! They've lost track of the fact that they're dealing with a Half-wit. They're hypnotized by his Facade!"

"That's Right!", Jacques said, "That's why he needs that white silk scarf, To Hypnotize Them!" Peter has commissioned Rene to make a scarf for him, 'regardless of the cost'. "

Frank continued, "The police won't look him in the eyes. They think he's a Rich German."

The Booze and Beer were flowing; THC smoke clouded the rooms. The Pace was picking up: A Band Of Jewelers broke into a stirring Rendition of "Jump Down, Turn Around, pick a Bale of Cotton", Frank was off on a story about Werewolves in Hollywood, Jacques was Changing the color of his eyes to Red, Rene was Getting Tired, Phil was spreading Confusion from Group to Group by Forgetting That He Was The Host, Hadass was reading and smoking Hash, and I was wandering around in 1968 In San Francisco wondering if there was any opium to be had in the Haight.

I overheard a Young European Hippy telling Black Diane about Steve Gaskin and 'The Farm'. I soon put a stop to That, "Oh, do you know Steven?", I asked, as though He were one of My Disciples.

I was leaning against the wall and Accidentally stepped on Phil's Puppy; it squeaked. Luckily, when I looked down, it was Peter's Fur Coat. It recovered in a moment and was soon chasing its own tail in the corner, while I followed Young English Helen out onto the Balcony. We talked about the View for a few minutes: Buildings. She told me that she craved Waves of Undulating Greenery. I told her we should have a picnic sometime in a big field near the sea. So Much Time: So Much To Do. It Must have been good hash.

We were joined on the Balcony by Peter and Tracy the Dancer, and the three of them found something interesting to look at on the floor near the Bathroom Door out there.

I left them to their Madness and went to see what Hadass was into. She was still reading, but had begun drinking GIN.

"Kiss me, Jack.", she said. I did, and with the Exchange of Saliva, all visions of Tracy dancing on me, and Helen Romping Naked Thru The Clover, instantly faded. It was a Secret Code between Hadass and me: I had been refusing to Make Love to her for days, "How can we be Lovers if we don't even kiss?", I would ask. "We cannot.", she would reply.

This was It! She wanted me, Finally. I went in to get her some More Gin. I 'lost' the Hash at this point and kept her glass full for the rest of the evening. We French-Kissed a few times and I think she was going to show me 'The' Kiss of the Desert', but we couldn't find a camel.

By about three oclock the party Got in Full Swing. Tracy had lights going off in and around her head, Helen was Being Generally Delicious, and Hadass was Holding Court. Frank said that ever since I began putting her in the book she thinks she's a Star.

"The Six-Day-War got everyone stoned, and the Yom Kippur War got everybody Horny.", Hadass was telling Phil, who was Wide Open for an Israeli Recent History Lesson.

She went on, "I got my period during the Six-Day-War, the volunteers from the rest of the world brought patchouli Oil and Drugs. It was The Beginning of a New Life for me." Coming of Age in Modern Israel?

"Everybody was High, Happy, and Rich!", she exclaimed, "It was good to be an Israeli!"

A few more people gathered around her now, "you have no idea what my Life is like. To Travel, All These Years. Raising on the Kibbutz. There is always war in Israel. The People all getting pregnant after the war. Everybody Fucking! It's Good!" Phil just stood there nodding his head, afraid to interrupt, aware that He Was Learning, even if he didn't want to be, and the Professora was A Little Bit Mad.

After about fifteen minutes, Hadass finally began to run down, and lowered herself gradually into a sitting position, where I was afraid she was about to break into Sobs. I comforted her with a kiss and a glass of gin.

Jacques, meanwhile, had finagled himself into a Beery Philosophical Argument with Two of the Jewelers, "I see what you mean, but I don't Agree with your Interpretation.", and shit like that. I can't remember the exact words because I have no mental system where that kind of phrasing can find a place to Rest. Jacques is a Master at it: Concept War. He's trained for years in bars all over the West Coast of the U.S.. With his Red Eyes and Multi-Syllabic Phrasing, he is Almost Unconquerable in Party Discussions. This time, however, it was a Draw: These were intelligent, experienced Beer-drinking Expatriate Jewelers who may have been to as many parties as Jacques has.

Frank had hypnotized a German, Tracy, and Helen and there was Continual Cackling from their corner. Phil and Rene began asking people, "What? Are you leaving?", whenever someone would stand up to get another drink or straighten their clothes or go to the toilet. The answer was Invariably, "No, not yet, I'm staying all night just like everyone else." Phil and Rene are really into partying; I would have been tired of it Way before five oclock, but not them.

A Group of Young Hip Europeans was trying to Devise a plan to "Burn Europe" without destroying the parts that they, The Anarchists, considered Valuable. I started to Join the discussion but decided that it was Just Too Wiggy for me.

Hadass, Energized by the Gin, had Phil mesmerized again, "She was Incredibly Beautiful. Zey Kiss. I, see zem. Zey Never going to see each ozzer again. I know zis. Zen zey split up and we go to the Party at the Communist Party. I meet him at Christmas years later in Rome. It's Fantastic!" She can't say 'th' on Gin?

"Hadass, you lead an Incredibly Surrealistic Life!", Phil told her, as I leapt for my pen and became a Drugged Observer rather than a Drugged Participant.

I've been teaching Hadass American.

Phil told her, "Hadass, you have one normal friend: me."

"Gimme a Break, Phil", she replied, completely cracking him up. I was proud of her; she used 'Gimme a Break' perfectly. I'm waiting for her to use 'Crazy as a Loon', which she's also been practicing at home.

Frank was Spearheading a Movement to head for a 'Granja' (ice-cream shop) and partake of some "chew-chews", as he put it, pointing at his mouth. Most of the crowd wanted to go to a Bar and drink more, but his enthusiasm for "chew-chews" was impossible to overcome.

Rene had taken over the Living/Bedroom to crash, and Phil was on the way out with us when he remembered again that he lived there. I made an appointment with him to work on the ideas for the English-Language Underground Newspaper, but we forgot to set a date and time.

Jacques brought the tape-recorder with him, and He, Hadass, and I finally emerged into the Barcelona Morning to find no trail of the Granja Crowd. We sauntered towards the Barrio, a couple of miles, with Jacques Dancing Like an Idiot to the Worst Disco Music Imaginable. And John Denver. It took him back to the time he worked with Retarded Children and they all knew the words to "Rocky Mountain High". I think those memories were affecting his dancing, because I had to keep a close watch for Ladrones who were attracted by his Disco Machine and his Obvious Lack of Social Awareness. Idiots are Easy pickings, but I had the 'Cane of Escudillers' and Hadass had her Expression. We were safe.

As we parted from Jacques, he was pissing against a building to the beat of Spanish-Disco and was drawing weird looks from early-morning passersby. I supposed he would be safe on the streets, as was Mr. Hyde in his day.

Hadass and I retired to the penthouse, climbed in bed and began our interpretation of "Rape in the Desert." My turban kept coming unwound and she would yell, "Stop!", so I would stop. It turned out that "stop" in Desert Talk means "More", but it took me a while to figure this out. It finally all began to make sense, and became Fun when I told her that I actually Had Lived in the Desert once. We found a camel.

In the end she said I wasn't weird enough for her, and we left it hanging at that til the next time. We shall see.

Patented Penguins

Jacques was in the Tapas last night when Hadass and I arrived. He was talking to Whiting Southall Tennis, a recently arrived 7ft Young American painter, who got the room at Pension Costa which I refused. Frank has christened him Whitey, which will probably stick. We were soon joined by Black Diane, an Australian, and her Friend Sergio, an Argentinian who is trying to sell computers in Barcelona, part time. Diane made 1000ptas yesterday playing Hadass' recorder in the Metro. She'd never played before, and had just learned how to make a Musical Sound on it. Yesterday, when I gave it to her, she put it in her mouth backwards. She figures that the Metro is better than the streets because people are in a hurry there and won't stop long enough to realize that she repeats herself every thirty seconds. Her heart is in it though, so she Will Make a Living. Sergio is educated, vacationing, working, laughs a lot, and somewhat resembles Mr. Spock, without the ears.

Santi was closing down, so we all migrated over to La Barraca, the bar on the ground floor of Pension Costa; usually Ahmed's home, but not since the head-bashing of a week ago.

The Conversation was Light and humorous until Hadass was heard to say, "A friend of mine patented penguins."

Maybe it was the Hash, maybe the Caffeine: I nearly split a gut laughing. She began explaining to Sergio, in Spanish, exactly what she meant by this. They talked for a couple of minutes, the rest of us anxiously awaiting a better translation or an explanation.

"Well,", I asked Sergio, "Did her friend patent penguins?"

"No,", he answered, "He Designed Them!" That was It. The crowd was Gone. My stomach hurt.

Jacques said, "The guy's not as smart as we thought, they can't even fly!"

Hadass began again explaining to Sergio just what it was she was trying to tell us. They talked animatedly for a couple more minutes. Jacques began to translate Hadass' words for me, as Sergio obviously wasn't doing very well: "She says that after he made a four foot penguin he realized it was a new animal. His original idea had been much smaller." I told Jacques to ask her if he'd designed the Kiwi also.

Hadass said, "Now he's working on Roofs. He build only roofs. He no care about house. Only build roofs!"

Jacques was beside himself, and his beer, with glee: "After he fucked up with animals, he only does buildings now!"

The Evening was obviously ending: we had reached the Heights of Mindless Hilarity, and our stomachs could take no more of Hadass' Conversation. It was a decent Baptism for Whitey.

Hadass' Pad/The Pad

Hadass and I are back at the Pad. Such a Pad. It's about twelve feet square with a kitchen slightly bigger than a phone booth. Everything is painted white, even the exposed pipes and wires which criss-cross the whole place. There are prints, calendars, wood-things, postcards, newspaper photos, and original drawings and paintings hanging, lying, and leaning all over the walls, floor, and ceiling. There are boxes and trunks of various sizes clogging one side of the room. These are filled with Hadass' Many Treasures. (She even has a Complete Auto Repair Kit, which she found one day on the street when she needed a hammer) There is a huge chalking, on paper, covering most of one wall. (You know what hash does for me? I keep dropping the little pieces allover the floor, and accidentally knock coffee cups over and drop lighted cigarettes in the bed, That's what it does.)

There are electric wires running all around the room, with bare ends hanging out occasionally; This is a Beatnik Pad if I ever saw one: I'm glad I finally got to grow up and be a Beatnik. I was too young the first time. The bed's on the floor, there's a couple of end-tables, and three wooden chairs and a Hadass-made-from-scratch Functioning and Functional Main Dining Table.

Things in this room don't seem to have any Special Place: they move from spot to spot from time to time. Hadass says that when I am not here Things usually stay in the same spot from day to day.

"You mean like Monks?", I asked.

"Yass", she answered.

She is worried that she may break her back some day while travelling, because of the weight of all the stuff she carries with her from year to year, back and forth from place to place, in country after country. This last year, for instance: from Israel to Spain to Belgium to Italy to Greece to Barcelona to Santi's to Calle Raurich. And on and on. I suggested lightening the load by jettisoning some of the Useless Treasures. So, she showed me a couple of Things she has been carrying around for years for no Logical reason: Two Beautiful little boxes, Chinese lacquered, varnished wood.

I told her, "Well, I can see why you carry them everywhere. They're Both Beautiful! I think you should always carry them." I was a big help. I guess she'll have to buy a car.

Years ago there was not a room here. This place was added onto the roof later. (of course, Later). So, the floor is the old brick roof. It seems like it, too. You can't play marbles and it's difficult to stand up and kiss in here: you end up on the low side of the room if you get lost in passion: you fall there. This is the Barcelona Mystery House: you wash the dishes in the bathroom sink and get your hot shower water from the kitchen. How Amazing: Let's sell tickets to the Beatnik Pad.

"you're gonna climb those 96 stairs."

Woody Allen Siesta

As it approached one-thirty I folded everything up and dropped it off for safe-keeping with Jacques in Plaza del pi. I headed over to the Anarchist Bar but was told by his mother that Juan (my prospective student) didn't come in today, but would For Sure be in Tomorrow. I stopped by the Huge Cheapest Mercado in Barcelona and bought some grapes, peanuts, cookies, and oranges for Hadass and I to eat for Lunch.

I met her at her pitch and she folded up her stuff and we headed for the Pad to Make Love During Siesta, something we hadn't tried before. We were very Happy and Anxious. We stopped off at a small store and bought some Pate of pig's Liver, Milk, and more Cookies. This was going to be Some Siesta, let me tell you.

I took a standing bath while Hadass made some Coffee and a few sandwiches: Bread, Pate, Cucumbers, and Tomatoes. AH! We can Make Our Own Cafe Con Leche! We ate the Sandwiches (not Bocadillos: Too Much Ingredient), drank the Cafe, and Talked.

I watch her mouth Carefully; I'm Naked.

He begins to make love to her; He is naked, she is fully clothed. He realizes after a minute or so that it's not going to work. He tries to remove her clothes but fumbles helplessly because they are European Fastenings, with which he is unfamiliar. She begins laughing. He tries , vainly, to cover Himself with some socks.

She tells him, "I have discovered new Truth behind Street Artists: If you work in a office you can't be Horny. What you going to do? You have to serve People: you can't be Horny. But, if you a Street Artist, you can be Horny all day!"

He Has to write down what she has just told him, so he jumps up to get his pen, kicking a small table with his foot, knocking a glass of coffee all over the pillows. She begins removing some of her clothes, but She Also seems to be having some trouble with the fastenings. He decides to light the Heater: The fucking little trick Spanish matches keep breaking off or not lighting. She finds it Hilarious, and is in the background Chortling his Hard-On Of The Day away. He finally gets the heater going, but it runs out of gas a minute later. They both work on getting it going (She has her pants, boots, and scarf on; he is wearing socks) .

"I hate to make love with socks on.", she tells him.

"You can't even see them under the boots!", he answers.

"Not you!", she says.

They begin again, but she knocks the red part of his cigarette onto the bed and they both have to fumble for a minute to find it. The Siesta Is Passing, and Our Heroes are not even close to Heaven's Gate. He decides to Go For It and lunges his head towards her groin just as she crosses her legs: "Crack!" He has a few loose teeth but doesn't care as His Ardor Is Growing. He Moves In and skillfully breaks down her Tribal Defense as she throws her head back in Ecstasy and cracks it on the bookshelf. They laugh uproariously when they realize that this has all been an Audition for Woody Allen's next movie: "Spanish Affairs".

Humor wins over Lust, but they give it a try anyway: A Joke is a Joke, and a Fuck is a Fuck, but You Shouldn't Quit When The Fuck is a Joke! They manage to use what he has left and rapidly complete the Afternoon's Siesta.

I wish I could say that the Church-bells had a Simultaneous Ringing, but they rang-off early: Premature osculation.

NEW YORK, 1990

A long black Cadillac limousine is cruisin' the slums of New York City. It screeches to a halt next to a large pile of garbage, a door flies open, another. Out the first door comes a tall woman, dressed to kill in a see-thru dress, high heels, make-up, jewels, stockings: A beautiful long-necked, erotick, smiling Israelita. Right behind her come Mick Jagger and Andy Warhol, "I am loookeen for somseen espeshiall!", she cries.

She begins to laugh, halting her search through the piles, "Oh, ha ha ha ha, I wass theenking I am in Barcelona, At thees time! Ha ha ha, I am haveen thee habit of lookeen in thee street for my theengs! Ha ha ha!" Mick and Andy have a good laugh too, and they all pile into the limo and it speeds off with laughter echoing off the garbage, as the Dawn begins to Break?

Pirate Steve's Recipe for Ali-Oli

HOMING JEWS

A Wednesday evening in the Tapas with the usual crowd: Frank, Peter, Jacques, Canadian Steve, Christopher the German, Hadass, Whitey, and me. Basically, the Pension Costa Dining Room gang.

Peter was telling us about the trouble he was having with his 19- year-old girlfriend, "I'm giving up my Catalan girlfriend because she's so into Caves.", he told me. I submitted the subject to the Group for Discussion.

Peter explained, "She said we were going to be together this weekend and now she's going to explore some fucking caves!"

Jacques counseled him, "Peter, you're running into the Catalan Consciousness head-on! The only time they'll visit you is when they're trying to get you. Once they've Got you, forget it. It's exactly what happened to me with Marta." Peter continued to complain.

"Give her a duro (5ptas) and tell her to call you in five years.", suggested Hadass. Peter wasn't cured.

Frank had a hand, "Peter, the Catalans are the 'Dutch' of Spain, and the Dutch are the 'Jews' of Europe."

"That's right, they're on Rails.", I added, for no apparent reason.

Peter confessed, "I think maybe it's better if I have one-night stands for the rest of my Life."

Jacques, half-way through his nightly bottle, added this, "I think we should all use Hadass and Jack's method of Communication in a Love Affair: Publish it at dinner every night!"

We took a break and discussed Hadass' Period for a while; or lack of it, in this case.

For some reason, Frank was in a pleasant mood and wasn't actively agitating this evening.

I asked Jacques to get my cigarettes out of the left hand pocket of my jacket, and he had to do the Cub Scout Salute in order to remember which hand was which. (3/4 bottle gone).

Hadass fellowshipped with Jacques on this Quirk, "Ah! You also have problem with That! It's Psychology: knowing right from left. In the Army, it's a problem when you don't know right and left."

"I can imagine.", I said.

Canadian Steve added, "Valerie has the same problem." The truth is coming out: The Majority of the Tapas Crowd doesn't know Right from Left.

Pirate Steve finally made his appearance and read his most famous poem, "The Very Bit of It!", to a standing ovation, cheers, and Hearty Clapping. (This caused the only injury of the night when Peter stabbed himself in the left hand with a toothpick he was holding in his right hand, while clapping. It's a simple mistake, especially when you are distracted, as is Peter. The bleeding stopped in a minute or two). Steve wallowed in his Fame for a few minutes and then announced that all were welcome to join him later Down at the Bodega. Very Friendly, for him.

The Conversation wandered.

"The Catalans know the Value of Art: twenty-five pesetas per hour!", Frank told Jacques.

"If you have body lice, get Hadass to breathe on you.", I told Peter, referring to the amazing amount of Garlick she consumes daily.

Pirate Steve asked Frank what he had done today. Steve works, begging, and resents Frank's Lifestyle.

"I count any day in which I've accomplished absolutely nothing a day Well Spent.", Frank replied, making Steve feel even worse. He left, pissed off.

The conversation turned to Carole.

"Christmas would be complete if only she would make an Appearance.", I offered. .

"Every time Carole see me in Tapas she want to fight me.", said Hadass.

"That's because your Commando Background is a challenge to her.", Frank told her.

Hadass continued, "Carole got a good Jewish Education: She Hate Arabs!"

Peter added, "Carole has bionic limbs, you know. She has plastic for bones all over her body."

"It's true, Carole has been in so many scrapes that pieces of her are scattered allover Europe and the British Isles.", said Frank.

As Hadass, Jacques, and I prepared to head for the Bodega to meet Steve, Frank had this final bit of information for us, "Remember, there are 132,000 legally blind people wandering around New York City every day!" We thanked him and headed out.

Hadass and I were playing Huggy and Kissy on the way there. She asked me, "Do you know the expression, 'Last time, on the Carpet'?".

"No, but I want you to teach it to me.", I answered.

We arrived down at the Bodega and joined pirate Steve who was sitting at a big table with a glass of ale, listening to the walls peel. I offered him a toke of my joint.

"I'm Irish! What's the Matter with You?", he answered, refusing the toke.

"What the Fuck do you think I Am, American?", I asked, offended. I took a toke and the room got unusually Bright. Jacques and Hadass ordered wine. We watched an old lady leave the bar for a few minutes. We watched the paint peel. Steve asked me when my book was going to be published; he's worried, now that his poem is in it. I told him it would be sooner than he thinks.

The Conversation turned to Art.

Steve said, "Barcelona Radio consists of American Seconds. When you listen to the words, it's Shit: 'had a cup of tea", Crap!, 'polished me boots, got into me car', All Crap!", he continued, comparing the radio lyrics to his own, which are Far Superior. He said, "I've been writing songs since before pink Floyd was in booties!"

The waiter brought Hadass a Large glass of wine. "Iss too much for me!", she exclaimed.

"No! You haven't drunk half of it!", Steve shouted.

"Get Drunk, Sweetheart! You're more fun.", I told her.

"you Swine!", Steve said, jabbing me in the ribs.

Hadass wanted to correct Steve's mis-interpretation, "I told HIM: I'm more fun when I'm Drunk."

"She IS!", I agreed.

The Bodega is probably the oldest in town, about 400 years. I told Steve, "You're practically furniture in here."

"I've been coming in here for five years.", he bragged.

I said, "Yah, I usta drink in here last year. When I want to get drunk I come here: I don't wanna hear any of this Disco Shit! I don't wanna hear any High Heels! This is where I come to get FUCKED UP!"

"This is the place to do it.", Steve agreed.

An Obvious African came down the steps. Steve commented, "He's been hanging about the Cathedral all day. He's been home and washed, and put on his best clothes and he's out on the town. And he comes HERE! He's stolen three cameras so he could buy two loaves of bread and get his Jacket cleaned. And forgot his Trousers!"

Steve leaned over towards me and began to tell me Exactly What to Write, just like Hadass did when I began quoting her.

"See, Hadass", I told her, "It's happening again: I quote them in the book and they think they can tell me what to write!" Then Steve leaned over me, tried to grab my pen, and showed me Exactly Where to write what he had been saying. It went on for a couple of minutes, but I stood my Literary Ground til his feelings got hurt and he gave in. Here's what he wanted me to write: "He's got more Front than Woolworths."

He explained, "It's an English Joke. That's how we could tell he was BLACK!" I was at a loss for words.

While Jacques was off in a little smelly room trying to figure out which was the pisser and which was the sink, we talked about him.

"How's Jocko doing these days?", Steve asked.

"Badly,", I answered, "I have to loan him money, and we had to buy him some hash so he wouldn't self-destruct. If his money doesn't come from the States in a week, he'll be back on the street, chalking."

"He'll Have To!", Steve observed, based on his years of street experience.

"Say, Steve,", I asked, "why don't you come on down to the Anarchist Bar for lunch tomorrow, and meet me before I start teaching?".

"What am I supposed to do? Stand on the street outside and play me flute til I can afford to buy a glass of water?", he asked.

"NO!", I answered, "I'll buy you a fucking lunch. Not too soon, though, come over when I'm Middle Class. I can't afford it Now, I'm getting my lunch for free."

Steve demanded that I put his recipe for Ali-Oli in the book. Here it is:

"First of all you have a bowl. (he imitated a bowl with his hands, cupping them, as if I didn't know what a bowl was), then you have to have a Pummeller (he imitated a mortar and pestle), and some Fresh Goat's Milk, which is blue, like yoghurt. Then you have to grind up your Garlic and pummel it and add some flour, (I was writing fast now, I didn't want to miss THIS Recipe), and bits of onion. You Pummel .for an hour or two."

"When do you put in the Eggs?", I innocently asked, assuming that he had forgotten one of the most important ingredients of mayonnaise.

"THERE ARE NO FUCKING Eggs!", he informed me.

He continued, "With the oil from the Rabbit, you add it to the shit you've pummelled."

"Are you sure there's not eggs in it?", I asked again.

"There's No Fucking Eggs. The shit Santi makes is made with regular oil. The stuff I brought you from the Mountains was very Thick because the oil comes from the Rabbit. It's a beautiful Sauce!"

Steve ordered another beer, I continued praising the 'Alioli' he gave us last week, while Hadass went to get an Alioli Recipe from the old lady who cooks here.

"We ate it on everything: bread, cheese, fruit. The next time you go to the mountains, bring me back a whole jar of it!", I told him.

"The next thing you'll be telling me is that you're out of Jars!", he said, missing the point.

Hadass returned with the real recipe from the cook. She began to tell it to me so I could write it down, "Garlic, Oil,... ". She was interrupted by Steve, who wouldn't let her continue until he had Clarified This One point, "The oil depends on what you're going to eat: If you're going to eat Fish, you use Fish Oil, If you're going to eat Meat, use Meat Oil. What you had was Rabbit Oil. That's the Difference. You use the kind of oil from what you're going to EAT!" Hadass continued, "Egg..."

"There's no fucking eggs!", said Steve.

She continued, "... egg, and garlic, put them in a mortar and grind them, slowly add oil and salt." This time I interrupted, "I want something else in the alioli! Some herbs or something."

"What?", asked Hadass.

"Oh, Yah! How about Elegant Slippers!", suggested Steve.

We talked about possible ingredients for the alioli for a while, with Steve rejecting most of them. We were joined at the table by a couple of Steve's weird local friends. They're deaf and dumb.

Jacques began to counsel Hadass, "You Have to go back to Israel!"

"Maybe it's changing. You don't believe in things changing?", she asked.

"Yah, but not the Jews!", I interjected.

"I'm on a Mission!", Hadass assured us.

Jacques agreed, "It's God's Work. It's in your heart!"

He told her a story from the Old Testament. He somehow felt confident counseling an Israeli. He's a born-again Bible Scholar.

Hadass responded, "Yah, I believe what you say about Moses and the Sinai, but sometimes I doubt it."

"Then why do you keep returning to a place you claim you hate?!", he asked.

"What?", Steve asked, "Hadass is going to Israel?"

"Always! ", I told him.

"I Dream About It!", she confessed.

"If you ever decide Not to go to Israel", Jacques told her, "You'll have Visions about it. It's in your blood."

Jacques continued , "When I finally go to Jerusalem, I figure my European Tour is Over. First, Rome, Then, Jerusalem, Then: Retire. And I don't have an iota of Jewish Blood! This happened to me just because of the New Testament. But you're Jewish! It's a 'Homing pigeon' thing with you: You have to die to be free of it. You have to kill yourself to stop it."

"I going there now.", said Hadass.

"You're a Revolutionary Jew, but you're a Jew!", Jacques told her, "Your cells will begin dis-engaging if you try to avoid Israel for even three years."

Hadass sat there seriously considering all this while I wrote it down and Steve laughed insanely.

Jacques told me, "Jack, you're going to change if you keep living with Hadass."

"I'm already half Jewish after a week. I'm probably ruined for Ireland already.", I answered.

"They probably won't even let you in!", Steve told me.

Jacques continued, "If you stay with her another month, you'll probably be rich. She gets her Power from Israel. It rubs off." I smiled at Hadass, I hoped he was right.

He turned to Hadass, "You're Programmed: You're like a bird. Birds have to whistle six hundred times a day, they don't know why: That's the way Jews are: They have to go to Israel!"

Steve said, "Birds have to eat three times their weight in chocolate before they can fly!"

"Good, Steve.", I told him.

The conversation wandered over to International Sex and Hadass said, "The first thing I ask in Spain is 'What the Spanish Women say to the men in bed?', and they tell me 'Mas! Mas! Mas!', and I just waiting for a chance I can use it."

"I'll dye my hair black.", I told her.

The Bodega was closing. Steve took off for the Deaf and Dumb bar with his friends, while Jacques, Hadass, and I fumbled around in the street for a few minutes.

"See That!", Jacques yelled, "They closed the door right after we left!"

"What does it mean, Jacques?", I asked.

"It means we were the last ones in the bar!", he exclaimed triumphantly.

"God! Amazing! You're Absolutely Brilliant! What a Mind!", I told him.

We gave Jacques some hash and left him muttering in the street about Israel and Perception and Stones. We headed for the Pad where we smoked some more hash and ate grapes and oranges.

"Well, It's Quite a Social Life, Isn't it?", I told her.

She answered, "Yes, here in Barcelona is my most social life. In Israel I have one friend: he can stand me all the time."

She continued, "We have Social Life. In Israel, I have many different kind of friend. But here, no. Here, my social life is Street People only. In Israel I am jumping from group to group. They all know me. I don't car. They no know what I'm doing there, but they all happy to see me: It's Great! But, it's confusing: The slang in Israel changes every three or four months - it comes from the Army _ in one year you may find yourself unable to talk."

We continued smoking and eating and talking for about another hour. She talked about her family.

"One brother, he is always funny, he know what to say that is funny. All the time he says funny things. My other brother (she cracks up), he can't tell One Joke! He tries: It's Never Funny (she's laughing). And my Father get pissed off because he is not funny, all the time."

"I always have to say the last word. They all waiting what going Hadass say. Then I say the stupidest thing in the world and they all laughing. Now it's change: because nobody understand any more. My sister asking me 'Ah, you are on the same trip as when you sixteen!', and she bitches about her life (laughs)."

Hadass told me about the 'Love of Her Life'. She was seventeen. They were together for three years. They were Very Good friends, Very Close. She had an affair with another man and told her Lover, "I in love with him", and he began drinking and drowned in the Sea of Galilee three weeks later.

"There wasn't room enough on this planet for both of us.", she told me.

We talked til about 3AM and finally fell asleep. I missed my 3PM class at the anarchist bar.)

The Cowboy Song

I ran into Phil and Rene the other day. Phil has been sick lately: Chest Congestion, but Rene has a cure for it: she makes up a paste of Hot Chilis and oil and grated ginger root on his chest while he lays in bed. On his forehead he wears a paste of Lotus Root and Whole Wheat Flour. He still feels sick, but she gets off on it and they make love all night, he tells me. Rene is from Jew York and is Macrobiotick. Phil says he will call a halt to it when she brings out the Leeches.

"She was Grating It Over Me, That's the Point!", he emphasized, reading over my shoulder.

She look Jew, I didn't want to say it, but she look Jew", Hadass told me when she found out Rene was a New York Jew.

Well, It's Saturday afternoon and I'm sitting in the doorway of Pension Costa again. Not much money being generated: about 50ptas. Hadass is working today. She is Chalking for Two. She assured me last night that the Reason she is going to Italy is because I smoke Ducados in bed. Then she told me that if she's Pregnant, she's not going to Italy. So, I conclude that if I quit smoking, We'll have a child. In some cosmick sense this is perfectly reasonable: I wanted to quit smoking anyway. And I like children.

Hadass and I were having a conversation last night which turned into:

THE COWBOY SONG (don't stand in the food)

> I'm not telling you, Hadass,
> "Don't Stand in the Food!"
> I can't help it, Darlin,
> If I'm not in the Mood.
>
> We Don't have to Fall In Love,
> Allll the Tiime,
> We can do it Sometimes,
> Darlin, Tell me Whennn.
>
> Well, I don't know, Sweetheart,
> How long this will last,
> But, Darlin, If you're Pregnant,
> Let's-get-a-villa-fast.

Cuz We don't have to Fall in Love,
Alll the Tiime,
No, We don't have to Fall in Love,
Buddy can you spare a dime?

None of my friends has ever growed UP,
Alli of Themmmm,
Only one is a woman,
Sixx are Men.

So, we don't have to fall in Love,
Allll the Time.
We'll just have same children,
And listen to the church bells chime.

I'm not telling you, Hadass,
"Don't stand in the food!",
I cain't hep it Darlin,
If I ain't in the Mood.

I sang it to her for a while last night and she Loved it.
"I'm going to shut that off.", I told her, indicating the candle.
"Go ahead, shut that off.", she told me, "You can do whatever you want, just don't smoke Ducados in bed!"
"I'm going to put out the light.", I said.
"So put out the light.", she said.
"I'm going to, you don't have to tell me that!", I told her.
"I'm Sorry.", she said. She thinks this is Funny; she just learned the phrase 'I'm Sorry', and has been trying it out. I hope this is not a glimpse of what our Life in Israel, on the Kibbutz raising children, is going to be like. Such a lot of conversation just to get a candle blown out.
She asked me, "You want me to go brush my teeth?", because of her overwhelming garlick smell.
"Don't bother", I said , "It's in your blood."
In the dark she looks great in Red Negligee. She told me that in case she is Not pregnant now, we can try again when she comes back from Israel.

El Monstro

At Hadass' going away Party last Saturday night there was almost a Murder, or Murders.

It began well; there were about twenty people in attendance: Frank, Peter, Phil, Hadass, Me, Black Diane, Sergio, two friends of his, Whitey, Maria, Gandalf, and a few others. There was plenty of wine, hash, and some Potato Chips.

It was nearing 11 oclock when Peter and Frank arrived. Frank came up to me beaming and exclaimed, "There's a Madman with a Knife on the landing below!". I thought it was a joke. I looked down the stairs and there was my Neighbor below, waving a knife and yelling in unintelligible Spanish. I tried to tell him that it was Saturday Night and we were having a Party. He waved his curved carpet knife at me and Slobbered and Drooled and Screeched and Belched something at me in Andalucian Spanish. I asked Gandalf and Sergio to please translate for me. He was saying, "I don't give a fuck if it's your mother's fucking birthday, I'm gonna come up there and kill everybody!" according to Gandalf.

I tried to talk to him again over the railing, and he went into a Madman's Dance, showing us how his Cane could not be broken and how it would bend in half. He wanted us to know that it was a Dangerous Weapon. He also produced his Other Knife so we could admire how fast the 8" blade came out when he pushed the little button on the handle.

The party-goers were either elated or frightened, depending on their assessment of the situation. I didn't know exactly what to do, so Gandalf and Sergio took over as I retreated to the Patio with Peter, Phil, and Hadass. It went on for about fifteen minutes with Gandalf and Sergio translating for the rest of us, "He says nobody can leave. If anybody tries to leave, he will cut their throat!" That caused a Stir amongst the Guests. A few minutes later, "He says he is going to come up here and kill everyone. He can't sleep, and he works all the time."

I asked Gandalf, "What do you think he wants?"

"He's Completely Crazy! He says he's gonna kill all of US!", he told me.

"Is he Serious?", I asked.

"Well, he's Crazy, Drunk, and Angry! He's Stupid, too. He's Really PISSED!!", Gandalf told me.

"I THINK HE'S COMING UP HERE!", someone yelled. Most of the people retreated into the apartment, with the exception of those of us who were already on the Patio. He came onto my landing and began Grunting and

Yelling. He had both knives and his cane waving around and he was slashing the door to the apartment and the walls of the landing while apparently waiting for some flesh. Sergio had the door open a crack and was trying to talk to him while Peter, Phil and I picked up chairs and wine bottles and prepared ourselves to either Kill or be Killed. Hadass, pregnant, was hiding behind a mattress at the edge of the patio.

He kept it up on the landing for about ten minutes and then stepped out onto the Patio. I tried to calm him, "Senor, Por Favor! Senor, par favor, es una Fiesta, No Queremos Problemas, Es Una Fiesta!", and shit like that. He answered with violent Lunges and Grunts. I had a firm grip on the chair to my right and was ready to bonk him with the wine bottle if he attacked. I was thinking that this was a stupid way for my life to end. I would have One Shot at his head with the full wine bottle before he stabbed me to death. He was built like an Ape: his hands were about as big as Frankenstein's and his arms looked like my legs. His eyes seemed to be Glowing Green.

"You guys be ready to get him with the chairs", I mumbled to Peter and Phil, who were standing five feet to either side of me. It looked like someone was going to be seriously hurt. If I'd had a gun, I would Definitely have shot him dead right then. No Kidding.

We retreated a few steps as he lunged forward and stuck his switchblade into the table full of drinks and food, and tried to pull the whole thing onto the ground. I advanced a little as he did so, "POR FAVOR! POR FAVOR, SENOR!", I cried, feebly. The alcohol and drugs were no longer affecting us: We were all high on Adrenalin.

It had been going on for half an hour. He finally growled some more threats and then swung back down to his landing one floor below where we watched him over the railing.

Sergio said, "He's going to call the Police." Gandalf was leaning over the railing trying to Reason with the Madman, in Spanish, "You are the One who is breaking the Law! You have been threatening to kill people!" And on and on it went. It finally seemed to work: he continued yelling and showing his weapons, but Gandalf was beginning to have some effect. Sergio joined in, as I went into the apartment to see how the rest of the guests were doing. They were either Scared to Death or Highly Excited, depending. While we were talking, El Monstro came back up to our landing, with his knives at the ready. Gandalf stayed out on the landing, while Sergio backed into the room, holding my cane just in case. I looked around for a deadly weapon (a knife would be useless against him because he would have You if you were close enough to use it), but couldn't find anything heavy enough, so I finally settled for a liter beer bottle. Through the partially opened door I could see him waving a knife at Gandalf's throat, while Gandalf was talking to him in a Reasonable voice. I pictured him stabbing Gandalf, and then Sergio and I bolting out the door to clobber him while he was distracted in his Blood-Lust. I've seen some Heavy Fights in the States, and a few drug-crazed Freaks with knives, but this guy could have taken any of them. I couldn't believe Gandalf was Trying to Reason with him.

Somehow, it worked out. The next thing I knew, Gandalf and Sergio were accompanying him down to his apartment, while El Monstro was still Semi-Raving. Sergio came back up a few minutes later and got a glass of wine for El Monstro and said that he was showing them his war medals and photographs from when he had been a prize-fighter, years earlier. Sergio was apparently happy and pleased that he was making a new friend. I was astounded. From Murder to Wine, in a few minutes. He was offering to cook a chicken for Gandalf and Sergio, and was showing them around his apartment. Sergio said that the guy never got to talk to people, and that they were becoming friends.

Sergio and Gandalf stayed down with the guy for about half an hour while the Adrenalin was wearing off at the party. The party was Ruined, as far as I was concerned, and I was having second thoughts about how good a deal Hadass' apartment was. Everyone was trying to be aware of how loud they were talking and the party was a Drag. However, No One was Leaving. There was no way out but past his door.

Sergio and Gandalf joined us and said that El Monstro had retired for the night. He had given Sergio a gift cocktail-shaker, made at the plant where he works.

Things quieted down for a while and then Ramon and Sally arrived. The first thing I knew of their arrival was Phil coming in and telling me that there were some people yelling for me down in the street, "Jaaack, there's a Madman down here and he won't let us in. Ramon's talking to him and I think there's gonna be trouble!". It was Randy, a friend of Sally's, standing in the street six floors below. Then, somehow, Sally showed up in the patio and I told her what had been happening. I foresaw the worst: a fight between Ramon and El Monstro. I was worried for Ramon and told Sally that El Monstro had a couple of knives. She headed back down the stairs, presumably to warn Ramon.

Looking over the patio edge, we saw the whole troop, including Ramon and El Monstro, head into the street and then into the nearest bar. I couldn't believe it. In a few minutes, here came Ramon, Sally, Randy and a couple of friends into the patio. I asked what had happened. Sally told me that Ramon and El Monstro had a talk and that everything was fine now. I was still on adrenalin, and didn't feel like partying any more. Everyone else could go home tonight but I had to stay here and live with Sudden Violent Death, one floor below, for the next six months.

Sally and Ramon stayed for a while and then split, with about half the party, to go bar-hopping. Jacques and Helen showed up a little while later and we all smoked some grass and Tried to Have a Party. Gandalf came out onto the patio and lectured me on Getting to Know Your Neighbors.

"How the fuck· can I get to know a guy who is basically an animal and doesn't even speak his own Language?", I asked him, pissed that he should lecture me.

I haven't been typing in the pad for the last week because El Monstro mentioned to Sergio that the clacking was bothering him.

It doesn't look like very many people will be dropping in on me for a Visit, in the Near Future: All of my friends were at the Party.

Kerouac's corpse is turning over.

PART THREE
FRANK AND BILLY

I Take My First Drink in this Book

Christmas Eve, 1984. Calle LLibreteria (Bread Street)

Starting late today: Five oclock. Went to a dinner Party with Sally yesterday evening. Many of her English teaching friends where there, Male, Female, and Both. I was introduced as "My American Friend". We sat and 'chatted' for a while, and watched the people in plaza del pi from the balcony for another while. I decided that since the Occasion was So Civilized, it wouldn't hurt to have a couple of glasses of wine with dinner. Sally agreed.

It was some kind of traditional English meal they were preparing, as far as I could tell. They kept talking about 'the pudding', which had me mildly confused: I never saw any the whole night.

We finally had 'Liverpool Stew', or some such English Dish. It was delicious: Meat, Potatoes, Onions, Carrots, and Celery, cooked in a big crock in the oven. It was great with the dark red Spanish wine.

About halfway through the meal An Uninvited Guest arrived: Me, as Crazy Jack the Maniack. He managed to completely dominate the Conversation and drove most of the English into the other rooms. He was left at the table to converse with a Portuguese Hippy who barely understood English.

I watched me for about an hour and tried to get me to shut up, "Come on, man, you're not letting anyone else talk!", I told him.

"Fuck You! I'm having FUN!", he yelled back at me.

"Just try to sit there. Try to Have an Intelligent Conversation with these English.", I told him. He wasn't going for it.

"I can't shut up!", he exclaimed, "What I have to say is Much More Important than all this Idle Fucking Chit-Chat!", he screamed at me.

I gave up on him and let him continue with his Gross Stories and Insults. Sally finally left with Him and Ramon, after He had insulted her Bosses Intelligence, she said.

They headed on out into the Barcelona Night to find a Bar where he Wouldn't get killed for Talking. I stayed with them, as an observer, until the early morning and was Amazed That, indeed, He seemed to have Absolutely No Control over his Actions or his Voice.

I took him home about four or five in the morning, which took a couple of hours because whenever we passed a door-step he wanted to sit there and mumble for a while. It was difficult to keep the Ladrones away, but he seemed to generate some Arch-typal Fear in their groins. He waved his knife at a couple of moroccans who were debating whether to steal his bag or not. It was enough to send them on their way. I finally got him home at dawn. Merry Christmas, Crazy Jack.

Tracy's Party, Peter's Shoes

CROW, VIVIAN

The Party at Tracy's in Barrio Chino was One to Remember: Tracy, Helen, Frank, Ralph the Kraut, Alejandro, Me, peter, Donna the Czeck (Howdy Donna) and her beau, Gandalf, Carlos the living mummy, and various Colombians, Bolivians, and Africans. There was live music provided by Whitey on lectric base, Gandalf on Acoustick, and myself on drum-pot til my fingers bled, when an African took over. The music was Hot, and people were almost dancing. There was plenty of booze and dope. Carlos, Tracy's room-mate, spent hours preparing an Italian Feast with great sauces. Another friend of Tracy's materialized about halfway through the party, dressed all in black with a cape and hat, a weird glow in his eyes. He sat down with me and smoked a joint while I drank gin at the kitchen table.

"Where are you from?", I asked, pleasantly.
"Atlantis.", he answered, staring into my soul.
"No, really?", I pressed, not wanting it to end there.
"Atlantis.", he said, grinning and daring me to doubt him again.
"How's the weather there now? wet?", I asked.
"No, it's dry now, it's under the sea, but it's dry."
"I see.", I answered, not really seeing.
"My name's Jack, what's yours?", I said, proferring a hand, trying once more.
"Crow.", he answered, staring at me and ignoring my hand.
"Fine.", I said.
He accused me of Doubting him. I let him go. Too Weird.
'Long About four or five in the morning Peter passed out on one of the beds after trying to fuck an African Girl. Someone took his shoes off him and threw them into the street. Somebody Who lived there, I never knew who, was mad because he wouldn't let them sleep in their bed. He had been drinking quite a bit. There was a 'Peter's Shoes Skit' for over an hour. It ended with Peter pushing some guy, down in the street, because the fellow tried to throw Peter's shoes up on to the balcony but landed them on the balcony one floor down. Somebody woke up the neighbor below so he could get involved also. Peter's Shoes were very busy. The first I heard of it was when Frank asked me to help solve the problem. I looked over the balcony to see what was going on. The guy from the street was threatening to Kill peter, who was

surrounded by about ten people. It didn't look like I could be much help, so I continued Drinking My Quart Of Gin in the kitchen. Frank came back in and told me that a guy with a Scimitar had just chased a girl into a bar while blood spurted from her jugular vein. I drank some more gin to ease the pain from my bleeding fingers.

The party continued til early morning. I kept hearing commotions about Peter's Shoes for hours but was too gin-soaked to leave the kitchen. Somehow I got home that night, traversing Barrio Chino and Barrio Gotico, I can't imagine how.

The next day Peter went over to Tracy's to try to find his shoes: it had taken him weeks to become a Fashion Plate, and he wasn't going to let it end on this note; His Outfit was Perfect with the Black Italian pointed Shoes; he had to get them back, his other pair was sneakers. I went along to retrieve my notebook and pencil. Frank was along to look for bloodstains in the street.

Tracy, Carlos, Helen, and Ralph were all there. The Party started again. We drank a few bottles of wine and then headed out for a restaurant. Frank thought I insulted the owner. He was wrong: I merely told her that her 14-year-old daughter, our waitress, was Beautiful, which she Incredibly was. I told her that I had one also. Frank claims that we can never show our face in there again.

After dinner we split into two groups with Tracy and me opting for Live Music at a Local Band Practice rather than coffee at the Opera. Tracy sweet-talked us each a mike and she sang lead while I accompanied her with the Biker Voice as we both sang and danced our drunken selves into ecstasy. It lasted for a couple of hours with the band and us parting ways about three in the morning. I lost Tracy in the maze of alleys in the Barrio Gotico, but managed to find La Barraca, the bar below Pension Costa.

The next thing I remember is waking up the next afternoon in my bed at Hadass, apartment. I headed on out into the town, where I encountered Harry, the one-eyed English bookie (retired), who loaned me 100ptas so I could buy some wine.

I spent the day sitting in La Sardana drinking wine and chatting with Pirate Steve, Harry, and a new friend, Vivian, another Englisher (who was named after his father and grandfather and has never forgiven them for it).

Viv and I talked for hours about the meaning of Life, Israel, His Construction plans for an 18-string guitar, and the new false leg he's carving for Steve, which he says will be easily and quickly removed in an emergency and used as a club, per Steve's specifications.

Viv lives in Barcelonetta, the local ex-fishing ex-village down at the port; his windows overlook the Sea, and he's in Barcelona to stay: he's married to a

Catalana, Aurora. He's forty-four years old and says he hasn't been the same since he fell twenty feet off a balcony onto his head about twenty years ago. He sometimes plays banjo on the street, but as he's still learning it, he sounds like a Demented Flatt. He's a pleasant fellow, though, even if he doesn't know which country he's from.

After a few hours of Wine and Talk, I wandered on over to Santi's where I joined Frank and Peter for an afternoon of bullshitting. I'd been telling people all day that I wanted to go to Israel; I don't know why this Fit was upon me, but apparently I was Tuned In to The Cosmo-Dance: Hadass phoned the bar while I was there and I asked her if she wanted me to come to Israel right away. She said she would send me the money or the ticket immediately from Athens, where she's chalking. She said it had been too cold in Italy, and that she was leaving for Israel real soon, and was happy that she would be able to take me on a tour there.

I was Elated about my Forthcoming Trip and Probable Marriage in the Wholly Land. I ordered a bottle of wine with a cork, to celebrate. I borrowed the money from Peter, who was Happy for Me.

Ah, Hadass! Ah, Jerusalem! Ah, Life!

A Fish is Dancing, Dark

The Day After Christmas. Pension Costa Doorway.

    Alejandro. He's from Peru. Lives in Paris. Studies Philosophy at the University there. He's a writer who met Frank in Barcelona a couple of Years ago. He looks like a Peruvian Indian, especially when he wears my felt hat. He's written a Story, and an Interview with a Peruvian Friend of His named Lam, Famous Artist: Disciple of Picasso's. Good Friend of Alejandro's.

    Alejandro and I have been hanging out together since Tracy's Christmas Eve Party. We spent the day yesterday wandering around the Gothic Barrio, yelling and singing and dancing and drinking and laughing. I did most of the Dancing and Yelling, but Alejandro DID contribute quite a bit of Laughing, Singing, and Drinking.

    Here is one of Alejandro's Poems. I don't understand most of it, only the first line:

PESCADOR PROFUNDO

Un pez ha danzado sambra	(a fish is dancing, dark)
en el arpa hundida	(in the sunken harp)
de pescador profundo.	(of the profound fisherman)
Su musica es resplandeciente	(his music is resplendent)
y su sangre ya es muerte	(and his blood is already dead)
Ha mirado el oceano	(the ocean has looked)
y ha sonreido y para	(and has smiled)
el cielo se va aleteando.	(and towards heaven he swims.)

                                               (loosely translated by The Gringa Maria)

A Light Case of DT'S

I had a light case of the DT's last night. Hadass' form kept appearing in my Visions. We were making love in the Desert. It was a positive Delirium, anyway. The Vision is a Good One: Hadass, Billy, Amy, Sally, and I driving in Our Camper, to Paris, where we will stay for a couple of weeks with Alejandro before continuing on to Brussels for the Juggler's Convention. We will have thousands of dollars from the sale of Hadass' apartment in Tel-Aviv. I will not be drinking at this point because I'll have enough money for coke. What a Plan! What a Life! When Jacques heard that I was going to Israel and might be marrying Hadass, he commented, "If you and Hadass get married, I will realize that Life is Indeed, Truly Gourdless!"

CANDY TURDS

Stop the fucking Presses! Frank has just shown me some of the Candy Creations available here for parents to give their kids for the holidays: Little Creations which look exactly like turds. There are also little candy urinals full of piss, and candy toilets full of little candy turds. That Settles It: Israel is in my future. I can't take this kind of candy-coated Shit. For those with a weaker sensibility: little candy frying pans full of candy bacon-and-eggs. What a concept! Who is This weird?

BARCELONA DIARRHEA

So, This is the Diarrhea of Barcelona. So, Someday I'll Edit It, and make a Few short stories out of it: Hadass, Frank's Rantings, Jacques' Painting Career, Peter's Clothes, Barcelona's Problems, Shit like that. I'm not looking forward to returning to teaching English on Monday, after all this thinking about Israel. Really Not.

Oh, Well, What the fuck. This isn't as bad as I've ever had it. Things were much worse a few weeks or months ago. Bitch. It's just that having my hopes pulled around like this is frustrating. I can pull out of this one, though. I can go back to the original plan of Teaching English. Boring, boring, boring. I like the plan where we sell Hadass' apartment, get married, have a kid, and travel around Europe in our van, with a home-base in our villa near Barcelona. Much better.

I'm really out here just begging, now. I've lost all interest in writing about Barcelona and it's little problems and ancient stone streets and all the little fiestas. It's Nothing. It's just a little back-water of history. Gee-politics doesn't give a flying fuck about the Catalan Independence Movement; it's barely noticeable to the rest of the world that Franco is gone. Almost Nobody but the Spanish have the slightest idea what is going on in Spain: Common Market, Socialist Government; they don't even know.

I've chosen to live here only because I'm a Failure as an American: I was raised by a family, and in an area, where it would have been very easy for me to go to Stanford and get an MBA. But, Did I?! No. Why? Because, like most of the other foreigners living here, I am a Lazy Slob. This is not an Artist Colony: it's a conglomeration of Ineffectual Slobs. I could've been a middle-weight contender for the American Dollar Sweepstakes Throne, but, NO, I'm sitting here in some Gothick Backwater typing my diarrhea in the street, trying to get money to pay back a thirty dollar debt to a restaurant which was foolish enough to give me credit, while waiting for that Bitter Shrew, my ex-wife, to arrive and harass me, while my elongated girlfriend keeps me hanging by the purse-strings, so Jewish. I'm having a glass of wine in honor of the occasion. I may as well admit it: I'm not a writer, I'm a Drunk. I've been practicing the latter about a hundred times longer than the former, whatever. I'm a Begging Drunk, really; A Poor, Begging Drunk with Delusions of Grandeur. Or Splendor, at least.

The crowds of idiots still gather around and read my ridiculous signs and throw their worthless money in the little box. I could be typing anything, as I said on the first day out here.

The quick brown fox jumped over the lazy writer1s back. see? clink. clink.

Stores in Spain

It is very simple to go crazy here: simply try to buy something. There are people who have spent Generations trying to get their scizzors sharpened here; It's a Commission passed down from Father to Son. They wander around with a glazed look, Grasping Bloody Scizzors. Even the points have been dulled and lost: They can only buy Tobacco. (Never on Monday afternoon).

The Natives are born with The Knowledge: You can get scizzors sharpened on Tuesday Mornings except in Februario and Julio, on odd years when there is not a Fiesta going on. If you want to buy a French Sausage, you have to do it on Wednesday Evenings between 7:30 and 21:15, but only after the signs are removed from the Traffic Circles leading to the Panaderias which are closed only on Thursdays from 8AM til 1115 except in Aprilo when you can Buy Absolutely Nothing from the 11th until the 18th. (Except when Easter falls on a Tuesday Morning.)

You can buy Candy at the Post Office (downstairs) when the Tobacco Stores are not selling stamps from 17:45 til 22:15 on Friday mornings during a Fiesta. If you want your teeth cleaned you must make a Monday appointment at the Tabaceria to confirm your Payment Schedulo.

Last night I had to wait ten minutes behind a lady in the Tobac Store while the Clerk was affixing stamps to her thing. It pissed me off because I missed my appointment to get my scizzors sharpened and teeth cleaned, unless I bought a Bottle of Gas from the Bodega and had my Poodle clipped at the Toystoreria which is open only every other Thursday immediately after Siesta. Tobaccoanistas close for church from 6PM til 17:00 on Saturdays, during Fiestas or Siestas, I'm not sure which.

If you want Pan Integral (whole wheat bread) you must first point to some weird crackers and say "no, no, no", or they will give you Them instead. I spent twenty minutes in a Panaderia the other day trying to cash a check so I could buy a pack of smokerias. They didn't have my brand unless I paid in Francs because it was the Thursday following Christmas, which falls on Januario the sixth.

If you want to get your pencil sharpened you have to buy a Vespa and have a Small Orange Person install a grinder on the back wheels. If you want a Caraquillo, Never, never ask for it: It is an Insult, especially to the Basking Spanish from the North.

You can buy a parrot here very cheaply: However you must only feed it dogfood because it is illegal to have a bird permit unless you were born under a tree on the Ramblas. Never get caught late at night' without a little paper cone of birdseed. If a Moroccan asks you for a light you must respond Instantly: Show Your Bloody Scizzors and he will know you are a local. Never take a window seat in a Cafe if there are more than three little women dressed in black inside: it's a church.

If you ever find yourself in a bar with Little Orange People, leave Immediately unless you are wearing a red beret, in which case Grunt.

The ·rules are easy to understand after you have been here for about twenty generations. (The Official Language is Castillano but you can make up your own as you go along because Everyone is a Foreigner anyway).

Don't let the ringing of the church-bells bother you: There is a Madman that decides when they ought to be rung. He especially likes to ring them 23 times at 4:18 on Thursday afternoons and 47 times on Sunday Morning at 7:43 or so. The Locals Like It; You Soon Will, Too.

There are eleven different kinds of policemen here but the ones that will help you if you are in trouble have been on strike since 1938. If you get in trouble, call a Tourista.

There is a Magazine here in Barcelona which is devoted to Showing pictures of people with Swollen Legs: Interviu Magazine. If they run out of swollen legs, they show pictures of children with parts of their faces fucked-up. Jacques reads it.

Howdy Donna, Doody's Sister

I sit here and stink. I can take it. It's not bad enough to make my eyes water. There's a photographer from a magazine in Columbia who's been here snapping my picture and I'm pretty sure that it's going to appear in South America soon. I'll be Famous.

I'm broke again because I paid back a lot of the small little debts that I've been running up during the last three drunken days. I've been sitting the afternoon away down at Santi's drinking CafeconLeche and one 'quinto', a very small beer. I also (to be completely honest) had a couple of glasses of wine earlier. I feel fine. I'm Drifting. Don't Much Care. Don't Give-A-Shit. Know what I mean?

Donna, the Czechoslovakian, and her beau, were down at the Tapas and it was all I could do to keep myself from asking her to Drop This Guy That Looks Like John Lennon and Come With Me to my pad for an afternoon of Mad Loving. I want her. She looks like Howdy Doody's Sister. (YAYY!!) She's given me her address in Sweden so I can look her up this Summer. Such a Life! Have I mentioned it before? She knows that I Want Her. I know that She Wants Me. What to do? What to do? I want all of them. That's the problem, sometimes.

But! Howdy Doody's Sister! That would be A Score! To get her to roll her eyes back and dance at the end of those little strings!

"Gosh, Buffalo Bob, This Is Fun!"

"Clarabelle! Put Down That Seltzer Bottle and Get Off Howdy's Sister Right Now!"

I can almost see it. The Peanut Gallery Goes Mad. Mothers Dragging Their Children away from this Disgusting Scene. A Marionette being fucked by a Madman in a Clown Outfit: Up on that little stage. The Mind Reels. The Soul Rocks. The Marionetta Has An Orgasm. What Pun!

The next time she shows that little face with that mouth that bobs up and down, I'll Ask the Only Question Worth Asking: "Do you want to Fuck?"

I just yelled down the street to Steve that I am having fun but am not making money. He offered to give me four pesetas.

I've got IT! I can Feel It! It is almost impossible for me to Fuck Up right now. Whatever I touch will turn to something Wonderful. This Feeling happens every few days. When You've Got IT, Use IT! Where is Howdy's Sister Right Now? Just Give me a Bath and I'll be ready to give you Multiples. I could even do my Papa Noel act right now, I feel that good. It scares some of the kids but gives others Memories they will cherish for the rest of their lives.

The crowd seems to be Fascinated by the rapidity of my Typing. However, Very Few Duros. What the Fuck? My Art and My Life are Not Really For Sale Anyway. (Oh Shit! What if the guy that was praying over at Peter's pitch today wanders over here and asks Me for forgiveness for his Literary Faults?)

This could be a Slow Night, but… then again… it could be Fantastically Propitious Economy-wise, or at least Orgasm-wise. Fuck, I'd PAY for a piece of IT, tonight, If I had the money, that is.

Almost Impossible to Fuck This Up. (yah, but if anyone can do it, Jack can). God! It's Christmas In Spain. I'm from Berkeley. but… I'm Here! Peter just walked up and informed me, "They won't give you money if they see you drinking." " I'm sure you're right," I said, " but they'll keep buying me beers, won't they?"

Lori, The White Donkey

Lori is rumored to be heading back to Finland again this year. His mother sent him the money for a ticket last year but he never went. This could be another false alarm.

Ian, Harry, Frank, Randy and I were discussing Lori for a while this afternoon in the Tapas. Harry said he has no pity for a man who won't even try. Frank said that Lori is completely worthless. Ian said that Lori's new name should be 'The White Donkey' because that's what a Spanish Moron called him the other day at the bar. Steve the pirate said that Lori is a stupid Motherfucker.

I don't know what to make of Lori. Finland must be a miserable place, if he is any indication. Jacques and Hadass both think that Lori is very intelligent. There seems to be quite a difference of opinion about him. It's The Blizzard that causes all this confusion: Lori takes it with him wherever he goes. I hope he makes it to Finland this time. It's got to be better than being a slave in Barcelona, where it never snows.

He showed up at Santi's the other night with his ankles red and swollen to about twice their normal size. I think he's going to enter the Contest for Swollen Legs that appears weekly in Interviu Magazine.

Everyone present had some advice for him.

Peter said, "Get some cabbage and heat it in water and wrap it in a bandage and wrap the bandages around your legs. Do this about once an hour. Don't use the bandages again: throw them away. This is the best thing you can do for swelling."

Lori thought for a minute, then asked, " Well, do you have to buy a whole cabbage?"

Peter answered, "Nah, about a half a cabbage should do."

Lori said, "I'll try it. It's cheaper than going to a doctor."

I told him, "Lori, you've got to bathe regularly, and eat a lot of different foods." "I eat only fruits now, bread is not good for you.", he answered. I told him, "Lori, you should be eating bread and meat, as well as fruit!" He is convinced that bread is bad for you, and meat is too expensive.

"You stupid Motherfucker, Take a Bath!", yelled Steve.

Jacques, an old friend of Lori's, tried to give some advice, "Lori, You're Dying!"

"you Stupid Motherfucker!", Steve repeated.

We tried to counsel Lori for about an hour, but I don't think much was getting through the blizzard. He is Gay, and has been for years, since he was raped in Finland, he says. He has a job as a housekeeper/slave for some weird guy in the Barrio Chino

Lori's Trip to Finland

Lori missed the train to Finland yesterday.

"I know the track from which the train leaves, I know the schedules, I know the train, I Just Missed the Train.", he explained to Jacques, Frank, and me last night at Santi's.

Frank suggested, "Lori, why don't you pin a piece of paper to your shirt with the city's name in Finland and pretend to be deaf and dumb. You know, just wave your arms and hands around, but keep the same expression on your face that you usually have. That should get you to Finland ," Lori stared at him, smiling vacantly.

Jacques asked, "Lori, does your train go straight through?"

"No, there is one transfer: Lyon.", he answered.

"That's your new city!", Jacques exclaimed.

Frank spent the next twenty minutes explaining to Jacques how a person goes about Catching a Train, while Lori sat there eating my bread and some cheese which he'd brought in.

Jacques said, "Frank, I Know How to catch a Train! Lori's the one you should be preaching to!"

Frank said, "Well, I'm hoping he's picking some of this up! Lori! Didn't you tell me that your last job was working on a Railroad!?"

"No, it was the one previous to that.", Lori answered.

"Well, I mean, you Should know how to catch a train, considering that you used to work for the Railroad, Don't you agree?", Frank asked.

"Frank, I already told you that I just got there too late: the line for tickets was too long. Oh Fuck It!", Lori told him.

Frank continued, "Well, Lori, I don't believe that you really want to go to Finland: You gave us your key to hold for you in case you missed the train, and Jacques and I both knew that you intended missing it. What do you say? You're Right Where You Want To Be, aren't you?"

Lori just grinned at the table, and seemed to be huddling up because of the sudden increase in the blizzard.

Frank went on, "Why don't you get a pad and a pencil and a little table and set up on the street like Jack does: He's rolling in dough, had liver for dinner, and has his own bread. You're always writing anyway: You sat Right Here on New Years Eve and wrote in your tablet while a party was going on all around you. You could even draw little pornographic pictures, the kind you like so much, on the cover of it. Yah! They'd Love it. And for that special touch, you could get a plumed pen. I really think you ought to give it a try, Lori. You don't really want to go to Finland, do you? You could go out tomorrow and spend some of the money your mother sent you for the ticket and begin work tomorrow. How about it?"

Lori continued staring at the table, grinning and fiddling with his bread.

Jacques said, "Yah, Lori, you could try it in Lyon while you're there!"

Frank added, "You could have a little sign saying that you're a writer that can't afford a typewriter. Give it a try, Lori, I'm trying to help you see that you can do something with your life."

"I Want to go to Finland.", he said. Then, laughing, "Unless I miss the train again."

"Well, You Will miss it, Lori, because you want to. The Life of a Scribe is not a bad life!", Frank told him.

The blizzard seemed to be letting up; Lori was coming out of his trance, "You guys laugh at me. You seem to like things like this: My girlfriend left me and you liked that. I lost my job. I missed my train. You laugh about it!"

Frank said, "What I love about all of us is that we're all monomaniacs. And you know who is our leader? Lori!"

Lori was grinning quietly, the wind was gusting a little.

Frank continued, "We all can only think about one thing at a time." He gave about five examples of people we know who can only be involved in one thing at a time. Lori saw a chance to redeem himself, "I'm playing my guitar every day, Jacques."

"Is that why you missed your train?", Jacques asked.

Frank and Jacques cross-examined Lori once more on exactly how he had missed the train. Everyone agreed, after a lengthy discussion, that Lori should arrive at the station an hour before departure time and should buy his ticket the day before.

Lori went a step further, "I will get to the station four hours early!" We all agreed that in his case it might be a good idea.

Frank brought the conversation back to one of his favorite subjects: Obsessive Behavior, "Lori, your obsession is You!"

"But, Frank, so is everybody.", said Lori.

"Well, yes, that's what everybody that is thinking only about themselves thinks that everyone else is thinking about. But for you it's good: the same as it is for frogs: the way their eyes see only their prey.", Frank said.

Lori didn't understand the word 'prey', and a few minutes of prime time were lost explaining to him that it was nothing to do with praying. Jacques, 1/2 bottle down, said, "An alcoholic can only see wine. That's his prey."

Lori finally Got it: "A Narco-maniac can only see heroin!", he said.

The conversation wandered for a few minutes with Frank demonstrating how a lion tears it's prey limb from limb. Finally, we landed on Art.

Lori told Jacques, "Chalking on the Ramblas is a waste of time!" Lori used to do it but quit last year to become a slave.

"God, Lori! You wouldn't want to do That! Waste your Time!", said Frank.

The blizzard was increasing. It was time for me to go.

As I was leaving I heard Lori ask, "Jacques, don't you think it's good sometimes just make time for living?"

"No! Not Now! I just want Money!", Jacques answered.

Lori will try again tomorrow to catch that train to Finland. Or Lyon.

Fucking Israel

What do you suppose it's going to be like for 'The Street-writer' in Israel? Well, Hadass assures me that most Israelis understand English, so I'll gather a crowd who will stand around and Read what I'm typing as I do it. She further assures me that I should (should) make about 100 dollars a day. I hope this is true.

I have some apprehensions that I will suffer culture-shock of great magnitude in Israel, that Barcelona is a colony of Europe but Israel is Completely Foreign. I'm not worried. Much. I'm afraid that I won't be able to communicate because of my inability to make those weird choking sounds that pass for language among the Semites. What if I go on a Rampage in Jerusalem and some fucking Arab machine-guns me to Death? What about that? I'll check Things out very carefully before I start drinking any God-Damned Arab Wine, I'll tell you that right now. I don't want to end up as some fucking kind of Martyr to American Stupidity! For all I know these fucking people take themselves seriously. It's Likely, in fact, from what I've read. Whatever: I'm looking forward to it with a Smiling Heart because I will be with my Little Desert SweetHeart, Hadass.

This Fucking Thing, That Fucking Thing: Why does he have to say fucking fuckingfucking all the time? He says it because that's the fucking way he fucking talks. If he wasn't fucking talking that fucking way he'd probably be off in the fucking bushes fucking. Fuck that.

A Jewish American Princess just came up and said, after looking at this page, "Fucking, fucking, fucking, it's not my style!"

I asked her, "WHAT'S not your style?"

"Yours!", she answered, walking on.

I was dumbfounded for a few seconds but yelled after her, "It's just a Fucking IDEA!" Yah! Fuck Her! Know what I mean? Let her sit out here and fucking Create, huh, guys? Yah! Jack, That's Right! You Got It! Fuck HER!! She's probably a terrible Fuck anyway! Fck!

New Year's Eve, 1984

January 2, 1985. Bread Street

Well, I'm back on the Wagon, again. Got to. Rebecca and Billy are due here tomorrow from Almeria and If I'm drunk around them they will have Extremely Negative Flashbacks. They don't like to be around me when I drink. They've Seen It All.

The New Year's Eve party at Tracy's was Great. The only problem with it was Me. I got Very Drunk and began accusing the Germans, Danes, and The Rest of the people at the party of Treating me like the Ugly American. It was a self-fulfilling accusation. I got So Beside Myself that I never even made it to the second course of the meal. I haven't the slightest idea where I was at the stroke of midnight. I remember heading out into the street with about a dozen people from the dinner party, but soon lost them due to my inability to see very far, walk, talk, or think. I was That Drunk. I next remember being down on the Ramblas in a large crowd of people. I went to sleep a couple of times in doorways before I finally bar-hopped over to my house. I sat there sleeping on the steps until early in the morning when I was awakened by El Monstro, my neighbor, corning home drunk. we greeted each other with Spanish Grunting. We were smiling and wishing each other a Happy New Year and he offered to help me up the stairs to my pad. I declined the offer and informed him that I wished to continue my celebrating at the bar next door. We bid each other good night and I proceeded to the bar where I passed out at a table and had my lovely black bogey hat stolen. The whole evening was a Forgettable Experience.

It's back to Hashish for me. Much easier to live with myself later. Don't have to ask people if I insulted them when I see them the next day. Don't have to listen to stories about how I fucked up this dinner or that party. Much Easier On Me.

I woke up yesterday evening and limped on over to Sally's where She, Ramon, and Randy looked like they had been in the trenches of Verdun. They had a worse evening than even I did, if possible. Ramon destroyed a bar, sent one guy to the hospital, and dragged Sally part way home by her hair. After which they made mad, passionate, drunken love? What a couple.

I had a shower and partook of a delicious Chicken Stew and a few bottles of wine and beer while we discussed whether or not alcohol was Really a problem for any of us. We continued the discussion later, downstairs at the bar.

The Three Kings

Jan 6, 1984. Street, evening

Gourdlessness Lives, I'm here again.

The Three Kings Parade was a FLOP, unmitigatingly so. There were only about five floats and they were erratically spaced about five to twenty minutes apart. The crowd was standing there stamping its feet sometimes for half an hour before something of interest would come down the slush-covered street. And then it would turn out to be a Coal Truck. They intersperse Coal Trucks with the King's Floats because the bad-little-Catalans receive only coal in their shoes in the morning. Nevertheless, I'm sure that some of the kids thought it was a wonderful parade. I knew it was doomed when I saw who they had for the Black King: a gringo. At least last year they could afford a real nigro. This year the most exciting thing was the street-sweepers at the end.

After the parade Billy and I repaired to the Tapas where we had a game of chess (I won), a coffee, and a hot chocolate. Judy and her friend Carolyn (Australian) asked us to join them for the Grand Fireworks Display in plaza Espanya. We rode the crowded Metro, transferred once, jostled the crowds, and arrived in time to find out that it was cancelled due to the cold weather. It was back to the Tapas where we continued to drink wine.

Peter, the English friend of Sally's who got in a fight with Ramon last year in Plaza Regomir, was there. He beat me in a game of chess. I lost 50ptas to him. I haven't paid yet and he bought me a couple of glasses of wine to console me for my first-ever defeat in that bar.

Jacques was there bleary. Frank was there spell-binding. I was there drinking. Billy left with his pal Amani; they're about the same mental age.

Randy came in an told me that there were a couple of my friends outside who wished to speak with me. I knew it was Ramon&Sally, but thought that they didn't want to enter the bar for fear of a Repeat Performance by Peter and Ramon. I was putting on my coat and bidding the crowd good night when a huge basketball-sized snowball landed on my back. There was much merriment and snow all over the cavern. That Sally&Ramon!

"See you in a couple of days!", Jacques said, as I headed out into the Bar-crawling Evening with my Crazy Friends.

Sure enough, after hitting a couple of bars with Sally, Ramon, and Randy, I saw them disappear into the night down a dark alley. I was, as usual, unable to maintain their Manic Pace. I sat down on a bench in plaza Regomir and meditated upon my Existence here in Spain, before deciding to take a stroll down Escudillers. I ran into a couple of my old Arab friends who were extremely. interested in the contents of my pockets and bag. After convincing them that I carried no weapons, they bought me a beer and we talked about how tough it was to make a living on the street these days.

Along about dawn, in the freezing snow, I headed back to the pad where I hunted for cigarettes and set one of my socks on fire by trying to warm my feet on the cooker. I gave up and crawled under the blankets. I woke up about noon and got up for a minute and stood in my room shivering and then said fuck it and crawled back under the blankets until about three this afternoon.

I headed for Santi's where I encountered Irish Ivan Kelly, English peter, and Judy and Carolyn, both Aussies. We bullshitted for a while, and I had three coffees before I could begin to act like anything resembling a Social Animal.

"I don't see why the women here are so Oppressed: they wear high heels and stockings and are definitely not Liberated.", said Carolyn.

"They're trying to look Good for the men.", I explained.

"Well, they should be trying to look good for themselves: They're Oppressed!", she continued. I noticed for the first time that she has short hair and wears baggy clothes.

Ivan said, "I Love the women here: They're Sexy. Much better than Irish women. At least the women here smell good: they bathe. Irish women are scummy hags."

I said, "It's a biological thing: The human race is a result of females attracting the best available mates: Carolyn doesn't have to dress up because she is going to attract a mate, if she wants one, because of her soul: Because she is a Being and wishes to be treated like one."

Peter said, "Jack, your ideas are foolish."

I didn't like the way he said it so I started yelling at him and jumped up from my table and leaned my face close to his and screamed, "These aren't just my opinions about history: I've lived in the fucking mountains and the women get pregnant and they stay by the fire, they keep the fire, and they keep care of the children while the men go out and hunt! I've lived this way for Ten Fucking Years, In The Woods! It's Not THEORETICAL!!"

"Let's not talk about it if you're going to yell.", Peter countered.

"Bullshit! You just insulted me with words and you can't stop the Fucking Conversation just because I'm Yelling!", I yelled. I was proving My Point through Actions, Louder than words, I'm told.

Eventually I apologized to Peter while Carolyn and Ivan continued their discussion. Carolyn must have got the worst of it because He is an Irish Lawyer. I further explained my theories of human evolution, always with an eye towards spending some time between the furs with Carolyn. For a Philosophical Discussion, it was Very Theoretical, and I doubt that anyone profited very much from it, although I do hope to see Carolyn again and continue my explanation of Human Reproduction. With Exhibits. (Chauvinish Pig!)

Frank, David Bowie, Howdy Doody

I went to the Opera Cafe the other night with Frank, Peter, Maria (it was her going away party), Jacques, Whitey, and Tracy and Helen. Maria was well on her way to having a good time: Something she is only beginning to learn. She was hanging on every word Frank spoke, A Dangerous Thing To Do: four of his disciples have committed suicide by hanging on his words.

Peter was wearing a tuxedo that he found in a pile of garbage: it's perfect and fits him as though he had it tailored: "If you go round the garbage you can make a bloody good living!", he told us. Rebecca could testify to this: Her Most Recent Boyfriend, in Almeria, was the Scavenger for the group of hippies that lived on the beach there; I can picture them in his sleeping bag eating bits and pieces, as Billy described it to me.

We smoked some hash and the conversation turned to Jacques' Recent Riches: he has bags and bags full of coins in his room; Frank says that it's difficult to even walk through it because of the Coinage Problem. Jacques never, never locks his door and there is a known thief living in the Pension.

"I have so much that if they only take a handful at a time It won't even matter!", he told us.

Frank was giving Maria the Encapsulated Version of the History of the Cafe De La Opera, "Bowie comes here still, dressed as a Black Transvestite, blowing a whistle; this is his way of avoiding attention." Maria bought it. He also told her that the Rolling Stones come in here to relax when they are in Barcelona.

Frank sometimes claims to be the Quintessential American, yet he was heard to remark, "I don't know who Howdy Doody is, I've never heard of Howdy Doody!" Is he an agent for the KGB? How can this be? Never heard of Howdy Doody? He's as Famous as Dwight Eisenhower, is he not?

It can only be explained by a comment Frank made a few minutes later, "This Is Barcelona, Man! The Home of the Gourdless!" Maria asked him Exactly what he meant by this.

He answered, "And then some people ask me why do you call it the Home of the Gourdless? Look at the information I'm receiving!"

SUE, Why I Hit Her

January 7, same place

Canadian Steve left today for Tangiers. There was something strange about that fellow: he was not nearly as straight and neat as he seemed. I believe that he Could Be Secretly Dangerous. He grinned too often, much too friendly. There may have been a Gary Gilmore hiding behind that perfect haircut. I'm sure we'll find out some day, one way or the other.

My Old Friends, Rebecca and Billy, will get Steve's room in pension Costa; the middle room facing the street, the same room where I left . Sue a year ago, the last time I saw her, after I hit her for the first and last time ever. Rebecca recently suggested that I write about Sue rather than her.

Sue was the best fuck I ever had. Always, for two years. I was madly in love with her, and I think we'd have stayed together if she could've gotten pregnant. And we hadn't run out of cocaine. It was A Blast while it lasted. She's in L.A. now, running a sailing School, just like I taught her. Her kids have all grown up and joined either the Air Force or the Drug Dealers. She always wore red lipstick and once gave me head for six months. Quite a Gal.

She wants to have nothing or very little to do with me because she now thinks that I am a Drug-crazed Maniac, or a Drunk Maniac, depending. She knows it's true.

I knew that The Love Affair was Surely Over when I threw away all the pornographic photos of Sue and me. More Final Than Divorce.

I met her when she came into my Sailing School one day to take lessons. It was Lust At First Sight for both of us. We were very careful getting started, however, because we had both been through about five or six Love Affairs. Once we did get going, though, a couple of weeks later, It was Click, Click, Click: We were inseparable. She left her kids, quit her job, and moved into my little trailer behind the office and began helping me run the school. We built the business up from eight to about twenty boats during the next year. We smoked grass and sucked and fucked our brains out for about a year, when a friend of mine who dealt coke came to live with us.

We drove around in my red 65 Cherry Cadillac Convertible, went sailing on expensive yachts, ate every meal in restaurants, and snorted just a little bit more coke than we could afford. After about a year we decided to check the books and see how much money we had. We were $25,000 in debt; it was Almost a Surprise. We tried to save the business, borrowed money, worked for a change, and were able, after a year more, to watch it dissolve. I personally supervised the destruction, as I felt responsible. I had created it from Nothing. And, that's just what I ended up with: Nothing. No Woman, No Boats, No Money, No Cadillac, No Porsche, and No Dope; Nothing.

So we came to Barcelona to get cured from Cocaine. It worked: I got drunk and hit her; I don't know why, I was drunk.

On The Street Again

FRANK, PETER; NORMA AND REBECCA IN LA SARDANA

Steve the Pirate is not out here yet today: he probably had a hard night. I left him at about eleven, drunk in the Bodega. He had spent the evening out here Absolutely Harassing the Passersby, "Give me some money! You Cheap Motherfuckers! Give me Some Money To Live!", he was yelling, and, "I can't fucking believe it! Sticks! Sticks! That guy with the cane bumped into Me!" The cane had bumped into one of his crutches. He was Outraged. He must not have been doing very well, peseta-wise.

I was supposed to meet Ramon and Sally down at the Bodega, but they were already off and running by the time I got there. I was delayed at Santi's because every American except Norma and Rene was Present for dinner last night. Phil returned from Seville, One of my tribe; I smoke Celtas. Ramon left Santi's pissed-Off at me because I had put my arm around Sally when I thought he wasn't looking, but he caught me and gently tapped me on the head with one of Steve's crutches.

The holidays are almost over. Barcelona will soon resume its normal pace: Only one Fiesta per week, and only one Siesta per day. The crowds are already much smaller. I've been here about an hour and I've only made about 300ptas. For the last week or two I've been Pulling Down about 500 per hour. Maybe the novelty is wearing off. Maybe my frowning and grimacing isn't helping much either. Maybe the Locals have finally realized that anyone who would sit out in this freezing cold doing this is Completely Out Of It. Beyond Help. Too Far Gone to be a Reality that must be dealt with. Maybe the word is getting out that this is just a Diarrhea, not a Novela. Whatever. Let Jacques figure out what this is: that's his job. Mine: Just sit here and Spew.

God, I bet it's Warm in Tel-Aviv right now. Sandals, Hawaiian shirts. Typing on the beach. Such a Dream. Such a Deal. If my feet weren't so Fucking Cold I could probably dazzle you with my observations and story-telling. oh Shit! There goes the little finger on my right hand. I can't type anything that has a 'p' in it from now on. Oh Shit! There goes the ring finger. I'm going to have to do this the way Jacques does: with two fingers. clink. Even with two fingers: clink! Ha! I sit here and rub my hands together because of the cold, but I look like a madman counting his duros.

I came into Jacques' room yesterday evening and caught him running his fingers through a pile of coins. He pretended to be counting them when he realized I was watching. He sits up there in his room smoking hash late at night and you can hear the jingling even though he turns on his radio to try to cover the noise. He's got the Capitalist Bug bad. Remember, Art Dies In Wealth. He's Proving the Axiom. So Am I?

Just had a glass of wine with Peter, Rebecca, and Norma at the bar across the street, La Sardana. We were joined by Frank who was mumbling about piles of dead bodies all over Europe, "People are piling up in Paris, frozen to death! God, I hate cold!"

Billy just joined them inside as I came out here to Work, as I call it: a euphemism for Begging. Ten minutes ago I was sitting at a table with two women I love. But Now: Idiot's Delight on the Street, while my friends, and old friends, chat each other up.

I am fading fast: There was No Ticket to Israel at the Post Office, again, again. I even had to bum 40ptas from Norma for the glass of wine. Rebecca and Peter just stared at me when I asked for some money. Such Friends. If you ask Frank for a Loan, he pretends that he doesn't understand English. Peter and Rebecca probably have Personal Reasons for not loaning me 40ptas. I'd like to hear them. It took me about five minutes of begging, with hand outstretched, to get That Glass Of Wine. It was a little bitter.

Norma is heading for London on Monday, and then on to Taiwan for a few months. She is planning to teach English there, but has made no arrangements ahead of time. (At what other time can you make arrangements?). Nevertheless, she is casting her kite to the Chinese Mind. She will probably be returning in a few months. I am still fascinated by her face, whether or not she wants to read about it. There is really very little that is Normal about Norma, no matter what her roots. While she was over here in the Barrio, Billy was over at her house looking for her. They had a re-union in La Sardana. It was touching to behold; I'm the One Who Almost Cried though. Such a Sentimental Fool. I love it. What is everyone else looking for? Not Emotion? Not Lust? Are the rest looking for Fidelity and Trust? Am I nearly alone in my Quest for Thrills? Sometimes it seems so. How is it that I got to be forty and still don't know how to have a Polite Conversation? Did I miss some Important Class about Polite Conversation? Where do they learn it? I think I'm Civilized, but It's nearly impossible for me to sit at a table and chit-chat. I Must be dancing to the tune of a Completely Different Orchestra, let alone the drummer.

I don't know how long this will last tonight: The little finger is starting to Go already. Enrique, the Columbian Magazine Writer, just brought me a wine. It's good. (editor goes into fit at shortness of un-necessary sentence). Tough.

Just want to make enough for tonight's dinner. Don't really give a shit about art. (I wonder how you translate 'give a shit' into Spanish. It couldn't possibly be done literally, could it?)

I can Just picture Peter, Frank, Rebecca, and Norma sitting in That Warm Bar, ha-ha-ing it up while I sit out here losing a digit. Shit, jealousy comes easy to me: Peter and Frank are both Well-dressed and Glib, the fuckers. Meanwhile, the idiot sits in the freezing street and types his diarrhea.

I just went into the Sardana to see if Norma was still there. She was gone, but Rebecca and Frank were there in Hot Conversation. Frank, after giving my frozen-finger situation a little sympathy, called me a Passive-Dependent Personality. This, because I'm waiting for Hadass to send me a ticket to Israel. He made Rebecca laugh. I told him, "Fuck you, Frank! I'm not a passive-dependent personality: I Use People, I don't Depend on them!"

He told me, "What bothers you is that Hadass is spending her money on herself, and not you!"

"Fuck You, Frank," I said, "I come in here for sympathy for my frozen fingers and you try to humiliate me in front of my ex-wife! Fuck You!", and I left. Yah. I could hear them still laughing as I entered the freezing. The Bastards! Some day they'll come crying to me and then what do you think I'll say? "Passive-Dependent Bastards!"

They came out of the Sardana laughing, arm in arm.

"Tonight, you are an Artist!", Frank told me as they Strolled down the street.

"Good Luck, Sweetheart!", Rebecca cheerfully trilled.

"Go get 'em, Tiger!", Frank added. The bastards.

This is not my beautiful wife. This is not my beautiful house. The thing that is beginning to piss me off is this: Rebecca keeps looking better every year. I met her when she was about 22 and was a little dumpy-seeming. Now, she's becoming Beautiful. What Fucking Luck. I suppose Lynda and Sue are going through the same changes now that I've done with them. Shit. Water flowing underground. Is this my beautiful wife?

One sure way I can make Frank happy is to write about how difficult it is for me these days to find something fit to eat in the piles of garbage where I shop. He Chortles.

"I thought you Wanted people to laugh at you!", Rebecca told me. God! I hope I never get any enemies, these are my friends. What I need now is for Jacques to walk up and "Hello Idiot-Box" me. I imagine that everyone else in the world is in a warm place doing pleasurable things to each other while the Idiot continues to freeze.

How did Norma get away? God-damn it! Sloppy work, indeed. She is probably with Peter enjoying a nice hot meal in some secluded little restaurant. Sure, That's got to be it. Shit. I Really Am Getting Tired of all this: even though It's Mine. You can't run away from yourself: Such Popular Bullshit.

On The Street Again, Again

SIX DIE IN BARCELONA

Next Night. Bakers Street. The Same.
  Well, I Live in Barcelona. It's Official. I got a postcard from Hadass: "30.12.84 Happy New Year. Hi jack- look at the cow!! (behind) I am back to the desert. it IS warm! very. I am looking for a place to stay. and in few days I am back to work (on the street) Playing a lot. I hope I can make some money here, (on the street). I am not so reach anymore. I am happy. MORE SOON! (in a letter). lots of LOVE----I miss you. Have FUN! And dont give up!"
  That's It! No mention of a ticket or money or my trip to Israel. I guess I'll clean up my apartment and get some gas for the heater. I might well settle in. Looks like it's going to be a long winter. Six people froze to death in Barcelona last night. Three in the street and three in their houses. This place wasn't built to withstand any Cold at all. There is virtually no insulation in any of the houses.
  The postcard has a picture of a Bedouin on his camel. The sun is shining and it looks very warm there. What a Gal! I miss her too. God Damn It! I was ready to go. Jacques predicted the contents of this postcard, almost exactly, a few days ago. He knows the Israelita well, I'm just beginning to understand her. He told me, "She missed the whole point of your phone conversation. That's Her Way!" Clink, clink, a cup of coffee at least.
  I've set the picture of the Bedouin right next to the sign saying "Ingles Lecciones 700pta/hora". That'll give them something to think about, eh? I may have to go back to the way I was Living a few weeks ago: cafe-con-leche, no wine, get my shit together again. These Holiday Seasons in Barcelona are Surely Fun, but they tend to head me towards the pit. Oh well, Next Year in Jerusalem. I'll keep the camel picture near me for heat. I'm sure Frank would approve.
  I gave the Opera Crowd (Frank, Jacques, Whitey, and others) the night off last night. Frank's reputation would suffer if I made a Scene there, at his table. Instead, I headed for the Bodega where I engaged in boisterous conversation with Steve, Vivian, his wife, and a friend. Vivian was specifically looking for me last night, he says, because he likes the way I bullshit. We headed down to the deaf-and-dumb bar when the bodega closed and remained there drinking wine until early in the morning. The next thing I remember is stumbling over my heater and knocking all my food on the floor of the pad, bumping my

head on the table as I went. I have a beautiful bump/scratch on my forehead and would be Instantly Granted Membership in the Denton Gang, if I applied right now.

My footwear alone would probably gain me access: Rags disguised as socks. If the members saw the rag I use to blow my nose, they would probably make me president for Life. I have descended to Jacques' Fashion Level for the first time this trip. Billy suggested that I get some plastic bags for my feet, to keep warm. clink.

Maybe I should put up a sign saying, "Don't let this man become number seven tonight!". That should bring in the duros. Maybe I should make a Spectacle indicating Just How Cold I Am Sitting Out Here, You know, blow on my hands, flap my arms, and moan.

It's the coldest here in twenty-eight years and I've been so spaced out that I've been living in a roof-top apartment with a heater, but haven't managed to get it filled. This is a Sure Sign of Quasi-terminal Idiocy. My socks are still sitting in the bucket.

Country Western Verse:
"My socks in the bucket, the bucket, the bucket,
My heater don't work, butt-fuck it, but fuck it."

Peter spent the day making some kind of australian stew out of potatoes and mashed-up brussels sprouts. I tried some of it and almost had to spit it out. I hope he finds a wife soon, before he kills himself with his own cooking.

I think I'll try to stay sober tonight so that I can go shopping in the piles of garbage. I need a new pair of pants. These brown high-waters are starting to permeate my whole being with bum feelings. I think brown polyester has a deleterious effect on one's nervous system.

There must be some Rational Explanation for this sudden change of fortune. Just Yesterday I was sunning myself on the beach in Tel-Aviv. Now, I have a 50-50 chance of freezing to death or falling and killing myself in my own apartment. Or setting myself on fire from the feet up. Shit! What a Life!

Frank has been accusing me, lately, of Ruining the Ambience of Our Little cavern at Santi's because I have befriended Steve and he occasionally joins us there for dinner, during which time he Belches and Shouts and interrupts otherwise Intelligent Conversations. When Steve is pissed (drunk) he can be as obnoxious as the best of them. Last night he assaulted a young American Girl, (with his mouth and what was left of his mind), named Ellen, who Jacques and I introduced to Tapas-Life yesterday. She is Confused about what to do with her life, so, Jacques, Frank, and I, have been Counselling her. She mentioned that she may start playing Music on the Streets and that was all it took for Steve to blow his top, "You Stupid Motherfucking Shit American Twit! It's My

Motherfucking Life you're talking about! You're too Fucking Stupid to do it!", he screamed at her, almost blowing her mind, and totally ruining any progress we had already made with her.

I thought we were about to lose her. I had to keep telling Steve that she was just young, and "C'mon, man, you're completely fucking-up the evening.", while Frank sat there Grimacing and Casting Evil Looks in my direction. Steve finally calmed down, talked for a few minutes with us, belched a few more times, and went to sit at the bar to wait for me to accompany him to the Bodega. I was torn between two loyalties. I decided not to risk the evening at the Opera: I joined Steve's Reality, leaving the Counselling to the Higher Classes.

Evidently, all went well: Ellen, and her friend, showed up at Jacques' today and she told him that she is planning to move here from France as soon as she can return to Paris and quit her job as a Nanny. We had to assure her that she probably wouldn't ever be attacked by Steve again. She's only nineteen and her eyes get big easily; it's difficult not to impress her. we'll probably be seeing more of her in the future, I know I hope I do. She has dyed-red hair and rosier cheeks than Helen, who I assume she has been sent to replace.

Steve just headed into the bar with this parting shot, "My balls are so cold you couldn't even warm them if you boiled or fried them!" I think he composed that especially for inclusion here.

clink. clink. all small change: no 100 coins yet. Haven't they heard about the street deaths'? This is not a Joke! This is Serious Begging.

"How did Jack die?"

"He fell down in his room."

I overslept my three oclock Anarchist English Lesson today. I'll try again tomorrow. clink.

Mcdonald's Suicide, Michaelangelo, Snot

King of the Cartoon People.

One oclock, Thursday. Bread street, as usual.

I am not in Israel. I am in Barcelona. It is good for me to remind myself of this. It has warmed up a little bit; nevertheless, I slept in my overcoat again last night. Four days ago it looked like something a German tourist might wear; Now, I'm not sure the Denton Gang would even pick it up from the street. And I have to wear it to my English classes tonight.

Peter is painting a series of Suicide paintings. They were inspired by a magazine article and photographs of a woman jumping from a third story somewhere in the U.S.... She landed on a couple (a man and woman) who were passing under. Luckily (?) a Photographer caught the whole thing on film. Everyone around here agrees that the photos are Excellent. In Peter's paintings she is leaping from the 3-story McDonalds at the corner of Fernando and the Ramblas. She is falling past the little red awnings which are above each little window. There is a Catalan Couple in red sweaters eating pastry directly below her.

Peter told me that he must have German Blood; he is interested in such things. I mentioned that he will probably have a hard time selling the Biggest One (about 4 x 6 feet) in Barcelona because in this town of two million there are probably only about ten people that would consider hanging it in their living room; and these would probably have whips and chains in there already. He said that he could sell it very easily in Germany. It's a Horror to Behold. Maybe he can sell it to McDonalds.

Frank has suggested that he do a painting of the view from inside McDonalds as the woman falls past the window. Big Mac, Big Splat. I would like to be one of the people sitting there eating, in the painting.

I stayed up late again last night, drinking at the bodega with Enrique, two young Columbian friends of his, and Steve. We had Quite an Evening, Jabbering away in Pigeon Spanish and Pigeon English. Frank had requested that I give the Opera Crowd another night off. I complied. Frank said that it was good for me to hang out with South Americans, they'll be good connections for, "Down and out in Bogota".

I really am going to have to stop this wine drinking. My pad is a Cold Mess and my hands are dirty. Even I realize that the bucket of socks in my bathroom is Ridiculous. There are six million people in Greater Bogota. Why am I not in Tel-Aviv? This is not my Beautiful Beach! This is not my Wonderful Life!

Last night at Santi's Jacques told me, "It's a sign of genius to wear rags on your feet: Michaelangelo did; he wouldn't change his socks for six months. When he removed his buskins his skin would come off with them. He was hanging out with Princes, Kings, and popes, at all times!"

"AT ALL TIMES!", Frank added, "And I'm sure there were imitators that would put buskins on and leave them on for six months in imitation of The Master!"

Five oclock Thursday. Barrio Diario.

It's Now Official: I am a Retired English Teacher; I gave all of my classes to Rebecca, with the exception of the Anarchist Bar, from which I was fired today.

Frank and Jacques spent the day lingering with the Denton Gang in Plaza St. Juame. I was bullshitting with them for a while when Jacques suggested that I Retire from teaching and Devote My Time to writing. I had been looking for just such an excuse to quit. I've missed the last four or five classes anyway. Now I can devote my time to Serious Drinking. No more pretensions of Middle-Classness.

Frank doesn't want to go On Record as having been an Advisor on this Career Move. I suppose he is afraid that I will Come Begging to Him when I Fail. Jacques lacks that Particular Fear because he knows that I will come begging to him no matter what happens. It's the same thing.

As Jacques predicted, as soon as I gave the classes to Rebecca, a Great weight was lifted from my Psyche. I no longer have to Keep Appointments. I don't have to get up So Early in the afternoon anymore. I got rid of those stupid brown plastic pants and am now wearing a pair of Norma's old blue overalls. I always did want to get into her pants. And now I am. Fashion Be Damned! I can walk around with dirty hands and snotty clothes as much as I wish now. It Feels Great! I can now hold up my head when I am in the company of either Artists, Bums, or Beggars. My Horizons have been widened.

Frank is threatening to avoid Norma's going-away party tonight because I have invited Harry. Frank's afraid of a repeat performance of last year's dinner at Meson David wherein Harry nearly leaped across the table to kill Frank, who was doing an imitation of me drunk. It was Very Intimidating for Frank: Harry's hands are like bear-paws, and his voice is likewise bear-like when he is angered. Tonight could very well turn into the Party of The Year.

According to Jacques, I get more attention at the Opera Cafe when I'm not there than when I am. Evidently I was the main topic of conversation there last night. I am Flattered. Frank said that he was enjoying his life right now because he is constantly dealing with 2- dimensional characters. He told

Jacques that I am the King of the Cartoon People. Frank said that it gives him an added dimension of Reality to associate with the rest of us.

Frank told me that I will have to produce at least 1500 of these double-spaced pages in order for Jacques to edit it down to normal book size. I may fire both of them. I'm going to publish this exactly the way I wrote it, and call it "Barcelona Barrio Diarrhea Diario". Has a nice ring to it. un-expurgated, Original,   As-typed-by-thecartoonrnan-actually-on-the-street-because-if-he-typed-it-in-his-roomthe-monster-from-the-floor-below-would-come-up-and.-stab-him-to-deatho I've taped the picture of the Bedouin on his camel to the front of the desk, right next to the begging notice.

Frank told me today that it is better for my ex-students that I am not their teacher anymore, "Imagine the Little Spanish with a sexist-racist teacher! They're much better off with Rebecca!"

"Frank, I'm not a sexist or a racist! I like to fuck black women!", I told him.

"So, you've solved the World's Problems at last? We can all live in Peace now!", Steve said in passing, on his way to play.

"I think I Am one of the World's problems.", I answered. And the years go by: Water flowing underground, teeth falling out.

Norma's Going-Away Party, the Happiness of Stones

CLINK SPRINKLE CLINK

Next Day. Friday. Calle Llibreteria (Bread St.)

It should be a good evening. I didn't even have the paper in the machine when a lady walked up and handed me a 100pta note. clink.

Got a letter from Hadass today. Says she is still looking for a place to stay. Misses me very much. If she can't get a good scene happening soon she says she may be heading back for Barcelona. That would be just fine. Then I'd have some heat) love, and clean socks. Shit, there's 200 in the box already. Go, Jack, Go.

Norma's party at Meson David was a Complete Success, with the exception of what I ordered for dinner. On Norma's Recommendation, I ordered one of the 'Specialties of the House'. Harry also told me that it was very good. I forget what it's called but when it arrived it looked like Old Macdonald had been performing an autopsy on a pig and had thrown some of the leftover pieces onto my plate along with the cabbage and potatoes. There was a Whole pig's Ear, a couple of unidentifiable pieces of pig, and a Pig's Hand with no meat on it. I ate what I could and gave the rest to Rene who said she was going to have them bronzed.

Everyone else feasted on their Normal Food, while I had to content myself with mainly bread and wine. Out of respect for Norma, the Anticipated Blow-up between Harry and Frank, or Me and Everyone, didn't happen. The Most Active Participants were Amani and Billy who were in some sort of Adolescent Trances and just couldn't stop teasing each other and jumping around. Things calmed down after they left, early in the evening.

Norma admitted that she also was attracted to me but has been purposely giving me almost no Encouragement because of what she has heard about my past love affairs and their usually messy endings. What a shame. We have tentatively agreed to go to dinner when she returns from China. This will be about the Slowest Love Affair on record, if it ever happens.

The Group, less Harry, Amani, and Billy, headed over to the bar with the Unpronounceable Name, which sounds like 'frog-way', where everyone drank their favorite drinks and shared a little of Jacques' Hashish.

Frank told me that as long as I write about him I would do fine. I dutifully pulled out my notebook and pencil, poised to write, and nodded at Frank.

He began, "Most of the people we know are secretly robots. They begin to live at Parties where there is free food. You can spot them: they're always on their way to someone's house for dinner. They all eat and read at the same time. When they come to Cafe del Opera they always sit facing the TV in rapt attention. They've deterred me from my suicide: 'In Death there's Freedom from Pain', according to Camus. This is called 'The Happiness of Stones'. It's Frightening! Margo would knit, read, eat, and listen to her Walkman at the same time, for instance. It's turned me around: I was ready to blow my brains out, but now I'm reconsidering."

I asked him, "So, Frank, does 'The Happiness of Stones' seem less desirable to you now that you've begun to examine it?"

"That's why I'M Alive!", he answered.

Phil asked, "So, this has scared you out of your Suicide?"

"You bet! They're minimal life-forms! You can put your cigarette out on their hands! Jacques' and I counted, 15 out of 22 people in the opera the other night were robots experiencing The Happiness of Stones. Christopher, the German, was one of them: the more dope we gave him the Stonier he got."

I told Phil, "Nothing works to keep them away. I've even tried multisyllabic words to no avail."

"Where's Christopher now?", Jacques asked.

"He's gone back to Germany to get a lube-job.", I told him.

Phil and Rene, Whitey, and I left ahead of the rest and Whitey and I parted from them in Barrio Chino. The night ended early for me with Whitey helping me find the Gothic Barrio and Calle Raurich. The rest of the crowd repaired to the Opera for the Evening's Discussion.

Frank publicized his theories about Robots and The Happiness of Stones for a couple of weeks and seemed to have driven most of them from our ranks. I suppose they became self-conscious. Lately, he's been discussing 'Cartoon people'. It may prove effective also, though there are still quite a few of us hanging around.

CLINK, SPRINKLE, CLINK

"Hello, Stupid!", Jacques says as he walks up and peruses my act.

"Well, Jack, you just have to think about getting some sort of umbrella act together.", he counsels. He's not aware of the umbrella deal in the works with Billy. Cosmic? clink. sprinkle. clink.

Jacques read the letter from Hadass, "Well, this just means that she's heading back for Barcelona.", he tells me. He knows her well. I sure would like to see my Desert Gal.

I tell him, "If Hadass was here my life would be Great. It would be stable!"

"you wouldn't be able to get drunk anymore.", he says.

"I wouldn't have to get drunk any more!", I say.

"Well, Jack, Health is Wealth. Bums are always healthy because they spend so much time outside. Your time spent out here is like money in the bank.", he tells me. I'm Greatly Encouraged.

He continues, "Jack, you know what you need to happen: Some Famous Writer, like Mailer, to come by and see you out here. You would be rich overnight just because of his contribution!"

"I'm expecting it.", I tell him. This Advice from the guy who talked me into quitting my Teaching Career.

He continues encouraging me, "Well, Jack, the night is young. Never mind the fact that the temperature is dropping a degree every few minutes." .

"Yah, Jacques, as long as it's not raining or snowing, I think it's a nice day.", I tell him.

"That is Truly Bum Consciousness!"

"I'll stay out here til eight, if the weather lets me!"

"Just get your ten pages!", he advises.

"I want the Money.", I say.

"You should be glad if you almost freeze to death, or starve to death: It means that you're on the Right Track.", he assures me, "Artists are famous for that!"

An old lady clinks a duro in the box.

"Those old ladies are incredible, they're good for about 200 per night in duros.", I say.

"Yah, but look: Now Steve doesn't get one.", Jacques says. It's true. I may have to move the pitch to another Spot if Steve mentions it again.

The rain has ceased, the temperature is dropping near the point where I won't be able to type 'p'. I continue, just Sit Here and Beg.

Jacques says, "I'm sorta gettin' in to lingerin' out here with you, Jack."

"Yah, I noticed that.", I tell him. I guess he figures it's just as cold in his room as it is out here.

He tells me, "Me and Rebecca are going to buy a heater together, Jack, that will change everything."

"Good for you both,", I tell him, "I'm running out of paper and ribbon."

He says, "Just think about when your typewriter breaks, Jack, then what are you going to do. Y'know why you get money out here, Jack? Because people relate to you as a Street-Drummer. If you were using a pen, you would get nothing. So, if your typewriter breaks, you'll be all right as long as you can make drumming sounds."

"Thanks,", I tell him, "It's Really Threatening to Rain, isn't it?"
Looking on the bright side, he answers, "It's Gonna Happen, Man!"
"This is really slow,", I tell him, "I don't understand it."
"It's because I'm lingering here, man, it's always that way: as soon as your friends come, you have reason to be depressed. See you later, man.", he picks up his paintings and heads for the pension.

It is Really getting Cold now. My feet are hurting from it. Maybe that English-teaching wasn't really that bad, after all. You never have to do it in the street. Ah, well, winter will be over in a couple of months. Then the Spring Rains begin. Ah! Shit, I think it's time for another glass of wine. Can Barely afford it but at least it distracts me from how cold I am.

Ah! That's Better.

Santi's, The Opera Cafe, Unconditional Love

Stones, Tolstoy, Custard Pie.
Tuesday, l0:30AM, Bread Street.

Got out here early today because I stayed up all night. Don't know why I couldn't sleep. Must have been anticipating getting to work early. I hunted around in Hadass' clothes bag and found a pair of sweat pants, some leg-warmers, and another pair of socks. Also found a couple of berets. Now my feet, legs, and head are much warmer than they have been for the Last; few days. Had 300ptas left over from yesterday so I went out this morning and bought some milk, bread, eggs and cheese and came back to the pad where I cooked myself up some scrambled eggs and had some home-made cafe-con-leche. Ah, I'm rapidly getting back on my feet now. Even had enough money left over for a pack of cigarettes and matches. Today may be the big day for me, if this ribbon holds out: I'll get to fill my heater tank and tonight I'll have heat. How Together can one get? Boggles the mind: I'm learning how to take care of myself! Eating and Everything! I've even begun the first step towards rescuing my socks from the bucket: I dumped them out on the floor of the shower. Next step is to hang them up on something. I'll probably do that tonight, If I remember. Clink. l00 already. yah! Shit! 350 already!

Santi's was closed last night, so Jacques, Peter, Rebecca, Billy, Frank, and I went to a new place for dinner. It was supposed to be Cheap, but the Menu (a complete meal, with drinks) was 350, about average. we were joined by Gandalf. It took us about twenty minutes to figure out the menu: Everyone had Opinions, there were light arguments, and translation problems. I was getting bored because I already knew what I wanted: a bowl of soup.

We finally ordered, except for Billy, who was having a lengthy argument with Rebecca about what he could order. I moved out from between them; it was driving me crazy; they were arguing about 50ptas difference in the price. When that was finally settled, the group discussed the prices of drinks for a few minutes. Frank was grimacing; we were acting like such stereotypical Americans.

It was cold in the restaurant, almost as cold as outside. Peter suggested that next time we should sit over by the lights. Brilliant.

Everyone I know in Barcelona sits around and talks about how cold it is in their rooms. Billy and Rebecca continued to argue about the water for a few minutes.

"The last thing Gilmore was involved in was illegal: the scattering of his ashes from an airplane.", Jacques told us as he slopped macaroni on my manuscript. Frank and Gandalf were Discussing Diet; Frank told him, "Coca-cola is very good for your digestion: it eats your meat for you." Gandalf was not moved. Frank continued, "y' know what I thrive on? My nails grow longer, my hair grows faster, I'm more aggressive on the street?" "What?", bit Gandalf.

"Pastry!", Frank ejaculated, "Pastryarians are Better People!"

"They use Animal Fat in pastry!", interrupted Peter.

"Yah, that's right, they use animal fat in pastry.", assured Gandalf.

"Uh-oh, uh-oh.", said Frank.

Rebecca asked Frank where he gets his Special Custard Creams. About three people began giving her directions. I helped out, "I'll tell you how to get there, Rebecca,", I said, "You face the Bar Del pi, from the outside, turn right and go down a block.

"Jack, how can you face the Bar Del pi from any other way than Outside!?, asked Peter. I had to think about that for a minute and I shut up.

Peter mentioned that a lot of young girls were taking second looks at Billy today while they were out walking around.

"Peter is using Billy for young-girl bait", accused Gandalf.

"That's Right!", said Jacques, "Why do you think he's wearing Billy's clothes!?"

I was counting all the duros (5ptas) that I'd made the day before, on the table, when Billy said, "That's the duro I gave you!"

"What?", I asked, "You gave me that fucked-up one?"

"Yah, they wouldn't take it at the store.", he snickered.

Frank asked, "Billy, how do you like having all these disciples? Just remember that you're responsible for them!"

I said, "Someday Billy can say: 'My dad was out begging one day when I was 12 and I put a duro in his box.'"

Frank said, "Yah, and later when I got home my mother beat me for it."

"I think there's some cockroach shit on my Flan!", added Jacques. We discussed Flan for a few minutes, that tasteless, odorless, pale-yellow, ubiquitous Spanish version of Dessert.

Frank was getting happier, now that we weren't discussing prices, he exclaimed, "I Love My Little Friends!"

"They love you too, Frank!", I told him.

He went Happily On, "Lots of times you think I'm being judgmental, but I'm just telling it like it is! I give you Unconditional Love! That's What it is! Unconditional Love!"

"That's the only way for a judgmental person to be!", Jacques told him.

Frank was beaming, "Rebecca! Billy! Gandalf! Peter! Jacques! Jack! No matter how fucked up you get, I want you to know I offer you Unconditional Love! I Love All My Little Friends!" All was smiles.

Gandalf left but returned a few minutes later with a windbreaker for Billy that he'd found in the street. Billy added it to the other five garments he already had on his upper body. Gandalf is becoming Billy's Michelin-man Guru.

We finished up the dinner and left, passing Barbara and Santi on their way in. Frank said that they check out prices at other restaurants on their nights off.

We dropped off Rebecca, Billy, and Peter at the Pension so they could continue their love affair with Peter's Heater. Jacques, Frank and I repaired to the Opera cafe where we each ordered what we could afford. Jacques: beer. Frank: Cafeconlech. Me: water.

THE OPERA CAFE:

"Well, when you get your book open, I'll start.", Frank told me. I assumed my role as Opera Cafe Reporter, opened my notebook, and he began, "Helen is quite concerned that she's being treated as a Sex Object. My advice to her was to do what I did when it happened to me: Develop a personality so that people will have something else to get their teeth into."

Jacques added, "And she took it all in, just sat here like a fireplug."

Frank continued, "And I asked Ralph, in front of Helen, 'Ralph, did your girlfriend have a good time here?'"

"And Helen was sitting right here getting none of it; she was in a Robot Trance! Jacques told me.

I said, "Well, Helen Does need to be treated like a sex object, that's My Theory."

"Yes, and Your Theory has gotten you where you're at today.", Frank told me.

I said, "Well, hey, I'm working my way back to middle-class right now! "

"Jack, we never told you to become Middle-class.", said Frank.

"Well, being middle-class to me is just having food.", I told him. "Yah, middle-class to him is sleeping in his bed and not in a doorway!", said Jacques.

"Ahh, it's just a different definition.", said Frank.

Jacques paid for his beer with fifty 2pta coins. I said that I thought he might be causing a problem by doing that.

Frank said, "We didn't get hit, knifed, or robbed, so I don't think it's a problem." I wasn't sure. I understand some Spanish, and I'm pretty sure the waiter was swearing heavily.

We talked about hash prices in the Opera lately and I said that I had the best connection in town: The piss Bar, where no one else shops.

Jacques said, "Well, it looks like I' 11 be able to rile the dope dealers tonight, as well.", as he headed for the front with a handful of coins. He returned in a couple of minutes, having made a Fair Deal: 400ptas for a gram. He hadn't been able to find his usual connection so it wasn't a Great Deal.

He explained, "Monday nights are slow on every level, restaurants And dealers.

Frank loaded up Billy's corncob pipe, took a large toke, turned red in the face, and gave us a couple of minutes of what he calls the "Moroccan National Anthem".

Jacques said, "That's good hash, huh, Frank?"

When Frank stopped hacking, he said, "I have no complaints, ever, about the hash I get in here, Unlike some of the shit I've gotten in Plaza Real". Frank then held the pipe for me while I took a hit. (He won't let me hold the pipe since last year when he says I swallowed a screen from his pipe. Earlier this year he gave me one more chance and then told a joke just as I was toking up and I blew away another screen, laughing. When Hadass was still here he would make her take a toke and pass it to me in a Jewish Kiss, which worked fine). I toked what little was left in the pipe, and got a little buzz.

I said, "All I know is that if Hadass was here I would have Heat, Food, and Love, and wouldn't have a bucket of wet socks ,"

Jacques said, "That's the main reason I don't visit you, Jack, I don't want to have to deal with that bucket of socks."

Frank said, "If Hadass was here you could get head whenever you want: just say, 'c 'mere baby, gimme some skull'." He did a little pantomime to show us how it would look. The dope was obviously working.

We talked about one of Frank's Favorite Irritations: How people we know don't know how to smoke dope without wasting it: sometimes they can't tell whether they've gotten any or not.

Frank said, "I Never have any problem telling whether I got any dope in a hit: It's Hot, and it passes through my mouth, throat, and into my lungs! These things have Feeling in ME!"

I exhaled the hit I'd been holding: nothing came out.

"I held it down; I don't think I got any that time!", I told Frank. "It's in your system!", he insisted.

"Yah, Maybe, but not a fucking thing came out! It sure wasn't much!", I complained. A big mistake, I soon found out.

I said, "Y' know, looking back from this year I can really see what a tourist I was last year. The way I spent money."

Jacques said, "Yah, and you'll look back next year and say the same about this."

" Frank added, "Next year he'll be in there rapping with Peter and Rebecca about seven pesetas."

Frank continued, "If you said 'Fuck' to Gary Gilmore he'd Come and Squirt in every direction; some of these we know, you just say 'peseta, peseta, peseta,' in their ear."

Frank gave me another of his Pretend Hits of Hash (he'd bought the dope tonight, and was in charge of disbursement), about which I again mildly complained.

He chastised me instantly, "I buy it! Jacques fetches it! I prepare it! And then we bring it right to your lips! You're a Virtual King in here! And you threaten to Get Even with Me? You should be Ecstatic!"

I backed down. He was right. I had it Made. I went to get another glass of water from the zombie at the bar. When I got about four feet from him he pretended not to see me and looked the other way. When I finally got his attention, he was very rude and slammed the glass down on the counter with a grunt. When I got back to the table with my hard-earned water, I told them about the bartender. Frank's eyes lit up, he grabbed my glass of water and drank almost the whole thing down before I stopped him.

"Ah, Gracias Amigo, but that wasn't enough for me.", he said, and grabbed the glass again and downed the rest of it.

I said, "Oh, Great Guru, are you giving me Lessons on Being Hip? 'Never Say You Didn't Get Enough'? Especially with Dope, Free Dope?"

"That's Right", he said, and grabbed my glass again. I grappled with him for it and said that I was tired of the Fucking Lesson. Jacques said that he would keep the glass filled all night, for nothing, if Frank needed more water. Frank said he did. Jacques went into the Funkiest Bathroom in Barcelona and came back with the glass filled. I asked him to drink some of it. He did. Then Frank grabbed the glass and drank all of it down. I was thirsty, but Frank was making sure that I Learned My Lesson.

Jacques went and filled it again, but this time I grabbed it and held on to it upon his return, to keep Frank from grabbing it.

Frank, at least, was Obviously stoned, he said, "Some of these we know, the only times they get excited is when it's time to pay, or the food comes, or when they say, 'this isn't as good for the price as the other place'."

"Yah, it's the continuing story of The Happiness of Stones.", I said.

The conversation turned to Tolstoy; Frank is reading his biography, and there was a Hidden Message for me in Frank's summation of Tolstoy, "You know what they said about Tolstoy, and mind you, He Is Gilmore, always hanging out with serfs, borrowing money, getting drunk, and fucking gypsy women; he was a lot like you, in ways, Jack. Tolstoy would begin each day by writing a list of rules for his behavior and then violate them all by evening, and end up repenting late at night, down on his knees wailing.

"He went on and on about Tolstoy, explaining how schizophrenic he was in his involvement in Russian politics; how he would take both sides of any conflict or argument, "Tolstoy never mentioned himself in his writing, he only bragged to his friends.", he said.

"He's not like me in that respect, is he?", I said.

"NO. He's not.", Frank answered drily.

Carolyn, the Aussie, joined us; I told her, "We were just discussing the condition of the serfs in Tolstoy's time."

"Oh, well, I'll stay out of it.", she said.

Frank told her, "We want to talk about whatever you want to."

"She didn't respond; she had noticed the TV, "Oh! A TV! I haven't seen one in so long!", she said, staring at it like a stone with its mouth open. I cracked up. Frank almost blew his mind, and sent Jacques to fetch him another glass of water from the men's room.

I said to Frank, "You get what you deserve, eh Frank?" He nodded grimly.

"I just saw a dog get run over.", Carolyn told us, struggling to pull herself away from the TV.

"Oh Shit!", Frank said, "Don't tell me that! I hate to hear it, it almost makes me throw up." Carolyn went on to explain that it was a 'good' dog-got-run-over story because a lot of people had stopped to help. They talked about dogs getting run over for a minute, til Jacques returned with the glass of water, which I stole.

Carolyn asked, "Frank, have you ever thought of being a comedian?"

"Well, yes,", he answered, "Once in Los Angeles, my friends all suggested that I give it a try, so I went down to the famous place for comedy in LA, The Comedy Store. There was a line of about thirty of them waiting to audition outside. I went in to see what they had to go through; they'd get up on the stage and start to tell a joke and the crowd would start yelling and a guy with a hook would come and grab the poor guy by the neck and yank him off. Here were Young Aspiring Stand-up Comedians needing Mass Love and receiving instead, Hate, from this crowd. I came back the next night for my audition. I had everything worked out: what I was going to talk about, and as I pulled into. the parking lot, a body came hurtling down onto the pavement right in front of me, from the roof of the Hilton Hotel next door. I recognized it as one of the aspiring comedians who had been on the stage the night before. It was the end of my Aspirations for Stand-up Comedy!"

Carolyn was amazed, and asked, "How many suicides have you seen, Frank?"

"Countless, ", he answered, "I used to work for an ambulance company in L.A."

Frank then told us a couple of his favorite ambulance stories. His first night on the job there was a car crash near his home. He was very proud of the way he looked in his white smock; Dr. Kildare-Box, he thought. He arrived at the scene and the crew tried to lift up a victim who was lying on the ground, but they were having great difficulty; Frank was standing on his left hand. Frank's whole family and his friends were out there that night to applaud his work. He saw the guy later at the hospital and asked him how he was doing. The only permanent injury was his hand.

Carolyn went to fetch us another glass of water. Jacques and I were arguing over who was going to get her gloves if she didn't come back, when she came back.

She said, "Frank, how 'bout some hash?"

"Certainly.", he replied.

"I have some.", she said.

"Ah, well!", he said.

Fulfilling a recent prophecy, they managed to spill a small bit of Frank's hash before they even got it lit. The Happiness of stones. Frank had a hit and then passed the ash to Carolyn, who looked at it and decided to do some of Hers. She pulled out 'the little bit'; it was about a half gram, a large chunk by the evening's standards.

Evidently, Carolyn had never seen a pipe before, "Oh, this is just like a Chillum!", she kept remarking.

I said, "That's like going to the Grand Canyon and saying that it's just as pretty as the postcards."

"You're right.", she confessed.

Carolyn told Frank, "I'm obsessed with the Cold, lately."

He said, "I don't care if it SNOWS! Even if it Snows tomorrow, I' 11 be just fine in my room reading my Tolstoy biography and eating one of the twelve custard pies and eight gingerbread pastries I have in my room; with Bowie on the box and the heater blasting out, and my twelve candles in bottles lined up near the window! I don't care if it SNOWS!"

"I walked around all day with my hot water bottle strapped to my stomach.", said Carolyn.

"I have one of those! But it doesn't seem to work.", said Frank.

"Do you put boiling water in it?", she asked him.

"No, I just use warm water. I don't want to walk through that cold hallway to the kitchen to get boiling water; I just use water out of the tap.", he told her.

"Try boiling water! It'll work for sure.", she said.

"Ah! Maybe that's what I'll do! Yah!", he said

I think it might work: with the hot water bottle filled with boiling water, his heater blasting, the twelve candles, the lights on for heat, five blankets, five shirts, two hooded sweat-shirts with the drawstrings pulled so tight that only his eyes can be seen, I think Frank has finally figured out how to stay warm. The Custard Pies should help too.

Another Night at the Opera Café

Last night at Santi's there wasn't much going On: when I left, Gandalf and Amani were having an argument about the Correct Way To Masturbate, in front of Carolyn. I headed to the pad, and brewed up some Cafeconleche, which I Put in a Jar and took down to the opera Cafe where I joined Jacques and Frank already engrossed in the Evening's Discussion.

"Do you know why I'm Stating The Obvious?", Frank asked Jacques.

"No! I don't.", Jacques answered.

"Because I'm High as a Kite!", Frank exclaimed.

I asked them if they could spare some change so that I could buy a coffee. When they hemmed and hawed, and looked at each other, I reached into my bag and pulled out a typical bar-glass and my jar of cafeconlech, and a little packet of sugar, and began pouring myself a glass of coffee.

"Well, fuck you guys then, I'll use my own!", I told them. I next produced a hard-boiled egg, a tomatoe, a loaf of bread, and some tangerines, which I offered to them.

Jacques said, "See, he doesn't want our money, he just wants our company."

Frank held his tangerine up and stared at it as though it were the Star-of-India, and said, "My little friends are the Kings of (pause, his eyes sparkle, he's on another planet) ... Stuff!"

I offered them each half of a hard-boiled egg, with salt if they liked.

Frank said he had been so hungry for heat lately that he had taken to sitting in front of his heater; snapping at the fire and gnawing on the edge of the heater element. He had Heat Munchies.

We got to talking about the Opera Cafe and recent events there. There had been a riot a couple of nights before among the drug dealers who crowd the smaller area near the front entrance. Jacques and Frank had seen it. It had lasted for about half an hour. The Bartender and the Waiters just stood by until it was over and then went in and counted up the broken furniture and dishes and cups and added up the cost and presented a bill to the participants. It was paid with no argument. Frank said that the Rolling Stones come to the Cafe Opera just to watch the owner sit in his corner, read his paper, eat his food, and control the whole operation without seeming to be aware of it.

He said, "While the others watch TV, I watch the owner. I get the best entertainment."

Frank says that the Waiters in the Opera are about the toughest guys around. One time, the waiter who looks like Tony Curtis was hassled by some German Tourists who wanted their table cleared Immediately: He bowed politely and disappeared into the kitchen. He came out a few seconds later with a lead-filled bat, raised it over his head, and brought it down smartly on their table, smashing the glass top into pieces and scattering their glasses and bottles all over the place, along with customers and the Germans themselves. "Clear Enough For You?", he asked.

"Who in History hasn't heard of the Cafe de la Opera,", Frank asked, "you can do anything you want in here as long as you can afford to pay for the damages. It's been here a hundred years!"

We watched the owner for a few minutes, chewing at high speed and speed-reading his newspaper.

"Now Billy's getting a new disciple: his father!", Frank said. There was a long pause.

"Who? Me?", I asked, as though I'd just realized I was Billy's father.

"Yah.", Frank said.

"I'm thinking of becoming Billy's disciple too!", said Jacques.

"So am I.", said Frank.

"Not me.", I said.

I reached into my bag and brought out my own dope and my hash-pipe made out of a toilet-roll: I'm not dependent on anybody. I toked up, which caused a small stir among the staff of the Opera: they hadn't seen such a unique pipe before. I was Proud.

Frank had promised, earlier at Santi's, to talk tonight about 'Peter and Succulents". I'd thought he said 'Peter and Succulence'. When I cleared it up I tried to explain the difference to Frank, and what it meant to me. He told me, "You just write down what I say: I'm the one talking about succulence! I'm the one who knows about Succulence."

I shut up and got out my pad and pencil. Sometimes it is best for us Little Folk to just accept our role as Audience, and hold our tongues.

Frank began, "I did a study of Succulence...."

I interrupted, "Do you mean 's-u-c-c-u-l-e-n-t-s', or do you mean 's-u-c-c-u-l-e-n-c-e'? It makes a difference to me; They're two different words." Frank glared at me as though I had less brains than a cactus, and told me to shut up and write.

Frank continued, "So, I did this study of Succulents, and found that there was this plant that had a will to live that was so strong that it Transmuted itself from what it was into a cactus called a Hydra that looks like a bunch of snakes raring up out of the ground!"

I asked, "You mean it didn't Evolve? It just changed from a Lichen into a snake-cactus when it saw horses coming?"

"No, No, No, It wasn't a Lichen, it was more like a… Life Form! Stop asking questions and just record what is going down. Observers should not Participate!", he told me.

"Sorry.", I said.

He continued, "Those plants that grow on granite, when they see a deer coming, change into granite-colored plants. They pray to God not to be eaten by the deer, and He changes them into granite-colored plants!"

"Are they like Lichens?", I asked.

He ignored me and continued, "Some People We Know are like this, also. They are able to Transmute themselves, like the succulents can, Whenever the need arises. They see the need to change because their will to live is so strong. They just Transmute themselves, like cactus and other succulents."

He began explaining about bugs that look like twigs for the purpose of fooling birds and I interrupted to tell him about snakes in the swamps that look like coral snakes but aren't really poisonous at all.

Frank said, "Snakes! Gawd I Hate Snakes!"

We passed the pipe around once more. When the Moroccan National Anthem quieted down, Frank began again, "I've been thinking that a good way for me to commit suicide would be to go, down to the poisonous snake pit at the zoo here and throw myself in. God, man, snakes are Horrible! I Hate Them! You can't plead with a snake, man!! No! They're cold-blooded! I was going to go to India to seek enlightenment from the guru who taught Baba Ram Das to fly, and it was going to cost me twelve cents a day but then I researched India, man, and I found out about Cobras!"

"What'd you find out, Frank?", I asked.

"Cobras, Man! When the monsoons come, in India, it washes the cobras down out of their holes right into the center of the major cities, and they're pissed off about being washed out of their holes, and they're biting in every direction, and they can't help but get a hit every strike because they're right in the middle of the teeming masses, man, and they're Really pissed Off! Why, man, if a Cobra squirts venom on you, you're paralyzed, and if it looks you in the eye, you're hypnotized, and then it bites you and you die in forty-five seconds. Hundreds of thousands of people every year are bitten by Cobras in India: Three hundred thousand! And Ninety percent of them die! But ten percent live and they are immune to cobra venom. And if you get bit a second time by a cobra and live then you become one of the Cobra People! Man! These Guys Are Heavy! They are the same as Cobras! If they bite you, you die. people throw them alms from afar. Mothers want their daughters to marry them because, except for the top caste, the Brahmins, they are the heaviest people in India. Well, man, when I read that, I decided not to go to India for enlightenment. I vowed never to set foot in India: Fuck it, Man! Cobra People!"

Frank continued, uninterrupted, "So, I figured since India was out, I would find out about Africa. You know what they have in Africa? The Black and Green Mambas! Yah, man! The Black Mambas, and the Green Mambas!"

"So, did you go to Africa, Frank?", I asked.

He ignored me and continued, "Man, the black and green mambas are driving the villagers into the sea! they bite and kill all over Africa! The people can't get away from them: They're twenty feet long and pencil thin. The first six feet rares up like a horse so that' they're right at the level where they can bite you in the face. The remainder of the snake propels it along faster than a speeding stallion across the plains. When they come thundering into a village the people go into a panic: mothers throw their babies to the snakes, and husbands throw their wives, in an attempt to slow them down, but nothing works, All Die! To illustrate how Mean these snakes are: they have been known to wipe out a herd of cows in seconds! The Black Mamba's bite kills you in eight seconds. with the Green Mamba you live longer: twelve seconds. That's the only difference. When someone yells "The Mambas are Caning!", no one cares whether it's a Green Mamba or a Black Mamba!"

He paused, "But, that's in north Africa. So I thought maybe I'd check out south Africa."

"So, you went to South Africa, Frank?", I asked.

"No, man! They got a snake in South Africa that comes into your house at night, man, through the window, and its Breath is poisonous! It doesn't even have to bite you, man, it just slithers up on to your bed, breathes in your nostrils, and you're Dead! So, I came back to Europe, man, where the only snakes are in the zoo."

Jacques, Frank, and I agreed that we will visit the snake pit down at the City Park in a few days. It was getting late so I slithered home through the alleys.

Visions from 'The Howdy Doody Show'

VOICES IN MY HEAD FROM ANOTHER DIMENSION

(Author's. note, 1992: one day as I was sitting in the street writing this book, I began to hear voices in my head, talking about me. I was used to hearing The Peanut Gallery; this was different. One was an adult, the other was a questioning child; they were discussing me. They began when I posed a rhetorical question, "Know what I mean?", and went from there. I faithfully recorded what they said, but quit, astounded, when they mentioned 'their world' the second time. They stopped talking when I stopped typing. I'm pretty sure they're not from my Normal Dimension. Maybe they were Catalan Ghosts.)

Bread street

Frank recently suggested that I change the title of the book to "Frank". He has also offered to tell me stories whenever I run out of ideas. He said that He will be available for story-telling twenty-four hours a day. I won't need to seek him out, though, because I have an inexhaustible stable of stories of my own from the Hippy Days, he'll be glad to hear.

It looks like I'm going to have to settle into some kind of stable life-style here for a while. Maybe I'll fix up the Pad, you know, sweep it out, move things around, wash the dishes, shit like that. Sounds like fun, eh? I guess maybe I'll start looking a little harder (sic) for a woman to hang out with.

I ran into Howdy Donna today and asked her if she wanted to come up to my Pad and get warm some evening. She said, "I don't have to: It's Warmer." I'm not sure that she knew what I meant, but I think she did. She leaves for Sweden in a week, so I better figure out how she wants to be seduced, soon. We've run into each other on the street every day this week; This is more than co-incidence; This is Fore-Ordained. Know what I mean?

"What does he mean?"
"He means he wants to fuck Howdy Doody's Sister, child."
"Would he want to fuck her if she didn't look like Howdy?"
"That depends, child, on whether she had money or not."
"What if she looked like Goofy?"
"She would have to have a lot of money, child. "

"Do his women have to look like cartoon characters?"

"No, but it helps, child, for he is a cartoon character himself."

"Why is he here, in our world?"

"Because, child, the Howdy Doody Show was cancelled just as he was entering puberty. If it had stayed on the air for just a year or two more, he would have grown up just like everyone else does, and he wouldn't spend his life trying to live out the plot of a children's show. "

"Didn't he know it was just a show?"

"NO, child, he didn't. No one had ever bothered to tell him that Television shows were any different than real life. He has spent most of his time, since the cancellation, acting like Clarabelle the Clown, but has recently grown up a bit and has taken on some of the personality traits of Buffalo Bob, the M.C. of the show. His only real fear in life is that he will end up like Howdy Doody himself, A Real Dipshit. But, the Actual danger to him is that he will end up like Mister Bluster, the Villain. I think this explains why he is attracted to puppet-like women. Let this be a lesson to you: Don't watch Howdy Doody re-runs, should they ever be brought back."

"Was this the only influence in his life?"

"No, but it was a Major One. Where he grew up was much like the set of a children's show, also. There was one other Television Show that had a Big influence on him, it was about a boy in a sailor suit who lived in a shoe with a dog. For a pet they had a frog that would disappear after telling off-color jokes. The M.C. of this one was a big, fat man named Andy Devine. This show had more of an effect on his Religious Life, whereas The Howdy Doody Show was his main Sociological Input."

"Does this explain his strange behavior, then?"

"Not totally, child, he has had to work with this basic framework, expand upon it, elaborate upon it, in order to come up with the cartoon character that we perceive wandering in and out of our world."

The Israeli Guards and the Tower of David

Next day. Same place. 9:30AM, earliest yet

I don't know the date or the day of the week; I'm that spaced. Haven't been smoking hash or drinking. Just lost track of all that shit. Know what I mean? (yes). It's foggy today; heard fog-horns all night long as I lay awake waiting for morning to come. It wasn't too bad, though: I had constant coffee and a good book to read: mine. I think Kerouac's corpse Must be turning over in his grave; I'm not able to write in the Pad, like I thought I would be; therefore my Most Insane Flights are not being recorded here. I go craziest at night, so this book will be the Sane Half of the story. I'll write the other side when I get a Pad where I can type at night, Tel-Aviv? God, Imagine what visions I could have in Jerusalem, Religious or Otherwise.

"What's that clacking coming from the Tower of David?", one guard asks the other.

"You can go look if you want to; I've checked it out and there's nothing there when I get there. Just let it be; must have something to do with the Cyanhydrin."

"Well, it's been going on up there every night since we caught that crazy, tall kibbutznik up there that night, howling at the moon. It gives me the creeps."

"Yah, that and the crazy laughing coming from the tombs makes me want to go back to the hardware business, even if it is half the pay."

"Say, what ever happened to the girl that was caught up there, anyway?"

"You know Schlomo? From the barracks? Well, he says he fucked her up there one night. Says he was just sightseeing one evening up there and everyone else left and it was just him and this weird, tall girl up there, and she was making weird faces at him, and walked up to him and grabbed his Peter and said, "Give me whiskey! Give me whiskey, and I'll fuck you!". He says he ran right out to the nearest liquor store and bought a bottle of whiskey and ran back and fucked her for hours, on top there. Said she was a great fuck, but she smelled like patchouli oil and garlic and kept saying "Mass, Mass" ~ I don't believe him, though"

"Nah, too weird to be true, girls aren't like that. So what happened about her charges of 'Disturbing the Peace of Jerusalem'?"

"The charges were dropped: she had an American Passport."

"Yah?"

"Yah, she was married to that American writer, the one who came through here drunk last year and caused that big fuss at the Wailing Wall; You know, the one who claimed that he Wasn't Jesus and this Wasn't the Holy Land."

"Yah, what ever happened to Him?'

"He was charged with 'Disturbing the Peace of Israel' and was asked to leave the country, but refused; said he was one of The Chosen Some, and the planet was his country, Appealed to the High Court, I don't think it's finished yet. Lives in Tel-Aviv, last I heard; does some kind of begging act in the street. Weird pair; allright."

"Yah, what was the name of the religion they said they belonged to?"

"I think it was… 'Walking Morons',… No! I remember, "Idiots on Parade", yah, "Idiots on Parade" was the religion, and their bible was called "Juggler's Handbook", something like that. Weird, weird.

"Yah, what idiots! Who would join a religion called 'Idiots' anything? Say, by the way, what's your religion? We've been working together for two weeks and I never thought to ask."

"Rastafarian."

"Oh, yah? What a coincidence! We're both Christians: I'm a Mormon!"

"I'll be damned!"

"Me too, I thought you were Jewish."

"Nope. Born in Provo, Utah. Moved here with my missionary parents when I was two, but I was raised in the True Church here."

"You mean the Christian Church?"

"No, the Church of Jesus Christ of Latter Day Saints. LDS, for short."

"LDS? Is Timothy Leary a saint with them?"

"I think so, I haven't studied it much, but I believe so."

"Yah, me too. I've heard of Saint Timothy."

"Say! If you're a Rastafarian, why don't you have weird hair?"

"It was announced last year in Ethiopia that it was no longer necessary. It made it hard for us to spread the word. People would take one look and wouldn't even listen to the Gospel. I cut mine six months ago and joined the Israeli Army right after that; the Reserves, it's important. My mother was Jewish; from California, Brentwood, but I used to spend the winters with my father in Jamaica; he was a preacher and businessman there, working with the church.

"Didn't you have problems in Jamaica, I mean, being blonde?" .

"Not until I cut my dreadlocks. until then no one seemed to notice that I had light skin and hair. I don't go back now: they mistake me for a surfer, I either get arrested or in fights. Besides, I have no family left there; my father is in Hollywood running a juice bar, and doing very well, I might add. He kept his locks."

"Say, now that you mention it, is Brigham young a Saint with the Rastafarians?"

"Yah, I think he is. I think all of them are in there: Abraham, Mohammed-Ali, Hailie Selassie, Hailie Mills, Jesus, Joe smith, Moshe Dylan, Brigham Young; Yah, I'm pretty sure I heard him mentioned quite a few times in church."

"Well, good. Amazing isn't it, that neither of us is a Jew and we're both Christians, and we're in the Israeli Army, the Reserves, huh?"

"Yah, cosmic, it's like we're actors in a play, or something. Say, how did you get 'into the Army?"

"Reserves!. It's Important!"

"Yah, I mean how did you get in the Israeli Army Reserves?"

"Oh, it's a long story, I got a special dispensation from Ethiopia, I think they were allies of Israel, or something, I'm not sure, my father did it, said it would be good for me, said it was the best army in the world, and after I flunked out of dental school, I didn't know what to do, so I said what the hell, and here I am. My father was Jamaica's Ambassador to Lebanon once, shit, we moved around a lot; they're in New Zealand now, raising sheep or something; haven't seen them in a couple of years. Shit, it's great here, so I'll stay, though I do want to go to Disneyland sometime soon, before they close it."

"Yah, I heard they were going to close it. I guess it's because of those rapes last sumner."

"Yah, who would know that they hired a Rapist to wear the Goofy costume. Terrible. Terrible. You don't know who to trust any more."

"Wait a minute, I thought you said your father was in Hollywood, and then you said he was in New Zealand."

"That's my step-father."

"Oh. "

"The one in New Zealand, he married my mother; saved her life after she went completely bonkers in Jamaica. Jews shouldn't live in the Caribbean: they get absolutely freaked out by the Giant Bugs. Drove her crazy. Dad used to eat them. She couldn't take it and divorced him. "

"He used to Eat Bugs?!"

"Yah, but they're Big, man, a full meal, they'll knock you down if you get in their way when they're in a hurry. They're delicious, cute, but delicious. Very High in protein."

"Uh-huh, well, I wouldn't eat a bug, even if it looked like a cow!" "There ARE bugs that look like cows, in Jamaica. They look just like small cows; they're really delicious; drove mom nuts."

"Yah, I can imagine."

"But, she was always going crazy; went crazy in Africa, too."

"Yah? What? More Bugs?"

"Nah, in Africa it was snakes; she claimed a snake was chasing her around the front yard. She had to be locked up. She claimed it was as fast as a dog and twenty feet long. Said she barely got away from it."

"Really?"

"Certainly. She's all right now, though, in New Zealand. They just have to keep her away from Kangaroos, they don't let her ever see a kangaroo, Which isn't a big problem because there are thousands of miles of kangaroo fences in New Zealand."

"Really?"

"Positively. As long as she never runs into a kangaroo she will probably remain sane. Dad is rich enough to make sure the kangaroo fences are always in good repair, and my sister told me that no one is allowed to mention them, or platypusses, in her presence; and no one is allowed to bring a National Geographic into their ranch. She'll be fine, she's almost sixty now; New Zealand is a good place for her.

"Say, have you ever seen an elephant?"

"Yah, at the zoo. Big Deal. Elephants, shit, a tank can wipe out a whole flock of 'em in two minutes. They're Old-Fashioned. You wanna win a war these days: Don't ride elephants; That went out with Clarabelle crossing the Alps!"

"Clarabelle crossing the Elfs? What's that?"

"Histry, man, only it's Alps, not Elfs! Alps are mountains, Elfs are small people that live in Spain, or Angorra, or somewhere."

"Oh, yah, I remember, Alexandra and Clarabelle crossed the Hamilton Alps on their way to fight Napoleon Solo, or something. Say, is that Out? Or is there enough for me to get another hit?"

"It's gone, man, gone. Roll another one."

"Yah, shit, might as well; getting stoned helps me forget about that goddamned clacking, and that moaning. You got papers?"

"Yah, here." One guard rolls a joint while the other takes a piss off the parapet. It's a Starry Starry Night.

PLAZA DEL REY

Ferd is still swatting the citizens in Plaza Del Rey when he feels some moisture on his head. He stops and looks up. He sees a guy in an Israeli Army uniform (A Reserve, this is important) taking a piss over the parapet. The guy is un-circumcized. Ferd begins yelling, "Off with his head! He's pissing on me! Guards! Get him! Kill that man!", and pointing up towards the wall around the cathedral. The guards grab their petards and start running around bumping into each other, and looking up at the wall; They see no one. Ferd is the only one who can see him, and the only one being pissed on. Evidently, it's His Karma; HE expelled the Jews. He's known for being Touched anyway, so the guards run around the plaza, shouting, for a while, thinking this will probably satisfy him. The pissing stops and a marijuana 'roach' comes flying down. Ferd picks it up and takes a toke, laughs maniacally, and begins chasing various soldiers and citizens around the plaza with his sceptre, shouting, "'The Gods may piss On Me, but You are Still My Things!" The crowd tries to escape, but never too far, because they don't want to miss anything. Ferd is a very popular King; he's Famous for putting on a good show when he's stoned.

The Andalucian National Anthem

THE CATALAN NATIONAL ANTHEM

THE STREET-BEGGARS NATIONAL ANTHEM
(All sung to the tune of "Goodnight, Irene")

THE ANDALUCIAN NATIONAL ANTHEM
(See "The Abu-Dhabi National Anthem" in Appendix)

Shit, I'm Hot now: there's about 700 in the box. The Abu-Dhabi National Anthem never fails to bring in the dough. It's very popular, even outside of the country of its origin.

Time for lunch: a tomato and some bread (good food) .

Frank said that "Abba-Dabba" is an unknown country, and that no-one would be interested in its National Anthem; that I should just forget it. Peter said that he's been there and that it is not a country, it's a city.

Frank asked, "Who would want to read THAT?"

"I don't know.", I answered, hanging my head.

"It's All Desert!", Peter told me, trying to help.

"I know," I said, "The National Anthem tells all about it!"

"Nobody wants to hear about it, Jack! You shouldn't even bother!", Frank told me.

"But, Frank, if Jacques tries to scratch it from the book, I'll just change the name to 'The Andalucian National Anthem', and then it will be pertinent.", I told him.

"Come on, Peter, let's go. Let's leave him alone.", said Frank, obviously disgusted and feeling sorry for me.

I even sang it for them, and they STILL didn't like it, even though Frank did try to dance along with it. Frank is obviously not an Arab. Neither is Sinatra. Fuck 'em! They're painters; they have little understanding of music or good song-writing.

THE CATALONIAN NATIONAL ANTHEM
(Bon Nuit, Urina)
(sung to the tune of 'Goodnight, Irene')

>Sometimes we're part of Espanya,
>Sometimes we're part of France,
>Sometimes we don't know what we're doing,
>But at least we have our own Dance.

>We love to wear red sweaters,
>We love our high-heeled shoes,
>We're taking on all bettors,
>We won't be long singing the blues.

>Goodnight Espanya, Goodnight Espanya,
>No matter how it seems,
>You'll see us in your Dreams.

That's Really Weird! The Abu-Dhabi National Anthem brought in more pesetas than the Catalonian National Anthem did. Hard to figure out. Nationalism is a strange beast. I thought they'd LOVE their Own Song. Ah, well, live and learn.

I just saw a dog try to bury his shit on a stone street. It was pitiful: he finally gave up and trotted away with a very confused look on his face. I'm thinking of calling it 'Quits' and wandering off. Maybe that's what I should call this book, 'Quits'. That's a name that's probably never been used before. Oh, shit, that dog is back and he's trying to bury the shit again. I think he's going mad.

THE STREET-BEGGAR'S NATIONAL ANTHEM
(sung to the tune of 'Goodnight, Irene')

>Sometimes we sit in the alleys,
>Sometimes we sit in the streets,
>And if you're not Cold-hearted,
>We won't freeze off our feets.

>We see the people go strolling,
>With full bellys, money, and wit,
>How do you think they'd like it,
>If they tried to bury their shit.

They seemed to Love that one: clink, clink, and a 100pta note. Shit, I've got about a mil; Can't quit now: gotta keep pumping out those songs.

Amani is Even a Worse Fucker than I Thought

I just returned from the Pad where I spent the latter part of Siesta. I ran into Jacques on Bread Street. He had a story to tell me about what The Greatest Bullshit Artist Alive, Frank, has been working on for the last hour or two: Amani.

As I left the Tapas near the beginning of Siesta, I passed Amani, who was on his way in. I told Frank, "Well, here's some more grist for your mill: The Be-bop Kid."It looks like he took me up on it.

According to Jacques, when Amani entered the Cave, Frank began to question him on his relations with other writers, "Well Amani, how do you get along with other writers? It's important that you have a good relationship with them.", and other such Fatherly Inquiries.

Amani took the bait, "Well, I only know one other published Writer, and I get along with him fine.", he answered. (According to Jacques).

"Well, how about Jack?", Frank asked, "Do you get along with him well?"

"I'm trying to.", Amani answered.

"Ah, well, what seems to be the problem?", Frank reportedly asked. Amani hedged the question. Frank mentioned an argument that Amani and I had, and inquired as to the details.

(The 'Argument': Amani had been explaining to me, a couple of weeks ago, how to go about getting published, and was further explaining to me the 'Correct Way' to write a book. I told him that I didn't give a fuck about the rules, that I'd lived my life, and survived, without following the rules and that I'd write any fucking way I wanted to. He kept patronizing me, I thought, and I finally blew up and told him to stop giving me advice, "I am older than you are! Just Fucking stop Giving Me Advice About Writing! " It WAS Irritating. I don't think he really understands who or what I am, to this day. That's how Heavy the 'argument' was. I mentioned the incident to Frank about a week ago.)

Jacques says that he saw the put-on coming from a mile away but that Amani had taken hook, line, and stinker, and after about two hours still didn't realize that Frank is a Great Bullshit Artist and was putting him on while pretending to be trying to smooth things over between Amani and me.

According to Jacques, Frank had Amani believing that I am almost constantly thinking about what Amani told me about writing, And that I have been writing a considerable amount in my book about what a fucked-up guy he is. According to Jacques, Frank has Amani believing that I am almost considering calling the book, "Amani Is Even A Worse Fucker Than I Thought", and the sequel will be, "Amani Is Even a WORSER Fucker Than I Thought."!!

"Unbelievable!", I said to Jacques, "You're Kidding, right?"

"No! Honest to God, Jack, that's what Amani thinks the name of the book is going to be! It's Incredible!", he told me.

Frank has been telling Amani, "Well, I've done my best to make things right between you two, but it looks like they've just gone too far." Frank told him, according to Jacques, that I am 'Thin-skinned' and was greatly affected by our 'Argument', and am "slaughtering" him in retribution.

As Jacques was telling me all this, he was in Near Terminal Ecstasy, as we stood outside the Santa Clara Cafe, where it was Still Going On. I went into the Cafe and greeted the crowd, giving special emphasis to Amani and Frank.

I said, "Amani, I hear that a lot of what you're writing in your book is about me." He denied it.

I then said, "Do you know what a Bullshit Artist is? Well, you're sitting at the table with one of the Greatest Bullshit Artists alive!"

Frank said, "Do you hear that Amani? He says you're one of…"

"No, Frank!", I interrupted, "You're The Great Bullshit Artist"

"Yah, he's talking about you.", said Amani.

I told Frank, "I'll get even with you for this some day, Box, I don't know how, but I'll get even!"

We stood around for a few minutes, Frank said, "I love my little friends.", and was having an Obvious Great Time, and then Jacques and I left. We ran into Black Diane right outside the cafe, who was searching for a place to buy some bread.

"Ah, well", I told her, "Frank is right inside this cafe, and he knows where to get some bread; he knows all the places and prices by heart. Just go in and ask him."

"That's right,", said Jacques, "He was talking about bread as we left him just now. Ask Frank." We talked with her for a couple of minutes and then parted company; We, supposedly to head for the Pension; She, to inquire about bread from Frank.

I snuck back to look into the window while she asked him: Ah! Revenge is Sweet. I waved and smiled at Frank as I walked by. He was grinning insanely at Diane as she talked to him. Ah!

Frank is proving that he has a Right to be the leader of the Neo-Pretensionist Movement, on a Daily Basis. I would vote for him, if he didn't already have the job.

Frank's Hot-Knife Conversational Delivery can cut through the Butter of Emotion-Based Self-Deception with ease. If he was Truly Vicious, he would be Dangerous. Luckily, he likes nothing more than a little action, a good laugh, and dope.

Sometimes it seems unfair for him to take advantage of people who have used a lot less dope than he has; they'll believe almost anything he tells them. It's like he's a Living Gullibility Test, at times, in this crowd. And these are supposed to be the Independent, Self-Sufficient, Travelling, Expatriates. The Talented Ones! The perceptive Ones! Shit, he could get most of the people around here to march down to the sea and drown. He even got me to quit my English teaching job, though he'll deny it.

I wish he'd go back to painting on canvas instead of using people and their minds. What if he slips with the brush? I'm the one who will have to deal with Amani and the weird ideas he now has in his head about me. No matter what I say to him, Frank has made the connections in his circuitry.

Frank just joined me and admitted that this is one of the "funnest" afternoons he has ever spent, "I wanted to stop a dozen times, but…. I couldn't. It was a down-hill trajectory and we were all locked into it!", he told me.

"All in all, it came down incredibly well.", Frank continued, "It's too bad it wasn't on film. Just watching the little tumblers in his head falling into place."

"Well, Congratulations, and Fuck You.", I told him.

As he left, Frank said, "You never know what a writer is going to write: his life comes out in his book.", and suggested that I get aboard and put it behind me, with pictures of Hemingway, Tolstoy, and Miller on it, to lend an Intellectual Air to what I'm doing. I told him I'd think about it.

I just told Billy that I'm thinking of calling the book, "Amani is even a worser fucker-than I thought", and Billy said that Amani mentioned to him that I was writing about him. This whole fucking thing has gotten completely out of hand.

There's a hippy sitting here reading what I've written today, and as Frank left, the hippy turned to me and asked, "Is it serious when he says that he is planning his suicide for next October?"

"I don't know, we'll have to wait and see; his herpes bother him quite a bit.", I told him.

Gandalf, Billy, Peter, Frank, Jacques, Vivian

On the street, Bread Street

There's a demonstration going on down in Plaza St. Juame, the government square. The demonstrators this time are all fourteen year old Spanish. As usual, my friends and I have no idea what the demonstration is about. They've joined hands and made a big circle all around the plaza and are chanting in a foreign language: Spanish, I think. This is probably the opening of the Demonstration Season; they started about this tune last year and continued for a month. These kids are amateurs compared to the police and firemen who demonstrated for about fifteen days in a row last year, marching around the plaza ten abreast, blowing their whistles, yelling, and honking their airhorns, causing a din that could be heard for a mile, and making life in Pension Costa nearly impossible. I hope they come back this year.

Well, Billy just started his street career; played the flute for a couple of minutes and then scurried off, embarrassed.

Gandalf just walked up with his hair arranged in a manner which a mentally deranged child would do its dolly's hair to be mean to it. He has a top-knot wrapped up on the front of his forehead which sticks up about three inches, made by drawing hair from allover his head. What's not in the top knot is arranged in 'little top-knots' everywhere else; it's outrageous. He must Really be scaring the locals today. I asked him why he did it and he said that he was feeling weird.

"You look like an Arapahoe with Scottish Ancestry!", Peter told him, as he and Frank joined us. .

"I get some interesting smiles with this hairdo.", Gandalf said, making a Mad Magazine face.

"I'll bet.", said Peter.

"Well," said Frank, "We're having an interesting time looking at pots and pans."

"Why are you looking at pots and pans?", I asked.

Peter said, "Because Frank is jealous of my cooking ability am wants to get a set-up of his own."

"Well, let's stagger down to the next pots and pans store and then stagger back this way a little later, and that way we'll be using up some of our day.", Frank suggested to Peter. They staggered off, on their Mission Ridiculous.

The Demonstrators from the plaza just marched by, the demonstration is over. Gandalf informed me that it was school-children demonstrating for better school conditions.

Jacques joined us, "Jack, maybe you should bring your stew out here and have a little stew kitchen for people to get fed while they're watching you."

"Yah, great Idea, 0 Editor.", I replied.

"Listen, Jack, whenever you can't think of anything to write, you have my permission as Editor to go Berserk on Howdy Doody stuff", he said, "Get into the Peanut Gallery for a while, man."

"Well, you know I would if Donna showed up.", I admitted.

"She's your catalyst for that stuff, basically, huh?", he asked.

"Yup.", I answered.

Jacques looked at Gandalf and noticed his hair for the first time. huh, that's why he's all fixed up?"

Gandalf said, "I get a lot more smiles from women on the street this way. A woman came up and fiddled with my hair in bar kiki today."

"Well, it's kiki enough, as it is, in that bar.", Jacques told him.

"Kinky?", asked Gandalf.

"Yah.", said Jacques.

"Man! There's a Smooching Act going on right there!", I said, indicating some lovers directly in front of me in the street.

"Well, write about it, Idiot! Don't Watch It!", Jacques ordered.

I wrote about it.

Jacques continued, "You ought to write something about how I tried to start my Renaissance Chalking School today and my first pupil didn't show up." He was referring to a Begging Franchise that he was going to do with his chalkings and Tracy.

"Well, why don't you phone her, man?", I asked.

"Because she's Out! She's Gourdless!", he exclaimed, "The School has rejected her and the Master doesn't even want to see her on the premises! I'm going to tell her that her only chance in the Art World is to hook up with one of the rival schools, like the peter Shaw Art School."

"Too Bad,", I said, "I thought it was a good deal for both of you."

"God! Mucous is Gross!", he said, blowing his nose. He decided to linger here for a while and catch up on reading this. I' asked him to go down and lean on the garbage can while he was reading, so as not to Visually Bum-Up the pitch.

I said, "This is turning into a pitiful act, money-wise; I was planning on paying back Santi and paying my rent from doing this, and I've been out here faithfully for days."

"I don't want to hear your troubles, Jack.", he told me.

An Old Spanish Lady just came up and rabidly babbled at me for a couple of minutes. She wasn't Angry at all; she wanted something: I caught 'letter', 'London', 'write', and like that, and thought maybe she wanted me to write a letter to London for her, obviously. I asked Jacques to came over and translate and she began telling him about 'The Rarnblas', and 'a guy needs to practice English', and 'washing dishes for no pay', and stuff like that, according to him. It got so intense (I was trapped, sitting down, between them), that I finally had to jump up and walk a few feet away. We told her that we only understood part of what she was saying. She apologized and said that she would be back later. Great.

"You love it when you're attacked like that, don't you, Jack?", Jacques asked.

"Yah, man, it happens every day.", I told him.

Jacques particularly likes the part in here about Howdy Doody being shipped to Barcelona in a crate. I'll tie it all together yet.

Viv just came by and I told him that Steve has headed off for England. Viv just got his new lathe and will probably start work on Steve's new leg in a couple of days; he's getting the wood tomorrow. For Steve's sake, I hope Viv stays on the wagon for a while; Steve could end up with two left feet.

Barbara is two months pregnant. She told me yesterday. They'll have a little Spanish/English person to deal with in a few months. Probably be born with a skillet in his hand.

(Editor's Note to the Peanut Gallery while I was gone) :

"Look kids ... you all better get on the stick and try and cheer Jiggilo Jacky up alittle. He's not making any money (BOOO NO MONEY) and on top of that he seems to be running out of ideas. I know you guys can yell sane jokes (YAAAAAA JOKES) to him just when he's least expecting it, or else tell him you want to hear some of the good old Howdy Doody stories from the first days when he was on the T.V. (YAAAAAA TELEVISION) That's the Spirit Kids, now come on, I'm counting on you, O.K.? (YAAA HE'S COUNTING ON US YAAAAAAM.)"

Well, I'm back. I see you kids have been having fun talking to Jacques while I was gone, but what about the exclamation marks? What happened to them? (YAYYY!!!).

I think I'll sit here til at least another hundred comes in. (YAYYY!!! ANOTHER HUNDRED!!!). Shut up, you fucking idiots, I said 'until' another hundred: It Hasn't Happened Yet! (OHHHH!! SORRRRY!!!).

I'm being scanned, but not related to, on a regular basis. I think I may have become Unrelatable out here. I hope it's just a phase. (DON'T WORRY, JIGGILO JACK, WE LIKE YOU!!!). Yah, that's great, kids, but I can't fuck the Peanut Gallery, and I can't eat you. Weill, wait a minute! (NO! NO! STOP THAT GIGOLO JACK! THAT'S NOT NICE!!). OK, OK, sorry, kids, I just spaced out for a minute there. Don't tell Buffalo Bob or Howdy, you know how straight they are. (O.K. GIGOLO JACK! IT'S A SEEECRETTT!!!). Gosh, thanks, kids.

Frank is reportedly carrying around a can of mace in case he runs into Amani or me because we're angry with him for fiddling with our careers. Amani has been gunning for Frank for a couple of days but Jacques has been standing lookout for him and luckily there hasn't been a shoot-out yet. Frank told me that Amani's Martial Art (Capoeira?) is effective against fists and knives, (unlike Karate, which Ramon has proved is NOT, by getting stabbed twice), but that Nothing works against mace shot from ten feet away. I hope I'm not around for the shootout.

On the Street. VIV. Mick. Suzanne. The Meadcm

Another week: gone. Just gone. Don't know where it went. It's gone. I'm still here but last Wednesday is not. It's joined the rest of the past. It's history. It's gone to the Elephant's Weekday Graveyard.

Vivian and Aurora just stopped by to chat for a few minutes. They're out shopping for a Wood-cutting tool so Viv can get on with making Steve's Leg. Viv and Jane had a run-in last night over who got to play in Steve's old spot: Viv won. He says he told her to get on her bike and piss off. She told me that she met "a dangerous man" playing the banjo last night. I told her that he was a friend of mine and had fallen three stories and landed on his head. She said that was no excuse for acting the way he did. I just don't know.

The Street is just not the same since The King of the Gothic Barrio departed. The rest of us are Rank Amateurs compared to Steve. He gave the place a little class.

I've just been joined by Mick, an English guy about my age who does stained-glass windows and owns a house and a little piece of land down near Valencia. He's 'busking' these days just to fill out his time and pockets while he's visiting Barcelona. He came here to buy some stained glass and same lead. He's gone over to 'La Sardana' to buy us a glass of wine each from the money he's made playing guitar. Ah, here he comes now, And, now I'm drinking the wine. Ah,

"I've had an octopus in my purse all night and I have to put it in my refrigerator.", Suzanne just said, explaining to me why she has to hurry back to Sitges, and can't come up to the pad for lunch.

"Dahling, I have to go to Sites and be a Fag-Hag tonight!", she further confessed.

"Well, come up to the pad anytime!", I yelled after her, as she pranced away.

"YOU Sweet Daahhling!", she yelled, seeming to be from Paris in the twenties, all heads turning lustfully as she drooled SEX through the narrow Gothick alley...

Mick and I discuss whether to get another wine or not: Yes, we do it, enough for two more. Mick and I have been here bullshitting for about an hour. He's lived in Spain for seven years and is a Local at this point. He's taken off for the other part of the street where he is playing his guitar for duros for a while. He says that there are many international freaks living at his place near

Valencia. He says they call it 'The Meadow' though it isn't really a meadow, it's on a hill. They even have schoolbusses. He's invited me to visit and stay any time I want. I'll probably be stopping by there in the near future. He says I really ought to meet his kids. He used to be an actor in England but sold the ranch and hit the road about ten years ago. He looks exactly, exactly, like Rex Harrison. He has four kids, aged from fifteen on down to five. He's a Very Nice Man, a Gentleman. He bought me a glass of wine.

I've invited Rabbit/Eduardo over to the pad for soup, wine, and bread this afternoon, along with Suzanne, and Mick. It will be great to get my head back on this afternoon. I'm slightly spaced-out from all this drinking for the last couple of days. When will it end? God knows. Rabbit is buying us another wine from the bar.

Jane has joined us for a bit. She's not going to make it for lunch today, she has to take care of the clown-kids or something. I offered to take her up into La Sagrada Familia and make love to her. She said she'll consider it. So? What's to Consider?

LATER THAT EVENING

So, now it's Saturday night. Ellen is standing just out of sight, about 150ft to my right. She's singing Simon and Garfunkel again. I just spent the afternoon with Mick and Rabbit/Eduardo. We had some of the Eternal stew, bread, cheese and a couple of bottles of wine. We had to pool our funds to buy the last bottle for 36ptas. I have almost decided to head south to Mick's place for the remainder of the winter.

I Fall in Love With a Clown

CRAZY ALAN

Ain't no use to sit and wonder why, babe, if you don't know by now. I wonder why. Sunday. Noon. Spain. Big Party last night. Lost my bag in a bar at the end of the line. Took the Metro, with Rabbit, rode around on it for a while drunk and got lost. Ended up at the RockandRoll Bar about ten miles outside of town. Hung out with the Clowns. They gave me a new black felt hat. They felt like it. I have it on. I'm in Love with the Clown Gal I met last night. She looks like Judy from Whitethorn. She danced while I played the drums. We danced while Rabbit played the drums. I drank while the band played the song and the Clown Gal Danced. And I fell Madly In Love and don't remember the end of the party after Rabbit and I took over the 'stage' and played our drums til our fingers bled. And the Clown Gal danced and danced and her red hair spun and spun me right out of my mind. And I woke up this morning at the pad. No Clown...

ALAN

Now Alan is calling me Happy Jack. He thinks he has a worse reputation than I do; he has just given me his knife, for protection, I suppose. I'm not sure what we're doing out here today; Having Fun, for sure.

"Being a Street-writer is not an easy life.", I tell him.

"Being a Street Person is not an Easy Life!", he replies.

"Who are you Telling?", I ask.

"Too many people in wheelchairs", he observes, thinking about the lacka-money in the box. In The Box. Sweet Mama. ("It's Shit, Jack!", I can hear them saying at the bar later.)

Alan tells me that there are two busses for hauling away the people in wheelchairs parked down in plaza St. Juame and things will pick up when they are Evacuated.

"Thank God, I don't have chewing gum on the back of my coat!", he tells me.

"Yah, things could be worse", I say.

"Yah, it could be raining."

I cough, hack, and spit.

"There is No Excuse for that hacking", Alan tells me, "You've just been smoking too many cigarettes for too long: The Cheap Motherfuckers won't give you five fucking pesetas to save your life! That's the one thing that really rubs me wrong about the Spanish People: They'll give you drinks and smokes all night long but wouldn't give you five pesetas to save your life the next day!"

"I know what you mean.", I say.

We discuss Vietnam for a while. "Tell them to take their fucking Purple Heart and stick it up their ass!", he tells me.

"And then they wanted to send me back: 80% disability. Fuck VietNam! I want to see the fucker that can send me back! It's the truth: I'll kill 'em if they fuck with ME!", he tells me, "It's very, very unfortunate: I can hurt them in a minute. When I DO Snap: their ass is out! Luckily, it doesn't happen very often any more!"

Alan continues, "War injuries, indeed. We are Injured. But, We're getting Even, aren't we. Taking over the Whole Fucking World. I see a line of cars and they're all painted black, I see the girls walk by dressed in their summer clothes, I have to turn my head until my darkness goes. I look inside myself and it's all painted black."

He continues, "That's why I don't fuck with Coke: I'm under the bed, looking through the drapes, ready to throw my knife at somebody: Normally I use a Uzi, high velocity, 223, I use a 9rnm, I want to kill them when I shoot. They all died: AK47, sprayed. We were playing a whole different game there, man. They should do it in Beirut: Blacktop, man. The American Way: Blacktop. Wipe-out the whole fucking way. The worst: Afghanistan: Half the road was made by the Russians, half by the Americans: Tank traps and all. Rolled the fucking tanks right down the road that they built. It's not US man, what more can they do to me? There's no Fucking Viet-Nam that they can send me back to! Kiss My Ass: I'm a Fucking Viet-Nam Vet! It's not us: We're Right! Walk into the Embassy 'Hey, Fuck You! I'm a Viet-Nam Vet! Give us our fucking charter!!' Manana, Manana, but we're not used to it: The American Way. The Only place I get quick service is at My Bookstore: They'll wrap anything I bring them! Cinco Pesetas! c'mon you Spanish Motherfuckers! Where have all the flowers gone? Long time ago? Where HAVE all the flowers gone? The fucking hippies are sleeping in the park again. Neither one of us gives a flying fuck for anything: When they saw us walk in the bar they pissed in their pants. I put a couple of guys down in there. They don't understand. When will they ever learn?"

Ah, a glass of wine. I feel much better. I'll be able to stagger in a straight line in a while. It's close to being Sober. Rabbit is throwing money in my box and Alan is reimbursing him each time.

Alan Continues, "They look at me with a mixture of Anger and Anguish. Then, when they're down I take my heel and kick their teeth in. It happens very quick. I show them how quick it can happen."

We tell Alan how it took us half of last night on the metro to find the RocknRoll Bar, he says, "I'm So Spanish, I could even fall asleep on the fucking Metro!"

I told Alan's fortune for him: "You Will Never Own a Washing Machine."

"I don't really give a Flying Fuck: I take my clothes to the laundry.", he answered.

Billy was just here; I gave him 17ptas, all there was, out of the box to pick me up some oranges while he's shopping. He hesitated and told me that you can't get very many oranges for 17ptas. I said, "I know, I know, just get me 17ptas worth of oranges, OK?". He finally agreed to do it. I'll start getting my health back as soon as I eat an orange.

An Evening with My Friends, at the Opera Cafe

SUZANNE AND GUMMING, TOLSTOY

I left the pitch at about 8 last night with 600 pesetas. Went to the Post Office; bought some onions, tomatoes, bread, smokes, garlick, and retreated up to the pad where I feasted myself and relaxed for about an hour. I then headed down to the Tapas where I joined the others near the end of their evening meal.

Frank was discussing Tolstoy, "I differ from Tolstoy in no material way. "

"Then you'll be a christian in no time!", Jacques said.

Frank began explaining Tolstoy to Peter and Ellen as Suzanne, Jacques, and I laughed it up.

Jacques told me, "Billy will be a Heavy in the street-scene someday, if the Brown Police are running him off now! I've never heard of them running Anyone off! Ever!" I admitted that I was Justly Proud of my son.

Jacques was reading my book, "Frank, this is a perfect profile of you."

"Yes, Jacques, I'm just like Tolstoy: one day he beats a slave am the next day he's asking forgiveness and kissing the hem of their peasant garments! I'm just like him!", he exclaimed, "Like Him, I don't like my Cleaning-lady to make my bed; but I don't like to make it myself, either: that's the trouble!"

Suzanne dropped me and went over to sit with the Painters: Frank and peter; she said, "Peter, your painting of the bag lady is right up there with the Sagrada Familia as far as contemporary life goes." Peter was basking in his Fame.

She continued, "When I saw the bag lady I nearly fell over! It speaks to me in a language I understand!"

Frank was trying to read aloud some pages of my book which he thought were good, but was unable to hold Peter and Suzanne's attention because they were looking at photos of Peter's paintings. Frank became irritated and accused Suzanne of being 'A Maximum Dilettante'. She admitted it.

Jacques was about half way through his nightly bottle of rose' wine, he said, "I'm starting to have a new Flash for the name of Jack's book."

"Gigolo's progress", interrupted Frank.

"Perfect!", said Jacques, "But I was thinking of 'The Last European Writings of Charlie Manson.'"

An Evening with My Friends, at the Opera Cafe

I faded into the Sober Background as Jacques and Frank talked about JACQUE'S BOOK!

Jacques said, "I've decided on the title for my book: 'Frank and Billy'"

I interrupted, "So, I suppose Hadass is gonna end up marrying you now, huh, now that you're a writer."

Around eleven O'clock Santi ran us out and closed up. We headed, en masse, over to the Cafe de la Opera were we took up our usual position .at Frank's table in the rear. Frank sat, in his particular kind of heaven, between Suzanne and Ellen; Jacques sat between Peter and me on the other side. We fired up Billy's bamboo pipe and passed it around. Frank got the first toke and coughed it out a few seconds later, serenading us with the Moroccan National Anthem. Everyone, in turn, joined in.

Suzanne was warming up, "Everything is Sexual!", she shouted, laughing, "Anything where you're using your body is Sexual!" We all agreed.

"Yah! Everything is! You put your finger right on it!", Frank said, "I have often thought that EVERYTHING we do, with the exception of straight sex, is perversion!"

A junkie, who Frank met the night before, wormed his way into our table, pulled up a chair and offered free tickets to a Disco. He struck up a conversation with Suzanne for a while and then finally wobbled off mumbling. We were glad to see him go: he would have interfered with whatever Topick was On for tonight with irrelevant observations. Frank hates that.

Ellen tried to bum a smoke from Frank and he grabbed my pack and offered her one of mine. I told her that they were very strong, so Jacques offered her one of his 'american' cigarettes and she took it instead, letting both Frank and me off the hook.

Peter looked across the table and said, "Suzanne, I want to paint you and make you immortal like Nepenthe." She sucked it up. Suzanne then said that she would like to have a film of me. I sucked it up.

Frank said, "Yah, we could make a great cartoon with Jack, he's two-dimensional already; it's so easy for him." I was flattered.

Ellen said to peter, "You could make the best cartoon character out of You!"

Jacques told her, "Rebecca has already done it!", referring to a painting she did of him. We were all becoming infatuated with ourselves: we were the Most Famous Looking crowd in the Opera.

Frank continued, "We SHOULD make a movie of us, we Really Should!"

"Honey, we could do a sit-com!", sang out Suzanne.

"We Really Could!", Frank agreed.

"Where's the screen, man?", Suzanne asked Frank, pretending to spill the pipe. Frank's mouth dropped open.

"Oh, here it is!", she said, pretending to find it. Frank relaxed. "She's famous for losing the screen and then finding it!", said Jacques.

"I'm a Gemini, honey! I was on the lost and found committee!", she yelled. We all talked for a few minutes about what committees we were on in school.

"I was the head of the Safety Patrol!", I ventured, which was greeted with General Disdain and I was thereafter ignored. For a while. More hash was passed.

"85% of Americans have an IQ under 100.", Frank said, out of Seemingly Nowhere. We fell for the bait and soon were congratulating ourselves for being in the other 15%.

I said, "Well, they don't start locking them up til they reach a low of 70 or 80."

Suzanne said, "I don't think this has very much bearing in Europe: they don't take IQ tests!"

"Be thankful for That!", said Frank.

"America is like a Great Big Insane Asylum, with TV's in the Sitting Room!", added Jacques. (Peter and Ellen weren't joining in: they were sitting at the end of the table, fingers entwined and wiggling, staring with deer-eyes at each other and mumbling sweet- somethings. Stoned and in Love.)

"What you're describing is Exactly the main character in 'Being There', with Sellers, Shirley MacLaine, by Kosinsky! Exactly!", shouted Suzanne.

"Yes, That's It!, said Frank, "Why, I know people HERE who talk about nothing but TV shows!"

"In the Bars?", asked Suzanne.

"Yes, Everywhere!", he answered. We discussed 'Being There' and Kosinsky for a while, some admitting that they'd read all his stuff, others pretending not to have read any.

Frank summed it up, "There's a moral to 'Being There': His advice to the president was just as sound as the advice of the high-powered advisors because he had focused in on one thing! Focus! You see!"

Jacques was discussing my Literary Pretensions, "Jack, luckily for you I don't read novels; I can't relate to them."

I said, "This is supposed to be good news to me? That my Editor has never read one novel?"

"Yes," he said, "That way I have nothing to judge yours against!" "Fucking Great!", I said.

A paper airplane, with a drawing of a horrible face on it, came flying from over at the bar and landed on our table; the Junkie had drawn and launched it at us. Frank accused Suzanne of having befriended the Junkie and she said that Frank had. He denied it vehemently. They discussed International Etiquette on Handling Junkies for a while. Peter still had the Junkie's Free Disco Tickets so he came under some abuse also. Frank claimed to be Blameless. He mentioned to me that I wasn't joining-in and seemed to be a wallflower experiencing the 'Happiness of Stones'.

I replied, "If I start talking, I'll start yelling."

Jacques supported me, "That's right! He only has 'on' and 'off', no middle ground."

Frank insisted, "Well, Jack, put that statement of yours, about your yelling, in the book, or there really is no book." At this point I was finding it difficult to take notes and turned on the recorder.

A NIGHT AT THE OPERA CAFÉ

Jacques: "I would like it to be noted that except for me and Frank, we have Pure Gourdlessness reigning; not only reigning but Pervading. Every word that's spoken 'cept for me and Frank is Pure Gourdlessness!" We began passing the pipe again.

Suzanne and Frank were talking about Suzanne's lover in Sitges:

Frank: "By now he must be used to you dragging twenty-year-old spanish boys by the hair up the stairs and when you're done with them..."

Suzanne, interrupting! "I never Drag anyone by their hair! And when I make love with twenty-year-old spanish boys I..."

Frank: "You throw them down the stairs!"

Suzanne: "I usually do it in the middle of the night in the sand, and in the rocks and I don't have to...."

Jack: "She doesn't have to drag 'em up the stairs and then kick 'em out: She Molests them on the Beaches and in the Forests!"

Suzanne: "... and I only do it where I don't live, on my Travels: I wander the lonely narrow streets late at night, breathing the smell of the wet Mediterranean Rain, and I'm walking down the street and some big-eyed gangly lad comes up to me and says 'Hola, Guapa!...'"

Jack: "And she Rapes Him!"

Jacques: "OOOHH Man!"   (Suzanne is laughing hysterically)

Jack: "She doesn't do it in her own town, man, she'd be in the Hoosegow so quick... Some Irate Mother come down there with her little boy..."

Frank: "For Sure, Man!"

Jack: "...That American Tramp Fucked My Little Boy!!"

Frank: "A school-teacher on the run, man, in Europe, staying just ahead of all the child-molestation charges!"

Suzanne: "I don't molest children! I don't molest anyone!! These people, when I meet them, they deal with me much more like a Man, more than men my own age or older: they're polite and sensitive, they're Romantic and Sensual, they…"

Frank: "Well then, my friends."

Suzanne: "I don't encourage them…" (Jacques cracks up)

Frank: "Great! Great! She doesn't encourage them!"

Suzanne: You Think I'm a Child Molester!"

Frank: "No, I don't: I was having a joke; what's wrong with you?"

Suzanne: "The first time was when I was on LSD in New Orleans one night, and I was about twenty-two and I was walking down the street, and you know there were all these cute little black boys tap-dancing on the street, and I was on LSD and his eyes turned into the uterus and the Colon of the Universe, and I looked at him and he picked up his little plastic gold cup from the corner and said 'HELLO MISSY, YO' SHO' IS PURTTY!'" (She completely cracks up)

Frank: "How old was the guy?"

Suzanne: "…and we went to the Moonwalk…"

Frank: "Was he like twelve? Billy's age Exactly!"

Suzanne is still laughing hysterically.

Frank: "And you initiated him into the…"

Suzanne: "No. No! Most of the Lovers Of My Life have been my own age. There've only been a Couple of Occasions where…"

Jacques starts laughing again. I start pounding on the table; Everyone is in Ecstasy. Frank asks if I've got the recorder on. I assure him that I am getting all of it. Jacques is still laughing. Peter and Ellen are moving their fingers a little faster, staring a little deeper, and mumbling a little more passionately, Glowing with Young Love. We pass the pipe.

Frank yells, "TELL US SOME MORE STUFF, SWEETHEART!!"

Suzanne continues: "You want to hear about the Old men? When I lived in the…" (The crowd goes Wild, pounding on the table, eyes watering). "When I lived in Studio City I lived in this apartment complex, tacky, you know, with a swimming pool and all these cardboard apartments lined up next to each other, with five families of five living in one room, and this old lady kicks them out and they've got little whores that kill their boyfriends, you know; a couple of blocks from Universal Studios and that's when I met Jack, he became my best friend. He was eighty-five and he'd been a bookie and a truckdriver, and he'd ridden a unicycle in vaudeville and he was wonderful and the great love of his life was a woman who came to see him once a week and they'd been having an affair since before she was married!'

Frank: "Did you Fuck him?"

Suzanne: Never! we never fucked, but we talked for hours and he always had a nice tin of real good marijuana and good, cheap california wine… I was living with my two faggot friends and Bobby and I would fight, and I'd go see Jack and he'd talk and tell me all his stories about vaudeville and he'd pour me wine and we'd smoke dope and drink the wine and talk and then he'd go berserk and I always used to wear a long dress then, with no underwear then, and Jack'd say Oh Lord I've got to taste that Sweet Pussy and he'd take out his teeth and put 'em down on the floor and I'd sit there and he'd Gum The Shit Out Of Me!"

The crowd goes wild, glasses tumble off the table.

Suzanne: "…and I'd just sit there smoking dope and drinking wine and he never tried to fuck me or anything and he had a bathtub with one of those things, you know, a jacuzzi, and he used to like to watch me because I like the water orgasms and he'd give me wine and watch me."

The crowd can't take it, they are Gone, laughing.

"…and when I stuck my hand in the garbage disposal, my faggy friends didn't know what to do, and Jack took care of me, gave me whiskey and bandaged me up: He was always there if I was hurt; that was Jack."

There was a pause as we tried to regain our several composures.

Frank asked, "Well, wait a minute, was he 'GUMMING' you? Did I get that straight?"

"But he never tried to Fuck her!", I said.

"Right. 'Or Anything'", said Frank.

"But he made her sit in a whirlpool bath.", I said

"He didn't Make me, I like the whirlpool bath!", Suzanne answered.

"You were probably the First One.", I told her, sarcastically.

"I Hope that I was the First, rather than the Last!", she innocently trilled.

We passed the pipe once more. Frank talked with Peter while Suzanne and I had a chat about lawsuits over the use of her story about Old Jack and Gumming.

Suddenly Frank yelled, "Peter, Peter, Peter, Peter! Peter, Peter, Peter! You've Still Got That Suck? Get rid of it Man!", referring to the hypodemic nerdle (sick) that he'd found earlier in the W.C..

Frank explained to Peter, "Here we are with a confirmed heroin addict, and you…"

"Who Frank introduced me to.", interrupted Suzanne.

"Please!", Frank insisted, "I pointedly spared you an introduction! You met him yourself! You started talking French to him and acting seductive."

"I never! I never!", she answered.

I told Frank, "She's a Loving Person: she just liked him."

"Oh, Man! Stop it, Man!", Frank moaned, "You know what happened to a person being nice to a friend once?...."

"This Came!", Jacques said, holding up the paper airplane.

"Look at the way the heroin addict is bouncin' at the bar now!", Frank said. We all looked. He was nodding and swaying.

Frank began to tell us all the story of the guy who came into Santi's and claimed to have fallen out of an airplane and Didn't Live, but he couldn't remember the story. It was Very Good Hash.

Frank and Jacques began discussing Frank's similarity to Tolstoy again.

Suzanne said, "You know, every time we go out you keep talking about this guy who kept on trying and kept on trying; you really admire Tolstoy, don't you?"

"Do I Ever!!", exclaimed Frank.

"It's his Guru, at this point.", added Jacques.

"He's found somebody that's Like Him!", I told her.

"He's become a vegetarian, for one thing, in the last week.", said Jacques.

"Yah, Seriously.", said Frank.

"He's starting to treat me like a serf!", I told her.

"Yes. He has.", Jacques confirmed.

Frank told me, "You notice when I abuse you I Repent Instantly, and come back!"

I yelled, "It makes no difference to the serf whether the master repents after the beating or not!"

Jacques told Frank, "If we're talking in terms of Tolstoy, you're doing exactly what he did! First he hates the serfs, then he gives them everything: you did it perfect."

I said, "Well, at the other Counts' places they probably beat them and then, to repent, beat them again. Tolstoy at least gave 'em time off and fed 'em well when he was repenting!"

Jacques said, "When Tolstoy repented he gave 'em everything."

"Right! But on the other ranches in Russia can you imagine what it was like?", I said, "THEY didn't repent: they just beat them mercilessly!"

"...And he was a good pimp: took her out for champagne dinners after he'd beaten her and taken all her money...", observed Suzanne.

"Something like that, yah,", I told her, "except when you're dealing with millions of people."

"It's All A Question Of Volume, You See!", Suzanne told me.

I said, "Yah, it just depends on how Bad a Pimp you are: the Czars of Russia were the biggest pimps in the world: they could send ARMIES out to get fucked!" We agreed.

"It's a Question of Volume!", she said.

"It just depends on how much Trouble you want to get in.", I said.

"Volume!", she said, "It's a question of volume! It always comes down to a question of volume!"

"That's because 'volume' means nothing.", I said.

"But that's always what it's a Question Of!", she told me.

"Well, of course. It applies to anything.", I said. It was Obviously time for more hash.

Suzanne continued, "Petty Fascism is No Big Deal. Imperialisf Fascism: That's Heavy Crime!"

"Useless or Gratuitous Fascism is the only kind I don't like", I volunteered, getting Way Out There.

Frank and Jacques were discussing Tolstoy's Originality, but were interrupted by Peter, who was claiming to have turned the airplane portrait into a Work Of Art by sticking a beer bottle through the nose.

Frank said, "I'll say this: I know how to make the whole mess a Work Of Art,", as he grabbed my pencil, "I'll just sign this, and Thus Transform this Unbearably Unmentionable Thing into a Work Of Art!" He signed the portrait with the beer bottle through it's nose and held it up for the crowd; He received Praise and Laughter.

It was the first time than any of us have actually seen Frank at work. Jacques, Suzanne, and I began praising Frank for having created such an amazing piece. Peter got jealous and claimed that he did most of the work, and grabbed The Piece from Frank and tore it into small shreds.

"It was a Piece of Shit til I signed it!", Frank told Peter.

"And", said Jacques, "by your own criteria, Frank, it was the Best Reaction you could have asked for!"

"Exactly, Man!", Frank exclaimed, "Art should move people emotionally.

"I want it!", I said, "Can I buy it?"

"It's Yours.", Frank said, handing me the torn pieces.

"How much?", I asked, sending Suzanne into Spasms with the realization that this was Art Psycho-Drama.

"It's yours, My Friend", Frank told me.

"No! No! no, no, no!", screamed Suzanne.

"It's not the same!", I told Frank, "It's all torn to shreds, and you kept your Signature!"

"Well, I did this as a homage to Marcel Duchamps, A Revised, Late One.", he said.

I kept complaining that Frank had sold me all the shit and had kept his signature, the most valuable part. Suzanne kept screeching.

Ellen Patronizes Me

Well, it's been a good evening: 500ptas. Made 600 this morning. Billy has made about 7 or 800 today also. He's getting much better on the flute and he's a natural for this sort of action. He was playing a while ago on Steve's Corner and some people asked him if he was Steve's son. Touching, eh?

Ellen hasn't shown up here today, probably because of the 'friction' that came down between us yesterday: I met her in the Tapas as she was heading out to work, at about four. I told her I'd be following her in a few minutes. When I approached my Normal pitch, there she was opening her guitar case on the ground, setting up right where I usually type. I said, "NO, no, you can't set up there!" She suggested that I move over to where she usually sings, a few feet to the left. I explained that my table would possibly be considered an obstruction by the people that ran the bar there, and that This Spot is one of the few I can use. She was mildly surprised that I was making such a big deal about it, but agreed to move. I was feeling a little like Steve; Beggar's Rights and all that. Still, all was well between us and she gave me a piece of chocolate.

She began singing and I began clacking. She was immediately joined by Gregorio, The American Flautist From Berkeley, who began accompanying her with his flute. A Minute later Billy joined them and chimed in. In another minute a drunken member of the Denton Gang joined in with them on his harmonica. The Noise was Horrible; and this was the day I was going to transcribe same of the stuff I had on tape. I was mildly irritated but waited patiently for them to fade away.

I waited. I waited. Finally only Ellen and the Denton Guy were left. He played for a few minutes more and then came drunkenly, smelling of wine, to me and began hassling me to put a rubber band in his hair. It took a while to get him off me, and he proceeded to a spot about five feet in front of me where he began haranguing the crowds and the heavens with a Drunken Sermon in Loud, Unintelligible Spanish, with me and God as the two main characters. I finally had to begin yelling at him in English, "Hey! Hey! stop that Shit, Man! stop standing there in the fucking street yelling! I can't understand a fucking word you're saying! You're fucking up my whole thing here, Understand? Entiendes? Go Away! Stop Habla So Much!", and like that for a couple of minutes until he finally understood, through the drunken veil, that I wanted him to Leave. He came up to me and leaned in close, with clenched fists, and began yelling at me in Guttural Spanish. I yelled back at him in Biker English, "Just Get THE FUCK AWAY FROM ME! GO! MOTHERFUCKER!!", and like that , It worked, he left. I could finally get down to typing. It'd been about twenty minutes of hassles so far, and this was supposed to have been a Perfect Day: I'd felt great, sober, confident, and all that shit. I returned to it and began to settle my nerves.

Ellen looked over to me and complained that she had only made 67ptas in an hour. (it had only been half an hour). I told her that she was complaining to the wrong person, "I've only made one-fourth of that: I've got fifteen pesetas here." She reacted as though I was being un-compassionate.

A couple of minutes went by and Ellen looked over at me, smiled, and asked, "Are you still 'On The Wagon', Jack?"

I answered, "Ellen, Don't Patronize Me! You're not allowed to ask me questions like that. There's only a few people in the world that I let Patronize me: My Mother, My Father, Jacques because I've known him for twenty years, Rebecca my ex-wife, Frank because he's older than me and I let him. I LET These People Patronize me. You, Amani, Billy, people that are younger and more inexperienced than me: I Do Not Let them ask me questions like that."

"I wasn't Patronizing you.", she replied.

"Yes you were!", I told her, "I'm not a Dumb Shit that you can look down on. When you've been an alcoholic for twenty years you can ask me if I'm still On The Wagon."

"I Wasn't Patronizing You!", she insisted.

"Yes you were: Look inside yourself, look at yourself, and you will see what motivated you to ask me.", I told her; I was patronizing Her, now.

"Why are you in Such a Bad Mood?", she asked.

"I'm Not in a Bad Mood!", I told her.

"Yes You Are!", she said.

"No I'm Not!", I said, "And, you don't know me well enough to understand whether I'm in a bad mood or not; I'm just telling you something: You Can't Judge My Moods Better Than I Can, and I'm Telling You That I'm Not In A Bad Mood, Do You Understand?"

"Yes You Are!", she said, not answering my question.

I continued, "Do you understand what I've been telling you? Please Answer Me!", I said, raising my voice to one-fourth volume and intensity.

"Why are you putting out such bad vibes, I can't work with these bad vibes!", she answered.

"Have you ever been a Drunken Bum? Have you Ever Been Drunk? Do you know what it's like to wake up in the morning in bed with some smelly wretch that you have been making love to because you were so drunk you didn't notice and then you look in the mirror and you see someone who is all fucked up: blood on their face and dirty, dirty, dirty!? Have you ever done that? Maybe some day you will, and then you will understand what it's like to be a drunk. Then, you can ask me questions about being 'On The Wagon'. You want to know whether I'm drinking or not? Just look at me: if you see me drinking, I'm drinking. If you see me not drinking, I'm not drinking. It's that Fucking Simple!", I told her.

"You don't have to get so up-tight about it!", she told me.

"I'm not Fucking-Up-Tight! I'm trying to explain something to you!", I said.

"You've been in a Bad mood since you got here!", she accused.

"No I haven't", I said, "I'm in a good mood!"

"Well, I can't work with these bad vibes!", she said.

"Oh.", I said, as she packed up her guitar and walked down the street.

I went back to typing. Within the next couple of hours about five people came up to me and asked questions like, "What did you do to Ellen?". I'd answer something like, "Talked to her about patronizing me." It's a tempest in an pisspot. Like the Amani Deal ala Frank. Second Hand Information is like shit: it's no better served Hot.

A FEW DAYS LATER

I just realized why Ellen and I have problems: when she was here a few minutes ago I asked her, "Have you seen 'The Shining', with Jack Nicholson?

She answered, "I read the book."

I asked, "Did you see the movie?"

She again answered, "I read the book."

She never Really answered my question. I guess I should have asked it again? No? I read the book. I still don't know if she saw the movie.

Or, maybe I should have tried to continue the conversation; I was trying to find out if she'd seen the movie because I wanted to show her the full page of "All work am no play makes Jack a dull boy" that I recently wrote here; maybe I should have said, "Ellen, I'm asking you if you saw the movie 'The Shining' because if you have there is something that I wanted to show you that I've written; I'm not asking you if you've read the book because that's not what I want to know; Do You Understand what I just said?"

She might answer, "Why are you making such a Big Deal about it: I read the book!"

"I'm Not Making A Big Fucking Deal about it! I was asking a simple fucking question which you didn't answer either time I asked it!", I might say.

"You don't have to yell. You don't have to get Upset.", she might say.

"Fuck You!", I might say, getting upset and strangling her there in the street. One of us has a problem. At least one of us.

El Monstro, My Bloody Neighbor, Again

As I climbed the stairs to the pad the other midnight, returning from Hash Night at the Opera, I encountered my neighbor, El Monstro, on his landing with a screwdriver in his hand. I walked blithely ahead, anticipating death, while he began yelling at me something about his door, and water. Evidently the leaky pipes in my bathroom have run down through the walls and swelled shut his front door. He was unable to enter his apartment. He was Angry, At Me. He had obviously been out there for quite a while, trying to force the door. My Spanish (speaking, Out-going) has improved in the last month, so this time I was able to tell him that the problem was in the pipes above and that he should complain to the owners of the building. He said that I was not supposed to be living there and that there never was any problem with water or people walking up and down the stairs (my guests) when 'the girl' lived there. I told him that she was my Future Wife and that she would be back in a month and then we were going to stay for a month and then take off travelling. He lightened up on me at this news.

I managed to get past him on the landing, after watching for a few minutes as he pried and threw his shoulder against the door. I entered the pad, locked the door, and sat there quietly for about half an hour listening to him growl and bang the door. I was extremely high on Hash and was waiting for him to tire of trying his door and come and try mine, knock it down, and stab me to death with the screwdriver.

After a while I heard a Loud Crash, and decided that I'd better see if I could help. I got a hammer and another screwdriver and descended the stairs. He had the door open; I showed him the tools I was holding to help him with. He showed me the bloody wounds on his head and hand, which he'd gotten from attacking the door.

It ended well: we bid each other good night. There was some sort of bond formed as neighbors, but what I'm having to go through to get to know my neighbor is somewhat overpriced, terror-wise.

I've since tried to keep the leak to a minimum with buckets, wires, and other Hadass Goldberg looking apparatii. I hope it works.

The Shit Page, Billy, Rebecca, and Jack

Shit, Billy made 1800ptas in an hour and a half today. And, he played again a little while ago and made 500ptas in a half hour. Shit, he's making more than either his mother or father, and he's twelve. Shit, what's happening?

I should have been nicer to him lately: he could be supporting the whole family. Oh, well, when Amy and Sally get here I can put them on the street.

Shit, Billy's made 2300 on the street already today, and he's planning to go back out again: he's making more than any of the street people, and more than most English Teachers, at this point. Maybe he'll lend me money so that I can pay my rent.

He just went down to the sweet store and bought me a piece of chocolate (YAYY!!), the little shit. Unbelievable! I'm Blown Out! Gotta pause and consider Life for a few moments here. Shit! My Son: The Richest Beggar In Europe. I can see it now; I gotta get him to travel with Hadass and Me this summer: then I'll be taken care of by the two Most Successful Beggars I know. Amazing! (YAYYY!! FOR KIDS!! SEEE, GIGOLO JACK!!! THAT'S Not PEANUTTTS!!!).

I've just added a note to the letter I wrote to Amy and Sally telling them to write and ask Billy to send them air-fare. Shit!

He's found a new place to play and won't even tell his Father! The little shit sure learns fast, eh? Shit, I been living on a tenth of what he makes now. Kid's Lib is one thing, but this is ridiculous! (YAYYY!!! FOR BILLEEEE!!!). Yah, yah, yah, keep it down, God-Damn It!

Frank says that I should treat Billy like Gold from now on, he will soon be hiring me as a Go-fer. I could probably make more as Billy's assistant than I am doing at this. Well, shit, this means that I better get on the stick with editing this and sending it off. Can't let the little shit start patronizing me and rubbing it in. Gotta keep things in their proper perspective: I was only joking those times when I said I was only an immature version of Billy: I'm a successful Writer, eh? I wonder what Rebecca's cut is going to be. I should get about half that much, I figure. I've got it coming. (THAT'S FOR SURE, GIGOLO JACK!!!) .

SCENE IN RESTAURANT:

Rebecca: "Umm, the pork chops look good today?"
    Billy: "No, you just have the salad and the soup!"
    Rebecca: "Can't I have just one piece of chicken?"
    Billy: "Yes, you can have the chicken if you get the small salad!"
    Rebecca! "Can I have a cup of coffee too?"
    Billy: "Si, pero un cortado."
    Rebecca: "But you let me get a large one yesterday ! " Billy: "Yes, but that's because you didn't have chicken yesterday."
    As they leave the restaurant they are accosted by a beggar, "Spare change? Ayuda, Por Favor!"
    "Fuck Off, Jack!", says Billy.
    As Frank says, "Life sure takes some strange bounces."

The Opera Cafe Again

MY GRANDMOTHER APPEARS
FRANK AND MATERIALISM
PETER EXPLAINS REINCARNATION TO ELLEN
THE PROBLEM WITH ORDERING

Tuesday. Feb5. Bread St. 12:30

Steve the Pirate is back from England. He's down at the Tapas right now, basking in his Return. Billy ran down there to see him as soon as he heard. I hope he doesn't mention to Steve how much money he's been making on the street. Oh, sure, there would be fellowship now that they're in the same Business, but Billy never served an apprenticeship to justify his higher wage. Ah, actually it's good to have Steve back, refreshed from his vacation in England: He's been taking it easy drinking Guinness and Irish Whiskey. He's wearing a red pullover sweater. Does this mean He's Back For Good as a Catalan?

I got out here late today because of that last bottle of Voll-Damm (the Rainier Ale of Spain) that I had last night at the Opera, mixed with generous portions of Hashish.

I walked the mile and a half to Casa Peret last night to meet the Gang for dinner, but they never showed. I sat in a bodega across the street, leaning on the wedges that keep the thousand-liter barrels of wine from rolling on to the floor. The bodega was old: the walls covered with dusty old bottles of booze and wine, some of which have probably been there since before I was born. Some of the Bottles had been removed to make room for the Television Set, which, when I was there, was playing a "Get Smart" re-run. It's strange to sit in a place reeking of Ancient Spanish Atmosphere and listen to American Idiocy. I didn't look at the set: I looked at the garishly colored, plastic, glowing, ubiquitous slot machines, which sang me a Spanish Version of 'Mary Had A Little Lamb' every few minutes. It sounded like a cross between classical musick and a Merry-go-round theme. They sing the little ditty to remind us that they are still alive and awaiting our duros.

I had a glass of wine and sat there watching the age age. There was an old lady, bent over, presumably the owner's mother, sweeping out the bodega. She was wearing a shower-cap, flowered cotton dress, apron, and combat boots. She was very active for someone her age, I suppose around eighty. It was obvious that she had been doing this job for years. She resembled my own Grandmother. Shit! It WAS my Grandmother! I pretended not to recognize her; she didn't recognize me either, because I wasn't wearing tennis-shoes and have aged some since she saw me last, eight years ago, right before she passed on. To Spain, evidently.

I snuck out and headed back to the pad, angered that I'd let the Hippy Contingent affect my life again by agreeing to meet Somewhere with them. I should've learned my lesson by now.

Back at the pad I had a 300pta dinner, bottle of beer, cafeconleche, and finished off with a hit of Hash, before joining Frank and Jacques at the Cafe Opera for the evening's discussion: Materialism.

Frank was equipped with teaching aids for this one: Photographs of his x-house in L.A., a dinner party in his fashionable x-dining-room, him getting into his X-KE Jaguar, the dash-board of the Jag, Seats in the Jag, front view of the Jag, side view of the Jag, back view of the Jag, his x-studio on Venice Beach, his beautiful x-wife (yes, that Was his beautiful wife, yes, that Was his beautiful house), and other photos proving that he was at one time Extremely Successful.

This discussion was supposed to have been held with some of the budding young materialists in attendance, but none of them had made it. They had gotten bogged down at a restaurant, arguing over the check. So he showed the photos to me and Jacques. I reacted as though I wished that some day I too could have all of these things. It was an almost believable performance, the best I could do on such short notice. I tried to keep a straight face and react as though I was Ambitious for the American Dream, as some of the others we know would have done. It came off pretty well; I assume Frank will carry the photos with him until he gets a chance to try them out on Real Materialists. He is determined that some day he will not be surrounded by continual chatter about prices and pesetas. He's got a real fight ahead of him, I think. (It's a good thing he got the photos developed in the states: it costs about 1350ptas to get a roll developed here, much more expensive. Although, I know a place where you can get a roll developed for 1150ptas. I should tell Frank about it.)

The Gang had dinner at another place, on the spur of the moment, but Jacques said that I didn't miss much: with Peter in charge, and Emma translating, it took about half an hour to place the order for food, and then the discussion centered on various different prices for a while. Billy, as Guru, took over the evening with a discussion about why Jacques was being anti-social by reading his book rather than joining in the conversation. Jacques told me that Billy actually Rebuked him for it in front of the others, (Not the proper Way for an experienced Guru to behave), and had them all discussing it for quite a while. Jacques said that when it was time to leave he waited outside the restaurant for about twenty minutes while the crowd argued over who had what, until he finally lost his patience and headed for the Opera. He had begun telling the story to Frank, who was wagging his head and clucking his tongue, when I arrived.

Jacques, Frank, and I smoked some hash, got high, and began discussing the dinner party that Jacques had been to earlier. According to Jacques, Peter explained re-incarnation to Ellen: The Basic Stuff about how you will come back as a Cat if you are a good person, and a Dog if you're bad. Ellen had never had re-incarnation explained to her before. Whitey confirmed Peter's theories, and Ellen was on her way to a Better Understanding of the Universe.

I asked Jacques, "It was Known Comedy, right? They knew this was Comedy!"

"No!", he said.

"Ah hah, this is the Rub!", I said.

Jacques continued, "It was a serious conversation, Jack, that just went on and on, and I was already blown out. I haven't even told you how long it took to order!".

He continued, "Peter took charge of ordering and it took literally twenty-five minutes to get our order figured out and then it took Emma ten minutes more to take it up to the guy. The whole time that Peter was in charge it was so lost of an organization that you wouldn't have believed your eyes!", he told us.

"Then, after that is when the cat and Dog thing happened. I took out the Cellini Book: I didn't want to do it, but just for my own sanity I took it out and started reading it and after about 15 minutes I was Gone, and suddenly Billy breaks whatever they were talking about and Rebukes me and calls everyone's attention. Everyone is looking at me: Wondering a little bit, but they're also thinking it's weird that Billy's bothering me, but Billy is Completely Telling Me, "I think that's rude, Jacques, I think That's Terrible, I would never do that!", and on and on like that. Stunned? Well, I was Stunned."

Frank and I sat there entranced, Jacques continued, "Right before that, Billy had made some kind of sculpture out of a banana with a knife in it, was putting plastic on it and finally Peter said, "There, that's Perfect, Billy", seriously, and Billy said, "Yah, I know, That's why I'm Stopping!", and it was left at that. Then, after Billy rebuked me, the only thing I could think of to say, other than get pissed and get on his case, was, "Billy, if I have to stop reading, and look at THAT, Is that a good experience for me?", and then, well, he was rude, but he took it apart. I was still stunned and went back to reading, and for five minutes he explained to them, seriously, (I pretended to be reading, but I listened), Why It Was Fucked, What I was Doing. Peter told him, for a while,

"You're Passing Judgement, and that's never good to do: people should be free to do what they want.", and Billy had a response to that, that got Whiting going, saying, "Well, that's good: at least he was honest.", and That went back and forth for a while, and the last thing I remember is Peter saying, "Yah, well I see what you mean, You're Together, Actually, Billy". They thought I was checked-in to the book and agreed that "Yes, it was Cool, what he did". Billy had brought it around to that, basically. He's their Guru, and the Joke Part of it isn't Even There Anymore!"

"Incredible.", I said. Frank just grinned into space, thinking, in ecstasy.

Frank said, "Well, I assume that Peter took care of the ordering OK, and that everyone got their food OK, and that everyone was happy."

Jacques assured us that this was not the case, and continued to describe more of his evening with 'Billy and the Disciples'. We discussed how serious Billy's Ashram was becoming, and how it seemed that most of the people were unaware that Billy was taking over. Frank wanted to hear more about what the dinner had been like for Jacques.

He asked, "So, Jacques, Was it significantly faster paying the bill and getting out of there tonight than normal? I mean, they didn't linger and haggle over the bill like normal, did they?"

"They did!", Jacques answered.

"How long? How long would you say that it took?", Frank asked, savoring the question.

"When they left they sort of had bad vibes for me, and I had bad vibes for them. But, Man! It was five minutes, ten minutes, fifteen minutes, and That's when I Definitely Noticed!", Jacques told us.

"Fifteen Minutes!?", I asked incredulously.

"More than that!", he said, "Standing, grouped around the cash register, after about fifteen minutes Billy and Peter were outside, and Rabbit, Whitey towering there, were still at it. It went on for another ten minutes. Billy and Peter were out in the street screaming, playing like classic twelve-year-olds while these guys were still paying. Finally, Conejo came over and gave me a cigarette and bid me goodnight. Some of them were walking around talking and acting like robots. To give you an idea, they had had a long, long conversation about what kind of water Ellen wanted to drink. That went on for another fifteen minutes. It turned out that she HAD to get a bottled water: Billy was buying it for her!"

"That's MY Boy!, I cried.

Frank said, "You know, it's a common ploy, for a man, if he sees a beautiful woman, as a tribute to her beauty, to send her a glass of water, I've done it a lot. 1 tell the waiter, 'Tell her it's from me."

I said, "Yah, I don't have a lot of money tonight but The Water's On Me!"

Jacques said, "Listen to this: After Peter finally had hassled Ellen enough, it was a bad vibe between them, to get a water, because Billy was buying it; by then Emma was up at the kitchen telling the guy what we want, Peter goes, 'Emma! Emma!', and she immediately comes back, doesn't place the order, squeezes back into her place, which was a hassle, sits down, 'What?', she says. 'There's another water.' All of this is at least a half hour; they talk about That for a while!"

Frank groaned, "Oh , Man…"

Jacques continued, "There was some more talk about Ellen's water, whether with-gas or without-gas, and finally the order was placed. And everybody but me was having fun!"

I said, "That's worse than going to dinner with Junkies: You ask 'em whaddaya want and they 'Uhhhhhnnnn'"

Frank said, "So you spent over an hour ordering and paying the bill tonight?"

"Y' know, Frank,", Jacques said, "When you get closer to the suicide and you're just waiting for That Thing to put you over the edge: A Night Like Tonight Could Do It! You'd go: 'I didn't think it was gonna get to this',. and you I d say, 'This is the Night! '"

"My Night!", said Frank, grinning into Space.

"That's the Level we're talking about!", said Jacques.

"What an evening….", moaned Frank, "I was lucky: I almost went to that dinner!"

There was a commotion at the entrance to the Opera.

"Great, Man!", exclaimed Frank, "Here come some of the remnants of the crowd now!"

Jacques moaned, "Ohhhh, Hold onto your brains!"

Santi's Again

FRANK PATRONIZES AND INSULTS PETER

I arrived at Santi's about ten oclock, after stew and coffee at the pad, and became aware that Steve was back before I finished coming through the door, "You Stupid Motherfucker! You Ignorant Son-of-a-Bitch!', he was screaming at Gregorio, the recently-arrived, young, black, American, Flautist, concerning Street-musicianship. Greg had been telling the group how much he'd made on the street that day.

As I took my seat in the back of the cavern, I heard Steve yell again, "You're a Right-Straight-Down-The-Line Motherfucker!". Greg was trying to take it in good humor; he hadn't been introduced to Steve and nobody had warned him. He kept trying to explain to Steve that he 'understood', and wasn't trying to make light of his profession.

Steve told him, "You better piss off out of town tomorrow, Motherfucker; if I see you on the street tomorrow, I'll kick in your fuckin' teeth!" Greg did his best to be sociable, difficult under these circumstances, and in a few minutes I heard Steve 'meep-meep', a sure sign that the fit of anger had passed.

Peter was playing Vivian a game of chess, Aurora was floating on an alcohol cloud, Eduardo/Conejo/Rabbit was counting his pesetas, Steve was Ranting, Billy was 'in school', and Jacques, Ellen, and I sat in the hole in the back while they read 'the book'.

Frank wasn't there, which was too bad because Jacques, Ellen and I had an interesting talk about Pesetas. Peter joined us, angry because he had just lost the chess game to Vivian, who he probably considers Working-class.

"Get your Gourd on Straight, Peter.", I told him, referring to his wobbling and stumbling as he tried to sit at one of the little tables.

"Fuck Gourds!", he told me, as he fell into a chair, knocking over some drinks.

"Peter, are you on a Drunk?", Jacques asked.

"Yup! How Perceptive of you!", he answered. He leaned on the table, next to me, and began bobbing and weaving while he explained why he and Frank were No Longer Friends.

Billy asked Jacques for a piece of his white bread, which Jacques sold to him for 4 pesetas. Billy was wearing a new pair of pesetaloafers, a golfing sweater, and a cute little cap: he looked like a miniature Arnold Palmer. While Billy and Peter were arguing about why Peter lost the game to Viv, Rebecca, Whiting, and Judy Arrived, filling the cavern.

"I'm not friends with Frank, anyway,", Peter told me, "You can write that down. I don't need this shit. I don't need this shit that comes down! I don't need people patronizing me! I don't need people telling me I'm ignorant when I'm Not!", he told us.

Jacques said, "Peter, you should see the pictures Frank has."

"I don't want to see his car! I don't want to see his house!", he answered, "You know what he said to me that finally pissed me off: 'You can't help it if you had a lousy education and can't afford to go into these expensive stores and buy things.'!"

Jacques said, "Peter, The Whole Thing started because: There was Frank. And, There was someone trying to be serious: That's a Bad Combination. Always." Peter was not moved.

Frank was in the cavern in spirit; His Personality was The topic of conversation. Everyone had an opinion.

"Well, Peter, Frank just hit a raw nerve with you.", I told him.

"That's Right! My Education!", he said

"He did it by accident.", Jacques told him.

"He doesn't do anything by accident: he insults people!", said Peter, "You ignore him: he wins. You hit him: he wins."

"Frank is faithful to his Neo-Pretensionism!", Jacques explained. Peter would have none of it. According to him: Frank is Vicious.

"Here Comes Frank!!", yelled Billy, acting as lookout.

"WHAT'S HAPPPPPENINNNNG?", Frank asked, in True California Style, grinning and shaking hands all around.

Jacques said, "We were talking about you insulting Peter in the Santa Clara Cafe the other day."

"Well, that's as Gourdless as anything I've ever heard in my life!", said Frank, "Incredibly Imbecilic!"

"See, I told you he'd say that!", smirked Peter.

"Yes, Frank, you reacted exactly the way we thought you would.", Jacques told him. Frank was non-plussed: puzzlement, humor, and confusion battled to control his face for a moment. Puzzlement won.

He asked Peter, "Well, what did I say that makes you think I insulted you?"

"I don't THINK you insulted me, Frank, I KNOW you did!", said Peter, "The thing that Upset me was what you said about my education."

"Well, Peter, you know that when I insult you I do it right to your face. I've insulted your in-breeding many times but I can't imagine why I would want to insult your education: I've never even thought of it!", Frank told him. They spent the next few minutes arguing back and forth trying to agree on what really had been said that day.

Peter said, "You said that because of my education I didn't have the potential to earn the money to go into the expensive shops! That's Exactly What You Said!"

Frank replied, "I said Exactly the OPPOSITE of that!", and proceeded to delineate his argument.

"No You Didn't!", said Peter.

"Yes I did!", said Frank. It was a stalemate.

Jacques, 2/3 bottle down, gave one more try at reconciliation, "It doesn't mean you don't have a good education just because you're inbred: look at Toulouse-Latrec!" It didn't seem to work.

Frank told peter, "Well, if that's what you really think, then I guess we're just not friends anymore."

"Suits me just fine!", said Peter. At last, they finally agreed on something.

The crowd was beginning to go their separate ways. It had been Very Entertaining for all concerned: everyone had their Own Observations to make about the Match.

Billy talked Peter into joining him at the bodega for a drink by offering to buy it. They departed: a night on the town with the boys. Peter was drunker than Billy.

As Jacques, Frank, Ellen, and I headed for the Opera, we passed Vivian helping Steve crawl to his pension. He's Back: I still don't know whether he was able to get the Government Pension he went to England for. We'll find out soon, I'm sure.

On the way down to the Opera, we ran into Gregorio in plaza St. Juame, who joined us for the walk. I asked him what he had done to start the argument earlier with Steve. He said he'd mentioned that he was working on the street. I told him he shouldn't have done That. He said no one had warned him. Ellen, an old hand at being called 'A Stupid Motherfucker', consoled him.

As we got to the Opera Cafe, Greg headed up the Ramblas, he had an appointment with someone at the cathedral, while Frank, Jacques, and Ellen entered through the front door.

As I was about to follow them in, one of the Moroccan Dope Dealers leapt out of his chair and came charging out the door, right past me, and walloped a guy who was riding by on one of those cute little bicycles with small wheels. The guy was knocked to the ground, and the Dealer picked up the bike and was about to Brain him with it when he scrabbled away and began running up the street, knocking tourists aside as he went. Greg, who was only about twenty feet up the street, was bumped, turned around, and was faced with the Dealer running with the bike raised over his head, screaming in Spanish. Gregorio started to say something to him, thought better of it, and stepped aside as the Dealer threw the bike after the runner, who disappeared up the street. A crowd of dealers from the cafe came out and tried to calm down their friend, holding him back, as I entered the Opera. I joined my friends at our usual table: Another Night at the Opera cafe was beginning.

YET ANOTHER NIGHT AT THE OPERA CAFE
FRANK EXPLAINS AURAS TO ELLEN

It took us a few minutes to figure out which kind of water Ellen wanted to drink, and Frank not-so-graciously lent her 2Sptas so she could pay for it. The Usual. Ellen said she had come with us tonight "because the conversation is So Interesting". I got Jacques to pay for my first beer of the night out of the Rent Money that his bank has been saving for me.

"Well, Frank, let's smoke some of your Hash for a while.", suggested' Jacques.

"Certainly, my friend.", replied Frank, reaching for his accoutrements.

We passed the pipe around. Ellen asked, "What was it you were saying, Frank, about Hash blowing holes In your aura?"

"Yes!", he said, "But Small!... compared to the Giant Holes that smoking cigarettes causes."

Ellen said, "I'm not doing cigarettes anymore!"

"They rip and tear your aura to shreds! It looks like a shroud hanging on you!", he told her.

"And what determines the color of your aura?", she asked, "Like, is yours green because you have green eyes?"

"No!", he answered, "People just have different color auras."

"Ah!", she said, "What color is yours?"

"Mine…was… polished to a Bright Golden Hue, by my Aura Therapist not nine months ago. Now, as you can plainly see, can't you, It looks like a rag! And the nicotine stains are threatening to turn it…"

Ellen interrupted, "What color is my aura, for example?"

Jacques told her, "I don't have an aura therapist, I can't tell." "What color is Jack's aura?", she asked Jacques.

He answered, "It's invisible, you can't see it unless you're an aura therapist. People like you and I, and even Frank, we can't see them. "

"Sometimes we can.", I said.

"I can, frequently.", Frank added.

"Really?", she asked.

"I can.", Frank told her, "Yours is purple, I've told you that. I see yours."

"But don't forget Reincarnation!", I said.

"Ah, how can I forget it?", Frank asked.

Frank had recently received his latest copy of the monthly scandal sheet, The Sun. He told us about the latest headlines: Children can remember their previous lifetimes.

"What's the 'Sun'?", Ellen asked.

"It's a paper from the states.", I told her, "Frank subscribes to it. It has things in it like: UFOs carry off Tony Curtises Bearded daughter, and shit like that."

"Ah!", said Frank, "Here comes Phil the Vampire and Jack the Jeweler!"

Jacques said, "Jack the Jeweler again!? How Gourdless can the evenings become in succession?"

Frank greeted them, "Ah, a crowd of Happy Larkers coming our way!" Phil and Jack sat down with us and we all said hello and proceeded to arrange for another hit of hash to be smoked.

We were joined by a guy that Frank met the day before who had spent the night sleeping in the train station. Frank had been telling him how to survive in Barcelona with nothing: Go to Cafe Zurich and pick up a rich girl and stay at her house. It's sound advice but I think it would be better to show him how to find the street first. I got on Frank's case for ruining our nice little Gypsy Cave Atmosphere by inviting all these Weirdoes to join us.

Phil accused us of looking like a bunch of hill-billies because we were smoking corn-cob pipes, but shut up when I told him that they were gifts from our Guru, Billy.

Ellen said, "I really like the part in your book where you say that Billy is King because he has the most money."

"It's a joke.", I told her.

"Everything is a Joke.", she said.

"Ah, you've heard of that?!", I exclaimed.

"...And, Nothing is a Joke.", she continued.

I told her, "Don't complicate it with Deep Philosophical Questions: Everything is a Joke."

"Come On, Jack! I don't see anything as a joke, really.", she said, seriously. I just looked at her wonderingly, sitting there at Frank's table, completely surrounded by Madmen, and not seeing The Humor. I was stunned.

We passed the pipe around a couple of times. I filled in Phil about Frank and Peter, about which he'd already started hearing rumors. I explained to Phil how to hang clothes that you find in the alleys with dog-piss on them out on the patio for a week to make them wearable.

"So, Frank, why doesn't Peter like you?", Phil innocently asked.

"Well, we were talking about something entirely different from what he thought; So, it Is a Misunderstanding, although I don't feel the need to discuss and discuss and discuss it with him to try to make him understand, because, relating with an inanimate object isn't that important to me.", he answered,"Unless I attribute anthromorphic qualities to the inanimate object, which I Have Done in the past!" Phil laughed.

I said, "It's ANTHROPOMORPHIC, Frank, PO-morphic!, Not Anthromorphic!"

"Right. Right.", he said.

Jack the Jeweler asked Frank, "Are you talking about my mother?"

"No, Noooo,", answered Frank, "Your Mother? What a guy!"

"Is your mother named Peter?", I asked Jack, signalling the descent of Conversation into Gourdlessness.

Jack, Phil, and I talked about drinking Tequila in Mexico, while Frank and Jacques tried to explain to Ellen who Lori was, a difficult job.

Frank finally asked the Drifter/Junkie to leave our group, which he "did. We were all proud of Frank's Direct Handling of an uncomfortable situation. Now, we were free to get on with the evening. Jacques got the guy high on hash and he set out for Cafe 'Zurich to try to pick up a rich woman. Poor guy. Ellen thought the whole deal was 'Incredible'.

Frank explained further how he got rid of the Junkie, "I thought to myself, what if I just deal direct with this guy, otherwise he might think I'm patronizing him." (This 'Patronizing' Concept that was being bandied about lately was one of my interjections into the Group Consciousness; I liked the way it was spreading).

Frank continued his explanation to Ellen, "It was an Incredible coup for Rationality, I feel." Ellen heartily agreed.

Frank further explained to Phil how Peter was the farthest thing from his mind when he said the stuff that angered Peter. I was explaining to Jack the Jeweler that I probably wouldn't be attending Amani's Dancing Show at the American Institute on Friday because of the Conflict of Authors Thing that Frank had created. I explained to Jack that Amani was Seriously Convinced that my book was titled "Amani is a Stupid Fucker." and that the sequel was "Amani is Even a Worser Fucker Than I Thought". Jack thought I was kidding.

Ellen was explaining to Frank how Peter was probably storing up his resentment for quite a while and that this latest blowup was just a release. Frank was listening attentively.

"People never say what they mean!", she told Frank.

"People often say what they mean, Ellen!", Jacques told her.

"Well, I'm just saying that because in a lot of situations I've been in lately, people haven't said what they mean.", she told him.

"Ah, well, I see what you mean.", Jacques replied.

Ellen returned to Frank and complimented him on his Handling of the Junkie, "That was very straight forward, and it was also very rare."

Frank acknowledged the praise, "Thank you, My Dear."

We were Descending the Ladder of Gourdlessness rapidly, somebody had better came up with something soon; we'd continued talking about the Junkie and Frank for another ten minutes. Jacques looked worried.

In a feeble try for Something Meaningful, we passed the pipes around once more. Would it work? No. The Junkie Returned.

"The Spirit of Lori has rejoined us!", said Jacques.

I was telling Phil what it had been like to be a hippy in the mountains in California while I tried to Bogart all the Hash. (sic). Frank grabbed a piece that I'd been hoarding.

"Frank, I wish you wouldn't grab things off from in front of me like that!", I scolded.

"Why?", he asked, as I grabbed back the hash.

"Because I had it there for a reason.", I said, "I put it there so that It Would Be There!"

He replied, "Oh, well, I thought if we were going to smoke this pipe that you would be just one of the ones that it would be passed to."

"That's a Good Reason, but notice how your hands anticipated it by entering my space!", I told him.

"OK, let's smoke MY hash!", he said, offering a solution to the dope-smoking breakdown. I handed him the piece that he had tried to steal and resumed my conference with Phil.

"Where's the other piece?", Jacques asked, "Where's The Main Piece!?"

"That's It.", I told him.

"Jack, look, all I want is a pipe to be goin'", Jacques said.

"We just wanna smoke some dope!", Frank added.

"Why has all this confusion settled on the table?", Jacques asked the Heavens.

I answered, "Hey, Man, I asked you for some dope and you gave it to me."

"It's True.", he reluctantly admitted, "It's All True!"

Frank agreed, "It's All True."

We finally got a pipe passing around the table, with the inevitable delay at Frank's position so that he could 'get the most out of the available drug'. Phil asked me if My Theory that Frank Never Passes Dope was true. I told him to watch. Sure enough, when the pipe got to Frank, he managed to keep it for about five minutes, through one maneuver or another.

Finally there was coughing all around.

"Frank, do you have a lighter?", Jacques asked.

"Certainly, my friend, it's one of my strong points.", he answered.

"It sure is.", said Jacques, High at last.

Frank and Jacques continued to discuss Peter for quite a while and I had a Hash Revelation that I had to share with than, "Frank, my theory is: You're getting sloppier and he's getting more Sinatra-like, and it's the partying of the ways; You met at the crossroads of Fashion, Now You're starting to look like an old golf pro; see what I mean?"

"That's It!", said Frank, "You meet the same people on the way down that you met on the way up! So you should be nice to everyone you meet!"

I added, "Don't shit in the trail, for you may pass this way again."

"That's right.", said Frank.

The talk went on and on, the pipes went round and round.

"He turned on me like a Rabid Dog!", I heard Frank tell Jacques, about Peter. It went on for another hour and I was finally so stoned and dizzy that it was becoming a blur. I was having difficulty telling what was going on and was on the verge of Taking Over the evening myself, so I decided to gather my things and split. I bid all a good night and passed Billy and Peter entering as I left. I slunk back to the pad and drank the liter of beer I had waiting for me there, while listening to Radio Israel on' the shortwave. It was Tree-Planting Week in Israel. "I'm Not Missing Jew", was the current number one song.

On the Street Again, Once More

LINGERING WITH NO VISIBLE MEANS OF SURVIVAL

Plaza St. Juame, Calle LLibreteria, Bread Street

Thursday, Feb 7, 1985. 12:30 PM

It's a Hazy but almost sunny day again in Barcelona. Spring weather for sure. Ah, the alarm clock worked. Woke me up about ten. Slept again til eleven. Got out here in time to make same bread with which to bailout the laundry. The campaign to get Hadass back to Barcelona, or get me to Tel-Aviv, is in full swing. I've pulled out all the stops: if she's not got a lover there, I've reminded her of a couple of times when we made love. Lust can move mountains'. I've also mentioned falling behind on the rent here. Double-barrelled attack. Money and Sex. If They won't get her back here, what will? Love? Yup, Mentioned Love, too. Three barrels. Pity? Yup, it's in the Letter. I may get run over by a truck if she doesn't get back here and take care of me. I'm That Feeble.

    There is a light amount of Catalan Churning going on: they seem to have forgotten what purpose brought them down to the Gothic Barrio today. They're mainly just standing or sitting around eating pastry and drinking coffee. There are a few 'scurrying', but not the usual frantic weaving and bobbing. I've got enough already, with what I saved from last night (YAYYY FOR RESPONSIBLE JACK!!!) to bailout the clothes, If I get there before they close for siesta. Which I doubt. It's mainly duros these days, with a few 100's thrown in occasionally.

    Jacques stopped by to tell me that he will be having the Menu at Meson Hadass tonight, again. Got to get some vegetables and beans to sweeten up the pot. Rabbit also stopped by to tell me that he will be staying at Pension Jack tonight. Getting Very Popular.

    Well, the tide is starting to flood. The Churning is picking up in this tidepool. 1m a sea-urchin waiting for the Cata-planktons. Sometimes the tide is rich in nutrients, sometimes it's not. I've moved the net (box) around to the side of the table, so that it's not so obvious. It's part of a plan that I came up with last night while I was stoned, to increase my take by appearing to not care about the money. You know, de-emphasize the begging, and emphasize the Art. Pretty soon I'll stop doing this in the street altogether.

    LATER. I got the laundry, made more stew, had a delightful lunch by myself, and am wearing clean clothes. Something is wrong. I headed over to

Puerta del Angel where Jacques is working and bullshitted with him for a few minutes. He'd spent the last couple of hours just sitting on a ledge near his paintings, reading. Made about 300 doing that. Frank joined us with the news that Ellen was causing some sort of Sixties Riot Revival down in plaza St. Juame. Seems the police came along and told the sunbathers on the tobacco shop ledge, there were only four of them including Frank, to move along. Ellen asked to see the Regulation forbidding sunbathing in the Square. The cop told her that she was not a dog, and therefore shouldn't be sitting on the ground. Ellen kept demanding her Rights and he asked to see passports. One of the guys took off running, followed by a police car and about six cops. Ellen walked away when her cop took off in pursuit also.

It's the Same Old Bullshit: Do I have a right to be here? Is this my Planet? Why can't I sit on the fucking grass? And on and on. These fucking cops have guns: it's as simple as that. You do what they tell you, regardless of how gourdless, because they will simply Kill You Dead eventually, if you don't co-operate. What a world! People's Plaza, indeed. I suppose that, as Catalonia stretches its independent wings, the local cops will become more and more obnoxious. That privilege used to be reserved for the National Police, but they'll all want to get in on The Fascist Act as the Power becomes available. Even Loafers will be polarized into becoming anti-something terrorists. Everyone who doesn't have a job as a plumber will eventually join the Army of Liberation. The Police will make sure that this happens. It happened in the good old USA, you know. Recently. I was originally just a loafer, but after getting beat up a few times by the cops I started learning how to make bombs out of turnips. (You have to boil them a lot). Well, at least Your Reporter is on the scene, in the middle of the Latest Act Of War: Lingering. Subversive Lingering with No Visible Means Of Survival.

Well, that's a Shame: I went to buy a cup of coffee con leche from the Santa Clara and they said that I couldn't drink it outside. I had to walk half a block down to La Sardana where the Jefe is a little less tight-assed. Shit, first my friends and kid are hassled for sitting in the sun, and now they think I'm going to steal their fucking coffee cup. Fuck them! They'll eventually make this place as bad as Harlem. Yah. Fuck them! We don't need any more up-tight assholes in this world. One of the Great Things about Spain, in the first place, is that the people are generally Tranquilo. Manana and all that. No Sweat. Organize all this shit, let Macdonalds and Burger King mentality in, and you've got Assholes everywhere. Someone ought to blow up the fucking television tower. Probably will, if they keep hassling Loafers. Give them something to do rather than Linger around the Square: Make Bombs and Blow Things Up.

Well, Kids! Guess What?! (WHAT? GIGOLO JACK!!) Howdy Donna's Back!! (YAYYYY!!! YAYYY!!! HOWDY DONNA'S BACK!!! YAYYY!!! YAYY!!! HIP HIP HOOOORAAAAYYY!!!). OK, OK, kids, settle down. I know you're excited now, but you'll get plenty of time to see her later. I've invited her over for lunch tomorrow afternoon. (YAYYY!!! HOWDY DONNA FOR LUNCH!!! YAYYY!!!). But, don't worry kids, Good Ole Uncle Frank has just walked off with her to show her where he lives. (BOOOO!! BOOO ON GOOD OLE UNCLE FRANK!!!). Don't worry kids, he probably just wants to talk to her about life. He doesn't even know who Howdy is! (WHATT?? HE DOESN'T KNOW WHO HOWDY DOODY IS??!!!). That's right, kids, so don't worry: he doesn't love puppets like I do. (YAYYY!!! HOWDY DONNA IS COMING!! YAYYY!!!).

Howdy Doody, Arnold Palmer, Muggings

HIT WITH A STICK, IT HURTS TO WRITE
"GIVE ME MONEY SO THAT I CAN LIVE, YOU MOTHERFUCKERS!"

Bread Street, (Pastry street), (Calle Llibreteria)

Evening, Winter, Barcelona, Gothick Barrio, Idiot Wind.
    I think I'll only work a couple of hours tonight. I don't really need the money. I have everything I need at the Pad. Except Pussy. (SEXIST! SEXIST! CAN'T YOU SEE ANYTHING ELSE BESIDES THEIR BODIES???). What do you want me to'do, look at their souls on the First Date? (YAHHH!!! THAT'S WHAT REAL POETS DO, GIGOLO JACK: LOOK AT THEIR SOULS!!). I wonder if Frank has finished showing Howdy Donna where he lives yet.
    There's an Andalucian Bum, one of the Denton Gang, looking like one of Howdy's pals, accosting the Tide with appeals for money to get some food. He decides who to panhandle by the simple expedient of asking whoever he happens to stumble into as he tries to keep from banging into the stone walls of the alley, which are about fifteen feet apart. He's not doing That great: about as good as me; about as well as I am.
    Ah, a beautiful, dark, Spanish Woman just stopped and gave me a quarter after I stared at her for a few seconds. I didn't want The Money, exactly. I wanted her kneeling in front.... Oh, never mind. (WHAT, GIGOLO JACK?? WHAT DID YOU WANT??). Just never mind, kids, It's not Really Important. (DID YOU SEE HER HIGH-HEEL BOOTS??). Yah.
    The Puppet-Bum-Andalucian has just headed upwind and I can smell the wine a half block away. He's got a good gimmick: he breathes on the people, they get high and give him money. Now he's wandered into a bookshop; I hope he doesn't eat the books. The One Thing that he Does do well is to point at his mouth while mumbling. He's wearing puppet-like cowboy boots, the kind Howdy wears (YAYYY!!), but he walks on the sides of the heels, like Jerry Lewis. The guy is a Sight! And, his face resembles Alfred E. Newman.

I think I'll quit early unless the Tide surprises me and rises. Clink. Ah, well, 25ptas. I wish Alfred E. Andalucian would split: he's giving Begging a Bad Name with this 'eating' bit.

I've Really Got To Piss; I hope someone I know comes along soon so they can watch this stuff while I go. The Ups and Downs of Street Life! Ah, I can hear the breakers approaching: the tide is rising. Clack, clack, clackety clack. Shit, payday was only last week: Is everybody broke already? Are the Pastry Shops almost empty? Give Me Money So That I Can Live, You Motherfuckers!

Billy, disguised as Arnold Palmer, just stopped by and told me that he did all right: 800 in an hour and a half. He IS the King of the Beggars: Even Jacques, who is the best Street Painter right now, doesn't come close. Peter is lucky that he got Billy for the trip to Italy before I did. Billy sure is a busy guy: His Job, pub-crawling at night with his bodyguards, Entertaining Nightly at Santi's: the whole social whirl. Too much! He eats as much candy, chocolate, and delicious pastries as he wants, with no thought to getting fat; if he does, he'll simply buy a new wardrobe. He just told me why he is spending most of his money in restaurants rather than shopping at the market like he and Rebecca used to: "I like to live comfortably, and Well, Rabbit just came by after his practice with the new band and bummed 30ptas out of the box so he could buy a gingerbread pastry for dinner. He told me he still plans on sleeping at my place tonight.

HIT WITH A STICK

Feb 14, 1985

I can barely type: I think my right hand is broken. My left elbow may also be broken: I'm in pain from the top of my head, where I was hit last night with a stick, to my ankles, and back, which were hit with the same stick. It was A Nightmarish Evening for me, and my friends. I remember a couple of skirmishes and have been told of a couple of others.

A man pointed a pistol at me right outside the pizza parlor near Plaza Regomir. I'm told that a man shoved me across some tables and chairs in the Opera cafe. I do remember the man with the 6ft stick, near my house, in Plaza Real, trying to kill me. I don't know why he was after me though. At one point I shoved him on to the ground, started to walk away after telling him that I didn't want to be involved with him any longer, what with his stick and all, but he got up and bonked me on the head from behind again. I put my hands up to protect my head while he flailed away at me until I was again able to knock him down and Back down the alley to my door.

I've lost my brown bag containing the last fifty or sixty pages of this book, along with the small tape recorder Hadass loaned me, and all of my personal shit. I have no idea where I lost it. I think it was stolen in the Opera Cafe. There's been a lot of discussion about what happened to the bag, today among the survivors. I believe I may also have a concussion.

Frank and Jacques both agree that I was lucky to have survived even the scene I caused at the Opera when I turned off the television set that was being watched by a gang of Moroccan Criminals. That bothered them, I'm told, but what made them even angrier was that I proceeded to lecture them about Idiocy and Television.

Essentially, I was almost killed three different times last night. I have quit drinking. This time for sure. It would probably be wise of me to stay indoors after the sun goes down: I have no idea how many pissed off people there are wandering around the Gothick Barrio, waiting for a chance to shut me up.

I have two new girlfriends as a result of staying sober today: I can actually talk when I'm not drunk. One, a German woman with an unpronounceable name, an Artist and Traveller. I think we've made a date for tomorrow evening, but I'm not sure because the pain is obscuring rational thought patterns, my spinal column is shooting messages all around my body indiscriminately, I can't tell what is going to come out of my mouth when I open it, I'm as surprised as the people I'm talking to. Very Spaced Out.

The other new girl is, like half the women here, named Maria Jose. She has a nickname which I can't remember or pronounce. She has been sitting here typing up her script for a cartoon that she is going to try to get an underground comic to publish. She's a Native, beautiful, dressed all in red, and extremely vivacious and sexy. I asked her if she wanted to be Lovers. She said that she will take it into consideration and let me know later. I told her, "That's what theyall tell me." Waiting Furthers. Sometimes.

I'm having a hard time typing because of the pain in my hand. When I stop typing and lean on my elbows there is an instant flash of pain. When I stand up it hurts. When I sit down, it hurts. It hurts to walk, and it hurts to sit. My body Just Plain Hurts. I want to retire to my beach front palapa. Just sit in the sun, swim in the ocean, and make love to one of my gals. That's the Vision.

Munch, Munch, Churn, Gabble, Stroll, and Chatt. That's the name of a famous Barcelona law firm. I may call this chapter 'It Hurts to Write'. I've got about 400 already, and may hobble on down to Santi's for a cafeconlech.

CARNIVAL IN SITGES?

Friday evening, five oclock, Bread street, plaza St. Juame, in front of the Santa Clara Cafe.

I slept (actually: tossed and sweated) from about midnight until noon today. I woke up every half hour or so and meditated on healing my body. I think it worked: I can walk today without wincing with each step. My head still hurts though, as do my elbows and hands, when I try to use them. I spent a couple of hours cleaning up the pad and added some tomatoes, onions, and garlick to the Eternal Stew.

It's a slow recovery, but it's beginning. I've counted up the pages that are missing: about forty-five pages. The Shame of the situation is that same of it was good: it was the week between two binges.

Tonight should be a fun night: it's the beginning of Carnival. Most of the Tapas crowd is heading for Sitges tomorrow, where Carnival is taken Frivolously; I may not accompany them: I have to work and recover. I don't think it would be much fun sober.

Carnival in Sitges is reputed to be one of the wildest in Spain. Sitges is the unofficial Gay Capitol of Spain, and they take their partying seriously, I'm told. Each Perversion has it's own group in the parade, with the Sodomites coming near the end.

Frank offered, in his usual wry and condescending manner, to obtain some Suicide Equipment for me. I told him that I was not a Suicide. He also told me that he Knew that I was going to be beaten with a stick the other night: that if they hadn't beat me with a stick, it would've been because they had stopped doing it altogether.

I saw Maria Jose today in passing, the girl in red, but she just waved and scurried on. I guess she's taken the 'Lovers' suggestion under consideration and decided against it. Too bad.

The churning is getting into full swing now; the usual strollers are mixing with the Halloweenies on their way to parties. I just need to make enough dinero to work on the stew and buy another bag of coffee. Mellow At The pad is showing tonight. I may even go so far as to wash some of my clothes in a bucket tonight. I have two weeks to came up with the 4,000 for January's rent. That figures out to about 300 per day that I should pay to Jacques to hold for me. I may make it. I like short-term goals like that, occasionally. Maybe I can sell some of my stuff; the stuff that wasn't stolen, that is. Maybe I should raise the price of the Menu at Meson Hadass to 150, and include pastry. Yah, that's it. Tonight is the night the German girl said she would get in touch with me; hope she does, it would be fun to share some stew with her. No Charge.

For some reason, the tide is out. I believe that it's temporary, and that there is another huge set due in a few minutes. After all, it is Carnival, is it not? Billy has stopped playing, Steve must be out of the bar. Billy's getting pretty good on the recorder; he's been playing for a couple of weeks now, and he's better than I am and I've been playing it for twenty years. Frank and Jacques told me that Billy has Redeemed himself as far as dope-smoking goes; he came into· Jacques' room last night and turned the two of them on with an unlimited offering of· hash. This makes up for his supposed Leeching, and not turning us on a few nights ago at the Opera.

Well, been out here for a couple of hours and there's 100 in the box. Maybe it's my Sick Vibes that are discouraging the duro-throwers. They see me and think, "He's almost dead, why should I give him money?". I saw myself in a mirror as I was walking around a minute ago, and I walk like a zombie because it hurts to swing my arms. Maybe that's it: I seem like a zombie to them, not even on the same life-plane.

The tide is out: all of the little goblins have disappeared and there is only a small flow of pastry-seekers. Billy made about 600 here in half an hour; I've been here two hours and made 90. Shit. He's headed off for Santi's to buy the house a round of drinks. I ought to go just to get a free cafeconlech.

Oh, well, there's always Manana. Bound to be good then. (YAH, WOUNDED-JACK, JUST LIKE IT WAS SUPPOSED TO BE TONIGHT!!). Say, where have you kids been. (WE LEFT WHEN YOU TURNED THE TV OFF IN THE OPERA CAFE!! WE WENT DOWN TO VALENCIA AND HUNG OUT WITH THE CLOWNS AGAIN!! WE HAD FUN!!). Ah, well, it's great to have you back. Clink. 25. (YAY!). Don't be sarcastic, kids; it's something. Well, here comes the tide again, for some unexplainable Spanish Reason. I guess that my life is back to Just Plain Getting By, again. I think the next time I get a lot of money I'll put some of it in the bank. (WHAT?? BANK!! BANK!! SAVE?? BE RESPONSIBLE?? STOP JUST COASTING THRU LIFE ON YOUR GOOD LUCK?? PLAN AHEAD?? GET SERIOUS?? LIFE IS NOT A GIFT??? IT'S A JOB!!). Sure, sure, sure. (PLAN FOR YOUR RETIREMENT??? FROM WHATTT??!!). Oh, forget it

Yah, Fuck it, I'll just go home and wash my clothes in a bucket, then hang them on the line on the patio. This will give me such a Responsible and Worthy feeling that my evening will be Meaningful, even If I can only make 60cents per day at my Chosen Profession: Street-Beggar-Writer. (DON'T GIVE UP FAITHFUL-JACK, SOMETHING WILL HAPPEN!!!). That's right, kids, something always happens: because of our positive Attitude. (FUCKIN'-A, RIGHT!!). Clink. Clink: see? A Hundred! (FUCKIN AYYY!!). ,

Hey, kids, here's a joke: 'Name two things that churn, one wears high heels.' (BUTTER, AND CATALANS!!!). That's right! How'd you know? (WE'RE IN YOUR HEAD, MEMORY-JACK!!!). Ah. (BUT WE'RE OVER ON THE RIGHT SIDE, AWAY FROM THE CONCUSSION!!!). Smart thinking.

Another hundred and I'm (WE! WE' RE GONE!!) gone. It's 730 already. That's It: clink, 100. (YAYYY!!! STEW TONIGHT!!!).

The Nightly Mugging and how it Came About

RABBIT, THE PAINTER AND POET

I worked here til about eight when Nuria joined me with some copies of the' photos she took of Hadass and me. I invited her to Meson Hadass for dinner at nine. I spent the 350ptas I had on more stuff for the stew, a liter of beer, and coffee. The Liter of Beer. Just one, thought Tolstoy. We had a mildly interesting conversation along with pretty good stew. We bought another liter of beer. Just one more, thought Tolstoy. Around eleven oclock we decided to head for the Opera Cafe to see what was cooking. Nothing was, so we parted, each heading for our separate abodes, theoretically.

I decided to head for Santi's, where I assumed the Gang would be. In plaza St. Juame I ran into Billy riding piggy-back on a Completely Drunk and Happy Rabbit. He'd played with the band yesterday for Carnival and made about seven mil. Billy told me that Rabbit had just drunk six whiskeys rapidly at Santi's. Rabbit Invited me to join Rebecca, Billy, and him for the evening, to celebrate.

Billy began treating me like a beggar; he kept saying, "Good Night, Jack!", over and over again, meaning I should leave.

I told him, "Hey, fuck you, man! Don't talk to me like that!"

Rebecca joined us and I followed them; Billy kept it up with the 'ditching' me, and "Good Night, Jack!", and like that. When they entered the Opera I turned back, not wanting to have to deal with the hangover from my actions there earlier in the week with the Moroccans and the TV. I started to walk home but as I thought of the way Billy and Rebecca had just been treating me I got angry and decided to head on back there and tell them so.

They were seated at a table with Gregorio, smoking volumes of hash, and drinking Voll Damm, the Rainier Ale of Spain.

I joined them and told Billy, "Just treat me as well as you would someone you don't know and I will have no problem with you. If you keep treating me rudely, I will hurt you." That seemed to settle the irritation for the night, and Rabbit began ordering me beer and passing the pipe. Rebecca was Being Madly In Love with Eduardo-Rabbit, and she and I had a couple of mild confrontations about her being rude to me also. They soon ended and we settled into High Inebriation for the duration.

Frank was sitting with a couple of young, female, San Francisco Anarchists who were in town to organize an anti-nuclear demonstration for today. Rebecca and Rabbit-Conejo insisted that I take some hash over to them, which I did. I fellowshipped with the girls about the S.F. County Jail and other hotspots in San Francisco for a while and then rejoined the New Little Family: Rabbit, Rebecca, and Billy.

Rabbit was far enough gone so that he was mainly staring at things, with occasional extremely loud outbursts like, "I Painter!", or "I Poet!", that would stop all conversation in the Cafe and draw the attention of the staff. He would then resume his stoney staring. Most people would have passed out under the influence of so much alcohol.

I had about five regular Beers, smoked continuously, and tried to stop Gregorio from talking like a god-damned Berkeley student intellectual (which he is), while Rebecca petted and swooned over Rabbi t and tried to get him to go dancing.

We all finally left when Rabbit's money ran out. I headed for Robber's Alley: Raurich, where I live. I entered my doorway where I collapsed on the steps and watched the pretty patterns that the Hash had unlocked from somewhere. I sat there for quite a while until I heard some people speaking English right outside. I unlocked the grate and went out into the street and joined the conversation about which bar to go to next. We were soon joined by three Spanish-type Moroccans. We all talked for a few minutes and then the English left. I unlocked the gate/door and all of a sudden the three entered also, one pushing me up against the wall while another held a knife to my neck and the third stood lookout.

One of them spoke English, so I told him, "If you want to rob me, fine, just don't kill me." He told the guy with the knife to relax, which he did, though he kept the knife near my neck, just not jabbing it, and we continued with the profitless (almost profitless: they got my empty wallet) robbery. We all shook hands and went our separate ways; they to find a more fruitful victim, me: to bed. Another Fucking Mugging.

ANOTHER MUGGING

Five oclock. Same spot.

At two oclock I had 100ptas and went shopping for vegies and fruit. Passing down Calle Avinyo, about a block from the pad, I heard, "Policia! Policia!", and looked up the road and saw four eighteen-year-old Moroccans (we always suppose that they are Moroccans) rounding the corner at Calle Fernando and heading towards me at Sprinter Speed. They were huffing and puffing; they looked like they had been running for a couple of minutes. I stood there in the middle of the street as they passed by a couple of feet away. I saw that the fourth one was holding something under his jacket, which I presumed to be a stolen purse, and I had about two seconds to decide whether to throw myself in front of him, try to trip him, or dodge. I pictured the other four stopping and returning if I dropped the one with the bag. I 'Passed' on the opportunity, partly because of my two recent muggings. MAYBE the bystanders would have joined in if I had tripped him, Maybe Not. I saw the Ladrones slow to a walk a couple of blocks further on, secure in their freedom, they thought, as the Victim carne walking around the same corner. He was out of breath, about fifty or sixty years old, walking with determination, and Obviously Foreign. He was pissed, for sure, but there was No Way he was going to get the money back; the Purse or Bag: possibly, if he could find where they threw it in the Maze of alleys down by Escudillers. By the time I got home I was ashamed of myself for not tripping the one with the purse. There's been an overabundance of petty crime and violence in my life lately, though.

Sitges, Sitges, Who's Going to Sitges?

According to Frank, Carnival is banned in Barcelona; has been since Franko's time. He says that the only party here tonight will be the Demonstration in Favor OF having Carnival. Doesn't sound too great.

Frank and Peter have walked off to see how Jacques is doing on the street today, with the instructions that I delay the two anti-nuclear American girls who are scheduled to meet Frank here before going to Carnival in Sitges, should they arrive. They will be difficult to miss: one has a ring in her nose and the other has her head shaved in strips. Frank says he's known one of them for years; knew her in Paris and many other places. She's only about twenty-five or so; must have been leading an active life.

Billy says that he is going to Carnival in Sitges tonight. I suppose he will be going with his new parents, Rabbit and Rebecca, although when I asked him he said, "I'm going with everybody!", whatever he thinks that means.

He asked me, "Why aren't you going to Sitges tonight?"

"Why do you ask that?", I asked.

"Ellen told me you weren't going.", he told me.

"Oh.", I said. There was a twenty second pause, while I kept typing.

"Well, Why aren't you going?", he asked.

"How do you know I'm not?", I asked.

"Well? Are you going or not?!", he demanded.

"I'm not sure, Maybe, Probably not: I don't know.", I told him, clearing up the matter once and for all.

Maybe I'll go to Sitges with Ellen, if she's going; I'll have to ask Billy whether Ellen is going, or not.

During Siesta today I bathed myself, with warm water heated in the stew pot. I also washed my other set of clothes in a bucket: The First time in my life I washed my own clothes by hand, since the Navy. I was almost laughing as I watched myself stooped down in that little bathroom, scrubbing, rubbing, and rinsing, All to save·200ptas. Reminded me of being a disciple at the Macrobiotick/Astrology Commune where I spent a year once learning how to cook rice and tell fortunes. (YAYYY FOR MAHATMA JACK!!. Hi, kids.

Peter says that even if I don't have enough money, I should just go down to the station and get on the train to Sitges: the conductors will probably be too busy to collect from everybody, "Just Fake it.", he told me. I'd rather pay my own way. Sense of Pride, and all that. (IS HE KIDDING??). Just kidding, kids, just kidding.

The Anarchist Girls just dropped by; they may be going to Sitges, maybe not. I gave them the address of my apartment in San Francisco, that is currently being used by the guy that ended up with what remained of my sailing business when I left. He got the business. And my apartment. Let him figure out what to do with a couple of Really Freaky Anarchists. They'll be heading back to SF in March, presumably after spreading Anarchism in all of the European capitals?

Shit, I'm still undecided on whether or not to go to Sitges tonight. Sergio, the guitar player, just passed by. I asked him if He was going to Sitges tonight. He said he wouldn't go even if he wasn't working tonight, "I don't want to see it.", he explained. That's a Mark against it. I'll just let the score build up, pro and con, until the scoreboard makes a decision for me.

Tracy the dancer just stopped by to pull my beard, give me 25ptas, and refuse my apology for what I can't remember the other night at the Opera.

"You're Shit when you're drinking, and I'm Too Good to hang around with Shit!", she told me. I explained that I am schizophrenic and that the Shit side of me is my Mr. Hyde, and I don't really care for him that much either, he recently gave me a concussion. Tracy 'may' go to Sitges. Ah, well, 400 total in the box, and I'm going to stay out here for another hour. Got enough for the trip to Sitges, now.

Amani is Not going to Sitges tonight: he says he's been to Carnival in Rio and that Nothing in the World can even come close to Carnival in Rio; it lasts a week and they spend almost the whole year preparing for it. He says that I can get to Rio cheaply from Bogota when I'm there, which will be in a couple of years, or three. Tonight is Amateur Night for Dancing In The Street, and since Amani is A Pro, he is spending the evening writing in his room. Score another.

The Question of the Night has changed to: "Would Dr. Jackyll have a good time in Sitges tonight?" We know Mr. Hyde would, but he's been confined to quarters as long as we can feel the concussion. Amani said that Ellen is Going, but we can't score with second-hand info.

Sam, an Egyptian who speaks English with a British accent, just stopped by to bum a light and told me that he too was robbed last night, the fourth time since he's been here, only in his case he put both robbers in the hospital, with his fists; He was sober. He said he'd like to stop by some time so we can chat about books. I said Fine, let's do it some time. He's going to Carnival in Sitges tonight.

Steve just stopped by with the news that the best time to have gone to Sitges was this afternoon: the trains will all be crowded tonight. And, besides that, the best Carnival celebration in Sitges will take place next Tuesday. I don't know how to score this information: Steve has been known to confuse his facts a bit, from time to time. He has beat me to the Punch: shaved his beard, and for the first time we get to see his face; looks like Hitler: he left a moustache.

THE NEXT DAY, WHY I DIDN'T GO TO SITGES FOR CARNIVAL

Sunday, Plaza St. Juame. 5PM

I made it through the night without getting mugged or hassled. I hope it's a precedent. I didn't make it to Sitges: stayed in Barcelona. I quit at about 8:30 with 7 or 800ptas, and was heading for the pension to drop off the stuff when I ran into Peter, Emma, Whitey, Billy, Ellen, Phil, and Rene (back from her month-long trip to Italy for a couple of days before heading for New York), on their way to the train station. I asked them if they would wait for me while I dumped my shit upstairs. They said they couldn't. I assume that party Momentum had them, that it was nothing personal.

Phil and Rene stopped me and said that I could accompany them to Sitges. I thought about it and finally decided that I wasn't going after all, probably, unless I ran into Jacques and Frank and they were on their way there.

Events and Attitudes were helping me decide, as I'd hoped they would. As I headed for Santi's I encountered Frank boogeying up the street with Shining Eyes and Joyous Expectation on his face, hot on the trail of the rest of the crowd. They were to meet at the station.

I wished him a Fun Night, which was likely because he was going to take LSD, as he says he does for every Carnival in Sitges.

I hit all of my favorite stores on the way to the pad and picked up ham, eggs, onions, beer, bread, and a special treat: mustard. I was planning an American Truck Stop Ham and Eggs Sandwich Special for myself for Carnival in the Pad.

I no sooner got back than I heard the knocker announcing guests below. I peered over the balcony and was delighted to see Phil and Rene, quaking in the Robbery Breeze of Calle Raurich, begging admission to the Castle. I dropped them the keys and they soon joined me for Stew, beer, olives and congenial carnival Conversation. It was Rene's last night in Barcelona, and with Phil, for quite a while. He may join her in the US sometime, but he and I tried to persuade her that her place is here, and that she should return as soon as she can. She said that she didn't want to be poor, so, was planning a career in the States. We finally agreed that she could get rich there and then spend about 6 months a year here, in love with Phil. He's all for it.

The ham, egg, and mustard sandwiches were Delicious: a little bit of home for the first time in a couple of months. Around midnight they decided to head for home; I accompanied them as far as Escudillers for protection, where I bought another liter of beer and we parted with hugs and kisses as the transvestites and drunken robbers churned and stumbled around us. I went home.

I celebrated Carnival, for the rest of the evening, by reading . William Blake's critique of Bishop Watson's letter to Thomas Paine, which was a public attack on Paine's 'Age Of Reason'. It made me laugh.

I retired around two or three oclock to the sounds of screams, drums, firecrackers and bombs, and generally riotous noises emanating from all around the barrio six floors below. I even locked the door just to be sure that no drunken robbers came up and mugged me while I was asleep. I had to break the pattern, and was taking no chances. It worked; I slept til about one this afternoon, still healing my battered body with too much sleep and good food.

This afternoon I encountered Jacques, leaning like a stone against the stone walls in Plaza St. Juame. He had just been run out of Santi's by Rabbit's usual ravings: "I ARTISTA! I FREEDOM! HA!", and like that. Jacques said he'd just wanted to read his book but was unable to because Rabbit kept good-natured-drunkenly interrupting. I moseyed down to Santi's where I found Rebecca and Rabbit perched on bar-stools in the Crowded front. Rabbit had been up for two days drinking. Rebecca looked like she had gotten some sleep. Rabbit was ordering Rainier Ale on credit and it looked like he had no intention of slowing down, as he had no place to sleep. I wondered out loud why Rebecca had not offered for him to sleep at her place. I told him that he could sleep this afternoon at Meson Hadass. He accepted and I helped him navigate the streets, the stairs, and helped him find the bed when we got there. He was asleep seconds after falling on the bed. I left, and haven't returned all day for fear of waking him up. He looked like he was going to become ill pretty soon if he didn't get some sleep. His cuts aren't healing very well these days, either, a sign of Terminal Alcohol poisoning which indicates a needed change in one's lifestyle, don't you think. I hope he isn't thrashing around and destroying the pad as I write this.

He and Rebecca were up most of the night dancing in the streets and plazas allover Barcelona, but I guess he was too crazy to go home with her and get some sleep. He missed his gig at 8 this morning with the three man band.

I've gotten Peter's, Emma's, and Whitey's reports on Sitges: Peter says that it was much milder than last year. Emma got drunk and passed out on the beach. Whitey partied until he got tired at around 4 this morning. All said that the transvestites virtually ruled the show; they were packed in allover Sitges, elbow to elbow, silicone breast to breast. The dancing was still going on when they all left at dawn. Whitey ran into Suzanne in a bar and says that she was wearing a homemade tinfoil dress, with her huge breasts hanging out. It's Her Territory, for sure.

I haven't had a report from Billy, Frank, or Ellen, yet, presumably because they are still sleeping, although Peter says that Billy was smoking hash for most of the night and was seen dancing and mock-fighting on the beach early in the morning. It turns out that Steve was right about the Main Parade being held next Tuesday; maybe I'll be ready for that one.

On the Street, as Usual

RABBIT, TRACY AND CROW

MESON HADASS

Five oclock. Tuesday. Santa Clara Cafe (in front of it, rather).

Stayed up til four last night, reading "The Catalans", a detailed account of who they are, why, where they come from, in English. Turns out there's more to this independence kick they're on than I first suspected: at one time they controlled about a third of Spain, southern France, Sicily, Mallorca, half of Italy, and Greece. They were the Greatest Power in the Mediterranean. This was around 1400 and lasted for about three hundred years. It's no wonder they don't like, even this far down the history line, being called a province of Madrid. They really aren't 'Spanish'. I just found out. And yet, the first time I ever heard of 'The Catalans' was when I arrived in Catalonia; and I've read a lot of history. Some, anyway. Well, a bunch.

This morning on my way back from the bread store I heard yelling, "Ladrone! Ladrone!". I looked up the alley and saw a 'Moroccan' running towards me with a purse under his arm. I saw the victims round the corner five seconds behind him. I had plenty of time to decide whether or not to tackle, trip, or hit him with my bag. I decided not to. I was scared. Two weeks ago: no problem, I would have thrown myself at him. Now: Uninvolved Spectator. I was afraid that the other robbers who hang out on Calle Raurich (in the Tanger Bar) would get involved or that I would become a marked man in the neighborhood.

Carrying a heavy cane or a gun are the only ways I can figure out to resolve my feelings on this Everyday Violence. Jose-Luis, the Newspaper Writer from Mexico, a friend of mine, says that he saw a guy get stabbed, during the day, in plaza Real, and the stabber left and returned a few minutes later with a Samurai Sword and was going to decapitate the guy but was unable to catch him after a three block chase. He says that the police acted like Keystone Cops the whole time and were not even able to see the would-be killer, let alone stop or arrest him. I said that we ought to get together and write an article about the ridiculous amount of crime taking place in and around plaza Real, like in front of my house. He said that it would, as usual, be pointless: everything is controlled by The Syndicate; the cops even have their own un-official rules about this sort of thing. All I know is that I have either been involved with, or seen, same sort of violence in my neighborhood every day for two weeks. And I don't spend that much time there. The Fix must be IN, for Petty Legalized Crime in that area, huh?

I guess this is turning into "Barcelona, Under the Influence of Purse-Snatchers…". Alan, an Englishman, and his unpronouncably named Chinese wife, who I met yesterday, were robbed yesterday afternoon near Estacion Francia. They'd only been in town three days and were looking for an apartment to rent. They planned to stay here for a while. They've been travelling in China, India, Egypt, and like that. They are going to be moving on now, because she is afraid to even walk around in the streets here. They were mellowly walking along, he about five feet in front, when a black and a moroccan grabbed her bag and dragged her while she tried to hang on to it. By the time Alan heard what was happening and turned around to look, she was about fifty feet away; she let go of the bag because she was being bumped along the ground at a high speed: she only weighs eighty pounds and both of the robbers were running with her between them. Alan, who is in good shape, about thirty-five years old, pursued the robbers but was unable to keep up with them even at his top speed. They are probably recently retired from chasing gazelles through the jungle. Score another PR victory for Personal Freedom in Barcelona; isn't it Great?

I find my self in the strange position (for me) of desiring more police protection, yet appreciating the lax attitude towards drug use. Robbers and Drug Use are not necessarily connected, I rationalize. Ivan, the Irish lawyer who has been living here for about ten years, says that part of the problem is that there is a conflict between the police and the judiciary: the cops feel that even when they do arrest someone, justice is not served. They're let go on bail if it's their first offence, a relatively new law on the books here. So, they don't police the town that well, as a result. Also, he adds, the police in Spain have, for the last forty years, been recruited mainly to harass and beat the public, and are not yet skilled at patrolling against crime. He thinks it will change when there are more complaints from other countries about the safety of tourists in Spain. I hope so. Drugs: yes; Knocking Down Old Ladies: no.

Ivan read in the paper about a woman who had her purse snatched the other day on Calle Boqueria, the shopping street just on the other side of plaza St. Juame, wherein the robber was knocked down by a civilian. The robber slashed the guy with a machete. The police approached and the robber started to attack them. They shot him, not killing him, but breaking his arm. This is not the news I wanted to hear: Now I have even less reason for stopping the next Ladrone I see. Maybe I could wear a disguise and linger with a big club on Calle Raurich, club the ladrones as they pass, then run away and remove the disguise. I suppose I would probably get hassled by the cops, depending on how weird the disguise was.

I am living for the post Office and The Stew, with an occasional distraction by Sleeping and Drinking Coffee. The duros per hour have dropped so low that I have to be out here each and every day just to get by. No Sightseeing or Carousing, at this point. One of the highlights of the day: my first piece of Chocolate. Now. (YAYY!! OUR LIFE HAS MEANING!! CHOCOLATE!!)

THE DAILY LADRONE REPORT:

1. Amani saw a girl's purse get snatched, and her boyfriend caught one of the three robbers and began hitting him. The other two came back to help their fellow robber but took off when they saw Amani coming, and all three escaped with the purse.
2. Gregorio was playing his recorder the other night near the cathedral, when a ladrone came up to him and tried to take some of his stuff. Greg made as though to hit him with the recorder and the guy went for his knife. He was stopped from further violence by the arrival of a man with two dogs, and made his escape.
3. Last night at the cathedral, while playing, Greg saw the same Ladrone, with two of his partners, accost three Catalans and demand money from them, threatening to pullout their knives. They were given money and let the victims escape. On their way past Greg they threw same duros in his box and told him to keep playing.
4. Jacques ran into a red-headed Swedish girl at the post office who has been here a week, has a job here, and intends staying for a while. As she was leaving he told her to be careful with her bag, which was slung over her shoulder. She said she already knew, showing him the red bruises on her neck.

Well, I've been out here an hour and a half and have made 30ptas. Ridiculous. ("What are you giving them, Jack?", I can hear Jacques asking) . Well, if you want to make fun of me, go ahead. Just remember this: I'm making more money writing My first book than Henry Miller made writing His.

Well, I got my rent money out of the bank (Jacques), all 500 of it and went to the Ramblas market, where for 200ptas I bought: a kilo of tomatoes, 1/2 kilo of onions, 1/2 kilo of oranges, 1/2 kilo of squash, some mushrooms, a head of lettuce, 1/2 kilo of green peppers, a kilo of carrots, and some olives. I also bought a loaf of bread, 3 eggs, a 100gram package of coffee, mailed a letter to Israel, and paid my 25pta dope-dealer debt. All that for 500ptas.

I'm now broke again but I have enough supplies for Days. What a place. I've been paying two or three times what I could have been, for the last month, by shopping in the 7-ll's near my house. I have enough supplies in stock to keep the place open for about a week, if we're not evicted for failure to pay the rent. Well, that's the way the restaurant business is; you never know.

Ah, well, I've made 30ptas so far, which I just spent on a gingerbread cowflop: Ah, living good now! (YAYY!! HE'S EATING COWFLOPS!! OOWFLOPS??). I'm happy, alright, either because I got more stuff for the stew, or, like all Americans, I'm satisfied now that I got to Spend. Or because I feel most comfortable when I have absolutely No Money to worry about spending. I don't have a Peseta to my name, or my pocket.

Jacques, sitting in the Santa Clara Cafe, is telling me in sign language through the window that my gourd has taken off. He is experiencing what the Catalans must go through every day as they sit in there and look out the window at the Hell's Angel sitting at a typewriter, begging.

Jacques suggested earlier, "Jack, just change your head visuals and you life will change also." He was referring to my wandering hair and beard. I'm still planning to shave my beard when I can afford a razor and some shaving cream.

Jose-Luis, the writer from Mexico, who lives here and writes articles for the local papers, invited me for a Cafeconleche in the Santa Clara. I carried my typewriter in with me, and proceeded to knock an old lady's cup of chocolate into her lap with my bag while trying to get into my seat. I explained that I had done it because I am an "Estranjero Estupido". Her friend agreed. The Jefe came over and angrily told me I couldn't bring my typewriter into the bar, and asked me to leave; he just plain doesn't like me sitting out there on the street, I suppose. We headed down to the Sardana, where I had a couple of cafeconleches and we chatted about writing and different books that we're reading or have read. He said that he will be bringing a book by Bukowski for me Tomorrow; but cautioned me that Tomorrow doesn't necessarily mean Tomorrow, "After all, I'm Mexican.", he told me.

Tracy is walking around town carrying a new foam mattress on her head. She is having trouble with wisecracks and propositions from every macho male that she passes. She and Crow have moved out to their new pad in the country, actually the industrial district, about ten miles north of here. They are setting up housekeeping. Tracy says that she wants a baby now that they have a washing machine; as I told her would happen, a few weeks ago.

"I have to start disciplining myself.", she admitted, finally realizing what everyone, Everyone, has been saying for months. "Years! Years!", she corrects me. She says that she is trying to find 'my little german friend'; she won't tell me if he's her lover because she said I would write about it. I told her that I wouldn't. I think he IS her lover.

"Where's Crow tonight?", I asked.

"He had to make a quick trip to Atlantis.", she told me.

"Ah.", I said.

She's taken off with the flute player for Casa Peret to get some chow.

"Stay off your back!", I told her.

She dropped about fifty lpta coins in the box, one at a time, to make me feel rich. It worked: I feel rich. 150ptas in 3 hours. Shit.

CATALAN BREAD

Thursday, Feb 21, 1985, Santa Clara Cafe

Well, at least if I am evicted, It will be in good health: I'm getting plenty of sleep. Slept til two today, helped by a bottle of wine I drank at the Meson last night. It's been a week since the last binge, but I have been drinking a liter of beer each night, without venturing out into the Barcelona Night. There have been no confrontations because I don't yell at myself. I finished reading the book about the Catalans and I've finally figured out why they say they're not Spanish: they're not Spanish. Barcelona has been attacked, defended, and sacked about ten times in the last thousand years: French, Castillan, French, and on and on. Most of the political action has taken place in the Generalitat, the building about fifty feet to my right, where the state government still sits. The Catalans have had their ancient rights, 'fieros', taken from them and re-instated over and over again. It's no wonder they're so adamant about being Catalan, and not Spanish. There is a Castillan proverb, "The Catalans can make bread from stones." Whether this means they are able to, or they should have to, I'm not sure. They Could Have Ruled The World.

THE DAILY BARCELONA, CATALUNYA, LADRONE REPORT

Last night, around 8:30, as I was approaching the pad with a bag of groceries for the Meson, I was passed by a running twelve year old Moroccan boy, carrying nothing. He looked terrified. About ten seconds later a Brown Cop (Policia Nacional, the second heaviest), rounded the corner at a full gallop with his stick out. I stood at the corner near my house and watched them disappear towards Escudillers. There came a scream and yelling from the direction of plaza Real and I looked up the other street into the plaza to see a crowd running, yelling, and surging towards Calle Fernando. At this time the first brown cop returned with. the kid in tow, while a second rounded the corner and headed into Plaza Real. He returned, followed by a crowd of about fifty excited Spanish, with a teenaged Moroccan in tow. They met about ten feet from me and tried to figure out what to do next. The crowd was surging around them, chattering like mad. I was the only one who had no idea what was going on, but I could guess. The cops kept pushing their prisoners around and yelling at them. The kid was not quite in tears, but was scared shitless. There were arguments going on between the cops and a group of Moroccans who had some sort of interest in either the kid or the teenager, or both. One of the Denton Gang, drunk, with his face painted up like Cochise, was relaying the cops' instructions to the crowd to stand back and move along, and like that. It had a mild circus atmosphere about it. After a few minutes of animated discussion, amongst the cops, crowd, denton gang, and Moroccan relatives, the cops walked off with their prisoners, presumably to the line-up. Another normal evening on Calle Raurich. Too bad it was only a kid; probably just a beginner, which explains his capture. END OF LADRONE REPORT. MORE AT ELEVEN.

BILLY AND THE BROWN PIGS, AGAIN
I PATRONIZE ELLEN, AGAIN

Ellen and Billy just joined me. Billy just had a run-in with the Brown Police:
"How old are you?", they asked him in Spanish.
"Twelve."
"That's very young."
"For What?", Billy asked.
"For playing out here."
"Is there an age requirement?", Billy asked.
"No Limitation,", the cop answered, "Are you here with your parents?"
"Yes."
"Do you live with them?"
"Yes, with my mother."
"Does she work?"
"Yes, she teaches English."
"Does she have money?"
"Yes, for her.", Billy wisely answered, "She pays for my pension, but I buy my own food."
The cops walked off, probably clucking their moral tongues.
I was telling Ellen about it and she found it highly amusing, she was squealing and laughing.

I told her, "Well, in the States they would just arrest Billy, put him in a foster home, and take the parents to court for being bad parents." This she found Absolutely Hilarious.

"It's not really funny, you know.", I told her.

Billy said, "Rebecca has custody of me; you're not supposed to take care of me anyway. It's no problem for you."

I didn't like either of their attitudes, at this point, and said, "You sure got that all fucked up! Do you think it says that I'm not 'Supposed' to take care of you? It's just a piece of paper! I don't give a fuck about it! Same as I don't give a fuck about any piece of paper! It's in the States! you're still my son, no matter what you think, or what the fucking paper says!"

Ellen walked away irritated, saying, "You're pretty aggressive today!"

"FUCK YOU!", I yelled at her.

Billy left, dropping a piece of candy wrapper in my money box, at which I told him, "And don't drop any more garbage in my box!" Fuck them, the little brats. She thinks cops are funny, and he believes lies.

Ellen probably thinks that this is a 'nice' world, and that 'aggression', whatever she thinks that is, is out of place here. She can't grasp that I wasn't being aggressive, in my terms, but only trying to explain something clearly and with some energy. I suppose that she thinks of talking in a loud voice as 'violence'. There are many like her. The word she was looking for was 'vehement'. Had she found even the correct word, she was misunderstanding that it wasn't 'vehemence' 'today', but just this particular subject. I'm pretty sure that she thinks that I am in 'a bad mood' again. This kind of conversation and social interaction almost drives me crazy because of it's total worthlessness, and it's potential rumor-mill value. 'Oh, I saw Jack, and he's in a bad mood again', Shit like that. Ugh.

Billy is temporarily prevented from playing, on this street, because Steve is out here, so he tried the street near the cathedral but was immediately run off by the Blues. Well, I've made about 400 so far and have bought a 'morene' (gingerbread cowflop) and 2 packs of Celtas, and a piece of chocolate. Moving right along: I wonder what is Different about tonight, compared with last night when I made almost nothing? I wonder? (YOU'RE WEARING YOUR WRITER'S OVERCOAT, CHAMELEONJACK!!!). Oh, yah. On top of this I'm going to put on my beret and pull it down over my ears; Looking Weird will probably help. (WHAT'S NEW ABOUT THAT???) .

Ellen just read what I wrote about the earlier confrontation and told me that it was. "not a Humorous Laugh, but a laugh of surprise". I told her that laughter is generally related to as a positive Response. She didn't want to hear that. I said it again. She refused it. In her case, laughter and shrieking are to be related to as something other than positive, I suppose. I'll have trouble with that, as I suspect others will. As she left to get a cowflop I said, "You're sure in a Sensitive Mood Today!" She didn't smile. She came back with the cowflop, we talked, and have come to a mutual understanding about our roles in the preceding interaction. All is well, I guess. Til the next time.

FRANK AND ELLEN PLAY TENNIS IN THE SANTA CLARA CAFE

Ellen has just joined Frank for a chat in the Santa Clara Cafe. He has her now: he's leaning over the table, gesticulating with his hands and attacking with his reasonable and insistent voice, slinging the ideas into her virgin mind with an accuracy and force which she will only appreciate in the future when they start bubbling to the surface. She is being molded right before our eyes. He's got her wide open now: she's laughing. She's even talking herself, occasionally: telling Frank what She Thinks about whatever subject he's introduced. What I find fascinating is that I even find any of this interesting: Reasoning, Arguing, Speculating, Planning, Comparing, Questioning, Considering, Analyzing: It's All Fishing. A bunch of little fishing trips being mistaken for the Grand Quest For Truth. Distracting by it's Ubiquitousness. (YAYYYY!!! YAYY!! WE LOVE IT!! YAYY!!!) .

Billy has joined Frank and Ellen after reading my version of what was probably happening in there. He's a spy for the Street-Writer.

Watching them in the Cafe is like watching a tennis match wherein Frank Serves, doesn't wait for a return, Serves again, doesn't wait, and then Serves Again. After four or five serves, with no return, he allows a hit from Ellen, which he then smashes into her court. Billy is a dysfunctional linesman/observer, I'm the Goodyear Blimp. She will eventually develop a good defense, but will never be able to serve.

FRIDAY, FEB 22. 11:30. SANTA CLARA CAFE, OUTSIDE

Still here. Still poor. No wounds or regrets from last night. Had the Regular Customers at Meson Hadass last night, drank a liter of wine and went to sleep about two. Wage-Slave Lifestyle, Waiting, Waiting: Don't know for what. Big Item on the Agenda: Pay the Rent. Living to pay the rent. I've placed an ad in the local paper: "Foreigner seeks position in Hardware Store. No Experience." I should be getting sane calls on that. (DID YOU LEAVE A PHONE NUMBER, WANT-AD JACK???). No.

Well, a guy just came up and gave me 175ptas in one swell foop. You see what Energy, Drive, and Thrift can accomplish? (YAYY!! FOR THE

EARLY-WORM JACK!!!). That's 'Early Bird', kids. (Oh! YAYY!! FOR THE EARLY-WORM EARLY-BIRD!!). Idiots. (SAY GOODNIGHT, JACK!!!). Goodnight Jack.

The Tapas Report: Ellen and Steve were singing Blues in the back of the cavern. Rabbit was drunk. Sergio speaks five languages. That's it.

The Street Report: Ellen has taken a break from playing and is sitting beside me, eating a cowflop in which she has found paper and hair. Billy hasn't been working but is eating cookies anyway. Rabbit has given him some beautiful jewelry: two rings and a bracelet. One of the rings is cast in the shape of a nude woman bending over backwards in a circle; Very Beautiful, in fact.

I asked him, "Are they Hot?"

"No, They're Cool.", he told me.

Billy offered to entertain Santi's guests for him last night if Santi would name a price. Santi did: "One punch for every note."

Rabbit and Billy went out bar-hopping last night; one of them was completely drunk; and ended up on the Ramblas with Rabbit accidentally assaulting passersby while giving Billy a demonstration of Tai-Chi.

According to the rumor-mill Tracy has broken up with Crow on their first night at the new pad. Frank's explanation is that Crow is a Passive-Dependent Personality and Tracy just found out when they set up housekeeping that he expected her to take care of him. She is back walking the streets with a mattress on her back, looking for some Kind Person to take her in. Looking for a place to live. Wish I could help her, but I don't want to get involved in a Space Triangle.

Gregorio just stopped by in his Moroccan disguise, a stocking cap pulled down to his eyes and a funky overcoat, and wondered why he isn't making much on the street these days. He was chewing on a piece of butter and munching on whole wheat bread. I wonder why.

COLD STONE STREETS (YAYY! 1)

Winter has settled back in; it's cold and overcast, seems like it will be permanent, though it's not Siberian at all. It's just brisk enough to remind you that you're alive, and should be wearing warm clothes and have a room to sleep in if you don't want to spend a Very Miserable Night sleeping in the Cold Stone Streets. {YAYYY!!! PROSE!!!). Cold Stone Streets. Cold Stone Streets. (YAYYY!!!). They're So Easy. Billy is playing his recorder down the street, accompanied by the baying of a german shepherd; a perfect duo.

MUSEUM HADASS

Frank thinks that someday Meson Hadass will be a Museum or Shrine, that admission will be charged to see where it all happened, "They will be coming up here saying, 'This is where they figured it all out! This is where it all began!', because we're up here, Renaissance Men of our Generation!", he said, while looking around the room with eyes shooting beams of light through clouds of Blue Hash Smoke.

Frank told us how some of his fingers, on both hands, became so deformed. He was a football hero in High School, played end, wide receiver, and would, in his Quest for Glory, play game after game with broken fingers. He'd break them on the first pass of the game and then swallow his pain, tell no one, and keep playing, All For Glory. At least he got it at an early age: The Rest of Us are still seeking it: I've been Almost Shot, Almost Stabbed, and Beat with a Stick in It's Quest, Recently. And Jacques is still trying to become famous as 'The Hunchback of Barcelona'. It Were Better For Us Had We Breaked Our Several Digits In Our Tender Years.(WHAAAAT???). It's prose, kids, I thought you would like sane Art, for a chanqe, (OH). (WE WANT CHOCOLATE!!! WE WANT CHOCOLATE!! NOT PROSE! CHOCOLATE!!). OK, OK, Chocolate it is.

RABBITS NEW HAT. THE PURPLE FAIRY. CHRISTIAN CLOWNS

Rabbit has bought himself a new Italian Straw Hat, to replace the ridiculous cloth ballcap that he's been wearing for the last month; a gift from Antonio. Now he doesn't look like a Complete idiot. He's upgrading his act, and spending his rent money. His deal for the 6 MIL apartment fell though "Because I South American", he told me. I don't know what he meant by that and when I tried to find out, we got lost in Translation valley. Phil, who is standing here reading (he made the mistake of asking me 'what's new' and I handed him a stack of pages), tells me that Rabbit says the reason the police hassle him, and Not Phil, is the same: "I South American". That's not all there is to it: he just happens to be Completely Socially Obnoxious, and Visually Offensive To The Max. He looks like a, yes, Rabbit. The purple fairy, one of my Regular Fans, at this point, just strolled by and said, "I don't have time to waste on you today, Sweetheart!" I told him, as he swished off, "1 consider that a blessing!"

Billy and Conejo just rejoined Phil and me; Conejo bringing me a Cafeconlech.

Billy said, "Wow, you're making more money than I am, Jack!"

"That's the way it's supposed to be.", I told him.

"Bullshit!", he answered his Father.

For a while there, Phil, Rabbit, Billy, Jacques, and a couple of girls I don't know, were completely ganging up on the pitch. I finally asked them to move along for a while and give the Tide the option of feeding the writer-Urchin. (YAYY!! URCHINS!!). Well, for sure the Tide is in: only it's the dreaded Estranjero Tide: Tracy, Peter, Billy, Jacques, Phil, Rabbit, and the purple Fairy. Great.

Tracy just came up with the Question of the Week, "Is he Gay?", she asked about the Old purple Fairy.

"Is this a typewriter?", Jacques asked her, pointing at this typewriter.

I just gave Jacques another 100 for the rent: total paid now: 400. Tracy is dancing the crowds over to the other side of the alley. My Catalan business advisor, a middle-aged man named Juame (pronounced Howma) has just informed me that the Catalan Newspaper 'Avui' printed an article about me a couple of days ago, and he has given me 100ptas and a gift from his heart: a little, old, book called 'visions of catalonia'. I'm Seriously Touched by this.

Five oclock. Same Spot.

I was just surrounded by Christian Clowns. They said they are attending 'Discipleship Training' here in Barcelona and were wearing whiteface in preparation for a skit they had just performed. The skit, as you might guess, is about The Crucifixion of Jesus, a famous Jew, and, of course, the famous Resurrection. They were ganging up on me, being led by the Chief Witnesser.

"Haven't you got a little tract or something you can give me?", I asked, sarcastically. They gave me a little cartoon tract that presumably explains Sin, Salvation, and the Blood of the Lamb, in Spanish.

They gave me a mini-quiz about who sold his birthright: Esau, I passed. The next question will probably be "Do you have a personal relationship with God?" They are hopeless lingerers. I've asked them to move a little bit back from the money-box. They've complied, but are still in an amazing lingering mode. I had to explain to them that I Live from the money thrown into the box, hint, hint. They gave me two duros and continued to surround me, staring obnoxiously. I finally got up and went across the alley and joined Phil, who was leaning against a building watching the show. They finally left.

My fame is beginning to spread; first the article in the newspaper here about me, and now a man from New York who is here doing an article for a travel magazine has taken my picture and said that he will be back in a little while to interview me and take some more pictures, which may be appearing in some New York Newspapers. I hope my mother happens to read them; or that the SF Chronicle picks them up" Then the money from the states will surely begin to flow.

"THANK YOU FOR YOUR CONTRIBU…"

Saturday 1PM, Santa Clara Cafe.

    I got out here late because I drank too much wine at the Meson last night. Tracy came over for dinner, bringing her young Spanish Lover, the one she calls 'my little German friend', because he's studying German at the university. He's named Eduardo, and is a pleasant young man, but I know what he wants. She kept apologizing for bringing him, and rightly so. Nevertheless, I charged them each 149ptas for the stew, salad, and coffee. The three of us drank one bottle of wine and I went out and bought another, which I drank myself after they left to go dancing, drinking, and fucking. The Happy Little Shits.

    Tracy told me, "I could never live with you!", after I tried to explain something to her in a clear voice. She kept telling me not to be angry and to calm down. She has Ellen's disease. Suzanne is the only woman that isn't afraid of loud talk that I've met in the last couple of months.

    It's a beautiful, crisp, sunny day; perfect for attending a concert in the park, or a funeral in the plaza. I've put up another sign, in Catalan, begging for help, and have put one up in English that says, "Yes…I am sitting here writing a novel/book/diary. This is how I'm presently surviving: people throw money in the box there. The name of the book is: "Barcelona, under the influence". I'm from San Francisco, originally. I live here now. I've been doing this about three months. I'll continue until my gal gets back from Israel & then we're going travelling. Thanks for your contribu…."

    At that point I ran out of room on the little sign.

EUROPEAN BABIES. MARIA-JOSE AND LOGICAL SADNESS. CHOPPED LIVER

Ah, well, I've had another cafeconlech and my ears are ringing. It's such a beautiful day to be famous in. I've made a couple of hundred already, and am planning to invite Rebecca over for Lunch this afternoon. All is well with the world, from this vantage point, even if I'm not getting fucked these days. In two months my sweetheart will be arriving with a shitpot-full of money. (YAYY!! A SHITPOTFULL!!!). Then? Off on the Greatest Adventure of our Lives: Making Babies all over Europe! (YAYYY!! EUROPEAN BABIES!! YAYY!!).

    The article and photograph from 'Avui', which I have hanging from the front of the table, seems to attract more dedicated Watchers than does the usual sign that's been hanging there with wine stains, written in Castillan; for the last couple of months.

All I have to do, as far as Responsibility is concerned, is Pay the Fucking Rent, and the rest is easy. To quote a Famous American Saying: "From here on in it's a Downhill Run!"

Maria-Jose, the Red Catalana, has just joined me. I've asked her, "Well, do you want to be Lovers? I've been waiting a week for your answer."

"Forget It!", she says, "I am terrible lovers."

"I can help! I can help!", I tell her. She laughs. They always do. Fuck it! I'm going to shave my beard for real this time: Irresistible then; none of this having-to-ask bullshit. When they see Redford peeking out of these blue eyes they will Throw me into bed. I've invited Mary-Jo over to the pad for lunch but she has also turned me down on this; she's been up all night (fucking?) and doesn't feel like eating. Shit.

Sinatra is lingering around, his planned trip to Madrid for this weekend didn't come off because he was double-crossed by the Twit from Texas, Jon-Claire, who is spending the weekend with her Catalan Businessman Lover.

Mary-Jo is going to take over the pitch for a while, while I go have a beer with Viv and Steve. Be back in fifteen minutes.

"Jack gone. Looks pretty -he- today. And the day looks pretty too; wanderfull. The sun shine over the streets and the people looks more happy. Is Saturday, people does'nt be hurry, the kids are by the streets, The clouds of the last long hours is gone and with them the logical sadness. I am in love with the sun, I am in love with God. And an old song comes to my mind…

'The Universe is singing a song.

The Universe is dancing alone.

The Universe is singing on a day like this.'"

So, I came back fifteen minutes later and she had written this; she is in love with the sun, she is in love with God; what am I? Chopped Liver?

Frank's Carnival Report

Wed, Feb 20. Noon. Santa Clara Cafe

Beautiful Day. Blue is showing through the clouds and there are patches of sunshine on the plaza. There is a slight chill wind blowing. I'm out here early because I'm trying to get the rent paid. I should be out here at this time every day I suppose. There is a lot more churning at this time of day, usually, than there is after siesta.

Meson Hadass was a Success last night. Frank and Jacques enjoyed their salad, stew, cafe, fruit, and pastry. They had no problem with the price having been raised to 145ptas, in view of the expanded menu and professional service. (The management will shop for drugs for you, if requested.)

We received Frank's Sitges Carnival Report last night: He spent two nights there and was only fully recovered last night. He took his acid and milled around in the streets for hours, occasionally entering bars and rapping, when possible, with the various friends that he had accompanied. Peter, he says, was on the Thrift plan for Sitges this year: he would drink his beer and then exit through a window, leaving Emma to fend/pay for herself. Whitey was the Constant center of attention of whatever crowd of Basketball Fans he happened to find himself in, and was at one point made Center on an All Spanish Girl's Team for a couple of hours. Frank ran into Suzanne about the middle of the night, wearing the most incredible and revealing costume to be seen there: tights, and a dress made completely out of tin-foil strips, from which her large bouncy tits were almost completely free, and covered from head to toe with glitter.

Frank was being followed this first night by Rosa-Jaws, the Catalan Mental patient, who scurried along behind him and Suzanne like a cockroach, darting from doorway to doorway in the hope that none of her students would see her in the company of Suzanne. At one point Frank was having difficulty keeping her from slipping to the pavement and asked Rosa to please give him a hand supporting her. Rosa complied and was instantly recognized and hailed by a number of her students, whereupon she scurried away in shame, to appear again from a doorway after the students had gone.

They entered the Most outrageous Gay Bar there, packed with the most Garish and Weirdly Costumed Transvestites in town, whereupon Suzanne went into her Movie Star Imitation (not really an imitation with her any more), prancing, preening, flirting, hooting, bumping, grinding, cackling, screaming, and instantly became The Star. The crowd went wild: fainting, hooting back, and fawning over her as she mounted the stage and began her well-rehearsed Fan Dance, without the fans; massaging her tits and holding them up for approval and generally carrying on as though Sodom and Gomorrah were small towns in Kansas. Rosa told Frank that she thought they were all in danger of being arrested because of Suzanne's appearance and behavior, while being constantly ashamed and fascinated by it. According to Frank, Suzanne would have easily won the Most Outrageous Costume Contest had she not required medical leave early in the morning due to alcohol poisoning.

Frank accompanied Rosa-Jaws to the rented house of some of her Catalan friends, where he found them watching Television and knitting. They come down to Sitges every year for Carnival, but Rosa is the 'Extrovert', and the only one who actually ventures out while the partying is Heavy, to gather a report for the rest. As the sun came up, Frank hit the sack as the Catalans were preparing to head out for the museum.

Jacques mentioned Lori, "I wonder how Lori's doing in Finland?"

Frank said, "He's probably in an insane asylum by now; I can't imagine him surviving in his own country in the condition he left here."

I said, "He's probably fine; I've heard Finland is like one big nut-house: so many people commit suicide that they don't even count them. "

Frank said, "That's Right! They don't take a census because at the end of the year there's none left that even know how to count!"

I ran down to the piss-bar and bought same hash for Frank and Jacques, who had shorted me 25ptas, which I found out while handing the money to the dealer after negotiating the amount of the dope, up. I promised to bring in the cinco-duro today. I'd better.

A Letter from Hadass in Israel

(LATE FEB 85)

"Dear Jack.
    I got your postcard and the letter. I love it. If it suposed to be a love letter. I got it. Maybe because it's the first one I got in my life, an also because I like your style. I'll tell you the plane- I can't stay here for long because I am not happy. stop. Not any more social explinitions and all the shit. The contract on my flat supose to finish 11 of march but no! the girl who living there asked me to one month more. So I gave her. You now my heart, She selling jwelerys the other side of the street where I am drawing and she poor and having nothing so after awile I gave her. So now will be finish 11 of april. The same date I have to pay my rent to the place I am living now. But I am not going to my contract on this place is for 1 year and a lot of money I am starting to look for somebody to live there and I'll move to my flat on April and then I'll start look for somebody to live there. I want all the money advance so maybe will take me some time to find it. but I don't car because I want all the money with me and not problems any more. So maybe will take me for a while to come back to Barcelona but I will came! for sure... I miss it... I miss you. I love it there. Fuck the polution and the noveler bum. I'll finish the drawing I am doing now. I'll try to work more as much as I can to pass the time. and I'll come. white for me there. I miss our child. I want to get pregnent from you. Don't ask me why. It's not the same love story I use to have before. I was trying to phon you but you wasn't there last friday. Why? and I didn't tryed again. I stope with grass. It was good. I took a brake. So I have 2 month here and then I'll come. for sure. we can do something there. faling love or something. the only thing I want to do is making love and paint. I am doing nothing absulutly nothing so I am poor very poor and depress. Buzy only with rent and bills. I hope soon the situation will change (depend on me). Yesterday falled in love first time since I am here, (You want me happy no?) so maybe today I'll have a good meal and a movie for free. I mean he'll pay it of course. I don't want a child with him (I want a child with you) so don't worry about it. I am playing a lot with my devil steak Pleas write me I love your letters. I'll be there in 2 month or 2 1/2. Please enjoy your self as much as you can. I'll try to do the same and don't give up our story.
    I have bad experience by saying "I love you" sort of, anyway, and I don't like to buzy my mind with this kind of questions especially if THERE IS something there. Don't come here now. We'll came here next year together

with the baby. If ISRAEL will be still exist and I'll be able to get in with the posebility to get out too. it's not a joke. It's all colepss here, not slowly anymore. ISRAEL like a jewes state became a big joke. Every body happy to see how it's falling down. It is a really bad jewes joke. But we are ISRAELIS not a Jewes what can we do? some escape, and the rest trying to ignore or to be religious. I hope I am not going to be the edialistic one who trying to change the world because that mean I am staying here to death. Plese No!

In 2 month I'll come to Barcelona. We'll built a new Jerusalem there. (Don't tell Jacques!!). But I am seriuce. And I want a place where my famelly could come in case. So my sister going back to America with her famelly and then they can choose. America or spain.

It is very sed. We like this peace of lend like home. But killing yourself just to stay alive? no why. And see the other ones killed. FUCK all this. I love Barcelona and you and I want to be there. so I will. see you soon and I'll try to phone and talk to you. Keep write to me your lovely and love letters. It's hold me on here. love. Hadass.

(there another page)

Hey- I got the onother postcard befor I went to post it. Stop drink! waite for me. Don't come it's only 2 month. I'll finish my beusnes here and I'll be back with the money. Will be a spring we'll buy a car and we'll travell and we'll make love, and money and we'll be happy. Be Patience. Me too. We have our time. Don't get lost it's only 2 month! and stop drink pay the rent. Have a stew. Have fun. Waite for me I'll be there soon. We'll do great together. kiss. Lots of love for you from me. Hadass."

What a gal, eh? Fuck: two more months. Ah, well, at least she'll probably arrive with some bucks. And, she thinks buying a car and cruising around Europe is a good plan. And, she still wants to get pregnant with me. Ah, In General: I love her attitude. She's Just the gal for me. We WILL have fun. We Will make love; it's in the stars, as are our minds, most of the time. She wants to be here, but is staying there to hassle around with the apartment she owns; renting it for a year in advance, so that she can have a couple of thousand dollars. I guess I shouldn't argue with her about it: she'll probably give me some of the money. Or even, All Of It. Heh, heh, heh. (YAYYY FOR JIGGILO JACK, HE'S BACK!!! YAYY!!!).

(Author's Note, 1992: So I waited and waited for Hadass, kept begging and writing on the street in Barcelona, for months. I'd already been waiting two months for the money or the ticket she'd said she was going to send me so I could get to Israel. And she kept sending letters or postcards that would say wait a little longer, 11m coming soon, but she didn't come. And then I met Hannah, one day, and fell in love that night and was gone to Ireland with Her when Hadass finally came back to Barcelona that summer and fell in love with another American, Scott. They fell in love while reading My Book, this Book! They've been together ever since, but I don't know why she hasn't had a baby. I miss her too. I miss little Jackoff [Hebrew for 'Jacob'], the name of our former baby-to-be. I've seen Hadass a few times over the years since all this happened, but we've never been alone and we've never kissed again. Well, not like that first kiss, anyway. If she ever dumps Scott, I'm still available.)

PART FOUR

HANNAH

The Clowns are Back!

Well, the Clowns are back (YAYYY!! THE CLOWNS!!). They're dancing and playing with their puppets right down the street in front of the Brusi Bar. Rabbit is in the Sardana hoping to catch a glimpse of the girl he met in the street yesterday. He's drinking Rainier Ale and lingering as though he owned the place. Billy is popping in and out occasionally, reporting on the day's take.

I spent about half an hour sitting in there, talking to Ellen, trying to bring her out of the depression Frank had accidentally sent her into by arguing with her about Germany and German Thinking. I had to explain to her that Frank sometimes engages in what could be mistaken for intelligent conversation, just for fun. She tends to take it all personally, and gets confused. It's an uphill battle sometimes: she accused me, repeatedly, of 'interrupting' her: this usually happens when she tells me something that I am supposed to have said, or something that I Think. She believes that she has heard things somewhere else right after she says them, and believes therefore that it is substantiated, or at least Common Knowledge. It's a Very Common Disease, I see it everywhere. Fact taken as Rumor, and vice-versa. Gosh.

I'm not sure if our little pate/talk helped matters: I may have confused her even further. She left with a puzzled expression on her soul. She's not sure Who She Can trust, and is tired of being treated like a child. I advised her to 'just listen' more often, and quit presenting her 'Opinions' if she doesn't like the reactions she's been getting. She Seemed to Understand, but began discussing what I was saying before I even finished saying it, making me wonder. It's hard being 'wise', even when called upon to do so. I told her that she . could be sure Frank was baiting her if, during a discussion about Germans she heard the word 'angst'. I'm not sure she got it, but if she hears the word it will came back to her.

Peter and Billy have just wandered off 'to go to the museum', arm in ann. Billy was being contentious, something he probably picked up from his friends. The Clowns have folded up their pitch and moved on to more fertile tide-pools. I was in love with the one that gave me the hat last month, but she hardly seems to remember. I wonder what her name is.

I just walked down to where the clowns had set up again and Found out the name of the clown I fell in love with last month: HANNAH. I can't seem to get away from this Biblical Shit: Judy, Rebecca, Sue, Hadass, now Hannah. (I'm not forgetting about Lynda, though).

It's getting chilly and it's getting late and I've had three or four beers. or five. Peter asked, "Ah, are you getting drunk?" I said, "Here, read this!", tearing the sheet out of the typewriter, "Does that seem like the writings of a Drunk?", I challenged.

"No.", he wisely answered.

It's very nice, nice, nice out tonight: expectation is running high. Gourdlessness is coming in a close second. (YAYYY!! A HORSE RACE!!). The Clowns Are In Town; you know how this affects me. (YAYY!! WE'RE GOING TO HAVE FUN! CLOWNS!!). I've always been in love with a clown, as Rebecca can well attest. Rabbit just stopped by with the girl I left with him at La Sardana, who had accosted me on the street for English lessons, and I dumped on him because My mind was in a clown whirl; I can't get it off the Hannah-Clown.

The Plot thickens: I've invited Hannah the Clown to dinner tonight at Meson Hadass, along with Jacques, Frank, and phil. They are pretty sure that she won't come. I think she will.

When I asked her, she said, "can I bring my friends?", indicating the other two clowns.

I said, "No, just you." She looked at them, looked at me, smiled, and said "OK, ten oclock?"

"Perfect", I said. We'll see. (YAYYYY!! CLOWNS FOR DINNER!!!). Jacques' advice to me is that I not drink alcohol until dinner; that I cease the beer-drinking for the evening. I think it's probably a good idea. Does a clown have a heart? I've just given her my address and directions to the pad. She says she will be stopping by about ten tonight. That will certainly be interesting: as the Gang is leaving, they bring in the clowns. I'm not sure that she knows the depth of my feelings in this matter: I would Love to Love a Clown. (YAYY!! CLARABELLE IS GOING TO GET LAID!!!). (How disgusting! Now he's got clowns fucking in his novel!).

Drinking does funny things to one's mind: I can't remember how long I've been here, or how I got here in the first place. After a few beers it seems like I've been doing this Forever. I have a Focus, however, the dinner tonight and Waiting For Hannah. God, I sure hope she doesn't change her mind. I need a clown for a friend; someone, finally, that I can relate-to. One of my tribe, you might say, if you said things like that. The Thing To Do is Relax. Have you ever tried relaxing when you think you may get fucked tonight after two celibate months? Try it. Don't want to? You Bettah Off. I'm just waiting for someone to hand me a mil. What else can possibly happen tonight? After all, a Clown is coming over for dinner!'

IN BED WITH CLOWNS

The Next Day.

(YAYYY!! YAYYY!!! YAYYY!!!! CLOWNS!!! IN BED WITH CLOWNS!!!) Well, I guess I won't get any peace from the Peanut Gallery until I tell what happened last night.

    Frank, Jacques, and Phil came over for dinner; all went according to plan. We drank some wine and smoked a little of Frank's hash. Around ten, according to plan, we were joined by Hannah, in Full Clown Regalia, with whiteface, polka-dots, and a funny hat. She had some stew, drank a little wine, and washed off the whiteface so that we could see what she really looks like. She was Beautiful. Frank said, "She's just like Sally!", referring to her looks and accent, which is upper-class, I suppose. She settled right in getting to know my Main Friends. The three left for the Opera Cafe, leaving Hannah and me to drink wine, smoke cigarettes, chat, and read the book. She found a lot of it funny: she read the parts where I had fallen in love with her last month at the RocknRoll bar.

    I don't think she was planning to stay overnight at the pad. Around midnight we heard the knocker signalling guests on the street below. I looked over the balcony, it was Rebecca and Rabbit.

    "Can we come up!?", Rebecca hollered. I could tell from six floors up that they were Way Into Partying already.

    "No!", I yelled down.

    Rebecca yelled, "Can I leave Conejo here?".

    I yelled, "No, We'll come down!", which we did.

    They were broke and half-drunk, Rabbit being the biggest half. He took his drums up to the pad for storage and the four of us headed out into the night to find a bar where Rabbit said we could probably drink for free. we were just out of plaza St. Juame when we passed four young hoodlums out looking for a fight on a Friday Night, all black clothes and pointy shoes. It turned into a minor scuffle with feints, chases, and diversions. I didn't want to turn my back to them as they chased me around the street, which further antagonized them. Rabbit got slightly involved in the scuffle a couple of tunes trying to extricate me from the gang, who weren't very coordinated in their attack. They managed to surround me a couple of times and did get in one fair kick at my butt, before everyone tired of the whole thing. They weren't really sure that they wanted to fight if it was going to be that much trouble. They wandered off and so did we, with a little more adrenalin in our systems than we'd had a few minutes before. Barcelona, Under The Influence Of Gratuitous Violence.

Rabbit led us down into the Barrio across Via Leyatana, through various Secret Alleys, to a couple of bars where, I think, he would ask if we could drink for free. Evidently the answer was No. We finally ended up at a late-hours bar full of paintings and babbling young Catalans. Hannah sprang for four Rainier Ales, and we spent the next hour or so laughing and talking.

As we were preparing to leave, Hannah said that she wasn't sure if she was going to spend the night with me or not, and asked Rebecca's opinion of me. Rebecca told her that I was "good with trucks", and was "a good guy" and was OK and that it seemed like a good idea to her. Hannah accepted this advice from my former wife as watered-Down Gospel and came back to the pad with me. We bid goodnight to Rebecca and a Delirious Rabbit in plaza St. Juame and wobbled home, got into bed, and made love most of the night, between coming to and passing out. I think we were probably too drunk to stand, and our lovemaking reflected this. Even so, it was Very Good. (YAYTI!! A NIGHT AT THE CIRCUS!!!) .

Hannah is living in a van with one of her sons, eight years old, and a friend. They are in Barcelona to make money, for a few days. She got up at about ten and headed for Park Guell (Guadi's Park) to do the Marionette Act. This is a simple act, with a lute, flute and about five Marionettes. It's not her main gig. She Actually IS a Clown and has worked with a couple of small circuses. She's also been the girl doing flips on a trotting horse. She's been on the road for about ten years, is about thirty, English, skinny, lively, pretty, flat-chested, very kind, and has a beautiful butt. I like her. She turns me ON. I want her.

She spends quite a bit of time living down at the commune near Valencia that's headed by Mick, the Rex Harrison look-alike, dropout, Old Hippy who I hung out with a couple of Binges ago. They all call it 'The Meadow'. He's invited me to come on down to his place, a hundred acres or so, with a house he built on it overlooking the sea. It's similar to the Open Communes that were ubiquitous (YAY!) in the Western US in the late sixties. I may take him up on it. Hannah has reiterated the invitation. We'll see. For sure when Hadass returns it will be on our itinerary. I don't know whether Hannah will be returning tonight: I certainly hope so; We could do a much better job of it Under The Influence of a little less wine.

Hannah and I are not nearly A Perfect Match, but we did enjoy talking and smiling at each other; it was quite easy. She possesses many of the qualities of both Hadass and Sally, and we Could do something together if it unfolds in that direction. Who Knows? (YAYY!! VAGUE JACK IS BACK). I'd almost forgotten how great it feels to hug and kiss, bite and squeeze, writhe and moan. Fucking! It's SO Good! (YAYYY! !! FUCKING CLOWNS!!!) .

On the Street Once More

THE SARDANA

THE PEANUT GALLERY

The musick is blaring, The dancers are bobbing, The Strollers are Strolling, The Chatters are Chatting, The Sitters are Sipping, and the writer is Typing: The Tide is In. I've got about 350 already, enough to pay Barb and buy a bottle of wine and some olives. Going to be a mellow night. (Really? What about the Clown?) (YAH, CLARABELLE, WHERE'S HANNAH??? I!! WE WANT THE CLOWN AGAIN!! MORE KISSING! 11 MORE HUGGING!!!). Don't worry, kids, let these things work themselves out. Be happy with what we've got. (WHATT?? WINE AND JUSTINE??? WE WANT THE CLOWN!! WE WANT THE CLOWN!! 1) . There's nothing I can do to alter the situation: It's her move; I've invited her to return whenever she wants. Remember, I'm getting older and don't always keep 'em coming back for more, these days. (JUST KEEP 'EM COMING AND THEY'LL BE BACK, LOVER JACK!!!). You Are the Peanut Gallery, not my Love-Life Advisors! Try to remember that. (WE WANT THE CLOWN!!· WE WANT THE CLOWN!! WE WANT THE CLOWN!!!). Thaƅs better: thaƅs more your style. (YAYYY1!). Enough, enough. Please.

It's chilly enough to make me shiver in the midst of the churning tide. Either that or I'm having some kind of mild alcohol withdrawal.

The musick has stopped temporarily and the plaza is buzzing like a cafeteria; they really are having fun tonight, in spite of the cold .. The band this week is the best I've heard in over a month; this one doesn't sound like the Tijuana Marching Band, more like a classical orchestra. What a wonderful night. Well, the volume of the chattering reached an expectant peak, the band took the signal, and We're Off Again. Am I in Love?

THE NEXT DAY. ON THE STREET AGAIN

I'm still a little out of breath from buzzing around town this morning looking for my lost bag. I left it late last night at the Opera Cafe where I'd been smoking hash (Billy's) with Billy, Rabbit, Jacques, and Tracy. The hash plus a bottle of wine and a beer put me in a mindless state, one wherein it was possible to leave all my worldly possessions, including My Work, under a table in a bar full of thieves. Luckily, I found it just a few minutes ago in Jacques' roam. Whew! That would've been another fifty pages down the tubes.

Billy was in charge last night: he supplied the hash, a giant chunk which he bought for 300ptas in Barrio Chino: less than half the normal cost, and he was the Trip-Master. He was the only one not drinking, which would help explain the ease with which he manipulated our minds and bodies. He was in Great Form: had me laughing almost continuously; jiving with the waiters to keep them in stitches, and just generally controlling the whole Opera Cafe Crowd. Jacques says that Billy has Mastered My Act to near Perfection, and is moving ahead of me in the Outrageous Race.

For about an hour he became The Face-Grabbing Alien: every time Rabbit, who was hopelessly, droolingly drunk, would relax his guard, Billy would Grab his Face; the arm would just shoot out and the little clamps on the end would latch on to nose, cheeks, and mouth. Rabbit would just sit there wondering what had happened and what to do for about half a minute with this claw clutching onto his face, until he would finally wrestle the hand loose. It was about the funniest thing I've ever seen. Rabbit finally got him to stop it after fighting with him in the aisle for a few minutes, and we began another conversation and Then: zzzzzzztt, out would come the Face Grabbing Claw again.

"Billy,", I lectured, as a parent should, "How many times have I told you Not to Grab People's Faces?" He ignored me. He tells people, "Jack's no longer my father; we're divorced."

Rabbit and Billy woke me up at about 1 this afternoon, coming to retrieve Rabbit's bongo drums. They said they had to get the drums and then go to the bank. Some High Finance Deal going on. They also brought me the Eviction Notice which was down at the mailbox in the front hall. I can't understand the exact details, but it looks like I'd better get the fucking rent paid quick.

Last night as Jacques was paying his bill at Santi's, in preparation for heading to the Opera with the Gang, he casually mentioned that we would all be eating at Meson Hadass tonight. Santi and Barbara, completely serious, asked where that was, they'd never heard of it. Jacques explained the whole deal to them about me operating a restaurant. Santi kept asking questions like, "Does he give credit?", no, "Does he wash his pots and pans?", no, "Does he cook your food the way you want it?", no. I am almost afraid to show my face in there tomorrow. I think this may signal the end of Meson Hadass. I Really Don't want to irritate Santi, and Jacques said that he has rarely seen Santi in such a serious mood. When his business is threatened he becomes a different person? Great.

Jacques (Idiot Wind) made about four mil in five hours down on the Ramblas yesterday, and is planning to make it his permanent pitch again. I checked for him down there this morning, while trying to find the lost bag, but I guess he isn't awake yet. clink 150 in the box. There is a high, slight haze, which the sun is able to penetrate every few minutes. Very eerie. There is a light idiot wind blowing also: perfect day for chalking on the Ramblas; But... where is the chalker? Probably out Hunch-Backing around.

Last night at Santi's was exceptionally mellow considering the crowd in attendance and their potential for Action: Me, Jacques, Billy, Rebecca, Rabbit, Ellen, Tracy, Steve, Vivian, Aurora, Peter, a couple of English film-makers, and an old friend of Jacques and Peter: Enrique (Henri) the world travelling, banjo-playing, ex-german with a Mexican Ski-Bum Sunburn. I know that Santi has had a Little Talk with Rabbit about keeping it down in the bar, but there is no explanation for Viv and Steve not flying off the handle and yelling 'Motherfucker!' every few minutes. The only thing missing last night was Frank complaining how the little gypsy cave has gone downhill and fallen into disrepute. In fact, Frank hasn't been' seen outside his house for a couple of days. May be having body problems. Or meditating. Or maybe he went to Morocco again. Thursday is Viv and Aurora's wedding anniversary and Viv says there will be a party at Santi's that night. He will supply the muzzles.

On the Street Again, as Always

WHY DO ALL THE SECRETARIES DRESS LIKE WHORES?

It's a Monday night. Or maybe it's Tuesday. It feels like a Monday. But, maybe it's Tuesday. Tuesday nights sometimes feel like Mondays. It feels like a Monday night, peseta-wise. There is a lax tide thrashing in and out of the Hamburguesa Tide-pools. (WHAT IS HE SAYING???). It's Art, kids: Hamburguesa Tide-pools. Ubiquitous Pastry. Day-Glo Butts. (WHY DO ALL THE SECRETARIES DRESS LIKE WHORES!!!??? WHY DO ALL THE SECRETARIES DRESS LIKE WHORES!!!???). Yah, yah. So, It's a quiet night, and Stew is Looming. (STEW IS LOOMING??? WHAT IS THAT???). Stew is Looming in my future. It doesn't look like there's going to be a demonstration in the plaza tonight; it's almost devoid. (DEVOID???). Yah, that's where you kids will end up if you don't quit this editorializing, Devoid. (OH!!! SORRY, SERIOUS JACK!!!).

Well, the kook of the hour is here. Gourdless conversation is the Rule of the Day, he's about the third in a little while: an Italian actor, involved with a theatre group here in Barcelona. I'm exhausted by my recent Social Whirling, and don't really want to get involved in another Scene, so I just let the opportunities pass by, sometimes. He is telling me that he has a library of 6,000 volumes and is also a professional photographer. He is completely blocking the money box, as usual. We have been joined by another friend who says that he Is a Marionette. We are having a discussion about 'The Arts', of which my new Italian friend knows almost everything: he's a singer, dancer, puppeteer, photographer, painter and just generally a Drinker of the Wines of Life. (WHAT??). Shut up. (SORRY..). He has wandered off to chatter about the arts somewhere else. There are a lot of wanderers like him in this city; the place is practically overflowing with them.

It's a Low Tide tonight, with little chance of getting much higher. The Marionette has just departed with a friend of his who also was wandering by. They're off to sit in same cafe and chat, chat, chat.

I've been out here for an hour and a half and have only got about 60ptas, about 40cents. I have never been able to figure out what causes the ups and downs. It Can be frustrating. I wonder when I'll start to get some response from the Hardware Store Ad I placed the other day. I've got my Writer's German Overcoat and my begging gloves on. I should be doing great.

Well, I guess Hannah has left town, what a shame, probably didn't came back because I made such a mess of our fucking when I got all tangled up in her strings. I'd never made love to a puppet before and I think I should be given a second chance. I guess I really Will have that 'Mellow Evening At Home' that I'm always talking about. (BOOO!!).

Frank's Trip to Morocco

WHY BILLY LIKES PUPPIES

PETER'S BROWN FAT

Frank has evidently gone to Morocco. Jacques and I concluded this after trying to decide whether to go over to his room and see if he's OK…It's easier for us if he's in Morocco than if he's hung himself in his room with pastry, or some other Famous Demise.

Peter and Billy found it difficult to believe he'd really gone, "Shit! He's paranoid Here, what's he gonna do in Morocco?", asked Peter. I told them not to believe me if they didn't want to; go ask Jacques. They've gone off to the bank; Billy goes there every day for some mysterious reason. Next week I'm going to have Billy sit here and tell everyone that he has a disease that keeps making him younger; I'm probably heading for Morocco to visit Frank while Billy mans the pitch.

"Was it hard to skin the puppies?" Ellen asked Billy, last night at Meson Hadass, as he was telling her what his life with John had been like, living in the caves at Gaudix.

"No,", he answered, "The hardest thing was to skin the bat."

Ellen was fascinated by the diet John had had them on.

Billy continued, to Ellen's Squeals, "I think puppies are cute, But, They're Delicious!"

"What do they taste like?", she squealed.

"They're kind of sweet.", he said, "Puppies are delicious, Bats are delicious, the Most Delicious is Moths, second to Chocolate." We talked some more about what John, Rebecca, and Billy had eaten on their trip to the south last year.

"How many grasshoppers do you have to eat to be full?", Ellen queried.

"About twenty.", he answered.

"How many grasshoppers have you eaten?", Jacques asked him.

"A couple of hundred, he said.

"How do you eat them?", Jacques asked.

"Well, you just catch them and then bite off their heads, and pop 'em in your mouth and chew. They're very sweet.", Billy said.

"Are they jumping around when you pop 'em in your mouth?", I asked.

"No, you pull off their legs right when you catch them, Then you bite off their heads. They're Really Tasty, Very Sweet; I love 'em!", he told us. Ellen could barely contain herself, The Peanut Gallery went wild. (YAYY!! GRASSHOPPER CANDY!!).

"Moths are better, though; they're my favorite.", he continued.

"You Ate Moths, Too?", Jacques asked, spilling his wine.

"Yup. The wings are the best part.", he told us.

There was silence for a minute; we all stared at each other and Billy.

Peter said, "I found out why I get cold so much: I have brown fat! People with brown fat feel the cold more!"

"I'm cold!", said Billy.

"You have brown fat!", Peter told him.

Hannah, Hannah, Hannah

Well, it's Thursday. I've just spent the last couple of days with the Clowns. The Hannah Clown and I are lovers; I, madly. She: surely. She's in town with her clown friend Sonia, a younger woman who is taking Acrobat, Juggling, and Busking (playing on the street for money, an English term) Apprenticeship with Hannah. Hannah has been doing all of this for six or seven years, travelling with her two sons, now aged eight and ten. She was with a circus for a while but says that they're 'too fascist' for her tastes. Their current busking act is playing Irish penny-Whistles while dangling marionettes from their elbows and legs, which hop about in time with the music. They dress up in bright Clown Outfits, and Sonia occasionally juggles or makes faces to the music. It is an uplifting little act. They make about 1500ptas per hour, most of which they're saving to pay the insurance on Sonia's van or the tuition for the acrobat school they're going to be attending here in Barcelona for the next month. I've invited Hannah to move in with me; she's considering it; there could be some difficulty because her son Tarn, the eight-year-01d, is Extremely Jealous. He and I had a couple of small confrontations yesterday during siesta in the van when She and I were snuggling, but we made friends last night at the pad over a wonderful little dinner for three.

They've gone off to the beach with Jean-Claude, the French clown, to practice a circus act they'll be performing at a children's school on Friday. She said she'd see me on Saturday when she'll be Rich from the money they're getting for the show.

I'm a little bit shakey this morning because I've been drinking for a couple of days. The Clowns like their wine, too. I've had no Ladrone problems for these two days because few arabs will assault a clown. They are hilarious and non-stop Fun-seekers. I've been in on a couple of Clown Conferences with them; their decision-making processes resemble a Marx Brothers skit. My head hurts from drinking, my stomach from laughing, and my dick (willie) from fucking. It's been Wonderful: Hannah and I Are In Love! She's been trying to hold back for a few days but has finally admitted that she is losing it over me.

I left my bag (again) at a bar the other night. I don't know which bar, or where, but Rabbit, who was with us that night, is going to try to help me find it this afternoon. There's the usual fifty pages gone.

Hannah said that I probably won't be seeing her this evening because she wants to get a lot of rest for the show on Friday. I hope she changes her mind. I Want Her. She's Just My Type. She can't believe she's gotten involved with 'Another Drunken Madman', but it is So. After having seen the way they make decisions, there is probably a fair chance that they won't finish the Acrobat training at all, and will be heading south for 'The Meadow' Mick's commune on the ocean. If it goes this way, I'll Go. I would really like a change; The Country rather than The City, for a while. If I've Really Lost another 50 pages I'll probably just quit this fucking writing for a while and live off what the clowns make. They're generous by nature.

I've probably blown out most of my more Normal Friends since I've been Clowning Around: I get so fucking excited just being with her/them that my energy just spins off into mindless hilarity.

Hannah is very good-natured and has a Joyous Heart, in spite of the trials and tribs she's been through with all this travelling and clowning. Her mouth is Extremely Sensuous and she uses it well: makes me seem straight-laced by comparison; she purrs and moans when we make love; I think I'm in bed with an animal, Which I am.

Sonia is Simply a Joy to be around; during siesta yesterday she kept all five of us in stitches in the van by trying on different outfits; trying to decide what her True Clown Self really is. Jean-Claude was counselling her; I haven't seen him in costume yet, though. At about midnight last night they took over the Ramblas with about half an hour of acrobatics, and beer drinking. I was drawn into it with My Version of Drunken Hopping also, but don't even come close to the coordination they possess. I can, however, Fall Down along with the Best of them.

I wandered down to the harbor to see if the clowns had changed their minds and stayed there in their trucks. They were gone; I was sad. I wandered around the town and picked up a letter at the Post from my daughter Amy in Oregon. She's planning to move to San Diego with her boyfriend and Sally. She plans to open a halfway house for teenagers with problems. And become a writer. Her letter had Absolutely No Spelling Mistakes, and the punctuation was perfect, with the liberal use of multi-syllabic words. I'm Proud. She'll probably do it: she's the Ambitious One, Sally is the Beautiful One, and Billy will be the Clown. He told me today, as we sat in the Sardana while I had a glass of wine, that he is getting tired of Barcelona and longs to be On The Road Again. I told him that I would introduce him to the clowns; that he would fit right in with their act. He Would: they play Irish music, same as he does, and he, dressed like a clown, would be Perfect. I wish I was twelve and had the option of joining the Circus Crowd. My Only Fatherly Advice was: "Join the clowns, son." Either that or get a job in a Hardware store.

Billy and I wandered around town for a while searching for Pan Integral, while he told me how his Busking has been going. He does just fine, when he works. Rebecca is moving up in the world: she's gotten a steady job at one of the English Schools, making about 50 mil a month.

It's so fucking windy out here today that my papers are blowing all over the street every few minutes and the signs keeps coming off. I've been telling everyone who will listen' that I am happy in my heart because of my new love, the Clown Hannah. Pretty soon the whole town will know that I'm in Love again. God, It's Great, let me tell you.

Jacques says that I probably won't make much money tonight because The Regulars have heard that I lost another fifty pages of the book, and they Hate that. That's the price of a Circus Life.

A truck just ran over my box, bending one of the latches but not breaking it. Is The Act going downhill?

My banker, Jacques, informs me that I only have 1250ptas on account now: not enough for the rent, by any means. Shit, I worry just like a Clerk. It would really be the shits if I lost Hadass' apartment for her, but not Completely out of Character. I try, I do.

Ah, the first clink: 9ptas already. This is the last piece of typing paper that I stole from Jacques' room today. Rabbit tells me that all that remains of his 30mil gift from his mother is about 12mil. He's had it almost a week; that's not bad.

Ah! Ah! Ah! Something almost as good as sex just happened: I got my bag back. Rabbit ran into the owner of The October Bar, where I'd left it, and they went over there and got it. Ah! I got the fifty pages back. I got my gloves back. My beret. Justine. Paper, Pens, and a Letter I'd written to Hadass. (YAYYY!!!). Ah! (DID YOU GET YOUR BEARD BACK TOO, REDFORD-JACK???!!!). No, kids, Ellen has it on a table in her room: she says it smells like smoke and Me. I wonder what she plans to do with it. Well, this calls for a celebration. Naturally. I mean a piece of chocolate. (YAYYY!!). Say, kids, where have you been while I was with the clowns? (WE WERE THERE THE WHOLE TIME!! WE'VE BEEN HAVING FUN!!!). You were there last night? (YAHHHH!! THE FUCKING WAS GREAT!!!· ALMOST AS GOOD AS THE JUGGLING!!! WE>RE GROWING UP FAST, GIGOLO JACK!!!). Isn>t She Great!? (YAHHH!! WE LOVE HER!!).

Frank finally appeared yesterday after a two-day absence. Jacques and I had already started the rumor that he was in Morocco, and he has had to deal with that. He got even by spreading the word that I had left for Valencia with the clowns. Ah, Mis-information will soon be back at it's Regular Level, now that ·the Master Stirrer is working on the Rumor Pot again. I've stumbled (really) across him a couple of times in Bar del pi, where he's taken up residence as Lecturer to Young Foreign Women, one of his favorite positions. I almost had a beautiful Norwegian girl half in bed the other day when Hannah popped in. I had to make a decision, fast. I left her with Frank and joined Hannah downstairs. A decision I'll never regret. Fine.

I have three great overcoats at home, but I'm sitting out here in one of my polyester arab suit-coats, on the coldest night of the month. Idiot. Steve told me that today was payday for many of the people, but the clinking doesn't attest to this.

Hannah, Tarn, and I got up at around noon and had a wonderful breakfast of coffee, milk, bread, marmalade, and orange juice on the patio this morning. We talked about our dreams, which had been weird for both her and me this particular night because we were drunk, stoned, and lustful til dawn. God, it was a Wonderful Night! Tarn slept like a rock through all the moaning and grunting; It was only after she finally had A Good Orgasm, A Nearly Endless Orgasm, that Hannah admitted that, yes, she was falling in love with the gringo.

I'm Too Happy right now. I feel like I'm the first person to ever make love. Last night was like the First Time. Know what I mean? (YAYYIT!! GIGOLO JACK'S NOT A VIRGIN ANY MORE!! YAYY, FOR COPULATION!!!). Stop swearing, kids. Copulation is a disgusting word. Just say Fucking, from now on. Or Making Love. (OHHH KAYYY!!).

Well, the tide is Flooding heavily; very little nutrient is finding it's way into this urchin's begging box, however. Ah, what the fuck. Just need enough for a bottle of wine to put me to sleep tonight, and enough for a glass or two of wine at Santi's. I'll seriously try to keep things mellow tonight. All I have to do is hang on for one day for my Clown to fetch me into her fun. And she will.

Rabbit

Five oclock, Friday, Santa Clara Cafe.

I feel O.K., considering that I stayed up drinking til seven this morning with Rabbit/Conejo and Paco, a local that I've hung out with a few times last year and this. He's a Dangerous Crazy; we had fun. We stayed at the Deaf and Dumb Bar (Meson Riazor) after it closed, drinking red wine and smoking Conejo's Grandmother's Hash with the owner and a waiter. It was a Fairly Noisy and Riotous Evening.

Rabbit hasn't been to sleep yet and is still sitting down at Santi's behind a bottle of wine, yelling, "I Poet! I no care!", and, "For me, No Time!". I offered, about five times, to help him over to my place so he could sleep, as Rebecca had earlier, but couldn't connect through the Beano Haze.

Paco, Rabbit, and I were the final celebrants last night of Viv and Aurora's first wedding anniversary. The party was a success at Santi's where Viv played guitar and sang Ribald English Dittys, like, "Tattooed Across Her Fanny Is Al Jolson Singing Mammy", and American Blues and Rock and Roll. The crowd waxed Boy-Scoutish: it seemed for a couple of hours that we were sitting around a campfire in Arizona. It Was Beautiful, at times.

When Santi kicked us out we headed, about ten or twelve of us, down to La Barraca where we took over the back room and drank ourselves silly, with a large Hashish Overlay. I entered Obnoxiousness at around two or three in the morning as the crowd split up, most heading for bed, Rabbit, Paco, and me heading for Riazor.

Frank and Jacques didn't attend; instead, they had dinner at Meson Box, Frank's pad. They had stew and cafeconlech, and then hung out in the Opera Cafe until there was a huge, bloody, chair-throwing fight. Jacques says that I missed the Adrenalin High Of The Week.

I haven't heard from Hannah, and am hoping that she comes by this evening while I'm out here, or comes by the pad later. I hate it when Love Affairs start becoming A Memory; it's already been one day.

I joined Steve down at the Brusi Bar where he bought me a beer because my hands were shaking. Drunks take care of each other. As we sat there discussing the State Of Barcelona Recently, we saw Conejo weave past the window, clutching a bottle of beano, yelling, and drooling. I went out to see if he was O.K., or needed any help. He just began ranting, "No Problem! No problem! It's My Life!". There's really nothing that anyone can do for him until he gets some sleep. I hope he doesn't get arrested. Billy went down to the cathedral to see if he could help him, am reported back that, "Conejo has serious problems".

I have one peseta to my name, but the stew-pot is full and there's three-fourths of a bottle of wine sitting on the table at the pad. I sure hope the Hannah Clown makes an appearance this evening, I sure do. I don't know whether I'm on a binge or not; I feel fine, but have Certainly been staying up late drinking a lot.

Rabbit has just wobbled up and is drooling and yelling at Billy and me. He is Way out Of It. Billy just wandered off with Rabbit in tow, to get some dinner at Santi's, I think; Rabbit has the money. I told Billy to take him up to the pension and put him to bed. He lost his bottle of wine and his new panama hat. He's trouble tonight.

Waiting for Hannah

5:30 Saturday, March 4, 1985

Bread Street. Windy as Fuck.

It's windy as fuck here. Billy is here standing in front of the liquor store window like I've asked him not to do. Phil joined me for lunch this afternoon while I took a shower. Steve just stopped by and told Billy that he'd break both his legs if he plays on this street tonight. The (I forget what I was going to write) .

I'm clean and fresh, wearing the writer's Overcoat: should do well tonight. Should. When the knocker went off this afternoon my heart leapt because I thought it was Hannah. It was Phil, a good friend, but not a Relief. (WHERE'S THE CLOWN, GIGOLO JACK???). Shit, I wish I knew, I wish she were here. I want to go down to the port and see what she's doing but I don't want to run into her twenty-year-old boyfriend.

One of my friends who works in the Hamburger Shop just told me that a tourist has been stabbed by a Ladrone in Plaza del Rey. What a fucking shame.

I shaved and drank two-thirds of a bottle of wine this afternoon, so I should do well this evening, right? (YAYYY!!! FUN IN THE STREET!!). But, mainly, my spine craves a Circus Show: God, Am I Missing Her!

Well, and Ah! Hannah just joined me. She's Here! We went down to La Sardana and had a wine and a cafeconleche. She's been hanging out with her young English boyfriend for the last day, but he's heading out of town tomorrow, on tour. She's staying. (YAYYY!!!). She's got a room in Simon the Yogi's house (where he doesn't want her bringing any more of her drunken boyfriends) , maybe for the month.

She said, "I'm confused; I don't know what to do." I told her I understood. I don't, though; she should Give Herself to Me Completely. It was So Great to see her. She's taken off to busk with Chris the Mandolin player; Sonia isn't working tonight because she's hanging out with her Israeli boyfriend, the one who's got dreadlocks and her pregnant. Hannah read what's been happening in my life for the last few days, and was amazed that I'd written so much about 'Our Love Affair'. I only hope that there is more to write. She doesn't know what she's going to be doing tonight, but may come over to my place. God, what other choice is there?

I told her that Billy wanted to join the clowns. She said it was a possibility. She also told me that I could head south for 'the Meadow' without her, if

I wanted to. I said that I wanted to go there with her, or I would stay in Barcelona because she is here. I asked her, again, if she wanted to move in with me for a while. She's not sure 'she wants to get 'so heavily involved'. I am. Why hesitate when it's offered to you? No?

It's High Saturday Night Fiesta. The churning is heavy. The pastry is out, yet I've only had two people throw coins in the box so far tonight, but both of them were hundreds. (YAYYY!! ONLY BIG IDNEY FROM NOW ON!!!). The wind is strong, I've gotten a piece of chocolate and am merely awaiting Hannah's decision on how she wants to spend her night: hanging out at the RocknRoll Bar with her young drunken lover, or hanging out with her new older drunken lover at his pad. The Choice is hers tonight.

Well, Hannah is back with the two little Irish girls, Tarn, her boyfriend, and the Mandolin Player. They're looking for a place to put their pitch.(?) They've just gone off to shop at the Magic Store and have left all their marionettes with me for a while. Jacques is coming over to the Meson for dinner tonight, and has just gone off to buy some milk and some bread for the stockpile. The clowns were thinking of setting up on this street if there was no conflict with Steve, but he just began playing right down the street.

I have no idea why there is no money being thrown in the box. I really don't. There are the same number of people stopping by and reading the signs, lingering, and perusing the pitch; but, not many monedas. Ah, what the fuck: I'm in love. Will she be able to ditch her boyfriend? She should certainly give it a try.

Well, she just came by again to collect her marionettes and has agreed to come to the pad for dinner around nine oclock, after which we have tentatively decided to join her boyfriend and his friend at the RocknRoll Bar for drinking and dancing. (and fighting?) .

She is troubled because, "I just want to Love Everybody, and Everybody to Love Me; and I don't want anyone to get hurt."

"I feel the same.", I told her. I didn't say, "You just go off and have a good time tonight with your other boyfriend and I'll see you tomorrow after he leaves." Fuck That! I Want Her Tonight!

The mandolin player just came back looking for Hannah and I sent him down the alley to where she's playing music and dancing her puppets. Shit, this is getting complicated: She's madly in love with me, I'm madly in love with her: Where's The Problem? Well, whatever: she's coming for dinner, that's settled; and my good friend Jacques will be there also: I'm a Happy Human tonight. Love in my heart, it feels so good. God, all I really want is for her to spend the night with me. Is this too much to ask? (JUST ASK!! YOU'RE GIGOLO JACK, AFTER ALL!!!!). You, just shut up. (HAHAHAAAH!!!).

I really do think that it is time to send some of this off to Ferlinghetti: it just keeps going on and on; and all I really need is a couple of hundred dollars a month to live: shit, that's Nothing! (HARDWARE STORE! HARDWARE STORE! HARDWARE STORE FOR JACK-THECLERK!!!). You Little Shits! I'm going to go down the street and watch the clowns for a while; you guard the typewriter. (OHHHH KAYYYY!!!).

Well, you did fine guarding the typewriter but you let the fucking book blow off the table and down the street. If it wasn't for all the Kind and Helpful Strollers, 'Barcelona, Under the Influence...' would be a Literal book of the streets. (SORRRRRY.)

Five oclock, Monday, Bread Street, I think it's March the Fourth.

I'm elated because Hannah is still in love with me and am sad because I don't get to be around her all the time and she says that she's not going to move in with me. She and Tarn are coming to dinner tonight and probably staying the night. Billy and Jacques are also supping at Meson Hadass this evening.

I didn't work yesterday; I took my typewriter with me and accompanied the Clowns up to Park Guell, where they busked and drank the day away. I was the Go-fer for the hourly round of beers. By mid-afternoon I was getting drunk, as were a couple of the clowns.

Billy, Rebecca, Rabbit, Peter, Henri, Ellen, Gregorio, and a couple of others joined Me, Hannah, the two little blonde daughters of Phil the English Hippy, Sonia, her Israeli boyfriend (who has gotten her pregnant and she's not sure she wants the keep the embryo because it will fuck up her burgeoning clown career), Jean-Claude, and Tarn, for drinks at the cafe in the park. It was almost an Hilarious Afternoon, I suppose. The two groups, both of which are my Main Friends here (except for Frank and Jacques), didn't mix very well, keeping to separate tables, but talking and passing beer and jokes back and forth, as did I.

I left the park in the afternoon in the company of the clowns and we walked a couple of miles, stopping occasionally at a bar for refueling, to Phil's Pad, which Is a Pad. He's a sixties hippy, and has decorated the place accordingly. He even had the good Rock And Roll tapes that Us Hippies Love. We went out to a neighborhood bar for a while so that Hannah could figure out which of her boyfriends to hang out with this evening. Midge, her main lover from The Meadow was up from Tarragona to fetch her, accompanied by his crazy friend who I met last month at the rocknroll bar. She finally decided, on Phil's recommendation, to just hang out with all of us and stick together for the evening.

We had a delicious Hippy-type dinner at Phil's pad, I got drunker on the wine, sang a bit, and we eventually headed out to the metro to get to the

Gothic Barrio. In the metro I went completely nuts with My Acrobatic Act, jumping around and falling down, teasing the third rail. I managed to falloff a bar/divider and landed on my back, doing enough damage to make it painful to walk today. I also was running and falling down in the station, on the escalators, and on the trains, and injured both my hips by sliding. I'm a mess of bruises today, but Hannah said that she'll give me. a massage tonight after the other guests depart.

Billy has been hanging around here for a while, stoned on hash and chocolate; he says that the combination has blown his mind: as he started to come down from the hash, the chocolate energized his brain, and he shows it: he's just sort of spinning around in the street, not finishing his sentences, and grinning like an idiot. I tried to connect him up with the little irish clown girls yesterday at Park Guell but he wasn't feeling well, and just sat there. They're ten and twelve and are taking acrobat classes with Hannah starting tonight and continuing for a month.

Sonia has headed for The Meadow with her father-to-be for a week or so, but has left her van parked down near the Colon statue. (YAYYY!!!). Midge, Hannah's other main boyfriend may be staying in town, because of his attraction for her, and to take the acrobat classes. She's said that she will be visiting me a lot, though. I'm So Fucking Happy about what I feel for her! And when 1'm with her! Our Lovemaking is Wonderful! (YAYYY!! GREAT FUCKING!!!). She's still in love with me, according to her, and we sat and talked for a while this morning down at the harbor. She's so Fucking Beautiful It drives me mad.

I lost the gang last night around midnight because I passed out at the Opera Cafe and then couldn't walk fast enough to keep up with their clown pace. Hannah said that she was worried about me last night and this morning but the other clowns told her not to worry about me, I could take care of myself. I don't know.

More Hannah

Don't know the day. I think it's Thursday. (THURSDAY, THURSDAY!!!). Same spot, sitting like an idiot in the street.

"Boring.", the editor told me last night at Santi's. "BORIING, Jack, anyone can write like this. The only thing that Bukowski does better than you is dialogue." He was perusing 'Factotum'.

"I thought it was great, this 'Under the Influence of Bukowski' shit!", I told him.

"It's just Boring.", he re-iterated.

"Well, you'll just have to put up with it until I finish his book, you fucker!", I said, ending the meeting.

The Question of the Day, as usual: Where's Hannah? I last saw her at Whitey's Exposition at around midnight. She left with Tarn and the yogi, not heeding my Loud Protests. I sat there with the Gang, on the third floor of the Bar/Gallery, not knowing what to do for a few minutes, until I finally decided to get drunk. I started my third bottle of wine and did a Robert Redford imitation. I got more heartfelt applause for my Steve McQueen, probably because he's dead.

I feel like shit today and my breath smells like it. I woke up alone this morning with all my clothes on. The last thing I remember is wobbling goodbye to my friends early this morning on Calle Fernando. We closed down the Opera. The Art Gallery Crowd took over the back room for hash and beer for a few hours after we closed the Gallery. The Show was a Roaring (literally) Success. My Favorite Painting is called 'Happy Jack'.

ONE P.M., FRIDAY, BOQUERIA STREET

Sitting on a store-front stoop on Calle Boqueria watching Hannah and Chris busk their puppets. Clink, clinkety, clink: A Constant Flow. Been hanging out with her since last night, Laughing, kissing, eating, drinking, smoking, and making love. She's staying at Simon's house: he's gone off to the Meadow for a few days with Tarn. We had a whole evening to ourselves; I stayed relatively sober in honor of the occasion. This morning, after an American Breakfast of eggs, sausage, coffee and milk on Simon's rooftop patio, we were joined by Another of her old Lovers: Clem, who brought her oldest son Chawakee up to visit his mum. They've been travelling in a van, busking allover the South. She hasn't seen them since November, and it looks like they'll be hanging around Barcelona for a while. Her boyfriends seem to be popping up all over.

Hannah and I are joining them for lunch later today at the van, which is parked in the fairground up at plaza Espana.

NOON SATURDAY, SANTA CLARA CAFE

Yes, we joined them for lunch. We brought a bottle of wine. They already had a couple. I'm not sure if Clem knew that I was coming with Hannah. The van is half Hannah's; they owned it jointly for about four years while they were travelling with their circus. Clem loves Hannah madly, also. It was slightly uncomfortable a few times during the afternoon, until I finally got mad, left, returned, and said that since we all loved Hannah madly, we should stay together for the afternoon. They decided to go busking at around seven and I followed.

I went into my usual Drunken Idiot Act in the metro, injuring my right ankle, left thigh, and left elbow. I can barely walk today. I stopped in a bar to get a small beer and managed to lose them. Maybe they ditched me; I don't know. I thought they'd said they were going to be working the Ramblas so I limped up and down the street looking for them for a couple of hours. It was pitiful. Hannah had said that we were scheduled to have an Evening of Love at Simon's that night, but I didn't want to limp the drunken mile to it, thru the Barrio Chino.

Hannah's Daily Life is so God-Damned complicated: sons, friends, lovers, busking partners, amigos, acrobat school, bars: shit, I can barely keep up with her. I just have to keep following her around, hoping that she finds time to squeeze me in: Sometimes I feel like a passive-dependent Fool. Why doesn't she just shine-on all of her other responsibilities and Concentrate on Our Love Affair? To hell with the rest of them! God, it's going to be painful to walk around this afternoon, trying to find Hannah. But, I must: I verily must. (VERILY MUST!! VERILY MUST!! VERILY, VERILY MUST!!!). Yes.

LATER

No Hannah; I went all the way up to Park Guell before I remembered that she said they were going to be busking up at the Sagrada Familia today, I think. I was hobbling around, with my cane, and didn't feel like I had enough energy to make it over there this afternoon, so I just sat at the park for a while and had a couple of beers. I feel fine; lonely, but fine.

One of the main reasons I'm out here is because then Hannah will know where to find me, should she so desire; which she should. I know they're somewhere in town busking today; it's so fucking frustrating. With this hobbling

I've reduced myself to, it makes it difficult to hit all of their usual hot-spots, though I've tried: passing Boqueria a couple of times today, checking out the van down at the port, Park Guell: Shit, maybe I should just let her find me.

Guess I'll just make a couple of hundred here and then head for the pad with a bottle of wine and intentions of cleaning it up, if I can find out what Rabbit has done with the keys; they weren't at Santi's this afternoon as we'd arranged when he took his girlfriend up there to fuck. I haven't been to the pad today, though: maybe he's still there.

Steve just stopped by on his way to the Sardana, to bash his head with another cognac; he considers that he is 'working' whenever he is drinking on this street rather than at Santi's. He mentioned to me that Hannah told him last week that she would be heading for Valencia today for Festival there.

Billy just came by with some little bottles of stinky liquid that he bought at the Magick Store, and was threatening to bust one of them here. I told him that if he did, it would be the last time he ever worked on the street: I'd fuck up his face. He laughed and left, without breaking one.

Where's Hannah? Where's Hannah? Where's Hannah? Where the fuck is she? (This Budding Love Affair is ruining the Novella.) Shit. I don't care. All work and no play makes Jack a dull boy, you know. I keep sending Thought Messages into the Barcelona Web, trying to influence Hannah into making an appearance here tonight: I'm not Joking, this is Not a Test. I'm not trying to prove Telepathy, I want to see her. Go man go.

Well, I just went and bought a beer, to mellow me out and make this Waiting bearable. It's working: I'm relaxing a little after a few sips. (RELAX, ALCOHOLIC-JACK, YOU'LL BE FINE!!!). Ah, well, I just bought a pack of Ducados, and my little American Heart is slightly satisfied by the Spending Experience. I know: the clowns are probably out busking somewhere and I'll see Hannah as soon as they finish. Shit, she's probably left town with Clam and Chewbaccy, headed south, and forgotten me.

I spent the whole 400 I made this morning getting around town, bread, olives, and beer. I only have about 100ptas for tonight, so far: I guess I'll hang in there for a little while longer. The typewriter tape (RIBBON!! RIBBON!!) is starting to go: I'll buy another one on Monday, if this one lasts that long. (WHAT KIND OF BOOK IS THIS, ANYWAY??). Fuck, who knows.

Well, the Tide is Way In, and Sinatra is standing here getting ready for his date with Emma tonight. He says, "You're going to kill yourself one of these days, Jack, Break Your Neck!" Billy told me the same thing earlier. Peter has been complaining to me about the cost of prophylactics in Spain. I told him to wash them and use them again. He may do it: he's borrowing 100ptas from Billy right now so he can afford the date tonight. Peter has been out on the street today for the first time in a couple of weeks because Jon-Claire changed her mind about paying his rent. He's invited Billy and me to join him and Emma at Casa Peret for dinner. Billy says he's not going if I am. Peter and I are trying to counsel Billy about saving money, and its proper use.

"It's only on Saturday that I do good; on weekdays I only make three or four hundred per hour.", he tells us, the rich little shit.

NOON, MONDAY, SAME SPOT

Didn't work out here on Sunday; hung out with Hannah all day. On Saturday Night, after buying more vegetables and a bottle of wine, I got frustrated and angry waiting for Hannah to make an unannounced visit. I drank half the wine, took the bottle and a glass, and headed over to Barrio Chino where I stood in the street below Simon's apartment yelling her name. She come out on the balcony and invited me up for dinner with Chawakee, Clem, her, and a mime whose name I forget. I told her about how I'd been pining away for her, how I've been suffering during her long, one-day absence. She allowed as how she'd been missing me a little, too. I was elated; The Love Affair was ON. Later in the night Clem and the mime left, and the kid, Hannah, and I hung around for a while, while he went to sleep. Then she and I headed out into the night looking for a bar to drink in. She'd made about ten mil on Saturday, busking puppets with Clem, her old Partner/Lover. She was rich and we were celebrating. We were in Love and Having Fun. We stayed out until we couldn't find any more open bars and went back to the pad and listened to rock and roll and danced and laughed and hugged and passed out.

Clem woke us on Sunday morning, said for her to come by the van when she got up so they could go busking, and left. We frittered away the morning rocknrolling and then had a rushed breakfast on the patio, cleaned the whole pad thoroughly in preparation for Simon and Tarn's return, and finally hooked up with Clem around one in the afternoon.

It took us about an hour to fight our way through the heavy traffic up to Park Guell, where they did their gig and made a couple of thousand; peanuts for them (YAYY!!); we arrived as the crowds were leaving.

My Job, while they played, was to watch the dog poppy and fetch an occasional beer, which I would drink most of. It's a perfect job for me, except I got tired of the dog pulling on the rope and gave her to Gregorio who I passed as he was on his way to play.

Hannah and Clem bought a bunch of sardines, cheese, bread, vegetables, and A beer, and we had a subdued picnic in the dirt on the hill overlooking the park and Barcelona. We left the park in the late afternoon, drove around for a while, tried to visit a couple of their friends, and drank a couple more beers. I was in what has become my Clown-Following Mode, and lingered with them until they parked the van as it was getting dark. I was trying to remain as sober as possible all day in preparation for Phil and Rene's dinner party that night. I succeeded fairly well: I'd only drunk about four beers all day. I was exceptionally sad as Hannah and I parted; I told her that she ought to start chasing me a little more often: I was beginning to feel like a fool.

SIX OCLOCK, SAME DAY, MONDAY, I THINK. SAME SPOT

(MONDAY, MONDAY!!! YAYYYY!!!). Yah, that's right kids, it's Monday and we're sitting out here in the street, as usual. Finally Bathed. Finally Washed my Pants in a bucket. Finally shaved. (Where's Hannah?). Feel pretty Good: Got some things done, Ate some stew, drank a bottle of wine, finished the Boocowski book, read my own, and Billy dropped by for a chat at the end of siesta. All Seems well tonight. Frank, Jacques, and Billy are scheduled to drop by for dinner tonight; should be an interesting Mellow Evening. If Hannah comes by, as she said she might, I'll drop everything else. (HIS DICK??).

Naturally, If I was independently poverty-stricken I wouldn't be out here typing tonight, I'd be sleeping. I have a new book to read: Tropic of Capricorn. Jacques gave it to me last night, trying to wean me from Boo-cow-ski.

I got out here too late to catch Hannah on her way to Acrobat Classes with her sons. She said she'd probably stop by at some point. I won't get all involved in telling about how Much I Love Her: It's getting hard for all of us.

The Tide is In. The Churning is in Full Swing: The Pastry is Dribbling into the Catalan Gullets; We're All Happy! (YAYYY!!!).

Some young Locals just gave me the 25pta quiz (in Spanish) :
"Why do you do this?"
"It's my life."
"Where are you from?"
"San Francisco."
"Is there no work there?"
"Yes, Plenty."
"Why are you not there?"
"I don't like it there."
"Do you like it here?"
"Yes, Very Much."
"But, why are you sitting out here writing? (like a fool)."
"Because it's not important to me, money, things, Not Important!"
"Couldn't you make more money in the united States?"

"Yes, I did once, but I snorted it all up my nose with cocaine."
"What?"
"I used to be a smuggler, now I'm a writer."
"You were a smuggler?"
"Yes."
"And, now you are in Barcelona? Why?"
"Because there is Personal Liberty here. It's New. Franco is dead."
"But, Isn't it better in America?"
"No, for me It's Fucked. I have problems there: It's where I'm from."
"Well, Good Luck.", they said, leaving me no richer.

I've been out here for half an hour and there hasn't been one fucking clink.)

12: 30 TUESDAY, SAME SPOT

I believe it's March 12th, however it may be March 5th. It's cold, windy, overcast: Gothic Grey. Got out here late because I had to drink a couple of bottles of wine at the pad last night with Billy, Frank, Jacques, And Hannah and Chawakee. She stopped by after her Acrobat class for a bowl of stew and some wine. Frank grilled her about her past for a while and was surprised to find out that she was born at Oxford and attended Cambridge. His eyes kept getting bigger and bigger to the point where they nearly popped out of his face when she was telling what it was like to live in a teepee in Wales.

She is happy, literate, intelligent, beautiful, talented, liberated, motherly, communicative, independent, and sexually attractive. Frank fell in love with her; he told me as he left that he wanted her to be his gal. Then he broadcast a disclaimer. I believe the former.

She didn't stay the night with me because she had to go do something in the other parts of her life. She has definitely taken control of herself; she's no longer Young and Foolish where Love is Concerned. Darn. I think she's coming over for lunch today; or maybe it was dinner: I forget, too much beano.

Frank and Jacques were complaining to me (and Hannah) that they no longer have Starring Roles in the book since she cartwheeled into my life; they read us excerpts to prove it. Hannah read aloud for about an hour from some of the recent pages, and we were all Laughing Heartily.

Fucking Wind, blowing through the holes in my socks, clink, a duro. And now I can't find the new copy of Tropic of Capricorn that Jacques stole from Phil and loaned to me the other night. Phil took it back from me earlier today but I got it back from him when Peter told me that Phil had borrowed it from Hadass, who had borrowed it from Jacques. I think it's the copy I gave him in Montana. But now it's disappeared from my bag. Phil just left also. Hmmmm.

Frank is reading 'Factotum' by Bukowsky. Peter is reading 'The Return Of The King', as is Billy. I think Phil must be reading 'Tropic of Capricorn'. I don't think Gandalf can read, or write. Whitey just finished 'The Executioner's Song', which he borrowed from Frank and has loaned to Jacques, and I've loaned my William Blake to Rebecca. Nobody knows what Amani is reading; or writing. Frank is writing a book; however, I am his biographer. Jacques is writing a story about my life, which he mails to my brother in installments. Jacques is also, writing a book called 'Frank and Billy', about Frank and Billy. phil is writing a book called 'The Barcelona Experience', mainly about me and Frank. I am writing a book called, 'Amani is a Stupid Fucker'. My brother writes to Jacques, not to me. Hadass writes me letters which I can barely bear to read. Hannah has been reading the book I'm writing about her.

6:15, SAME SPOT. TUESDAY STILL

Ah, had a delicious and satisfying lunch with Billy and Rebecca at the pad. I ran into her on Calle Fernando as I was on my way home during siesta; invited her over for some stew; she brought the wine; I bought vegetables for the stew. It was great. I wanted to lay with her, at least, but couldn't remember the Right Words for seducing an ex-ex-wife. Oh well, we Are Good Friends. The Memories Flow in her Company: I still think she's cute; she hardly shows her forty years. She looks the same as when I met her. Cute as a Bug, with the Experience to be Fun in Bed. What the hell, I had a hand in it.

We talked about our daughters: it looks like they may not make it over here this summer: money problems: Life Direction Problems. What a shame. Billy was his usual Obnoxious Self for about half of Siesta, but I did get to teach them how to shoot craps, as the wine took hold. I feel Great Now, hope it lasts. Still want to stay sober because it looks like Hannah must have said she'd see me tonight: she didn't show up today.

Well, it's an Idiot's Night tonight: a lady did a Complete Stumbling Prat-fall right in front of me; another got the wheels of her little pull-cart hopelessly stuck in the drain grating, and another just unconsciously dropped her umbrella as if it were a turd. They're stumbling around all over town. Something to do with the Vibes, I think. Now, two Africans have just asked me if the fucking typewriter was for sale: they were coveting it heavily. I told them that it was my Main Thing, that I am a writer,_and it isn't for sale. I'd better stay indoors tonight because of the weird feeling in town; just got over the last Concussion.

NOON WEDNESDAY, SANTA CLARA CAFE, IN THE STREET, AS USUAL

Woke up at nine oclock this morning: No Hannah. Flick it, went back to sleep and dreamed about her: she came walking up to me in Clown Dress, incredibly happy to see me, And: No Kids or boyfriends. So… Dream Lover, I guess it is. Shit.

Wowee, Zowie! Hannah just walked up, just like in the dream, Smiling, Happy to see me, been thinking of me, been missing me. Ah! God, I'm Falling in Love again, after a long day of loneliness. She and Chawakee are busking down on Boqueria, along with Simon. They're coming to the pad for lunch today: I'm glad. Clink, clink: Hannah just dropped 20ptas in the box. She's gone over to the bread store to get a cowflop, one of which she has plopped into the box: It's gonna be a Great Day.

I've got enough for a cafeconleche, trying to stay straight today. For Hannah? Just stay straight. Only drink Beer for lunch, wine moves us along the incoherence track a little too rapidly. The coffee will go well with the cowflop. Hannah's Back! (YAYY!! CHAWAKEE'S BACK!! YAYY!!) .

Cigarettes, matches, pastry, coffee, My Gal, a friend: I have it all today. I feel great; I could drink ten cafeconleche's, if I had the bread. (WHAT???). Beatnik talk, kids, before your time. Scratch. (WHAT??). Dough. Moolah. Dinero. Jack. Sheckels. (OH! MONEY!). Yah.

6: 30 SAME SPOT

Another perfect siesta; I'm getting to love it here. Friends, lovers, kids, salads, stew, beer, wine, cigarettes: from two oclock til 5:30, Life is Nearly Perfect. The orbit of the earth had changed enough so that the sun shines on the patio til about 4:30; when I first started living there, there was no sun after two. Perfect.

Hannah and Chawakee joined Billy and Me for the best salad yet: we spent about 500ptas on it and it overflowed with redpeppers, onions, green onions, olives, squash, spinach, and oil and vinegar. And Garlick. Fucking Great! Then we had the Usual Eternal Stew, with pan integral.

Billy split and Chawakee drew a picture of Hannah busking while she and I snuggled in the bed. I lobbied lightly for copulation but between Chawakee and Hannah's hesitations, I soon gave up and settled for hugs and kisses and reading the book aloud. They both loved it. (THAT'S BECAUSE THEY'VE BECOME THE STARS, MANIPULATIVE-JACK!!!). Yah, yah, well it IS Funny, even if you're not a character in it, I've been told. (ONCE!). They're invited back for dinner and intimacy this evening, and will be bringing English Phil's two little blonde Irish daughters, one of whom is named Tara, I think. I've invited Billy also, but he may be going to a movie instead. Too bad for him: the two girls are out-of-sight.

The plot is: have dinner with the kids, put them on the metro at eleven (after absorbing their intense energy for a couple of hours), return to the pad, and let nature have its way with us. That's the Plan: sounds great to me.

Hannah and I have agreed to try to conduct this Love Affair as though it were a Modern Romance: everyone is free to do exactly as they please, although both of us admit that we sometimes have Jealous Tendencies, Liberated though we may be. we'll see; I'm hoping we end up Madly, Madly, Possessively In Love.

How I Came to Love Clowning, Aid Clowns

Ah, A Happy Little Human: me. Hugging, Kissing, Talking, Rubbing, Snuffling, Eating, Drinking, Laughing, and Making The Love: What more is there, what more could I ask for: The Nearly Perfect Evening. The only Negative: my sleeplessness, caused by a slight withdrawal from alcohol last night, after a couple of weeks of steady drinking. I sweated heavily and slept Delerious Nightmares, but being reassured by the closeness of Hannah, with whom I was Simianly Entwined. (YAYY! MONKEYS!!).

We are getting closer; the Love Affair is getting better. The Fucking is Superb. She is heading for Valencia for the Fallas, the Statue-Burning Festival there this weekend and has asked me if I'd like to come along. I actually would, but don't have the money for the train ticket, which I hesitate to ask her to supply, though she has offered. (YAY! FOR NON-GIGOLO JACK!!). I'll probably go. I haven't been out of town for about four months, and have been working out here almost every day; I could use a vacation. (WORKING???? VACATION???)

The Tentative plan is for me to accompany her and Chawakee with Irish Drumming while they are busking with whistles and puppets. I'm not sure if this entails me wearing some kind of clown outfit, but I think so. Jacques is afraid that it will signal the end of my Writing career once I start being a clown: it's more my style.

Hannah says that the money is Very Good at the Fallas, and that the party itself is worth seeing. I may do it. As usual, I'll postpone a decision and let Events Decide. Hannah and Chawakee are down on Boqueria busking today, and are scheduled for dinner at the pad with the two young Irish blonde girls, and May come over for lunch today. (WHERE'S HANNAH! '?) .

Billy dropped by after dinner last night; the blondes didn't make it because they had to go home to their father Phil. Billy brought some hash which he smoked mostly himself, while Hannah and I split a bottle of wine. I wanted more wine, and, trying to corrupt me, Billy offered to pay for it. I won the battle, opting for Sweat and Love instead, and didn't go out to buy one, though Billy kept insisting that I do, knowing that it would fuck up the Love Affair for the night if I got too drunk. What a kid. I told him that maybe he should come to Valencia with us this weekend. He said that he doesn't think Rebecca will let him go, even with Hannah along as The Adult. I told him to think about it. He is. He probably needs a break from this intense Barcelona Night Life. He has had a lousy attitude about busking lately, it's not much fun for him; and Rebecca, since she doesn't get paid til the end of the month, asked him to give her 300ptas a day so she can eat. I've already been charging him about 50ptas per meal; he must wonder what is happening with his 'parents'.

Yah, as I think about it, I'll swallow my pride (WHAT PRIDE???'?), and let Hannah buy me a ticket to Valencia. Maybe I can pay her back out of the busking money we'll make when I drum with them. Yah, that's it. (YAYY!! DECISION-MASTER-JACK!! YAYYY!!!). That's it: I just made a Decision. A change of scene from Post Office, Market, stew and Wine. Maybe even go to the beach. Yah. A Train Ride, A new place, A Big party, Great potential for Fun, Fun, Fun. Yah, with my Lover.

Hannah doesn't have a 'partner' for busking today, so she will keep all of the money for herself; she does just as well by herself and makes more money; she'll need it for my train ticket. (YAYY!! THE ORIGINAL GIGOLO-JACK, THE ONE WE KNOW!!!). It's Love, kids, Love! I wouldn't accept a penny If I didn't Love her so. (YAYYY!!! A COUNTRYWESTERN SONG! !! OH, I WOULDN'T TAKE A PENNY IF I DIDN'T LCN'ER SO. SHE COULD TAKE THE TRAIN WITHOUT ME BUT I REALLY WOULDN'T GO, AND SOONER OR LATER ONE OF US MUST KNOW ...). stop, Stop! You're starting to steal Dylan's stuff. (WE MADE IT UP!!). Sure, you just can't remember, you were never RocknRollers. (OOOOOH, HAVE YOU SEEN YOUR MOTHER, BABY, STAND IN' IN THE SHADOWS!!?? HOW ABOUT THAT???). Yah, you only know that because I sing it to you sometimes to make you feel secure. (YAYYY!!! HE'S TALKING TO US LIKE REAL PEOPLE! YAYY!!).

As we lay in bed last night, Hannah and I talked about The Golden Ocean, The River of Life, God, What We Are, and how we feel about it. It gives her the Constant Joy that she experiences; It almost makes me cry; we're Crazy in the Same Way: We Love Living. There is a Real Potential for Us Together; We arrived here, at the same place, by different routes: I don't think she's seen as many of the Weird Uses to which people put this Universal Energy as have I. Who knows. (ONLY GOD AND US, QUA-SI-PHILOSOPHO-JACK!!). Yah, She's basically more Consistently positive than I am; hers manifests as Mild Joyous Ecstasy, mine as a Sense of Humor. I love her.

Chawakee, her oldest son, just ran by and dropped a croissant in the box: they are given a bag of them by an old lady every day. If she forgets to buy the pastries for them, she gives them 100ptas with an apology. Even croissants bubble up out of the Golden Springs. (YAYY!! MYSTICAL PASTRY!! THE CATALAN RELIGION! 1). God.

Hannah used to sail and live on boats, as did I, and I want to sail on that ocean with her. (YAYY!! CROISSANTS SAILING ON A GOLD OCEAN!!). I don't want any of this 'ships that pass in the night' shit. (SO THE FLYING SAUCER GOES SWOOPIING LOW OVER THE GOLDEN SEA AND PASSES RIGHT OVER A GIANT CROISSANT SAILIING ALONG WITH A BUNCH OF CLOWNS DANCING ON IT. THE SAUCER HAD TO GO TO MONTANA FOR NEW BOOTS, AND THEY REALI ZE THAT THEY HAVE BEEN SHIPS THAT PASSED IN…). Stop! You're mixing up the whole book: I was trying to write a Love Story here, not a Space Story. (OH). Besides, I don't really like croissants that much, anyway. (SO… THIS GIANT CHAPATTIE COMES SAILING ACROSS THE GOLDEN OCEAN…) Stop! Never Mind! Just stay out of this for a while. This is not a proper Peanut Gallery subject: It's My Love Affair, and none of your own. (GIT ALONG, GIT ALONG, GIT ALONG, LITTLE LOVER-BOY!!!). Forget it.

There is not much of a tide tonight, but I'm getting by. As always, I suppose. (WE LIKED THE CHOCOLATE!! HAVE ANOTHER CIGARETTE, HEALTHY-JACK!!). Billy has finished reading 'The Lord of the Rings' for the umpteenth time, and Gandalf is back from Italy; they've gone to sit in the Santa Clara Cafe and have CaféConLeches.

I think Hannah is going to bleach and then Henna her hair; in return I'm going to shave and bathe twice weekly. Billy told her not to do it because next I would probably want her to get blue contact lenses. He thinks I want everyone in the world to look like me. I do. (YAYY!! A WORLD OF HOODY-DOO-DYSI!! YAYY!!! WE ALREADY LOVE TARN AND CHAWAKEE! !! AND BILLY!! NOW HANNAH!! YAYYYYY!!!!!). Beauty is more than freckle-deep, kids. (YAYY!! FRECKLES!!).

The tide is in, the duros are not; my nose is turning redder the longer it takes for money to drop in the writer's box. polka-dots are beginning to appear on my pants, and the toes of my shoes are beginning to turn up. Come on, people, Save Me from a fate worse than Fooling Around: Clowning. Help, help, I'm turning into a clown! (YAYYY! !)…

The 'Fallas' in Valencia

What a Fiesta! What a Trip! What a Love Affair! Hannah, Tarn, Chawakee, Billy, and I spent about three days travelling, and busking in Valencia. We made and spent a mini-fortune, about 25mil; Hannah on food, Me on Drink, and The Boys on Firecrackers. We've been back since last night's train ride from Valencia, during which the kids turned the train into a playground for clowns, I turned it into a bodega, and Hannah took a nap. We ended up with both of Hannah's sons because it looks like She and Clem have finally split up. Clem decided not to take Chawakee with him to join the circus in Madrid; Hannah has them both now, at Simon the Yogi's house. She's probably staying in Barcelona for a couple more weeks and then moving back to the Meadow to live in her teepee.

We left Barcelona and drove to the Meadow in Simon's van on Sunday, I think, accompanied by Gandalf who was heading for Morocco on the spur of the moment.

The Meadow: Hippy vans, converted school busses, Rocky terraces, Mick's home-built house, Another house inhabited by another of Hannah's ex-lovers, a few acres of gardens, hilly and rocky, a beautiful view of the Sea about two kilometers away, broken cars, trailers, bicycles, motorcycles, goat-pen, chicken shed, outside shitter, orange trees, olive trees; a beautiful spot for an old hippy to retire to. So many agree with this that they linger around being a burden on the Permanent Residents: Mick, His wife Terry, their two grown sons, and a girl-child. Mick likes music and wine and has a Similar Attitude towards Responsibility and Ambition as do I.

As I sat on the hitching post in front of Mick and Terry's house, watching Elam, Sonia1s Israeli boyfriend, digging furrows for the garden, I flashed back to New Mexico in the late sixties: he could have been up on the plateau near Taos, planting an Alternative Vegetable Garden, except that the Political Emphasis is noticeably lower, Here and Now.

I brought a couple of bottles of wine, of which I drank most; the locals, about twenty of them, were recovering from a party/celebration the night before. We listened to rocknroll and later I played drums while a couple of Hannah's ex-lovers sang and played guitars: I was having a party of my own until very late, when I joined Hannah in her sleeping bag in one of the out-buildings.

The wind was gusting about fifty knots, we were on the second floor, and there was nothing covering some of the windows. We spent the night inside a drum-set, being awakened every few minutes by the banging of various boards, covers, chairs being blown over in the room, and the incredible whistling of the wind; it was a nearly sleepless night.

Earlier, at dusk, Hannah and I went for a walk to the top of the hill, where we made Wonderful Love on a terrace underneath an Old Olive Tree, to the delight of the herd of little hippy urchins who were spying on us from the branches of nearby trees. She spent the rest of the evening sequestered in Her (and Clem's) Van, discussing the direction of their lives, while I sat outside in a wine trance on a rock, occasionally throwing pebbles onto the van's roof to get attention, and other childish activities.

When we awoke in the morning, Clem had already left for Madrid in the van, alone. They've been splitting up for about six months and it is often an uncomfortable situation for both of them. And me.

We lingered around all the morning, drinking tea, and eating bread and margarine, the English staples I've learned to fancy a bit. We finally raced to the train station in Simon's van after about an hour of lengthy good-byes, and caught the train for Valencia.

We bought wine, food, and candy, and set off for what we knew was to be a Wonderful Adventure. Our Excitement was High; playing, drinking, laughing, and talking for the next couple of hours. It was Great to be On The Road again. Yah. Gandalf was still travelling with us, but was sitting in the non-smoking section for his health.

We arrived in Valencia at around two, in the middle of Intense Celebrating, and walked the two or three blocks to the Main Plaza. As we were passing through the flower-infested center, a scuffle broke out between two gypsy women: hair-pulling, screaming, dress-ripping, and like that. Their men were trying to separate them, with the help of a cop, to no avail.

One of the men got punched, then another. Now the fighting began For Real. There were Serious Punches being thrown, a couple of guys went down, along with the cop. One gypsy bonked another on the back of the head with a small ladder. The plaza was full of hundreds of celebrants, who cleared a 100ft diameter circle to make room for the fight.

We had been in town for about five minutes and I was thinking, "What a festival this is going to be!" Another of the fighters had a hammer and was chasing his opponents into the crowd, to Its ecstatic and terrified screaming and scattering. There were about ten gypsys involved in the melee now, running, screaming, and fighting all over the plaza; and the women were still at it too.

One gang was obviously winning: after a few minutes they'd chased the others into the crowd, and the guy who'd been hit with the ladder proceeded to destroy all of the other tribe's musical equipment: drums, tables, horns, boxes, etc. The crowd who'd been gathering for the parade went wild: it was a beautiful, sunny, perfect day for watching a Gypsy Fight. Hannah was almost Gleeful; she told me later that she's seen fights like this many times before, and this one wasn't really Serious.

I did see a couple of the young men begin to reach into their pockets at one point, but I suppose the Gypsy Adrenalin had not yet reached the point where Stabbing begins.

I know I got My Daily Rush, as I scurried away from the action when it got close to me, pulling the cart with the puppets and the sleeping bags. We retired to a sidewalk table in front of a tourist bar, facing directly onto the 60ft-high pile of flowers in the middle of the plaza. Tarn and Chawakee followed the gypsys around for a while after the fight, Hannah went off to see if some friends had a place for us to stay, while Billy and I sat at the cafe drinking and sun-bathing with the ever-increasing crowd of tourists.

After about an hour, Hannah returned with the news that she couldn't find her friends, just as the first of about two hundred bands began trumpeting by. Each band represented a Guild, or group of some kind; I'm not sure what exactly, because of their language problem.

Each band was accompanied by about fifty 'virgins': little girls dressed up with those Spanish Doilies on their heads and wearing high heels, make-up, and jewelry. They were immaculately beautiful, pimples or no. This was all a celebration for the virgin Mary, I think. Each girl carried a bouquet of flowers which she handed to one of the men whose job it was to throw it on the Huge pile. It went on like this for a couple of hours, or four beers. The girls were accompanied by full-grown men, like virginity guards, and followed by a similar-sized group of young men-'virgins'. Quite a show. Some of the slightly older girls/women were Really Preening as they passed the Reviewing Crowds; there were fewer virgins in Valencia come dawn.

The most ludicrous aspect of the 'virgins March' were the groups which contained middle-aged, pot-bellied virgins. Lust was running neck and neck with hilarity and drunken-ness in the crowd. I was keeping up as best I could, staying cool with liberal doses of beer at regular intervals.

We headed out to busk with the marionettes, me playing the bongo drums behind Hannah. She gathered crowd after duro-throwing crowd for a couple of hours until we took a cafe-sitting break and counted up the take: about five mil. After cafeconleche and beers we played again for a couple more hours. I was in an Irish-drummer, beer-and-wine-sotted Trance, madly in love with Hannah, and enjoying the fuck out of myself. Billy played his recorder around the corner for a while and then joined Hannah and me on tambourine. It was a beautiful evening, and I was forgetting that I'd ever done anything other than sit on the curb behind my Clown/Lover and bang on a drum, looking and feeling like Jesse James.

We quit for a while, and on the way to a cafe we unexpectedly came upon Clem; also dancing his puppets and playing Irish music. He joined us at the cafe, and it was decided that we could all stay at the van on the beach after busking together one more time. Funny Bounces, Funny Bounces.

We busked for another hour or so, and went to a cafe where we dumped piles and piles of money onto the tables, and then all five of us spent the next half hour sorting and counting it. It makes you feel incredibly rich to dump bags of money on tables. We repeated this process, in various bars around Valencia, about three or four times a day for a few more days. God, Is It Fun!

The Last Day In Valencia: World War Three started at about 8 oclock in the morning; I was wakened from my sleep by Bombs exploding all over town. It was almost deafening, even though we were about a mile away from the main action. Hannah and I were sleeping on the beach in front of the van, and tried to ignore the explosions by making love, but at a Most Inopportune Moment, someone in the van began throwing firecrackers into the sand right near us. Explosius Interruptus.

We had a tea, coffee, bread, croissant, and margarine breakfast on a blanket on the beach, then headed into town to busk; leaving the three boys at the van for the morning. We made a few mil, piled it onto a table at a cafe, ate expensive snack meals, walked around town looking at the giant papier-mache statues in every plaza, had siesta down by the river, and went to meet the Tractor People.

The Tractor People: Joe, an incredibly weird German hippy, his wife: a Jesus Freak, Joe's English girlfriend (Chris the Mandolin Player's old gal, Joe stole her from Chris at the Meadow when he passed through), and their toddler sons, have taken a year and a half to travel to Valencia from Germany, pulling their home-made gypsy house with a tractor at 15mph downhill, 8mph on the flat. In Germany the licensing for mobile homes and trucks is so bureaucratically sticky that many hippies figured out how to get around it by using tractors for pulling their houses. Tractors have much looser paperwork.

Joe is an alcoholic-lecher, rocknroller hippy of the classic sixties West Coast Type: we got on great when he found out I was from 'Frisco' and knew Pigpen. They have dogs, kids, bikes, a trailer behind the house, chairs, pots, pans, a foot-powered organ; drums, flutes, clarinets, and all the accoutrements for a successful travelling life.

We shared a couple of bottles of wine, sat in the dirt outside, played with the kids and dogs, and then headed back into the city to busk some more. We set up in front of the giant statue of 'The Fool', who was dangling various life-sized puppets from his hands, The gist of 'The Fool' statue was Anti-Nato, as were a few of the other three hundred or so scattered around town. The Fool was about sixty feet high, paper-maiche, air-brushed in beautiful pastel colors, extremely life-like, and was looking sideways and down, directly at us. We made a fortune there.

We were joined by Clem, Billy, Chawakee, and Tarn for the evening; I became the Go-fer: escorting the kids to get hot chocolates and drinks, fetching the occasional beer needed by Hannah to wet her whistle, along with mine. The frequency of the bombs was increasing as the evening passed; the bands, who had been marching all around the town at all hours anyway, began passing every fifteen minutes, blaring and preening. The Celebration was interfering with our duro-earning because we had to cease until they passed.

Excitement was building, they were getting ready to burn all the statues that had been a year abuilding. The streets were crowding, the bombs were constant, and the kids were attacking the sidewalks with little firecracker bombs everywhere. We continued being Irish buskers, drawing stares, duros, and street-blocking crowds; it was fun, and lucrative.

We began moving around town, fueled by a couple of bottles of champagne, compliments of Clem, following the crowds from statue to doomed statue until the crush became too great and we joined a throng to watch the first of the 'children's statues' be burned: they are smaller, adjacent, more (if possible) cartoonish versions of the large ones. I was getting a hint of How Weird this evening was going to be: the crowds go wild when the statues blow up.

We moved to a large plaza where Clem and Hannah set up again; I drummed and drank wine that Billy was finding on the street for me, while the boys went nuts lighting off firecrackers; bottle rockets, and the little throwing-bombs. Gandalf, in the company of a woman he was hustling, stopped and threw me a flower, chatted; and bid us good luck and good-bye: he was off to Morocco in the morning.

I, under the increasing influence of wine and beer, began clowning a bit more, falling down, and generally goofing around for the amusement of the excitable crowd, while Hannah and Clem kept dancing their puppets and playing music. The crowd loved it: I set off rockets in my hand, some of which didn't take off, exploding on the launch pad; same flew into the squealing crowd, and one shot straight up, turned around, came back, and exploded right in front of my face, to the extreme delight of the fire-and-adrenalin-seeking Valencianos.

They cheered for more, but I stepped aside and let Clem and Hannah proceed with the more pacific parts of the program, which they did until the crowds began surging towards where the Real Burnings were about to commence. We followed them to the nearest statue/display. We stood with the jam-packed crowds about fifty feet from the explosions surrounding the display, until the whole thing burst into gasoline-induced flames and generated a heat which caused the whole crowd to back up in fear of face-blistering; except for me, who approached to within about ten feet of the conflagration, dancing, hooting, and threw my wine bottle on the fire, to ecstatic cheers and applause.

The flames were shooting about fifty feet in the air, firecrackers (bangers) exploding Everywhere, rockets shooting hundreds of feet, and the crowd was in ecstasy. We followed them to the next burning where the whole process was repeated again until the firemen doused the flames once it had burned down some. We did this for about an hour, until we got tired of risking our lives with a death by fire. The Valencianos kept right on marching to the next statue. And the beat of a different drummer.

We tried to catch a bus to the beach, but were unable to get on the one with Clem, Chawakee, and Tarn; so Hannah, Billy, and I retired to a bar to have a beer and relax and wait for the crowd at the bus-stop to thin.

Billy has the habit of drawing tourist Americans into Strange conversations whenever he hears them talking American as they pass. He did it again this night in the bar to two young pseudo-intellectual college students on holiday from Berkeley; as they passed our table he drew them into his Web of False Innocence by singing "I'm a Yankee Doodle Dandy." They thought he was a ten year old girl because he had the drawstring of his hooded parka pulled tight around his face; he did nothing to dispel their illusion, even answering them in a higher-than-normal voice, and leading them, by his answers, to ask more questions. I thought it was slightly humorous until they began talking to me about, "There is no War! There is No politics!", and other college-coffee-house type bullshit, and referring to Billy as "She". Billy kept baiting them, and they kept responding and lecturing us until I finally lost my temper and began telling them to go away. Even Hannah had a few harsh words for them. They wouldn't leave and thought that we should become automatic friends because we spoke the same language.ß One of them kept telling me that we ought to have a talk because there was a lot I could learn from him about world politics. I blew my top and jumped up, pretending to reach for a knife in my back pocket, screaming that I was going to slit their throats if they didn't back off, and proceeded to chase them the length of the bar, to the amusement of the Spanish, Hannah, and Billy. I was dressed all in black: pants, shirt, coat, boots, and fedora, and the Spanish must have thought we were English Clown Gypsys and this was probably normal behavior for us.

We exited the bar and waited out in the street for a bus, mainly to escape our American tormenters, but they soon renewed their collegiate attack, whereupon I had to repeat the whole performance by chasing them down the street. Adrenalin is where you find it, I suppose. Next time I'll let Billy deal with the results of his gringo-baiting; let him chase them through the streets. We gave up waiting for a bus; and finally took a cab out to the beach; where I was supposed to sleep under the van with Hannah because there was a light rain:

I declined her invitation, somehow feeling it would be an insult to sleep under her boyfriend's van. I took a bßlanket and walked out onto the beach and lay down in the rain. Fuck it, I thought; I wasn't co-operating very well in a difficult situation. Unusual: I woke up freezing at dawn and crawled under the god-damned van and got into the bag with Hannah, tried to eat her, but ended up with humble pie:

Ah, well, in the morning it was a New Day; another English Breakfast on the sand, an almost tearful good-bye with Clem, shave my face, wash the kids, and like that; until we split and headed for the train station, leaving Clem preparing to head for Madrid in the van to join the circus.

Even I was slightly sad, though I've only known him for a couple of weeks and we haven't exactly become the best of friends: He'd been with Hannah for over four years; I think. It would have been fine with me if we all went off to join the circus; as long as I didn't have to sleep Under the Truck. After all, Hannah has the capability to raise all five of us.

We lingered on the lawn in front of the train station for most of the afternoon, drinking wine and eating home-made bocadillos, until we caught the Barcelona express around six. I was still in Love. Still Am.

Barcelona News/Pad News

Saturday noon, Bread Street, in front of the Brusi

The Brusi Bar, Steve's Bar, is closed on Saturday. I can type here today without being hassled by the owner. My original spot on this street.

BARCELONA NEWS/PAD NEWS:

It's almost sunny, perfect temperature, happy tide In, 30ptas in the box, dirty dishes in the sink, ashtrays full, glasses have scum in the bottoms, patio covered with olive pits and cigarette butts, bed disheveled, table covered with papers books and junk, carpet dirty, raisins smashed on floor, gas running out, clothes smell, four sheets of typing paper left, need a shower, need a shave, streets covered with litter, pigeons flying everywhere, people up-beat, have cigarettes, have toothache, left leg still hurts from metro clowning a few weeks ago, mad bell-ringer at work, pastry feeding ubiquitous, paucity of duros, (YAYYYYY!!!), Peanut Gallery back, Howdy Donna back from Switzerland, (YAYY!!), Frank's money due at any time, Jacques and Marta ON, (YAYY!!), Steve in the Sardana bashing head with cognac, Old purple Fairy leaving town, Ray Charles on his way to tennis court, American Tourists Obvious.

 Five of the clowns are busking down on Boqueria: Hannah, Sonia, Simon, Chris, and Roy (and Chalky) (YAYYY!!!); they look like a Medieval Street Gang. Chris, who's dressed like a Fool, has a little puppet dressed similarly, which spins and hops around like an idiot; it doesn't dance, as do Hannah's; It's perfect for his act. They're only making about as much money as does Hannah when she busks solo.

 I spent the night solo, also; Billy came for dinner and stayed to bullshit until about eleven, when he departed into Friday Night to find someone with hash. I stayed at the pad, drinking wine and reading Tropic of Capricorn until retiring early, at one. Slept peacefully til about eleven this morning: an actionless night. Hannah was too tired to come last night: she stayed at Simon's: I missed her, but I'm Grown-up Now, and can take these emotional ups and downs without batting an eyelid. Sure. I've invited as many of the clowns as want to, to come to the pad for lunch today. Billy's gone off to buy a new recorder.

 That's The News, Up To The Minute!

Snuffling with Hannah

Barcelonetta Busking

Noon Sunday, Santa Clara Cafe; the liquor store is closed.

The clowns are busking today up at Park Guell but I decided to come here instead of tagging along like I usually do on Sundays. Besides, Hannah is becoming Hard-Hearted Hannah starting today: she's not going to give me any more money Not To Work and hang out with her. Though and still, I may just pack this up about two oclock and head on up there anyway. Anyway? Take the Metro to Lesseps, then transfer to a number 24 bus.

Still and Though, I may just buy a bottle of beer and continue cleaning up the pad, which I've been doing for the last hour. Woke up early this morning and talked, laughed, and snuffled with Hannah. I'd never snuffled before; she showed me how, she's been doing it since she was a child, to dispel loneliness; it's Really Fun. You put your face in something soft (pillow, blanket, hair, neck, armpit, groin) and sniff and snort and humm and squirm and bury your nose there and inhale deeply and Snuffle; it's Very Primitive. She's an Expert.

She's really been following me around a lot lately, coming to the pad, visiting me at the pitch; I love it. Serves her right: I put in my stint. Ah! Ah! and Ah! Ain't Love Grand! (YAYY!!).

I had all of the clowns for lunch yesterday: Hannah, Chawakee, Sonia, Chris, Simon, ROY and his gal Pilly, Billy, and American Phil. Salad, Stew, Wine, and Cheese: Ummm. (UMMMMM!!! YUM!!). Yah. I'd made about 200ptas which I spent on food, and the clowns made about 5 or 6 mil; they chipped in some fish and bread and helped pay for the second bottle of wine, which I fetched.

Along about five, they decided to go busking in BARCELONETA, while waiting for the Poetry Reading/Puppet Show which was scheduled for about six. Hannah made a deal with me: she'd give me 240ptas (she bargained me down from our usual 300) if I would accompany her, and not come out here and type. It seemed O.K. to me; I probably would've made 100 here.

Chris, Sonia, Hannah, Simon, Chalky, Billy, and I set up near the Barceloneta Metro exit and played for about half an hour. Rebecca, as Official Mother, watched Billy's first 'clown' act: He fiddled with the life-sized dog-puppet while wearing my red clown nose; he was embarassed at first but soon got into it. Hannah and Sonia on pennywhistles, Chris on mandolin, Chawakee on diabolo, and I drank beer and played the drums. The Take was small: about 800, I think. We then headed over to the puppet theatre where the poetry reading/puppet show was to be, and found that the Hippy Puppeteer/poets were having a parade all around Barcelonetta in order to draw a crowd to the show.

We hunted for, found, and joined the parade. It was a motley crew; no different in appearance than was our group; with drums, guys with swords, clowns, bigger drums, jugglers, and like that. We marched around Barcelonetta to the amazement, joy, and confusion of the citizens, stopping every couple of blocks so that one of the poets could harangue the crowds; it was bizarre in the extreme. We didn't gather much of a following, but the parade set the tone for what was to follow back at the 'theatre'.

There were about four poets, taking turns reading, mostly in Spanish. The crowd loved them. I couldn't understand their words, but enjoyed the show because they were all weird people, expostulating, gesticulating, grimacing, exhorting, shouting, and generally carrying on like anarchists, which they were all advertised to be. The puppet show, however, didn't need explaining, and consisted of extremely strange puppets: insects, monsters, neurotics, puppets that fall apart, and like that. And was Completely Hilarious in any language.

I was tempted to get on stage and Rant in English a couple of times, under the influence of Beer, but restrained myself, for better or worse, I don't know. As it ended and we were leaving, I turned to the crowd and yelled, "I have seen the best minds of my generation ruined by the fear of nuclear war!" Someone said What?, and I repeated it. As we left, Rebecca said, "I didn't understand your poem, Jack?" What?

The clowns had decided to go busking on the Ramblas and were going to walk the mile or so to get there. I said I didn't want to walk, as they always walk faster than I want to, but would rather take the metro. Hannah gave me a handful of change for the fare, and I parted company with the rest of them, saying we'd meet a little later on the Ramblas. I jumped the toll-booth in the metro, rode to station Juame, bought a liter of beer, and headed for the Ramblas.

On the way to their pitch I passed the guy with electric guitar and amplifier who plays and looks just like Jimi Hendrix, and stopped to encourage him. I fell in with a 75-year-old Spanish Woman who was also dancing along with the music, and who assured me that her heart and spirit were as young as mine, shared my beer, and generally cavorted and danced with me, to the crowd's delight, for about half an hour, til the beer was gone and I wobbled up the Ramblas looking for my clowns.

I found them, in full busking swing, and joined them on drums and beer; they had mixed feelings and some discussion about my condition, but Billy assured them that I was always like this and that everything was OK. We played for about a mil, and then Hannah, Billy, and I headed for the pad for dinner, where they critiqued my behaviour and sobered me up with coffee and stew. Billy told Hannah that it was her fault that I was drunk because she'd been giving me money for beer. She's decided not to, anymore. Shit. Billy left around midnight and Hannah and I retired for a Night Of Love. (YAYY!!). Yah, Great.

An Island of Drunken Calm in a Frothing Sea of Civic Pride

Bread Street, Evening

There's a Huge crowd down in Plaza St. Juame today, filling the square with chanting and flags: Barcelona must have won the football (soccer) championship. They're going mad, absolutely Mad. The young men are coming, the girls are getting Laid for the first time in their lives: They Won! (BIG FUCKING DEAL!!! SPECTATOR-SPORTS-JACK!!).

The Intensity of the Celebration is almost driving my headache over the wall. God. It's not the Usual Tide, at all, at all. It's Teenagers on the Make: celebrating the Latest Conquest. Kicking a little ball around the grass: They Won.

Kicking a little ball around the lawn: fuck it: these little shits have no more of an idea what is happening in their lives than does the rest of the world. They act like It was something They did. It's not. There are professional Soccer players to Take Care of That. Shit.

They're marching by, screaming at the top of their lungs, wearing flags: What Fucking Idiots: they don't even realize that the Rest of the World Couldn't Give A Shit Less. And Me? Not a Fucking Duro! Does the rest of the world care? They Have their little Celebration, while I sit here, talented, observant, aware, doing nothing. Do I Care About Any Of This? Not A Fucking Whit: I want My Clown!

Now there are Incredibly Loud Cheers emanating from the Plaza: someone must've kicked the little ball well. Ah, well, one of the Celebrants, who I recognize, just gave me 50ptas, with a smile; I guess football isn't really that bad. Clink, goal, clink.

Well, I've been bumming beer off the celebrants, It's really not That Bad, this Sports-thing. I'm still drunk: to sober up this afternoon I drank a bottle of wine.

About every third person, really, is wearing the Catalan Flag. This is the biggest street Orgy I've seen since I've been here: better even than the Three Kings of the Catholic Persuasion: These Are The Nationalists! Puck 'em. Kick that little ball! Watch that Television! Cheer the Fucking Home-Team! You'd think they'd just won 'Freedom From Misery', the way they're carrying on.

They do well in Groups, but it is sometimes difficult to get One of them to Relate. Cheering? They're great at it. Communicating? Something to be desired, left. Staring? Great. They're Almost Chinese. Easy to Manipulate? Really. Is Television going to Ruin this Country? Indubitably. Too Easy. This is one of the most disgusting displays of Emotional Manipulation that I've ever seen; and I was raised in the US, where it's An Art. Disgusting.

Even the Older Folks are being swept to new levels of un-natural Happiness. Fuck! The Singing, The prancing, The Unusual Smiling: I'm going Mad just being a block away.

The TV cameras, on fire-truck ladders, are filming all of this False Hilarity; They're Falling for the whole fucking thing: Honest, It's really revolting; They're using up Adrenalin, which could be used to feed pot-bellied babies in Africa, like this was a National Knife Fight. Fuck! Now, every few minutes there is a Deafening Cheer lasting for over a minute. The Pre-Adolescents are having A Time. It makes me feel like a wise old man, or an old crab. Fuck.

The TV only eggs them on: they'd be doing much better if they were naked in bed, with the girl-(-or-boy-)-of-their-dreams; it's a good thing I'm drunk tonight: I couldn't take this sober.

Now? They're shooting off bombs and fireworks: Fuck 'em. Even some of the 25-year-old women are getting off on this: Shit! I'm ready to cry: What A Waste. Barcelona has won the All-Spain-Kicking-The-Little_ Ball-Around-on-The-Grass Championship: BIG FUCKING DEAL! They may all be blown to Smithereens in a few minutes, Jesus Christ! (YAYYY!!!). Shit, I'm embarrassed for all of us, at this point.

Here's how excited I am: ZIT. Every few minutes I bum a swig off of a beer-drinking youngster: That's IT. Am I Patronizing these folks in Their Moment of Glory? I hope so, because, It's Feeble. It's So Elating for many of them that they have their faces painted up in the Catalan Colors. God. Bombs going off in the Plaza! Skyrockets! I wouldn't be here tonight except I don't know what else to do. I'd rather not be writing about all of this: let the TV record this Insanity, for the Record; Let Posterity Know that Madness was Worldwide. I came to Spain to get away from this Bullshit. Even the Fat-Assed Girls are having a good time tonight, dancing around as though they were normal, no one cares or notices.

I just went down to the Plaza, about 100ft from here, and lingered for a minute until one of the flag-waving idiots nearly slit my throat with the sharp end of her flag; I grabbed it and told her she was a fucking idiot, in English, and to be careful. I hope this Nationalistic Bullshit, This Tribal Bullshit, This Football Bullshit, doesn't end up causing much harm. Shit, it Really Is getting out of hand tonight: They're going absolutely Bonkers. The plaza is packed, shoulder-to-shoulder, there are little rivers of movement, alleys which you can push through, throughout the Throng. The alley, here, is Jam-Packed right now, with people bumping against the desk every few seconds. I am like an Island of Drunken Calm in a Sea of Civic Pride and Anachronistic Nationalism.

I won't forget This. Ninety percent of the people here have gone Completely Mad, and the other ten percent are wondering where they went wrong. This is a good spot to linger, though, for the rest of the evening; I have nothing better to do, And, I can cadge a few swigs of beer. They're Absolutely Swarming now: I'm becoming a Traffic Obstruction; I've never seen it this Heavy before. There probably hasn't been this much action since the siege of 1647. Or 1349. Or 1152.

Kick that little ball! Who really gives a fuck? Who? Will any of these frantic screamers really go home tonight and scream in their living room? In their bedroom? Not a fucking chance. (Well, maybe she will). It's Artificial. They're ruining my Pitch. Is America ruining their country? Is Television?

I'm in pain: my head hurts. A Hangover. It's too bad that I can't feel Anything about this Great Soccer Victory. I used to feel something back home, When the Football Championship was won by the Home Team, but nothing like what I see here tonight. I feel the same way about World War Two: We Won. (YAYYY!!!).

I don't guess there's a chance of getting my 300ptas for the gas tonight, so I'll just fold this up in the Football Frenzy; there's too many people chanting and wandering glaze-eyed past the pitch to make this a Profitable Evening. Where's Hannah? That's what I've forgotten in this Adrenalin-Crazed Atmosphere. Good Night. (YAYYY!!!).

Idiot Wind; The Wind Blew' My Book in the Street

One oclock, Tuesday, Same spot, Windy.

The Hannah Thing is completely out of control: my Emotions are a Mess. I want her; I'm now throwing myself in her path; I'm making a fool of myself; she's making a fool of me. I profess Undying Love; She says she Really Likes Me A Lot: foolish. I have the unbelievable bad fortune to have gotten involved with Hannah at a time when she's decided not to get all fucked-up over men. Especially me.

She's down at Plaza del Pi busking with Simon, Tarn, and the two blonde girls. I'm 130ptas short of enough money to get my cooker tank filled, so that's why I'm out here today: one hundred and thirty fucking pesetas.

Ellen stopped by for a few minutes and told me that her life is changing for the better: she's found some friends her own age and has been hanging out with them as well as the Tapas Crowd. She's found a young American girl who is going to accompany her in her street-singing act. She's even wearing a dress these days and seems less confused now that she's not getting her main social interaction from Frank and Me.

Jacques just stopped by to fill me in on what's been happening with him lately: he had his bag, with all his art supplies, stolen when he turned his back while folding up his pictures yesterday. Just a Moment, and it was Gone. Next, a small retarded girl clamped her muddy feet all over the painting of the bread that he was going to sell today. Next, the wind blew a bunch of his paintings into the air. It's same sort of Cellini Karma.

The Soccer Celebration went on almost all night; the streets were clogged with flag-waving idiots all over town. It took about twenty minutes to get from here to the pension last night, dodging through the alleys, about four hundred feet. The Rumor is that they will be at it for about a week. Barcelona won the All-Spain Championship, a Really Big Deal! I don't Care At All, but the Joy was slightly infectious last night.

Last Night With Hannah: I went over to her acrobat class and watched her for a while, waited down in the bar while she took a shower, and kept almost crying and leaving. I was extremely confused about my feelings toward her. I began to End It by Just Walking Away, about five times, every time she tried to tell me that I Should Cool It A Little. I'm still confused: I don't know how to Deal Sanely with A Love Affair: my style is to throw myself at her feet; I Hate This Part of Growing Up! Planning Ahead! Clear Evaluations! Ugh.

Since I didn't have any fuel to cook with last night, Hannah invited me over to Simon's for dinner with her kids and the blonde girls. I drank wine and made puppy-dog eyes at her. I was disgusted with myself, as I suppose she was. God, I hate it when things go this way. Fuck it! I don't want to be Strong, and Adult, and Conscious. I want to swim in a Sea of Mushy, Erotic Emotion. Yah. I want her to throw herself at me, with no thought for the future or consequences. Yah, Like I Do.

Clink: a duro. Even If I do manage to get 130ptas today, the fucking gas store will be closed from two til five, for siesta. Ridiculous. Fuck it, I've got enough for a bottle of wine, even though the last thing Hannah said after she gave me 200 towards the gas, was, "Now, don't spend it on drink." Oh, well, I guess I'll just spend siesta napping in a wine and rocknroll trance again today: what the fuck, eh?

"It's an Idiot Wind Day, People don't like it when it's like this.", Jacques told me as he lingered Right In Front Of The Box. We were joined by Conejo and his gal for a few minutes as the Idiot Wind blew Jacques' paintings over, my book into the street, and Conejo completely away.

HANNAH GETS PREGNANT

6:30 same day, same spot

I think she's pregnant. She's a week late. I'm in Love and she's pregnant. She says she didn't plan it; I believe her: I Did. I forgot that I wasn't supposed to come inside her when she was Ripe. We cried this afternoon on the patio: she didn't want to get 'This Heavily Involved'. How much more involved can you be? If She Is, then I have six weeks to come up with a villa for her to live in. I'm Happy. She's been talking about drinking a quart of gin to abort, after looking deeply into my eyes. I played Leonard Cohen's Greatest Hits today, (he's dead: suicide after listening to all of his albums) and Infidels by Dylan, in order to make us cry this afternoon: it worked.

She's pregnant. She thinks a quart of gin will cause a miscarriage: I know it won't. I've drank quarts of gin by the case, as did my Nanny, and we're still here. I'm in love.

She's pregnant. I hope she can break the spell and come up with a Normal Name for this one, (Hadass was going to name our son "Jackoff"), like 'Jack', or 'Jack Junior'. I wonder which is dominant: Blue, or Green. She has green eyes, as do both her sons, though their father was Irish and has blue eyes. She's never been married; this will be her first time. (WHAT HAPPENED TO HADASS, GIGOLO JACK???). She'll be back, she'll be back; it's been three months, you know.

Well, I got gas for the cooker; Hannah, Tarn, Chawakee, Billy, Frank, and Jacques are scheduled to come over for dinner tonight.

"God, I hope she gets an abortion!", Billy just told me as he headed out to get a loaf of Pan Integral for dinner tonight. (DINNER TONIGHT!! DINNER TONIGHT!! DINNER TONIGHT!!). Yah, yah, yah.

The Deal is This: If Hannah IS Pregnant, I'm going to try to get a lot of money so that she doesn't have to work to support all of us. The Plan is to do it either by selling this book, drugs, or boat-rides. Something. I can Do anything, almost. Such Weeping, Such Emotion, Such a Life! A New Child! Yayyy!!! Another Little Vickland Shit.

"Oh, Man! Don't name him Vickland!", Billy told me as he read this over my shoulder.

Billy is standing in front of my table chanting, "NATO NO! BASES OUT!", in Spanish, trying to be more Politically Involved. He's trying to get me involved in Politics. Now he's playing an Irish jig on the pennywhistle and dancing around the money box like an idiot. Now he's telling passersby that I am "The Famous Novelist of the Streets of Barcelona". Idiot. I think he secretly wants to be a Clown. Not a Clone. He's going to go play about ten feet to my left and get up a hundred so we can buy some eggs and some beans for the stew tonight; he makes enough in a few minutes to support all of us for the evening.

IT MIGHT BE TUESDAY

FRANK'S TEEPEE

It might be Wednesday, It might be Tuesday, It Could be Thursday: my head clock is almost completely inoperative, though I know it's a little after eleven oclock in the morning, and I know I'm sitting on pastry Street. I've drunk two pots of coffee, eaten nothing, bathed in a pot, washed sane clothes in the same pot, and refurbished the Stew. I feel fine, except that I'm Very Hungry and have those kind of shakes that old people get, the kind where you can't quite get the key in the door, or pick your nose properly. I don't have a hangover, even though I drank a bottle of wine with dinner last night.

The Gang came as scheduled: Frank and Jacques, Hannah and Chawakee and Tarn, Billy am Me; the stew, wine, and some hash. Hannah read about fifty pages of the book aloud; the parts about The Valencia Trip, as requested by Chawakee, while Tarn and Billy fought on the bed and generally wreaked havoc at the Meson. Everyone split around midnight, leaving me to swoon and twitch to the rocknroll on the radio, as I passed out.

Frank fell further in Love with Hannah again last night; he told her that the teepee he's building in his room is corning right along, while making eyes at her. Frank and Jacques spent quite a bit of time explaining to Hannah why I would be a good father, like, "He Don't Car". Billy corroborated what they were telling her. What Pals. I think Hannah's plan was to put the boys to bed and then go out and find a quart of gin. I expect to see her for lunch this afternoon; I think she said she'd be coming by, after busking solo today. We'll see.

I woke up at 8:30 this morning and spent about three hours cleaning, cleaning, cleaning: I don't know what got into me; once I started I couldn't stop; maybe I better go see a doctor.

11: 30. SAME SPOT

"WHY IS THERE A YANKEE BEGGING?!"

I think it's Thursday, but it might be Wednesday. (YAYY!!). Woke up at six this morning, sprawled fully-clothed across my bed; it was the third bottle of wine that did it. That, and the Grass that Jimi Hendrix gave me yesterday afternoon, which I shared last night at the pad with Frank, Jacques, and Billy. Hannah didn't show. Nor did Phil.

It's sunny, it's churning, it's Not Clinking. A friend of mine, I suppose, has just parked his bicycle right in front of the box and is sitting here whistling.

A Catalan man just came up, stood in front of the desk, and yelled, "Why is there a Yankee sitting here in the street begging? They are throwing Yankee Spies out of this country, and there is one sitting here, making his living, begging! Why is a Yankee sitting in the street begging?!" He's the husband of the woman who runs the Tarot Shop over by the cathedral, who once called the cops on me and had me run off of the plaza by the goose-cloister.

I yelled back at him, "Who The Fuck Are You?! Who The Fuck Are You?! Who The Fuck Are you?!", until he hit the road. What a shit, nationalistic little shit. My bike-friend told me that the guy lived in the U.S. once, and doesn't like Americans. Fuck him. Walking around on My planet spreading bad vibes; Fuck Him. Yah.

I'm Not a fucking American; I'm from San Francisco; fucking California! Not America: I'm not from fucking Kansas, fucking Philadelphia; fuck it.

It's cold here in this Idiot Wind Alley, and I'm wearing my Hawaiian (American?) Shirt, with my begging gloves added. Maybe I should wear a red, white, and blue top hat also, the little shit. Yah.

"California isn't even on the same friggin' planet! Where's the guy's friggin' geography?!", Frank said, when I told him what had just happened. yah! So, I got a gratuitous rush of adrenalin from the little bastard.

Frank is trying to figure out a good way for him to beg on the street; he's been run out of the house by the weekly visit of the cleaning lady. He's thinking of making a sign that says, 'I need money for a cafe-con-lech. I've been run out of the house by the housekeeper'. I suggested that he add, 'I'm a Retired American Spy', because that's what he looks like.

"If that guy comes back, just give him some more of the same.", Frank told me as he headed off to sit in the sun in plaza St. Juame.

"Yah, I'll just yell 'Who The Fuck Are You?' whenever I see him.", I said.

"That's it!", Frank yelled.

LUNCH ON THE PATIO WITH THE GALS EL MONSTRO AGAIN

Well, it's about a half hour later; I'm sitting on the patio at the pad. Beautiful sunshiney salad, wine, and bread; the constant barking of the stupid little dog in the adjacent patio is the only item detracting from this Perfect Scene. I'm waiting for Rebecca to join me for lunch; I ran into her in the plaza as I was leaving after making 199ptas, which I've already spent. I'm down to my usual one peseta, but I'm Rich with Life: food, wine, sunshine: yah. Rock on the box, palomas flying above, olive down the gullet, gulp of wine: Ah, what a life, I'm Satisfied. Now, the Hawaiian Shirt Fits. Perfect; this is Where I want to be.

Rebecca showed up, we had lunch and discussed how best to raise the family. I didn't have any new ideas, so we decided to let her stay in charge. I 'Where's Hannah'ed over the balcony a few times; it worked: she joined us for lunch at around three. Billy came about four, after I went out to fetch some wine for the girls. Hannah and I are heading for Sitges this afternoon so she can Suss out the busking situation there, I think. It's a Mellow Afternoon, with sappy rocknroll on the box; I want Old Stones and other Quality Rocknroll, not this shit. Billy is playing his recorder and listening to suggestions about his 'career' from the 'adults'.

As I was chatting with Rebecca on the patio, she suddenly toppled over backwards, throwing her bowl of soup over her shoulder, through the door, into the hallway allover the floor, and on into the pad. I thought for a moment she'd Gone Nuts. It happened mid-sentence, as she leaned back in one of the trick chairs that I've found in the street and littered the patio with. She wasn't hurt, she landed on some cushions that are laying with all the rubbish. I went into ecstasy and couldn't stop laughing for a couple of minutes. we chatted for a while, and I went to get another bottle of wine, leaving Rebecca to explain to Hannah Just Why I'd Be A Good Father. At least that's what I asked them to discuss while I was gone. I don't think they did. I heard them talking about Gin as I came back up the stairs with the wine.

Hannah and I headed out for Sitges at around five, both of us dressed in black; she, Exceedingly Beautiful, me imitating Johnny Cash while sipping the wine. We hugged, kissed, talked, and drank all the way there, falling ever farther In Love as the afternoon wore on. By the time we got to Sitges we'd almost decided that Keeping the Baby was a good idea.

Hannah, however, is doing Preliminary Research into Spanish abortions, Just To Keep From Going Insane, she says; but admits that she may keep the child. We boogied around Sitges for a couple of hours, researching the Theatre Arts Festival which is coming up in a couple of weeks; she wants to put on a clown show for it. We hit a couple of police stations for info, and cafes for cafe-con-leche to try to keep me sober. We discussed how I/We could make enough money to support Hannah and three kids in the future: sailing? Doping? Clowning? Writing? The 'Sailboat plan' was the favorite.

We were being so erotic on the trainride back that we drove a couple of businessmen to another car. It wasn't enough; I finally convinced her that we could make love in the toilet, after asking a couple of Spanish guys to vacate the vestibule because Hannah was too embarrassed to enter the toilet with me while they were watching. They leeringly co-operated, and we were having a Grand Time until Trainstationus Interruptus occurred after about ten minutes: we were in Barcelona sooner than we'd expected.

She had to go meet her kids for dinner at Montserrat's, and I was too drunk to accompany her; she was afraid that I would scare Monsty; so we agreed that we would meet at the pad later that night. It was about 9:30; I headed for the pad and passed out til 11:30, when I came to, drank a pot of coffee, cleaned the pad, lit a candle, and waited with a hard-on for Hannah until about 2:30 when I finally realized that she probably wasn't going to show up. I put plan B into operation: "If I don't show up tonight, why don't you just jack-off and think about me." I woke up three times with a hard-on and let her have it again and again; she was great

Around midnight, Juan (El Monstro) spotted the candle-light coming from the open door and came up and asked if everything was all right. I told him that I was waiting for my 'Amiga' and was a little drunk. He said that he had shut the street door down below. I had to keep running down the stairs to unlock the front door every time one of the other tenants would come home and lock it. Juan said that he had two keys, and, since he lived alone, didn't need the extra, and gave it to me. I told him that he'd have to come up for dinner some night. Hopefully when Frank is dining there.

El Monstro and I have become friends. I've given the other key to Hannah. She came by around noon, and we had coffee and continued the train ride.

The Peanut Gallery Again

ATOMIC BOMB DREAM

5:30 Friday, Same Spot

"I guess we're going to have to start looking for another country to live in.", Hannah told me as she gave me the news that Spain officially joined the Common Market last night. I suppose in a few years they'll be tearing down all these shitty old buildings and putting up some decent condos. Next, join Nato, so they can get cheap atom bombs. I knew it was only a matter of time when I saw McDonalds go up at Calle Fernando and The Ramblas last year. Portugal, here we come.

I spent the afternoon at the pad with Phil, reading his book and eating; I haven't been drinking today, for the first time in a few weeks, Am Sober, and am hallucinating occasionally: seeing patterns in the clouds, seeing flashes of light out of the corner of my eyes. It'll probably be a couple of days until r resemble a human being again. Hannah said she Might join me this evening to help me stay out of trouble by making love; Keep the Visions to a Minimum, with Activity. If she doesn't come, I'll just read and eat candy.

The Old Purple Fairy just came hooting by with the news that Chagall is dead, and that I look more like Kathryn Hepburn than I did last week; I shaved again today; I think he's hitting on me, and that's his idea of a compliment; a True Looney.

Billy just stopped by, he made 600 this evening at Plaza del pi, and has gone to a cafe to count his money to try to decide whether he has enough to came to dinner at Meson Hadass tonight.

Billy says that Rebecca has forbidden him from hanging out at the Opera cafe with Frank and Jacques because of their bad influence on him; they've been advising him lately to ditch her, because she is temporarily dependent on the money Billy has been making. She's been living on credit because the Gangster Language School where she's been working for the last three weeks has refused to pay her and say they don't know when they will be able to, if ever. I've suggested that Whitey, Rabbit, Frank, Peter, Billy, Jacques, Amani, Ramon, and I accompany her to their office and see if we can't influence their decision. She's thinking about it.

Chawakee and Tarn just ran up. Tarn has his incredibly funny clown outfit on, with the bright red nose, but it looks like Chawakee isn't working today. They've run off to check whether Steve's pitch is occupied. Hannah is evidently busking down on Boqueria; she left her stuff at my pad all day, but was able to retrieve it with Her Own Key. Maybe I'll have them over for dinner tonight, instead of Frank and Jacques, or Billy. Maybe I'll eat alone. The Boys have gone down to ask Hannah if they are all coming for dinner tonight.

(COMING FOR DINNER TONIGHT!! COMING FOR DINNER TONIGHT!! AT THE PAD!!! AT THE PAD!!! WE'RE LEARNING HOW TO WRITE THIS BOOK IN CASE JACK TAKES OFF SAILING!!! COMING FOR DINNER TONIGHT AT THE PAD!!). There's more to it than that, kids, that's just Filler. (CLINK, A DURO, SHIT! CLINK: ONE HUNDRED, YAYY!! AT THE PAD!! AT THE PAD!! AND LIKE THAT!! AND LIKE THAT!! I SIT HERE AND STINK!! I SIT HERE AND STINK!! BILLY JUST CAME UP!! BILLY'S TAKEN OFF!! ETERNAL STEW!! ETERNAL STEW!! AT THE PAD!! ENOUGH FOR WINE!! ENOUGH FOR WINE!! FUCK 'EM!! FUCK THAT!! ENOUGH FOR WINE!! AT THE PAD!!) That's much better; I think you're getting the hang of it. (YAYYY!! FOR THE PUBLISHERS-GALLERY!!). Shit. (GOD!! FUCK!! SHIT!! GOD! FUCK! SHIT! YAYY!! THE PORN-NUT GALLERY!!) . Never mind. Don't know what time it is, may split soon. (DON'T KNOW WHAT TIME IT IS!! DON'T KNOW WHAT DAY IT IS!! IT MAY BE TUESDAY!! IT MAY BE FRIDAY!! WHERE'S HANNAH!! WHERE'S HANNAH!! DINNER AT THE PAD TONIGHT!! YAYYY!!!). Yah, yah, OK, you've got it: you can write the fucking book from now on, unless I'm talking about something serious, like politics, or sex.

Eleven oclock, Saturday

I'm down to my last 10ptas, better than usual for a morning, but a nice lady just gave me half a pack of Ducados when I bummed a smoke, so All is Well.

Hannah has gone busking uptown today, Paseo de Gracia, after spending the night with me. She's probably decided not to have an abortion, but is eating lots of celery because Sonia told her that it will sometimes bring on menstruation. We talked about how it could turn out to be wonderful to have a Chile, a female Chile, 'Daisy', if the celery doesn't work; we're both slightly confused and wondering How, at this age, we could have been so careless/stupid. It's in the Stars? Well, for sure it's in her belly. I need a couple of more days without drink before I can trust my thoughts on this matter. She says she's going to bleach strands of her hair today, and then Henna the whole thing: light red hair with orange streaks; I told her I'd find her even more attractive. Sonia is going to do it also; their 'take' should increase: more clown-like.

Hannah pointed out to me this morning, as she read the book, that my Political Understanding is Lacking: Spain has been in NATO for a couple of years, and it may not have joined the Common Market the other day; and Portugal will be right in there with Spain, anyway. I told her that I didn't really give a shit about politics, a feeble response. I've only read one newspaper in the last six months, and It almost made me sick. I'm better off in Ignorance, for the nonce. (FOR THE NONCE!! FOR THE NONCE!! WHAT'S A NONCE!!?). Half a Yonk.

There are squeals coming from the crowd of teen-agers who are admiring the Gigantic Chocolate Eggs which have popped up in every candy store window. Some of them are intricately decorated with flowers, birds, eggs, bunnies, elfs, and shit like that. There are huge chocolate candies in the shape of houses, cars, pianos, and other meaningless things. Evidently Easter means Chocolate in Barcelona. They are incredibly expensive, and I suppose they are meant to be gifts for children on Easter Morning. To every season there is a candy. Well, at least they're not as offensive as the little toilets full of candy turds that were so popular at Christmas.

ATOMIC BOMB DREAM

Saturday 5:30

Got the sausage, got the eggs, got the chocolate. Fried 'em up and sat in truck-stop ecstasy for a while in the sun on the patio, eating it up and drinking coffee. A definitely Non-Spanish type of siesta. Phil dropped by with a bag of food for the stew and I made him a salad. Billy came by to eat and bullshit and after a while I took a nap, leaving them to play on the patio. Without the alcohol stimulation my metabolism changes completely: I was even able to sleep right after drinking three cups of coffee.

I dreamt I was hanging out with Lynda, my old friend/lover, trying still to work out our Love-Affair, when a Russian cruise missile circled overhead and crashed in a field right across the street from us. Our Imminent Demise, as the missile was about to crash, finally spurred us into admitting that indeed we did love each other. we hugged as it crashed. It didn't explode: a dud, maybe just a test. It had served its purpose for my dream, bringing Lynda and me back together again. Another one circled overhead and also crashed near us, failing to explode also, but again causing us to admit that We Loved Each Other. I guess my subconscious needed further confirmation from her. I realized, even while dreaming, that this had something to do with Hannah; like Lynda was the flip-side of her; or it was a similar emotional experience for me; something like that.

I knew that I had to wake up soon, that siesta was nearly over and I had to get back out here. When I opened my eyes I heard rustling and talking in the room; there were two guys putting all of the things in the roam into a bag. I asked them who they were and what they thought they were doing. They said they were the landlords, and I, and Hadass, were being evicted. It was another dream, but I wasn't yet aware of that, within it still. I argued with them, pleaded, almost begged, but they were adamant: I was out, Hadass was losing the apartment. I told them that I could borrow the money and be back with it in an hour. They said that they knew that I was, In Reality, Jack White Rose, a . famous non-rent-payer, and that I was Out no matter what I did. I tried to prove that I wasn't this famous crook, which I am, but while looking through my bag for my passport they found a letter addressed to Jack Rose. The Game was UP.

That dream ended and I woke up to four knocks from the street below. I looked over the patio wall and saw Eduardo/Conejo/Rabbit. I let him in. We were happy to see each other. He was elated to hear about Hannah's pregnancy, "Love! Childrens! Normall!", he told me. Neither of us had been drinking. Was this another dream?

Time to cheer up the peanut gallery, how about a piece of chocolate? (YAYY!!). Ah, much better, we'll candy Away that mean ole Atomic War. We'll get happy in the face of Total Destruction, with the simplest means available: chocolate. (YAYY!!).

If you took a world-wide poll and asked which thing people would rather do without: Candy, or Atomic War? What do you think the results would be among the under-forty crowd? (YAYY!! WE WANT CANDY 1 ! WE DON'T WANT TOTAL DEATH!! YAYYY!!).

In light of this poll, I suppose I should stop making fun of the pastry-eaters, seeing that I come from the bomb-dealing country. Candy only destroys your teeth, and gives you a little Buzzzz, not a big one. (YAYY FOR THE LITTLE BUZZZZ!!). This dark chocolate virtually explodes on your taste buds, not on your town. (YAYYY FOR TASTE-BUD FIZZING!!! BOOO FOR NUCLEAR FISSION!!!). OK, ok.

Busking

LOVE, BABIES, SAILING BOATS, AND MUSH

OPERA CAFE WAKE

ANOTHER LADRONE REPORT

DAISY, AMBER, AND ROSE-PETAL

6:30 Monday evening, same spot

Warm weather, perfect weather; spent the afternoon with Hannah, Chalky, and Tarn about twenty miles north of town, near Las Planas, sitting in the grassy woods, right below an old church. We had a picnic, dozed, and watched the boys try to pull down an old dead tree. we'd gone there looking for Sonia and Chris, who'd had their busses parked out there, but they were gone, so we decided to make a Country Day of it. It was another welcome change from this Stoney Gothick Life.

    Now we're back to the usual grind: they've gone to acrobat class and I'm out here typing. Even though it's warm, I'm wearing my Charles Dickens Begging Gloves, It doesn't feel right without them.

    On Saturday night Peter, Jacques, Phil, Frank, and Billy came to the pad for dinner; everyone but Peter was high on Hash, he was getting drunk. He's gotten one of those semi-punk haircuts where it's short everywhere except in the back, where it dangles over your black overcoat, preferably. He's also obtained a pair of Elvis Sunglasses; with his Sinatra Hat, and new look, he was setting off that night to 'get laid'.

    I told him, "Peter, it's a difficult thing in life when you see someone you have been close to going over the edge." The rest of them agreed with me and we spent most of the evening getting on his case, to which he was seemingly oblivious, as he pursued his drunken high.

    It was partly a going-away party for Phil, who is leaving for France on Sunday. It was the Old Tapas Crowd.

    As The Gang was leaving around midnight, Hannah and her boys arrived. It was a blessed night of Friendship and Love for me; one of those nights in life when you know that you must have had your personality arranged pleasantly, because everyone seemed to like you and was enjoying your company. This was true for me this night, with the exception of Tarn, who can spot a tongue-kiss with his back turned, and never lets one pass un-obstructed.

They also had dinner, and decided, against Tarn's wishes, to spend the night. Hannah and I discussed the various life-plans we have come up with, and their variations, Made Love, and Snuffled. I couldn't sleep most of the night for thinking of the future. A Good Night.

We had a great English breakfast again, and she asked me if I wanted to play drums with her while she busked at the Zoo and Park Ciutadella for the day. I said I would do it for ten percent, probably 3 or 400ptas; what I would make if I was sitting out here. She agreed and we were joined later by Simon, and headed for the Zoo.

Chawakee and Tarn were both dressed as clowns, and the plan was that they would be performing also: they didn't, spending their time sulking (Chalky), or just goofing about (Tarn). Chalky was coerced into performing his Diabolo, (he has a stick in each hand, with a string between them, with which he spins an hourglass-shaped top, and flips it about seventy feet in the air and then catches it), which he did by getting it all tangled up, kicking it down the dirt path, and flinging his sticks into a tree: he didn't want to perform; I thought it was a good act; It was a Perfect Sulking Kid Show. Tarn, meanwhile, was supposed to twirl a twenty-foot multi-colored silk scarf on a stick, a very beautiful display when done right, but was only managing to get it all tangled up in bushes and on his head and feet, while grinning like a stupid idiot. I had to stop drumming a few times to untangle it for him. Chalky managed to throw his sticks and diabolo into the pond by accident, while trying to get them stuck way up in a tree.

Nevertheless, we made about 4000 in a couple of hours; it would have been more had the kids performed. Simon, who had agreed with Hannah earlier in the day to play "for a couple of hundred", when Hannah had told him that she really wanted to play without him today, Now said that he thought that it was fair that he got 700, because we'd made so much. This put Soft-Hearted Hannah in a bad mood. I demanded my 365ptas anyway. She was surrounded by 'helpers' who were draining her.

We headed for Simon's apartment in Barrio Chino without him, he went off to 'get laid', but as we passed across the Ramblas there were thousands of people promenading, and we decided that just Hannah and I would busk there for a while, and Billy, who we'd met at the park along with Frank and Rebecca, would take the boys back to Simon's and then return to pass the hat for us. We played for about an hour and a half and made 4500ptas. It was Fun, and I think Billy and I were an Asset because we Look Irish, and the theme of her music and puppets is 'Musica Irlandes', Irish Music. To celebrate we took the kids and ourselves to the only open restaurant we could find, a tourist-trap Pizza Parlor. We blew 2200ptas in there, enough to buy vegetables for a week.

We went back to Simon's, put the boys to bed, and then followed Billy out into the night to try to find some action. I was off my alcohol fast: I had two beers with the pizza.

Most of the usual bars were closing, Sunday Night, Two oclock. We found Frank, Jacques, Whitey, and his girl Alice, at Chez Popoff, the late-night Mafia Hangout in the alley behind the Opera Cafe, where all the weirdos congregate when the other bars close. The doorman has to approve you through a peep-hole in the door before he lets you in. I think he recognized Billy. They were deep into Hash, and Billy joined them while Hannah and I had a couple of beers each, held hands, looked into each other's Puppy-eyes, and talked about Love, Babies, Sailing Boats, and Mush. We left early, around three, and went home and snuffled and made fucklove. We've Completely Fallen. It's not sickening, but is Mushy. We don't care.

This morning, after going out shopping for breakfast, Hannah came back and got in bed weeping because a man wouldn't sell her gas for the bottle so she could make tea, and she's going to have a baby. I consoled her as much as I could and then got up and made her cup after cup of tea until the caffeine finally snapped her out of it. She wanted me to stay with her today so she wouldn't weep anymore. I went with her to the country because I wanted to be with her, and if she wanted me too, then What Could Be More Perfect? And it was: picnic in the country, sunshine, some wine, kids playing, snuffling…

Tuesday morning, Bread street

Hannah and the boys came over for dinner last night, along with Jacques and Billy. It was superior fare; the usual excellent salad, stew, coffee, and wine, and for a special treat: strawberries and chocolate provided by Billy, who is obviously being influenced by Frank.

I was moping around for a while, when I found out that Hannah had an appointment at the apartment of a Social Anthropologist who wanted to interview her about busking.

I said, "Yah, sure, what's he look like? How old is he? Do you like him? Why are you going to his apartment? You're going because he wants to fuck you, aren't you, Hannah?", and shit like that for a while. She found my Jealousy touching, and assured me going to his apartment? You're going because he wants to fuck you, aren't you, Hannah?", and shit like that for a while. She found my Jealousy touching, and assured me Bum from a fall at acrobat class, so we headed over to Simon's where we finished off this Domestic Evening by sitting around sewing costumes and clothes; my jacket had a rip. So far this evening I had Shopped with my Son, Prepared dinner, Cleaned Up and washed the dishes, gone for a walk with the wife and kids, and mended my coat; I think Hannah was Unpressed with my domesticity and stability. My Husband/Father Potential Rating is definitely rising.

Frank is upset: the owner of the Opera Cafe, a Barcelona Institution himself, is dead. The place will never be the same; the little old elf will never again be sitting at his usual table in the back, chewing his cud, rapidly flipping through newspapers, and invisibly controlling the action in the most dangerous bar in town. Frank is worried that the old guy's relatives are going to turn the Opera into a Fern Bar, or a Disco, thus ending Frank's Smoking-Room-After-Dinner-Hangout of six years. He's in a Tizzy about it, imagining the worst. He, Jacques, and Billy had a wake there last night.

LADRONE REPORT: Two nights ago, as Jacques was waiting on Calle Fernando for Frank to finish his toilet and join him for their evening session at the Opera, he noticed two obvious Ladrones boogeying towards him, about a half block away. He knew that he wasn't a Prime Target for them, so decided to just ignore them and look away, rather than cross the street to avoid them, as he usually does. The next thing he knew he was lying on his back on the sidewalk; one of them had given him a mighty kick in the back of the leg, dropping him to the ground. He couldn't believe it: it was completely gratuitous violence. He got up and just stared after the guy, who, about a block away, turned and waved as if to say, "Well, no harm done, it was just a spur-of-the-moment thing". Frank, not knowing that Jacques had been attacked, came out his door and said, "Well, my friend, I really like the way you wait for me." Jacques was too stunned to tell Frank what had happened, and also assumed that Frank had seen the whole thing and was making a Cruel Joke. Jacques now has bruises on his leg and shoulder. Welcome to the Gothick Barrio Club.

A while ago I overheard a Decent American Chap (he wasn't pretentious?) discussing with his son "which way they went", and asked if I could help. Yes, they had been sitting in a milk-bar (granja) across the street, and the two well-dressed, dark-skinned men sitting near them had casually walked off with their camera bag, which contained their camera and passports. They lost them in the crowd by the time they got out onto the street after realizing it was gone. I told them where the thieves market in plaza Real was, and told them to buy a beer and sit at a table as near to it as they could and watch for someone with their bag. I also told them that the odds were against recovering it. My good deed for the day; they weren't Typical stupid Tourists, just a little careless, a little too trusting: the thieves were well-dressed, and weren't wearing tennis shoes. plaza Real will open their eyes to the Real Third World. At least they'll get an education, if not their bag back.

1:30 in the afternoon. Same spot. Tuesday, I think, but it might be Wednesday

Jacques came for dinner last night, alone; we discussed the progress of the book; he thinks it's worthy of editing and publishing; however, in his opinion, it's only half done. He intends to rebuke Hannah for distracting me from What's Important: writing.

I told him, "Jesus Christ, Jacques, she's carrying My Baby! That's more important than some fucking book! It's what's Happening in my life right now."

"Well, Jack,", he said, "As your editor it's my duty to keep you writing, no matter what happens in your personal life!" He finally admitted, after about a half hour discussion, that Yes, the baby is very important, but he still has his duty to do.

"It's taken five months to write. what I have so far,", I said, "It's taken a million years to be able to create what Hannah is carrying! Which would you care about most?"

As my 'editor', he's afraid that I'll be leaving Barcelona with Hannah and won't be able to finish the book. I told him that Hannah is trying to get me to wear clown make-up. I told him that even if I leave Barcelona for a while, to go to Portugal to get a boat, that I'd be returning and finishing the book anyway. He didn't believe it; he thinks he can see my future better than I can. What A Fool.

Hannah and I are planning to go to Sitges and busk this weekend; I won't have to sit out here and do this Shit.

The Ladrone Report will probably be taking up more and more space here, now that the Tourist Season is beginning; plaza Real is full of them, unaware that all the 'colorful' people around them are thieves, junkies, and muggers. It's astounding to see them sitting around at the little tables with their purses, cameras, and bags sitting on the chair next to them, and watch the thieves checking them out, waiting for them to turn their heads. (When their accomplices create a noisy diversion.) It's going to be a wonderful summer, for all of us Street Workers.

AMBER, DAISY, AND ROSE-PETAL

Six oclock, same day

In the morning we're discussing how to get to Portugal, at the beginning of Siesta she's telling me how she could get a cheap abortion in the south of France, and at the end of Siesta we're deciding on a name. Is this confusion?

I'm not sure, neither is she. All we know is that we're having a Wonderful Time, and she's pregnant.

Amber, Daisy, and Rose-Petal, these are the New Daughter's possible names. If it's a boy she says she will throw it in the lake; she's just using me to get a daughter: she wants to put ribbons in her hair and have a friend; I think it's Lovely. If it's a son maybe I can talk her out of drowning him and get Amy or Sally to raise him.

I told Hannah today, while we made love on the patio, "We've got to stop this Hippy Day-Dreaming, grow up, and settle down sometime." She laughed. If we stay together it's more likely that we'll strengthen our already counter-culture ways. I'm for it. I want chocolate, not bombs; daughters, not sons.

Daisy is Dead

"LET'S SEE THE BABY"

BLEEDI HANNAH

BLOW-JOB AND BROWN RICE

Thursday, April 4, One Oclock, Same Spot

"I have wonderful news!", she exclaimed as she mounted the landing last night; she was grinning from ear to ear; I thought she'd gotten us a van.
    "What?", I asked.
    "I got my period!", she exclaimed, hugging me.
    "Let's go get drunk.", I said.
    I spent the next couple of hours in a Post/Pre-Natal Psychic Depression, trying to celebrate the Loss of Imminent Responsibility which the recent pregnancy had thrown us both into; I could feel that a burden was lifted, but I missed Little Daisy already.
    I would no longer have to come up with riches in a few weeks; I could take my sweet time.
    "Did you Love me just because I was pregnant?", she asked later.
    "No, but it certainly speeded things up.", I told her. We drank a couple of cups of tea and smoked some hash Sonia had given her; we didn't have enough money to go out and get drunk. We snuffled; hugged, and laughed; I was looking for an excuse to cry, but couldn't find it
    After a couple of hours I remembered how I'd loved her before she got pregnant, and we took off where we were two weeks ago: Lovers. She has her period. Full stop.
    Later, she even had the ovaries to say that we could become 'Friends', 'Good Friends', again. I said I would do my best to get her pregnant again. She said that now, we could get a sailboat first, and then have a baby.
    This is the second time in four months that this has happened to me; the next time a woman tells me she's pregnant, I'm going to say, "Let's see the baby." The Emotional Changes these pregnancies put me through are intense; why am I being tested? We agreed that the recent event had caused both of us to re-evaluate our lives, and consider where we were heading, and what we really want. Hannah is much happier about the blood than I am: the burden on her would have been greater; I simply feel like a Fool: all that work for nothing,

all that sweating and grunting nullified by a bunch of celery. Fuck Celery! Now she's Beaming, Busking, and Bleeding.

You can imagine how much I was looking forward to being the Authority Figure for Tarn and Chalky: now all that has passed; also: The Problem is that I've gone and sobered up for no reason at all; my house is clean, my beard is gone, I've washed my clothes; and I've tried to think clearly: all for nothing!

Well, at least we've gotten to know each other well because of all this; a Good Love Affair was Conceived, I hope it doesn't miss-carry also.

We're heading for Sitges tomorrow, if I can come up with my 185pta trainfare, to busk on Good Friday. I'll be playing the drums again; and then she's heading for her teepee at the Meadow on Sunday. I'm supposed to join her there in a week or so for a week or two, if I can get the 700pta trainfare There.

When I told Jacques the good news about Hannah bleeding, he had a mini-celebration because now I am a writer again. He said that this now clears the way for me to impregnate Hadass when she returns, I can get Hannah later. What an Editor; there's been a death in the immediate family and they're all celebrating.

The Most Injured of all: My Reproductive Macho Ego: I can make them miss their periods but they don't have kids. Shit. Well, It's Good for Hannah: now she can get on with her Independence and her Career, or, as she put it, "I can fuck around now!" Great. Now, she can fuck around as much as she wants. I told her that I don't care what she does as long as I remain her Lover. Except get pregnant with some other clown. I'm Possessive that way. Fucking Clowns.

"Hi, Schlock-Head!", Jacques greets me. He's here to tell me that the market is probably open, even though it's "Good Thursday", and that I will be able to scurry over there during siesta to buy vegetables for the dinner at Meson Hadass/Hannah tonight. I guess I will.

5: 30, Same Day, Same Spot.

Hannah cornered me at the pad, pinned me down, and put a white clown-mouth on me; I must admit: it looked pretty good; I think I'm a Natural. I told her I'd wear clown make-up in Sitges for 15%; she's thinking about it. She wasn't feeling very well; because of the mis-period, so spent the afternoon sleeping at Simon's. My balls hurt: we haven't fucked for a day or two, and I get all excited every time I'm with her; I guess this isn't unusual. For teenagers.

The Land of Drowse is calling; I'm obvious prey for sleep this evening; I want to lay right down on the typewriter; I'm tired; queasy, and my balls hurt: what a combination. I want a nap, a fuck; and a quart of fresh orange juice,

Fuck; juice; nap; in that order. Also, I think the emotional let-down about the missing child is finally getting to me; I was riding high on expectation and new-found ambition because of the 'pregnancy'. Now, it's back to the regular grind. Oh, I'm looking forward to the trip to The Meadow; and the trip to Sitges, alright, but like I say; "Let's see the baby."

Anticipation and Enthusiasm are not coming very easy to me tonight. Expectation seems like a ridiculous frame of mind to be in right now. I've been riding the god-damned roller-coaster for a few months now; and I think I'd like to try the fun-house; or the merry-go-round for a while. (YAYYY!!!). Or, maybe just lay on the beach and get a suntan; then go back to the teepee for a blow-job and brown rice with chapatties. (YAYYY!! MAHATMA-JACK!!).

Easter with Clowns

Next Monday. Sitting on the Patio at the Pad.

Three oclock, Siesta on the Patio

I've got beer. The RocknRoll Station. Built an awning out of a big blanket. I'm sitting in the Shade. It's almost Hot. I've spent the last three days with Hannah, busking in Sitges, fucking, sucking, snuffling, eating; We Even had an Argument.

Yesterday, Easter, we had a Working Holiday in the City Park. Billy dressed as a clown, with Top-Hat, and passed the hat for Hannah, Sonia, Chris, and Simon. I drank wine, juggled, ate, and Bullshitted with Rabbit, Rebecca, Frank, Whitey, Canadian Steve, English Phil, and a few others.

The evening ended early and drunkenly for me around 9 oclock. I slept til one and then joined Frank and Naomi, his new cute little Canadian girlfriend/disciple, for Hash and Beer at the Opera.

I don't know what happened to Hannah: I presume she's still out at the busses in the Country, Las Planas. I'm waiting for her now. She's scheduled to leave for The Meadow tomorrow, I think, with Simon in his van.

I've been Crying. You Know: The Resurrection, Hashish, Beer, Wine, Lack of Sleep, Gal Not Here, Love out the window, Reggae Musick: Enough to make me cry.

I've become a Hindu: I'm wearing all white clothes, with black vest and red sandals. I feel Turk. Been Waiting, Waiting here all day for Hannah. I don't want to have a Life, Right Now, Without Her. It's simple: She's focused my JOY. Oh, I can do it alone, But, Ratherr! At some point last night she was here: she left a note, "See You Soon." I'm waiting. Think I'll take a nap.

SIX OCLOCK, SAME DAY, BREAD STREET

Well, in four hours in Sitges on Friday, Good Friday, we made twelve mil; Hannah on puppets and flute, me on drums, and Billy on Hat Passing; Tarn and Chawakee were dressed for it but rarely performed; Chawakee is having emotional problems: he just sits around while the busking goes on; as soon as it's over he comes alive and wants to play; I guess he's against Child Labour.

It was a Jam-packed street scene in Sitges the whole day; we busked til about 10PM and then bought a roasted chicken which we ate in a cafe where I got in a slight argument with the owner because we were such clown/street people that we were upsetting the 'ambience' of his establishment by tearing the chicken to shreds with our hands. We managed to miss the last train to Barcelona at 11:30, and spent the next couple of hours wandering around Sitges looking for a place to sleep, or a friend.

We finally ended up sleeping underneath a boat down on the beach, with the exception of Hannah and me, who slept right under the stars for a couple of hours until we caught the 5:30 train in the morning.

We were spaced and tired by the time we arrived back at the pad. Hannah and I made Psychedelick Love for a couple of hours and then passed out. I wish I could describe it to you, but she says that She's Gone when I start going into detail in here. our Bonding, however, is Ever Stronger, That I Can say.

On Saturday we again busked; this time down at the port with Simon, Sonia, Chris, Billy, The Boys, and Me: I wore a clown mouth for the first time; I had stage fright. It was fun but unprofitable; Hannah said 'Fuck it, I don't want any of the money': there was only about 2 mil after a couple of hours. I forget where we spent that night, Simon's or My Place: I was drinking just a bit.

On Sunday, Easter, yesterday, we all met at the 'Park Ciutadella' and busked and had a picnic. I lost the crowd at nine last night and don't know what they've gotten up to; they're probably all out at the busses. I've spent a couple of hundred of the 1000ptas that Hannah gave me for trainfare to The Meadow next week, so I have to be out here in order to replenish the fund, before I see her, hopefully.

I miss her: The Love Affair is in Full Swing and I wonder where she is on such a beautiful day; I've jacked-off a couple of times just thinking that she might be showing up soon, she makes me that horny.

Ah, well, I had a nap on the patio this afternoon and am refreshed in spite of all this drinking; I had a couple of cups of cafeconleche right before coming out here: Feel OK. It seems to be a fiesta day; most of the shops are closed and there is relatively little traffic: it's Monday.

Some Spanish hoodlums just came up and tried to read what I'm writing, snickered when they realized it was in English, and stood there in amusement, while my adrenalin began pumping in preparation for the Coming Fight: it happens every couple of days; I'm vulnerable because I'm seated, and I have to stand up so they can tell that I am a Man also, and not just a thing attached to the typewriter; it almost always works. They left.

Christ Is Risen; So's The Bread, So's the Street-Writer.

The Brown Pigs and Billy, Again

Six oclock, same spot

Billy and I just had a mellow siesta: ate garlick, oil, pepper, salt; all smeared on bread, with vinegar to sweeten it a little: A Mediterranean Treat; we learned it from the clowns; Billy's favorite meal. I washed myself, the dishes, and the kitchen, drank one beer, and fixed cafeconleche for Billy and me. He's still up there reading horrible Spanish Violence and Sex Comick Books, but is heading for plaza del pi to busk for a couple of hours this evening. He's got over a mil saved for the trip to the Meadow on Monday, I have 900.

I feel Good, and Normal for the first time in a couple of days. Or is it weeks? The crowds are out; the Tourists are wandering around, The Pastry is Ubiquitous.

I must be Curing: I just bought a piece of chocolate: a sure sign of Impending Stability. When I'm on a Bynge I can't stand the stuff. (YAYY!! CHOCOLATE!! YAYYY!! IMPENDING STABILITY!! YAYYY!!). Compounding Senility. Suspended Tranquility. Up-ended Fertility.

Billy reports that the Browns visited Rebecca at the pension today, scolded her for not having a Residence Permit, and told her that they'd Rather have Billy in school than playing music on the street. Well, I'd Rather have all of them in Australia, Rather than carrying guns around in my world, hassling my kids. She told Billy that she thinks he should quit busking. I disagree: it's Absolute Bullshit: Billy probably knows more about Life, and the World, than do Any of the little brown fascist pigs.

This fucking town is crawling with robbers, whores, mafia, and every sort of petty street criminal that you can think of, and they're hassling a kid who plays a flute: Fuck 'em! Let them pull a gun, or threaten us with jail and then maybe we'll co-operate. Fuck Them.

He's trying to decide whether to head down to Plaza del Pi, right now. He's going for it: I told him that I'd bail him out if he has any trouble. All he's got to do is keep his eyes peeled for a couple more days and then we're off for the south, and this will all be blown over by the time we get back, whenever that will be, probably a couple of weeks. Fuck it, we could all move to Gerona, or Valencia, or Madrid, or the Meadow? Fuck this Cop Shit. What do they think of all the ugly old fat whores that clutter up the Gothic Landscape? Shouldn't they be in Home-Making class instead of peddling their disgusting pussies on the street? Huh? What about that? I find Them offensive: what if I was drunk and ended up in bed with one of those Spanish Whales. That's Offensive, not Billy. Yah. Next, they'll be telling the cripples that they should be out having a picnic or playing soccer, Rather than begging. Ratherr!

Sonia, Chris the Minstrel, and Roy the Clown just stopped by to chat; they're on their-way to busk down on Boqueria, and dropped about 50ptas in the box. Their busses got moved on yesterday, and they've had to park in a less beautiful spot; I've invited them over for lunch tomorrow afternoon.

Well, got enough for the night's bottleawine, and the eggs. All is well. Sober, too, feels different, feels fine: Too bad I don't have a Husband Eligibility Quotient anymore: just vague plans, just vague plans.

There's tons of activity on the street this evening: the orange sweepers are practically running amok, the tourists are reeling in confusion, the pastry shoppers are on the march, and the wind blew my book in the street.

The mad bell-ringer is playing songs, and the high-heeled Catalanas are beating a stoney rythym as they sway past, attracting the wayward fuckers, and ruining their posture for life; I suppose a couple of good fucks is worth being crippled from the age of fifty up. They obviously think so. Even the old, old ladies wear modified high heels as they waddle along. You can spot the foreigners: they're the only women who wear sensible shoes: never mind the butt-wiggle. The trouble is that when these Catalanas get to be about forty or fifty, their buttwiggle works against them: it's like jello on the hoof. Udderly disgusting. Yet: they wear those high heels to their own funerals.

Tracy

Six oclock. Saturday. Brusi Bar

Tracy is back from her week-long trip to the south, where she did the usual tourist shit, and ran into 'The Tibetan-Ukranian Mountain Troupe,' a travelling group of hippies and clowns in busses who do shows similar to Hannah's. Tracy said that their music was good but that their clowning was terrible and disorganized. She said they were drinking and smoking dope before and after the shows, and she hung out with them and fell in love with one of the women.

She's hanging around me, asking for kisses and hugs: I told her to come over and fuck me tonight; she can't, though, because she's only 'In Like' with me. Too bad, could be fun, active dancer. She's changing, may even become a nun. It's good to see her again, and she's probably going to come over for dinner. She inquired if anyone else was coming before she agreed. I lied to her, told her that a lot of people would be there; I'm going to seduce her if I can, you bastard.

She ran into Billy, busking with the clowns, and he taught her how to juggle. She's hanging around in front of the pitch practicing with the bean-bags I carry: she's making a spectacle of herself. Billy just joined us; the same police just ran him off from the clowns, telling him that if they caught him having anything to do with money on the street in the future he would be in serious trouble. What the fuck? He's got about 1400 for the trip, so I guess we'll leave as scheduled, hitching on Monday.

I'm making Tracy pay me beforehand for the dinner so that she'll show up. I suppose Billy will probably be coming too, along with Jacques and Tracy.

Silly, silly, silly: Tracy has that effect on the environment. Now she's got me in a god-damned light-hearted mood, too. She is actually becoming a beautiful woman, and is going to make a good little wife for Some lucky guy someday.

"I want to have a baby.", she told me.

"Well, you've come to the right place: I can do it.", I told her. She stuck her butt out at me and I made a face and stuck out my tongue. Let's finish this in private, I thought. Such Hilarity. Such Teasing.

Billy and Tracy are rotating on the juggling now; there isn't a fucking duro in the box yet.

(Author's note, 1992: a few months later Tracy came up to me on the street one day and said "Let's go somewhere and fuck". We went to Hannah's truck, where I was living. I thought it was Great. Tracy said it was too weird for her. I saw her the next day on the Ramblas with Crow again. Moral: Plant seeds, Never Give up.)

PART FIVE

ON THE ROAD

The Meadow, A Paradise

I'm sitting in the shade of an ancient Carob Tree in front of Hannah's teepee. I've been here about four days; sober for two of them, the last two.

Things are different here than I expected, yet not much. I expected Hannah to be Joyous upon my arrival; she was only glad. I expected to arrive with some cash; didn't. I expected the Love Affair to continue on a constant basis; it hasn't: only about half time. I expected Tarn to harass me; he does, but so does Chalky, now. I expected that I would get to go busking with the rest; I haven't, I go as spectator: they don't need a drummer at all when not in Barcelona. I expected to improve my juggling a little while here; I've improved a lot. I expected to drink wine constantly with Mick; it's only been two nights. I expected to finalize the Ireland plans with Hannah; we have: she says I'm not going. I expected making chapatties (with oats) for the folks here; I have, (no oats), and washed dishes and gathered firewood in the bargain. I expected a few adjustment problems; I've had them: cigarettes and matches are luxuries here and I'm Flat Broke. I expected a dunk in the Sea; I haven't had it: the time we went to the shore, the beach was rocky and the water was full of needle-sharp sea urchins; the time we went to the lake it was cold out. I expected Ubiquitous wine-jugs (it's only about 40pta/liter), but it also is a semi-luxury for the folks here. I expected that I would be writing a lot; this is the first time in four days. I expected arriving here Monday night; it was after dark Tuesday when Billy and I finally walked up, after Getting Lost On Trains for two days, my usual mode of train-travel. I expected finding Hannah with Red Hair; I did.

Basically, It's Great here. I've mellowed out, it started yesterday; I've reverted to the hippy mentality I had in the late sixties.

About half the people here are eating in an outside communal kitchen; everyone pays about a mil per week for the food, except me; Hannah is paying for me; Billy is paying his way by passing the hat for the buskers, and juggling. It's OK though, because I'm officially 'On Holiday', according to Hannah, who tries to assuage my guilt about 'being useless'. The majority of the twenty-five or so people here are English, with a Smattering of Germans, a couple of Spaniards, and Me, the only American, especially when I wear my white bell-bottoms, sandals, and bright yellow Hawaiian shirt. Billy says the way I look is California Surfer Disgusting.

"Lets's get one thing straight: you're not coming with me to Ireland.", Hannah told me the other morning as she was reading 'the book' under a tree, soon after we made love.

"Fine, Fine!", I lied, hurt.

Meanwhile, to make myself Useful, I'm trying to get a van running that's been abandoned here, well, almost abandoned, for about six months. It's a diesel, four cylinder perkins, with which I'm not exactly Familiar. I've rarely worked on diesel engines, just a few times on boats; if it was gasoline I'd have it running already. I've trouble-shot the extremely rough-running engine, for a couple of hours over the last three days, and just about an hour ago I found that two of the injectors (Diesel for 'sparkplugs') weren't working: this could be great news: they're relatively inexpensive. I've got them soaking in kerosene (paraffin, petroleo) right now, and this may clean them out. It's a big small van; large enough to pull Hannah's caravan (trailer), if she wants to. She said she probably will. Then she said she didn't know; It doesn't matter, according to her, because it's a Good Deed for me to get it running no matter what the outcome: Mick and Terry don't like so many vans cluttering up their Paradise, and have ineffectually been trying to cut down the number for quite a while. The Eternal Hippy-Van Eyesore At The Commune Problem. Between Chapatties, Fixing the Van, Washing the Dishes, Juggling, Smoking, Watching Hannah, Fucking Hannah, Eating, and Just Lingering, My days have been full, and relaxing.

I just went and tried to start the van; the injectors are still not working; I've got them soaking again; give another try in about an hour. Looked for the bag of sardines that were left over from lunch yesterday at the lake, but was unable to find them. I'm getting hungry again.

Hannah is Even More Beautiful here, in her Element, than she is in Barcelona. She's always Doing Something: "Chalky, go wash your face, now.","Tarn, quit breaking that chair!", "Who's going to do the washing up?", "Who's going busking?", basically being a Light, one of many here, but A Major Light for this place. She gets Beautifuler and Beautifuler in my eyes, while I get Stranger and Stranger in hers. "It's Not Fair!", I told her the other night.

She's gone off busking in Castellon with Simon the yogi, Billy, Chris the young clown brother of an old friend of Hannah's, and Martha, Mick and Terry's five-year-old daughter,.and Tarn the little clown. Chalky and I, along with the rest, stayed here. Chalky keeps running over to read what I'm writing whenever he hears the typing. "Good!", he said when he read the part about me not going to Ireland with them. Sweet kid.

The Layout at the Meadow: Terraces, Ancient Terraces, probably built by slave labor about two thousand years ago; Stoney Landscape. Each terrace is between twenty and fifty feet across and follows, naturally, the contour of the hill. Looking down and to my left I can see the Mediterranean about three kilometers away, with orchards and a small town on the flat between us. Dead ahead, one more Meadow Terrace, then a twenty foot drop to the farmer's orchard below.

To my right, vans, trucks, trees, tents, naked hippy women, kids, and rocks: The Meadow. Behind me, about ten terraces leading up to Mick&Terry's House, which they built about six or seven years ago. They've cultivated about an acre or more for gardens; the watering of which is almost a full-time job because the water has to be pumped up from down below and stored in the huge cement place built-in under the house, I forget what it's called. There are olive and carob trees about every fifty feet, still here since The Romans or who knows when. They've planted some fruit trees up in the gardens. Laundry hangs on various lines strung between trees at many of the visitor's campsites. There are usually about ten permanent residents and ten to twenty visitor\ guests. Most of the visitors are English Buskers, with a sprinkling of Just Plain Travelling Weirdoes, of which I suppose I am one. There are about ten kids living or visiting here right now.

Every couple of days a van or busload leaves or arrives, necessitating an Arrival or Going-away Celebration. There is usually dope, wine and music: Some of our Favorite Things.

There are a couple of other home-made houses that have been built on the top terrace also, though not as substantial as Mick and Terry's. The houses blend in with the brownish-yellow of the mountain. The red, blue, green, and black vans do not. This, it is often remarked, could some day be a problem for Mick and Terry; like: there's a new police chief in the nearest town and it is rumored that he made 'some remarks' in a bar one night that he 'would have to check this place out': The Usual Commune Paranoia, justified or not, I don't know.

The higher terraces are peopled by the more serious, permanent, committed residents; whereas where I'm staying, on one of the lower terraces, is the domain of the Transient Crazies; although Mick is known to make frequent Midnight Appearances at the campfire parties, and the separation is more Misleading than Real: Everyone here seems to have a good heart. They have succeeded in creating an environment here that I've seen fail many times before: A Home, And an Open Commune. I'm sure it took a lot of patience and work. A Paradise.

Shoestring Circus in Sitges

Two weeks later, Sitges

Sitting on the Promenade in front of the beach in Sitges, sitting in front of the trailer (English: caravan) writing for the first time in a couple of weeks. Been Too Busy: Fixing up the old black van that was abandoned at the Meadow by paddy, an old friend/lover of Hannah's. Mick said if I fixed it and got it out of there I could have it. It's ours/Hers, now. I fixed it. I figured out what was wrong and Hannah put in a couple of mil and it runs. It Runs! We're On The Road Again.

We've been having a Wonderful Primitive Life at the Meadow, Living in the TeePee, eating brown rice and chapatties, making love, drinking wine (not to much for me, thank you), smoking a little dope, and generally having a Lovely and Splendid Time. We've come to Sitges to join up with Sonia's Circus; they've got a 60ft diameter red and yellow bigtop (small top?) set up right on the beach across the street from the main gay nightclubs. There's about ten clowns, jugglers, acrobats, and hasslers in the show, along with about ten hangers-on, one of which is me. My attendance at this Scene is barely justified because I am Hannah's Mechanic/Lover.

Billy and I have both improved our juggling; we went busking a couple of times in Castellon with Hannah and her boys to make some cash for our stay at the Meadow. Billy is usually Hannah's 'bottler', or 'Hat-passer', and has been busking with her about ten times; it pays our bills. My Job, should I decide to accept it, is Driver/Mechanic/Baby sitter/Food shopper/Kisser Deluxe/Prime Snufflee/Sometimes Drummer and Juggler/Morning Coffee Maker; it sounds good to me.

Hannah is appearing in the show, for the first time, in about an hour. It's about four oclock now; we just arrived here last night from the Meadow.

They Laughed At Me when I said I was going to get the Black Van running. It'd been sitting there for Months, Various Hipsters and Fake Mechanics had perused it and concluded It's Fucked, Never Run Again. They were almost right, I almost gave up; didn't though because it was Hannah Bait: she said if I got it running she would travel with me and we could pull her caravan. I did it. She's delayed her tentative plan for the trip to Ireland; at least if the van keeps running; she won't be going with Simon in a couple of weeks. Instead, we may take the Long Route through Portugal and France, to England. On The Other Hand, she may decide that the New Circus is so out-of-sight that she may want to stay on with them for a while as Star and Queen. Whatever! I'm A Happy Guy! On the road with my clown gal! They Laughed.

There are two busses and four truck/vans in the Troupe, not counting Black Jack and the Quack Attack (Me/Us). It's a Motley rag-tag crew for sure, with lots of energy and almost no money. It's a Shoestring Soup Circus; funny though, and has that large Catalan-colored tent; it probably won't bring in enough money to support all of the people involved without them doing a little side-busking; but, you never can tell.

I'm not 'in the troupe', as I was rudely informed last night as I queued up for some soup. It ended with me angrily, inaccurately throwing a spoon at Roy, Sonia's Latest, which missed him and unfortunately hit Gary's pregnant wife in the tummy, for which I was unceremoniously escorted from the small-top. Gary owns the small-top, and has a goatee and tattoos on his muscles; I went relatively quietly. They definitely want Hannah, they don't especially want me; though it looks like we come as a package, together, these days. I'm Too Happy!

Charn, Tawakee, and Billy are in constant idiot attendance, and we all seem to have worked out reasonable, though not perfect, methods of relating to each other. The Travelling and Camping parts of my life these days are Flashbackingly Wonderful: I didn't realize it was any longer possible to hang out with a group of people who think Chapatties are Reasonable Fare and living in a truck is Fine, but it is.

It's Sunny, It's Beautiful: Hannah is sitting here having her last off-stage cigarette before joining the Clown Fray, which I will spectate.

THE NEXT DAY

The next day, same spot, the beach at Sitges, sitting in the sun, just finished breakfast on the sidewalk promenade; Hannah is sitting here grinning; she's listening to Pink Floyd on Chalky's Walkman. (YAYY!! CHALK-MAN!!).

The Shows yesterday and last night were Artistic and Monetary Successes: about fifteen mil altogether; Hannah made about four mil busking with Billy yesterday with which we bought all sorts of goodies, including a bar of chocolate and some fishies. I cooked the fishies and served up a Delightful dinner to My Working Clown Wife. I've become a Trailer-husband again. We just finished with toast, coffee, garlic, and eggs, cooked by Me.

What's going on here in Sitges is-this: The International Theatre Arts Festival; there are various shows going on all over town; there were a couple of Space-Age Foam and Mime shows down here on the beach last night:

Mountains of Foam and some fireworks, all crawled over by Machines of Loving Grace. We've crawled out of the slime; now, let's not blow off our heads with our toys, eh? That was The Theme, as far as I could tell.

Billy is lurching around on the sidewalk, bumping into things stoned, wearing a Bogart Overcoat and a black felt hat for the heat. I've had to have a father to son talk with him this morning because of his behavior last night: he went to bed early, before midnight. I told him he was no son of mine if he retired before two.

Hannah and I took a dump in the Sea this morning, my first since I've been in Spain. She and Billy are going busking in a few minutes but I'm not going along because she thinks that it doesn't make any difference when I Help. Fine with me, I suppose: I'll just linger around the kitchen for a while, planning the evening meal or something. Or maybe I could brush my teeth. If I can find a toothbrush.

I've just sent Billy over to kill the little two-year-old German girl who is sitting across the sidewalk from me wailing because her mother won't give her any more snot to play with. They've been with us for a couple of weeks, staying at the Meadow and Caravanning up here· with us, trailing snot the whole way. They have a Deluxe Mercedes Van, and live off money sent regularly from Germany. There are two women, each with a snotty brat; I sometimes retch just being around them, and have told the mothers How To Wipe A Nose a couple of times, which they didn't quite understand, obviously.

Billy is bringing me down: he's lingering around hoping to get sick or hit by a truck; he's wearing an overcoat in 80-degree weather; he's hanging his head and rubbing his eyes and moaning; he keeps talking about his various symptoms of fatal diseases; the usual Hypochondriac Bullshit: I think he caught it from Rebecca, All I have is bad teeth, which can't be lied about. I've been trying to drive him away from me, but he's only moved to a park bench in front of me and continued his moaning and wailing: it's absolutely disgusting. I say Good Riddance when he goes busking with Hannah; I'd rather have the Mongoloid Spanish Idiot Kid who is staring at me, for company, than that moaning little shit of a nerd kid of mine.

Well, I just finished a bit of sewing, and now I can just take it easy until it's time to prepare the mid-day meal, except for cleaning up the breakfast dishes, of course. Hannah left me some of the pesetas from yesterday in case I might need to buy some little thing, like cigarettes or wine. Charn, Tawakee, Tara and Jesse (phil's Irish Daughters, who are here with Phil and Angie selling food in the tent) are rubber-dingying down at the beach; the promenade is filling up with people strolling; I don't have my begging box out, I don't need it: my wife and kid work.

Later, Still sitting on the promenade; it's Siesta and the crowds have thinned. Busked with Hannah further down the Promenade for about two songs; I played the drums while wearing my new clown outfit: red and yellow pants with blue and white striped shirt: Looks Good! Just had lunch: sardines, salad: the usual Great Meal, Yah.

Hannah's gone off with Sonia to get ready for the five oclock show: they just worked out a new act about a flea/louse named Esmerelda who is a trained acrobat and they have this complicated clown interaction where Hannah keeps daring the louse to do another, more complicated flip. It finally does the flip and Sonia is so overjoyed that she starts clapping along with Hannah and the audience... (I hope I'm not killing the joke by explaining it)... (actually, I'd better not tell you how it ends: you'll just have to come to France to see it).

Meanwhile, Hannah has almost decided not to join up with the Soup Circus; hopefully, we'll be heading south instead.

We ran into Peter today on the promenade, down from Barcelona with Emma, on Holiday, and he informed me that my/Hadass' apartment has been sub-let to a Scandinavian Girl. It's still in Hadass' name, presumably, but I'M OUT. Back On the Road, Again, I suppose. I don't mind: that City Life was killing me. out here, in the wilderness, I seem to get on a bit better. Or maybe it's the Steady Fucking. Maybe the Country is good for me.

Next on the Agenda: Get A Pack Of Cigarettes. (presumably to mix with that wonderful country air, which can be healthfully lethal when taken undiluted, it seems.). 0 Me 0 My, I Love That Country Pie. Shalom.

THE NEXT AFTERNOON

Oh, yah, The Next Afternoon, same spot. Sitting inside the caravan because it's thunder storming outside right now: Sunny Sitges, Pearl of the Mediterranean Coast, indeed. Ah, well, at least there are no tourists wandering around; we have the beachfront to ourselves. Billy and Chawakee are reading books, Tarn is off with his two Irish girlfriends, and Hannah is sitting in a Cafe somewhere being interviewed for a magazine article about clowns or something.

It looks like the Soup Circus will be splitting up for about a month: Roy, Sonia, Hannah, Me, and the kids, heading south, maybe to Portugal. And Gary, Mandy, Chris, and a couple of others heading for France. There is dissension in the troupe these days; some want everyone to stay together, some want to head out individually for making more money busking. Hannah and Sonia, as best friends, want to stay together, along with ROY and Me as their Lover-Sidekicks, and do some busking in Barcelona, and possibly a few small clown shows in some schools there. We're probably heading for Barcelona tomorrow; we've gotten an Eviction/Parking Notice here this morning, nothing heavy really, just 'Move Along, Freaks'.

There was an incredible Blast from Mother Nature last night during the last show at around midnight; a thunderstorm passed directly over Sitges, flooding the beach and almost blowing the tent away. Everyone except the performers on the stage, and me and the paying audience, rushed out and began tugging on the poles and digging a wall of sand around the tent, and digging a trench to the Sea to try to keep the show from being flooded out. I couldn't move: I'd been drinking wine and beer and smoking hash and grass and was incapable of any type of organized thinking or movement. I just found a place upwind in the tent and waited for God to blow the whole thing away. Everyone else spent a couple of hours scurrying around and Saving us

The Performers kept the show going with added verve because of the noise of the thunder and the lightning's incredible electricity. The forty or so customers in the tent were trapped there for a couple of hours because it was coming down gatos y perros outside; nearly impossible to walk across the beach to the promenade.

Billy smoked a chillum with Chrissy and Tim and then went and stood out in the rain stoned. It was reported to me and I just shrugged it off with, "He's too dumb to come in out of the rain." As the rain let up a bit, a group of us went out and serenaded the trench-diggers for a while; I played bongos and told them what a Fine Job They Were Doing. Then I followed the sea back to the van and crashed.

We took the Marquee (tent) down this morning in about half an hour; there are about twenty people involved in this Deal, in one way or another; It's a Good Karma Scene, and it's probable that it will Re-Form, if indeed it does split up in the next couple of days. There's going to be a festival in a town near the Meadow in early July and everyone wants to continue on with the show then. We'll see. If it doesn't happen, I'll be lobbyinq for Portugal to try to find a cheap or free boat. We may be heading there anyway, Oh, my.

The German women with the snotty kids are just now taking off for the Meadow again; they're taking Gregory, the violin player from Idaho with them. He was in the show as violinist and Indian Dancer; Another Crazy Young American on the road, good guy, mellow.

There is Change in the Air these days, It's got all of us spinning.

The Trip to Ireland, 1985

PAMPLONA, BOREDEAUX, LA ROCHELLE, BRITTANY

Life is only hard when I'm not.

July 21, Pamplona

Well, here we are in Pamplona; left The Meadow, and Tortosa, a couple of days ago after a couple of weeks of hanging around swimming and eating. Hannah, Sonia, Roy, Enrique (the Barcelona Mime), and the boys, did a few shows for the Theatre Festival there and got paid 90 mil. We're now down to about ten mil after buying a bunch of shit and fixing the truck some more. The truck is running fine, for it. Hannah actually thinks that the collection of rattles, knocks, and squeaks that it makes can be described as 'purring'. Sounds more like a Death Rattle to me. One thing that the truck Did Do Wrong was to drive us into the Ebro River yesterday-eve in/near Zaragoza.

"Let's drive into the Ebro so that we can say we did it.", was the last thing we heard me say right before we had to spend the next few hours trying to get the damn thing unstuck; and finally Hannah got a tractor which pulled us out Immediately, as I watched, covered with sweat and mud.

Hannah just returned from the shops with some wine, gaseosa, and a bunch of salami: she met a bunch of randy old men there who gave her a bunch of free grapes and a bunch of other stuff, for 470ptas: she has a Way in the World; for instance: do you think the tractor driver/farmer would've stopped plowing his field if I'd've asked him to come and pull the idiot-van out of the river?

We are averaging 20mph (about 100 miles a day), and drive Uphill at about 12, Downhill at about 30 or 35, drawing stares from all the Spanish, who love to sit in their wooden chairs by the side of the highway whenever it's hot (most of the time), "Well, look at that red van, Did You Ever? And did you see the Driver?", and like that, I suppose.

We're camped right beside, like five feet away from, the plaza De Taros, in the Heart of Pamplona, in a sort of secret place, covered with Elm-Like Trees (it's cool here), right behind the Fire Station, with a view of the mountains to the north, and a view of the roads and the park about fifty feet below us. Hannah camped here last year, and thinks it's a good place because there's weeds growing right down the hill that she can pick and then put in our food later, after she puts them in bunches, ties them with string, and hangs them allover the place so they can shed on everything. She knows the names of all of them, and I just Have to Believe they're Herbs, because they look just like so many god-damned Weeds to me.

    I'm still learning to play the whistle and juggle so Billy and I can have a busking act in the near future. Hannah, Billy, and Chawakee made about five mil in an hour yesterday in Zaragoza. The Plot is to head for Brittany, probably arriving in about a week, and stay for a while with a friend of Hannah's, and then catch the ferry to Ireland. However, she recently got a letter from her old friend/lover, Clem, who is also visiting in Brittany, and in it he said that maybe, sometime in the future, she could have her old Library Van back. I said, "How About Tomorrow?"

A few days later, La Rochelle

Hannah and the boys made about thirty mil in three busking shows in Pamplona, so we're rolling in dough again, although Hannah keeps salting it away in various secret places, in case of a rainy day, or the ferry fare to Ireland. Anyway, we've been making about 150 miles a day for a couple of days and are now only about 70 miles from her friend's house somewhere in Brittany (I forget). We've stopped here to do some busking so we don't have to go into our reserves (the ferry).

    We've been in France for a couple of days, I think. We had some fun at the border: they were thinking of searching the van and the caravan, to look for the little bag of dope that Billy hid under the stove, but decided against it when they saw the mounds of mouldy fruit and piles of dirty underwear scattered allover the caravan. And when I told them the back door of the van doesn't open, they clucked and babbled in French for about half an hour, gave us back our passports, and told us to go. Since then we've been mainly driving, eating, and swimming in the Atlantic.

    The beach near Bordeaux has waves like Santa Cruz, California on a rough day: huge, noisy, and dangerous. Lots of fun, but hundreds of thousands of French vacationers lining up to pay outrageous prices at 'The California Pizzeria'. Just like Santa Cruz only much more Middle-Class: What Perfect Tans!

    We got the fuck out of there even though the waves were Great.

    It's muggy, humid, wet, and feels hotter here than it did in Tortosa and Spain, though the French keep their place looking very neat by comparison. They are definitely into shopping centers; something that I Wasn't Particularly Missing. This is a beautiful place to pass through but I can't Imagine staying here for Any Length of Time.

Billy spends most of his time talking about the various diseases that it is possible to contract, and imagining that he has symptoms of any number of them. He is also predicting a Coming Heat Wave, ala Frank, and we try to keep him off the dope and caffeine as much as possible.

With the exception of the Old Quarter, La Rochelle could just as well be San Jose. France is like that: a lot of it reminds me of Tucson or Watsonville. And the Language! Completely Incomprehensible, although Hannah has somehow mastered it. Billy and I hold our noses with our fingers and make weird noises and then Hannah tells us what we've just said in French; it Is Like That.

My Job, for the next couple of hours, is to clean up the pad and prepare some lunch for the workers when they return. I've also got to unbend the supports of the trailer which got all fucked up yesterday in Bordeaux when I hit a stump in a campground.

We bought about twenty-five liters of Spanish Wine at the border, so we are pretty well fixed up for a couple of weeks anyway. We also got a few kilos of olives, a bunch of olive oil (five liters), and a few kilos of sausage. It's Not So Bad. The Love Affair continues: Life is only hard when I'm not.

BRITTANY

Here we are, camped in the front yard of an old Chateau, or Farm House, or Something. Billy is lingering around drinking coffee and smoking grass; Hannah is laid-up in the van with a crinkly shoulder blade, upon which we have just put a poultice made of some of the weeds she gathered fortunately the other day. I think she calls them 'marshmellow' plants.

We're visiting a friend of hers, Joy, who rents two rooms of the old mansion (about thirty rooms, made of old stones) and they have a campfire in the yard, and have built a hippy cabin up the hill in the back garden, and her Dutch boyfriend, Martin, who used to live in Boulder Creek California and Venezuela, who has gone off busking in Vannes with Tarn, but Chawakee and 'Free', his Dutch-Boy son, are here catapulting a rubber ball into Billy's tent, which Tracy gave him.

I have an infection in my left ear, from swimming in the Ebro, and am deaf from that side, except for a constant ringing noise which I take to Be Cosmic. I have quite a hangover today because Hannah and I had to drink the rest of the Spanish Cognac last night because she couldn't go to sleep with her shoulder hurting.

It's Raining and Sunny; we're about seven hundred miles north of Tortosa.

"I can't even manage to smoke a whole joint! How can you manage to smoke a whole cigarette?", Billy asked me.

"It boggles the mind.", I told him.

"It's a Known Fact.", he conceded.

"It's a Known Fact.", I agreed.

"That was a stupid conversation.", I told Billy, as he stood there feebly trying to hold a board over this typewriter so the little shower wouldn't get this wet, not noticing that the rain had stopped a few minutes before.

"Well, is it Stopped?!", he asked the Cosmos, looking up into the sky and trying to figure out if it was still raining.

"You want some, Jack?", he asked, proffering the joint am dropping it in my lap.

"Hey! Don't Start Stumbling Around!", I warned him.

Chawakee, meanwhile, was standing beside me, trying to read this, and engaging his Frankenstein Imitation Mode. Scary shit all around.

Billy was still bumbling and stumbling around, hurting himself and the General Ambience, "Don't do stupid things, man!", I warned him again.

"OW!!", he replied, burning his fingers while trying to put the kettle on.

"You'll have to go away from here if you keep doing stupid things!", I told him. He snickered.

He sat down next to me on a folding chair (Look Out!), still snickering.

"Don't get on my case, man!", I once again warned him, as he fell over backwards, "If you manage to hurt me even a little, I'll Fuck You UP!", I told him. He snickered louder, began snorting and chortling.

"Where's my lighter?", I asked, "Where's My Fucking Lighter?! Billy?"

"Where'd I put it?", he asked the universe.

"You can't use my fucking lighter if you don't give it back!", I told him, increasing his Social Awareness.

The Plan has changed: Now, Hannah and Clem are trading vans. She gets the Big Ole Library Bus, 'Plum'; he gets the red (formerly black) van I fixed at The Meadow; it's taken a couple of days of mooning around and mooching about to accomplish this, but now the yard is filled with Things being transferred from one van to the other: it Could Be a Heart-breaking Situation, because he's still in Love with her. Meanwhile, I linger around as the Future Mechanic, trying to pretend that I'm not Famously In Love with her, and covering her mouth when we fuck, so as not to rub salt.

It's started doing what my English friends call 'Pissing', and the Idiot Sons are sitting out there In It, with umbrellas, giggling and generally acting like, "Man, how come everyone else has brains?" They're saying things like, "Boy, it's really raining, huh?", answered by, "Yah, it's really raining hard." Complete Idiots.

"Is it raining?", Tarn asked the other two from the door of the trailer, as he looked plainly at the rain pouring down.

"Of course it is!", Chawakee answered.

"Oh, yah.", said Tarn.

"Dimmy, Dim, Dim.", said Chawakee, tapping his forefinger to his head.

Now Billy is over digging a ditch around his tent in the pouring rain, while the other two stand at the trailer door and howl and laugh as the water pours into it anyway.

This is France, good weather for frogs. Everywhere very green, and everywhere people talking to each other in an un-understandable language. They haven't noticed that France stopped being the center of the world in about 1600.

We're still having Fun, and are probably leaving for the coast, and Ireland, tomorrow morning, although Hannah May decide to just let me go at any moment and then Billy and I will be showing up at Santi's ready to start the rest of our lives. I suggested it to her last night because I was getting bored trying to figure out which van we were going to be travelling in, and whether we're heading for England, Ireland, or just going back to Spain, or what-the-fuck?

I may try to get a Rock and Roll Band together somewhere: The Armageddon Boogie Band. Or get a boat in Ireland and sail it back to Barcelona.

We are a cute little clown family, 'The Fugawi', which I've painted on the front of the truck. And what passes for Problems in our midst generally would be considered minor irritations otherwise. Nothing Serious seems to ever go wrong: Our karma seems to be Grade A. So far.

August 12, Brittany

We spent the weekend at Vannes, and Lorient, where we touristed a Celtic Musick Festival there, drank beer, listened to the Irish and Breton Music, drank beer, lingered around, and danced. I ran into Cecile, Little Cecile, selling jewelry and plastic birds at the fair; she had spent the winter in Greece and Turkey, was glad to see me, and was Beautifuller than ever. we chatted for a few minutes and then I got out of there, let me tell you.

Hannah said, "Don't let me interrupt, stay and talk with her if you want.", as she came upon us chatting.

"Nah, that's OK," I said, "That's Cecile, she was my girlfriend once."

"Stay and talk to her if you want.", Hannah said, her eyes shining mischievously.

"Nah, let's go take a siesta.", I said, turned on by both of them at once.

We put on a Dancing Spasticks Show for a couple of the Musick Crowds at an open-air theatre/bar, when Hannah and Joy began dancing like sex-crazed, possessed Irish Hippies; I did my imitation of Jerry Lewis having a fit, and Martin, all 6ft6 of him, did his imitation of Ichabod Crane doing the shimmy. Tarn, Chawakee, and Billy pretended they'd had an overdose of strychnine, and the crowd generally quit watching the band and watched us for a while. Just another Normal Evening with the Fugawi. We re the Fugawi.

Hippying thru the Universe: subtitle of the Life. Geeking around every corner: expecting the seen: constantly amazed when things work out: teeth the only sign of decay: constantly learning; forgot how to keep track of growth: no scale seems sufficient: still love the Beatles, Jon's my fave.

And: Guess where the Milky Way is tonight? Right outside my door! And guess where the Atlantic Ocean is tonight? The same: the door: I walk out and I could drunkenly fall into either. (just to get away from the grateful dead) .

So, instead of making love tonight (she wants me to: I'm not falling for That), I'm sitting here writing, drinking red red wine, eating white white bread, and smearing Dijon Thereon: and protecting myself from the ocean and the stars by concealing my self in this latter day cave.

CENTRIFUGAL ENERGY (POSSIBLY MCNIN3 ON STRINGS) :

Sometimes it's like this: I can feel my life as a string.
Sometimes it's like this: I can feel my life as energy.
And, at others: My life is a string of energy.
The woman loves me, the boys love me, the rest can go to hell.

An Un-knowing Posthumous Letter to Frank

"August 26, 85, A monday in Brittany

Frankly,
    I'm Miserable, so I thought I should tell you about it to cheer you up. Sure! I've got this incredible lover/woman as a constant companion; but: How long will it last? Sure: I live in an incredibly comfortable new library van that we picked up a couple of weeks ago; but: it's not quite a palace. Sure: We're heading for ireland in a few days; but: what'll we do when we get there: will it just be the same old shit as everywhere else?
    I'm out of wine for the evening and won't be able to get any til tomorrow. I'm out of tobacco; same story. God, Am I Miserable.
    Even though I spent a great day with the boys paddling around in our new little boat (which I stole in some french seaport one night) , and splashed in the sea and flew kites and drank wine all day it wasn't that great: Because: I Got Stung By a Fucking Wasp: ruined the whole day. The wind has died and the sun is setting pinkly into the atlantic and I sit here: Miserable because I'm out of wine and tobacco and the god-damned french keep weirder hours than the spanish do. What kind of creature am I? I SHOULD be ecstatic: I have everything I want; and yet: I'm a fucking creature of my vices; writing (writhing) in uncomfortability in the middle of paradise.
    As I was lying on the bed a few minutes ago, hoping that the caffeine I just took would take effect quickly, and pondering the Uselessness of It All, I thought of you and decided to write this letter asking your advice about Suicide: are you pro or con? All Joking Aside: my teeth are getting worse and worse and I suspect that in a few years I won't be able to survive on my Good Looks alone. Not to mention my mental powers which are obviously on a Rabid Decline: Is there any kind of encouragement you could give me, Frank? Can/Could you sit right down and write me a letter that could shine some light on this depressing feeling of worthlessness in general? is there, Frank? If you can find the time, send a letter to me care of: general delivery, cork, cork, ireland, where I'll probably be living in a hovel of some sort, and drawing welfare. Any light at all, at this point in my downward slide, may keep the Inevitable Conclusion to my Ridiculous Existence delayed long enough for me to find same sort of Real Meaning out of all this Horseshit. All this

just because I'm running out of smokes: just one more left; should I smoke it now, or save it for the morning when the nicotine weasel arises? Ah, Fuck It! I'll smoke it now and then throw myself from the cliff in the morning when the nic fit hits me. Hannah, who recently came very close to quitting tobacco, claims that she lost the meaning for her existence when she couldn't smoke; i think it's happening to me tonight. (could you send a few smokes along with the letter, preferably carabellas).

God! why did I ever leave Barcelona? Beautiful, Friendly Barcelona! The Friendly Smiling Spanish Faces of Raurich Alley! The Fun! The Funk! I had a Career there, but, now, where am I: in this fucking french shopping-center of a country where everything costs too much, and the people are impossible to talk to; 0 why did I leave my friends; just to wander north (north! for the winter! To Freezing Ireland!) 0 what a fool I've been. Why didn't someone, anyone try to stop me; tye me down; lock me in Hadass' apartment; anything would have been better than to have been led astray out here into the cold, cruel unknown. Arrrrrrgh!

The plot is this, Frank: We're going into business in ireland: same kind of boat business, or car business, or monkey business: whatever turns up: we're going for the cash so that we can return to spain next summer and buy a house, or a boat, or both. We're going to live in ireland for about a year, with me hustling whatever I can: possibly start a sailing school, or just buy and sell shit: we already got a boat and an outboard motor for a very good price. I also plan to make a few bucks (pounds?) on the side by making beer and selling whatever I don't drink.

So, stay in touch, tell Santi not to worry about my bill: I'll pay it as soon as I get same bread, man; and tell some of the people that I miss them but tell some others that I never really liked them very much, anyway.

Good Luck with the rest of your life, tu amigo, Jack

P.S. Has Billy arrived in Barcelona yet?"

A Letter to Jacques, Frank is Dead

"Sep 3, 85

Cork, Ireland.

My dear friend Jacques:
    I am very sad. Sad for Frank, sad for you, and just plain sad. It's taken a few hours to sink in; i don't know whether to cry or shout. Sometimes, though I never admitted it, I believed he intended to do it. Sometimes I saw that it was A Great and Good Game of making everyone aware of Life; by his constant referrals to death. God, I'm Shocked. He was one of the funniest people I've ever met: this is definitely a tragedy. I have a tape of you, frank, and me one night at the pad; I'll listen to it and then send it along to you for the Box Archive, as soon as possible.
    I hope you are OK; i hope you are finding comfort with others. I know that Frank meant a lot to you; I Respected him; his mind and his perceptions, and his Philosophy and Demeanor of Life, but I know you loved him more than I did: he taught you a lot, me too, and I guess we should be thankful that we did get as much from him as we did. I wish you the best, Jocko: hang in there.
    Try as I might today, I've not been able to recall the very last time I saw Frank, unless it was one night with Hannah and the boys at the outside opera, or one morning at Santi's, Yah that's it, i think, one morning at Santi's right before I left for Tortosa. Well, I miss him already. I had been thinking about Frank a lot lately, was even telling or reminding Hannah and Billy about this or that thing that Frank did or said just yesterday, and I wrote a letter to him, via you at poste rest, just last week: I figured it would cheer him up, and I wanted him to know that I cared: fuck! a little too late, I suppose.
    Billy says that the last thing frank said to him as he left on the train for tortosa was: "Hurry back or you won't see me again." Hannah says he said much the same: "Hannah, this will be the last time I see you", or something very similar. I can't remember what he said to me, although we did part as friends, and I was Intending on seeing him again. God-damn it.
    You'll be glad to hear that some of frank's idiosyncrasies live on in the boys' young minds: Billy occasionally does frank's rocking out in a sitting position thing, even when he's standing up; he did it automatically this morning when we had Cafe-con-lech, and was instantly slightly embarassed when he realized

that things have changed somewhat. Tarn, also, sings, in a Very High Squeaky Voice, the song that Billy wrote in honor of frank a few months ago: "I love happiness, I love spring, I love flowers and birds that sing… But, I hate winter, I hate ice, I hate snow and weather not nice". Let me tell you, it's Shocking to the Earbones when his 8 year old voice tops out the register. Chawakee, also sometimes joins in, although his favorite high-pitched ditty is one that he plagarized from me: "Dingbat! Dingbat! Goody, Goody, Goody!", which can be an Equally Shattering Olfactory Experience: all in all, they are completely nutso kids, which is fitting, considering their role-models, I suppose.

It looks like 'Barcelnoana, under', is finishing itself: the cast has dispersed, The main player has self destructed. Shit, frank dead, phil gone, peter gone, hadass gone, only you remain of the original cast, and even the fucking author isn't in barcelona. Do what you like with it: there's plenty about Frank, and plenty of his quotes in there. I'll keep sending 'Ireland, under the influence' to you, anyway. New Cast.

It's Good News that Sally is staying on in Barca, though, thanks for that info.

Well, amigo, fill me in on what frank was up to before he died. What did you know about it? Did you believe he was serious. I know these are difficult questions, but we all need to know as much as we can about franks last weeks and days, for our own sanity. Like: did he have cancer? You know what I mean. Shit, Jacques, I loved the guy, and admired him in many ways. I share your pain of loss in this, i do.

Well, Good Luck in your life, ed, and God Bless you.

Love, from Jack"

Taking a Shit in Ireland

BANTRY MENTAL HOSPITAL, MAUGHANACLEA DIVISION.
Last night the inmates almost took over this division: it was a near riot, and I as the Senior Psychological Attendant, almost had to call out the local Guards. We were sitting around the hearth when it began with Chawakee, usually the leader in these riots, being Possessed by the Spirit of Dim. Tarn said something which caused Chawakee to break into a chant, "Dim, Dim, Dimmy-Dim-Dim", which he kept up for about ten minutes. It was obviously infectious, after a couple of minutes Tarn began chanting, "Tock, Tock, Tocky, Chocky, Locky, Sock, Sock!" Billy soon joined in with, "Karanja Naranja boppy de loo loo!", followed soon by Hannah with "Craydad, Hodad, Hoodad, Crammy Dop Alee!". These are rough approximations of the chilling chanting that was filling the Irish Night.

I was tempted to join in, drawn by the obviously ancient ritual, but resisted and pulled back, which was fortunate; had the Staff caught it, we all might have been permanently stranded in Nutso-land. By my example, I think I kept them from Actually Dancing About Madly and losing themselves completely.

After about fifteen minutes they seemed to collapse back into their Normal personalities, and resumed their carving and whistle-playing, the usual activities for Crafts Period; and which seem to be helping them adjust to life in Arland.

When I felt that it was safe, I dressed myself in my down vest, Down Coat, scarves, cotton gloves, leather gloves, rubber boots and ventured outside with the kerosene lamp to answer a call of nature: I had to piss and shit.

I took the shit-pick and the bog-roll (Irish for Toilet paper) with me. Thus equipped, I wended my way down the hill towards my favorite waste-spot. (Everyone has their own)

It was pitch Black and the Sleet was blowing against me in a Gale as I balanced on the steep goat-path above the lake. I set down the lamp, which blew out, and tried to unzip my pants, which was impossible because of the two pairs of gloves, so I took off the leather ones and was finally able to find my Willie (English for Dick) and spray piss allover the bottom of my coat and the ends of the long scarf wrapped around my neck, which I couldn't see because the lamp was out. I finished pissing and remembered that I had to shit. No Problem: Simply find a spot where the ground was soft enough to dig. I hunted around with a bic lighter, actually only the spark from it, it wouldn't stay lit. I dug the hole, dropped my pants, and proceeded to shit right next to it, which I discovered later with the lighter. I scooped the turd into the hole with the pick, which already had shit on it anyway because I'd used it to chip the turd out of my asshole when it had frozen there mid-grunt.

I finally got the hole covered, after chasing the used bog-paper down the hill, slipping, stumbling, falling, and unable to catch it because of the wind, which blew it into the lake. (NO Problem, the lake is low and mucky and the goats will eat it later.)

I found the lamp, pick, bogroll, and one of the leather gloves. I looked around for a few minutes with the spark of the Bic and finally came to the conclusion that I had buried the other one in the shit-hole accidentally. I decided to leave it til the morning and headed back towards what I thought was the house, but which was actually one of the sheds, on the way to which I stepped in Cow, Goat, Chicken and Dog Droppings. Country Life has Many Variations. After a few minutes of wandering around in the yard cursing the weather, I heard the faery-like refrain of "Dimmy-Dim-Dim", and followed it back to the house, where I joined the Family Division around the hearth for another Wonderful Arsh Night.

The next day, after I'd dug up the glove, I decided I'd had enough of wandering around at night getting lost trying to take a shit, and that everyone shitting wherever they wanted was inefficient. I decided to dig a deep shit-hole just on the other side of the driveway, which I did in the 'calms' between the gales. It was about five feet deep and two feet in diameter, covered with some boards to squat on, a piece of plywood to cover it, and some stones for weight. I also leaned a piece of plywood on a tree to make a roof. I was the first to use the 'outhouse' and it Worked perfectly; no more of this shitting allover the place. I bragged about how Clever I was to the rest of the family, and berated the 'lazy irish'. They were suitably impressed, Hannah said, "Well Done, Jack.", and patted me on the head. The boys fought over who got to use it next. I drank some poteen to celebrate my manhood.

It poured 'hard' rain that night. I went out to take a shit. I lifted off the stones, lifted off the plywood; lifted up the lantern, and almost lifted up my dinner. I was looking at a two-foot diameter circle of turds and bog-roll, floating at grass-level. When the ground became saturated and the hole filled with water, the plywood had sealed it in. It sure had rained a lot.

The house was 800 years old and never had electricity, inside water, inside toilet, or an out-house. Now I knew why. I filled in the hole the next day. The boys laughed at me for days. Fuck Technology.

The Weird Trip to Mlrepoix France

JACK AND BILLY AND UBIQUITOUS LADRONES

Spring 1986.

BARCELONA

I left Hannah at the beach in Gava, and drove back to Barcelona with Circus Fuckoffkoff. She was leaving soon for Granada. The Love Affair was Officially Over, she thought.

Billy and I settled right into Pension Costa after having been gone a year; I went to the Tapas and had a few beers, was only Mildly Drunk and went home early, about midnight, and smoked a few hashishes with Naomi and Billy in her room. We were laughing and talking when Awkmedd came in and rampaged at us so we retired to my room where we continued laughing, only quieter, and Again he Attacked us and told me and Billy that we were OUT of there as of Now and gave me back my money. I refused to take it though, and he stood there for about fifteen minutes yelling at me, but I Sat Firm. on the bed, knowing that it would all be OK in the morning, which it was. .

Everything went fine for about a week; we were husking and even saving up some (about two mil) for the Rent coming up in two weeks. We hardly busked, though, by Hannah's Standards at least: about thirty minutes a day when we could get it together; I got drunk a few times with Fuckoffkoff. Sometimes I couldn't even hold the whistle until about four in the afternoon.

We were cooking our own Eternal Stew in our room for about a week there. We had two pitches: Puerta del Angel and the Liceu Station on the Ramblas which was incredible sometimes: we'd make 1500ptas in about twenty minutes at times. All was fine until the day Hannah called from Valencia. That afternoon, a Thursday I think, we busked down at the foot of the Ramblas, moved from Liceu by the Blue police. Billy made a weird throw and the fucking diabolo landed on/near the top of one of those 60ft trees, stuck in a branch. I couldn't see it. There are nuts hanging on those trees, in pairs, which look exactly like a diabolo, and my eyes are getting no better. Finally, David Bowie came along with a camera with a telephoto lens and we were able to spot the thing. We had gathered a crowd by this time. I began throwing juggling balls at it, which Billy would chase all around, to fetch. Some landed on trucks, some on whores, some on old people, It Was Insane. I couldn't hit it, but we made some money from people who thought it was part of the act. We gave up and decided to try again the next day when the light would be better; it was getting dark. Fuck! No Diabolo.

That night Ahmed confirmed for us that we were leaving Barcelona: he went on the Rampage again because I was playing the whistle or something, I can't remember.

The next day I still couldn't hit the diabolo, and Bowie didn't show back up with his camera. So, we began busking with just juggling and whistling and same clowning: it went OK but not Near as well as with the diabolo. We had about two and a half mil at this point and were Officially leaving on Sunday. It, rained. Fuck.

We left some of our shit in the room and headed out on Sunday morning for the train, each of us carrying four heavy objects: juggling suitcase, typewriter, backpacks, my papers, Billy's papers, clothes bag, bedrolls, Everything we now owned in the world. It was almost impossible to walk, but what did we care, we were heading for Adventure.

We bought tickets to Gerona and boarded. We were immediately confronted with Ladrones, who got on in Figueras, eyeing all our shit. The Paranoia was Constant.

GERONA

Gerona was fine for a start, though we only had about a mil left. We walked around and found a place near the Old Roman Wall where we could stash our stuff and then after siesta we went out busking. We only busked for about twenty minutes when a Catalan named Carlos came along and invited us up to his house for dinner. We were wined and dined with a Fabulous Feast and then he took us out and showed us his favorite bars. Billy and Carlos drank champagne, I drank beer.

While we were out running around we met a girl named Margarita who fell in love First with Billy and Then with me. Nice Girl. Theoretically we went back over to the wall to get our stuff so we could take it up to Carlos' and sleep there. I was too drunk to make it up the hill to where the stuff was hidden and layed down in a parking lot at the bottom of the hill and told them they should go on, which they did.

In the morning I was Wasted. I waited and waited for Billy to show up, which he'd said he would do by nine in the morning. I waited til 10: no Billy. I loaded up all the shit and went. and sat down on a bench on The Ramblas and sat On the Shit because of the ubiquitous Ladrones.

Sitting on the Ramblas in Gerona, Completely Hungover, surrounded by ladrones, waiting for Billy. He never showed. I was thinking, 'Fuck! Is this where I lose my Son? Is this where It All Comes Down?' It was horrible. I sat there for about four hours, when finally Margarita came along and told me that she knew where Carlos lived. I didn't/couldn't remember, and didn't want to start searching around all those alleys carrying an unbelievable load and risk missing Billy That Way, did I? No. So, after taking her daughter to school, Margarita returned and we walked to Carlos' house where we rang and his wife woke up Billy.

Billy had a hangover, the first of his life. I admonished him for staying up half the night with Carlos drinking champagne in bars. Carrying all our stuff, we went with Margarita to a friend of hers for Siesta; about ten Catalan people/friends who meet at that house every day for Lunch: Another Fantastic Meal; Gerona was turning out to be great.

Since Margarita had to go to work at three, she showed us where she lived so we could meet her there at ten when she got off work. Fine. Back to the Ramblas for us, and some busking. It wasn't That Brilliant: Not many people, and we weren't very mobile, though we did make our beer and pastry.

Margarita's at ten. We went out for a few beers, she paid, she insisted. Back to her house for a bottle of wine and then, and then, we went to bed. Nasty Sex, Fun: I didn't come; neither did she. I was too drunk; she's only twenty-four. I felt like I was being unfaithful to Hannah, which didn't help much either.

In the morning we all lingered around the flat for a couple of hours, drinking coffee and talking. Billy was feeling better now, so was I. Margarita took her daughter to school and I jacked off in Hannah's mouth, she was great as usual.

We were invited for lunch again, but declined; we'd decided that it was time to be heading for France. We only had about a mil left so we decided to go husking and then Margarita would meet us and give us a ride to the station, which is what happened. We busked the Ramblas cafes and made another mil or more, which was fine. Billy was getting funnier, and better with the clubs and rings. We were even thinking that it was a blessing in disguise that we'd lost the diabolo because we were coming up with new ideas for the 'act'.

Thinking, 'this travelling ain't so bad', we kissed Margarita goodbye at the station and caught the train for Port Bou, which was a mistake because the end of the line is one station further: France. No Matter, we just snuck the last part with No Problem except for having to be Constantly Alert to the threat posed by the Ubiquitous Ladrones.

CEREBERE, FRANCE

We crossed the border with no problems: Just Weird Looking Tourists in Black Fedoras. We had 1000ptas, changed it into 45francs, not even enough to catch the train to the next station. Fuck! Now we were into it. Walked into town; took a long time because we couldn't walk at more than a baby's pace with all that shit. Center of town: fuck, incredibly small. No Matter, we bought some bread, cheese, wine, juice, tobacco and had ourselves a Fine Little Lunch sitting on the quay overlooking the beach. Dale, a Liverpudlian who was ripped off for everything he had on the train and had been in town waiting for a week for the money from his father to arrive at the post office, joined us and we became friends: a decent chap; with tattoos and a plastic leg; scarey-looking, big, but a good guy, you know. I bought us another bottle and we bullshat the afternoon away. Then we busked in the town square: about twenty little brats and their mothers and about five tourists.

A funny little show and we made 20francs but the brats attacked Billy while I was off shopping: they tried to rip his cape off and shit like that. He finally got mad and screamed at them, then I came back and chased them and they scattered, to some light applause.

We rejoined Dale down at the beach where he'd been sleeping and living, and were soon joined by the most Motley Crew I've seen this side of a Hell's Angels Funeral: Italians without Anything, Anything at all, a completely down-and-out Portuguese, some assorted weird French, and like that: about six of them in all, along with a Scottish hippy. So, we all drank wine as the sun slowly set on this Bums Paradise.

Before I passed out/went to sleep I told Billy to tie all the things together to make it harder for one of our 'friends' to steal them. I also told Dale that I thought our friends were a bunch of thieves. He agreed. I went to sleep. After a while Billy got sleepy so he woke up Dale who sat up half the night watching the stuff that Billy and I weren't actually laying on. It worked. In the morning we still had all our stuff.

Well, except for Dale, the rest of the gang was planning to head north by getting on the train with no ticket. Billy and I decided we would try our luck hitching. It was a beautiful day, we had bread, cheese, wine, water, and fruit. All was well. We sat there for three hours, no ride.

We gave up and headed, slowly, for the train station. Some Frenchmen we passed were cracking up at my/our appearance: the weird Portuguese who had adopted us a few minutes before, translated for me that they thought I looked like Charlie Chaplin; I was flattered.

When we got to the station, there sat the whole gang from the night before, waiting for the same train we were going to take. Everyone in the station was staring at us; I'm not being paranoid: it's true. By this point in the trip we were beginning to feel tired; our shoulders and backs and feet were starting to hurt. Little did we know we still had four days to go before we would get to Mirepoix and our friends.

The train finally arrived and we all 'snuck' on, destination perpignan, because, for some strange reason (I'd visited it once a few years ago) I thought the busking would be good there. Little did I know. our 'friends' offered to share a compartment with us, I declined and instead we sat in a compartment with an American/Mexican we'd met in the Cerebere station; a film distributor; we got along fine; he was amazed at our story about who and what we were, even though he was Hip.

PERPIGNAN

Perpignan, and we run off the train, beginning Act Two of our Clown Careers in France. I ask the stationmaster where the stairs are in Spanish, he yells at me in French, I ask him in English, he yells at me again in French. He steps down off the platform and begins to cross the tracks, I follow, he yells at me in French. I am over half way across, so, even though he is obviously telling me to go back, I continue across. So Does Billy. He yells at me in French some more, the people waiting in the station crack up. I plead ignorance, he kicks me in the butt as I'm climbing up the other side. The Audience Roars. I bow and we exit through the station. End of Act Two.

Perpignan. Where the Fugawi? It was a lot bigger than I remembered. Billy guarded the stuff on the main street in front of the station while I headed out to scout for busking. I walked about a mile or more til I finally found a small ramblas and some shopping areas with 'rue peatones'. I returned and Billy and I loaded up and began heading in that direction. I simply could not walk another ten feet. We stopped and I slept on the bags while Billy watched to make sure we weren't ripped off. (We had to do it that way: we'd already met about ten people on this trip who had Lost Everything) End of Act Three.

When I woke up I went and scouted for a place where we could sleep til siesta was over. I found it, under a bridge over the cemented-in river that runs through the middle of town, a grass verge between the cement wall and the river, behind same bushes. We crashed for a couple of hours.

After siesta we stashed some of our stuff in a large drainpipe, hoping it wouldn't rain, and headed downtown to the shittly littly rue de peatones that

I'd found earlier. We busked: pretty good: 20francs in twenty minutes: I went shopping: wine, bread, cheese, milk: we'd live another day, anyway.

Even though it was only about, six oclock, the streets were beginning to thin out and we realized that we'd gotten out there too late, too fucking late. We still didn't understand the French Way of doing things and we were still carrying quite a bit of shit around with us; we'd only stashed the clothes and a bedroll in the pipe. We kept on anyway and ended up with the food and another 40francs: alright.

I'd been on a Binge since Gerona I suppose, so this night I only drank one liter of wine and we retired about nine when it got dark. We felt fine, just exhausted and sore, and a little bit spaced because it was so fucking hard to get things done and how were we going to hop the train out of Perpignan if the stationmaster recognized us as the clowns from the day before, and if we didn't take the train, how the fuck would we find out how to get directions to the highway, let alone walk to it. Like that.

Billy faded off to sleep immediately and I lay awake having visions of fucking Hannah, and smoking and fidgeting because I hadn't drunk myself into a stupor like I had every other night recently. I had finally begun to drift off when I heard some weird clicks and whirring and the fucking sprinklers started watering everything, including us. I guess it was about four in the morning. I woke up Billy and we dragged all the stuff through the moist dirt, not yet mud, to a place that was sheltered a little better from the water, and then went and found a rock to put in front of the nearest sprinkler so it wouldn't spray us. THEN we went back to sleep, supposedly, in our slightly wet clothes and bedding. What fucking luck!

About nine oclock we got up and had breakfast: apples, croissants, milk, bread, cheese; fine. We packed up all the shit and began the hour-long, mile-long, trek to the station where we planned to hop aboard 'sans billette'. The train came at twelve and we got on. Within a minute, the conductor was upon us; we went into our act of 'I thought you had the tickets', which he wasn't going for; he'd seen it a thousand times, and he told us we had to get off at the next station: Narbonne. He also wrote us a 'citation' and I think they plan to mail us a 'bill' at our address: 'San Francisco'.

NARBONNE

We exited the station and sat in the hot sun in front of it and ate cheese, bread, wine and water: all was well, but now what the fuck do we do? I guarded the shit from the arab-types who were eyeing it while Billy took off to scout the town for possible busking. I struck up a conversation with some Spanish hippies who were also lingering with their packs in front of the station: they'd been kicked off the same way we were, but they told me that This was the way they travelled and that there was another train heading north at about 4:30 and that they'd simply get on it and ride til they got thrown off and then do it again until they got to Paris: they did it all the time, No Problem. .

Billy returned and told me that it was same sort of Fiesta and that the town was virtually empty: No busking that day. No problem, we'd just wait til 4:30 and jump on the train. Yah. So we waited til 4:30 and the platform was crawling with people, and we found a 2nd class car and climbed aboard with our new Spanish friends, but the station-guys had been following us and they immediately boarded and asked if we had tickets and we were kicked off before it even left…Fuck!

The Spanish hippies said that they were going to hang around the station til the eleven oclock train and then get on it, No Problem. Well, I didn't want to sit around there any more, so Billy and I decided to try hitching. Fuck, it turned out to be about 3 kilometers to the AutoRoute. we began walking, stopping at a crossroads where we tried hitching on the regular route for about an hour, and I went out to try to find a Alimentation open so I could get same wine: I was down to about a fourth of a bottle. I found bread and milk but no wine. Shit. My day was ruined. Getting kicked off the train after waiting half the day was bad enough, but This was Too Much.

Walk walk, stop and sit, walk walk walk walk, and finally we got to the Peage for the AutoRoute where we collapsed and began waving our sign 'Toulouse' at the people who stopped to get their ticket. We looked like clowns, for sure, without the red noses, and were getting lots of friendly reactions, but no ride. We sat there for a couple of hours, Billy juggled, no ride. Fuck it.

We found a nice spot in some trees right nearby and clumped over there and collapsed again and ate cheese, bread, the remaining wine, some water and then we retired when it got dark about nine. Billy, naturally, went to sleep. I lie there having sex and thinking about Hannah. WHY WAS SHE IN GRANADA?

Morning in the trees: we were down to 10francs, no food, little water, no wine, no tobacco, (I scrounged dog-ends off the street the night before and in the morning), so we decided to head down to the Supermarche over a kilometer away and busk up some food. We took a whistle and three balls and wore our costumes and red noses. We busked for about ten minutes near the entrance: nothing. Fuck it, we moved into the entrance-way between the electronic sliding doors and in another fifteen minutes we got 25francs. Cheese, wine, bread, milk: fine again.

We headed back for where we had our things stashed and had a nice little breakfast there in the trees and the sunlight. We felt pretty good and were sure that we would soon be zooming down the road on our way to Toulouse. We wanted to be there by Friday evening for good busking and this was Friday morning.

We still didn't have a map of France and I had forgotten that Carcassonne was the place with the castle where we'd busked with Hannah about a month before and done pretty well, so we were heading for Toulouse. Billy never knows where he is, map-wise.

We sat next to the ticket-machine for about another three hours while other, single, compact hitch-hikers came up and went off in trucks or cars. We were getting depressed again when a car finally stopped and the fellow said he wasn't going to Toulouse, but was going to Carcassonne. We took the ride. I Still hadn't realized that Carcassonne was the town with the castle, but I think Billy had, but I don't think he mentioned it to me, though he says he did, but I'm not sure.

We were dropped at the AutoRoute Carcassonne entrance, about four kilometers from 'La Cite', The Castle, which we could see, and Then I Did realize where we were, but, Fuck if we were going to walk another four kilometers with That Load... we were committed to the Autoroute as far as I was concerned. Billy went to find some water in the buildings near the entrance and I flashed the Toulouse sign at two cars, the second of which stopped. I tried to tell them in French that there were two of us, I think I succeeded. It was a small car but we crammed everything in, and Billy and I sat on it as we zoomed right into the middle of Toulouse in about an hour. They dropped us right in the middle of the Teeming Shoppers, right downtown.

TOULOUSE

Where The Fugawi? Where's the Pedestrian Street? This Load is Heavy.

There we were, loaded with an incredible amount of junk, standing on the incredibly crowded, busy sidewalk, not having the slightest idea of which way to go, not knowing how to ask for anything except 'Le Bar Espanol'. I didn't even know how to say 'river' in French. Still Don't. I decided that heading downhill would probably bring us to the river and then I could get my bearings. Trouble Was: which way was down? Hard to tell, but we headed off. About a block later I spotted a cathedral spire about a half mile away. I thought I recognized it as where we'd busked a big market one Saturday a month before. we headed for it: I was right. From there it was easy to find the Pedestrian Street where we knew the busking was good in the evenings, though we were getting tired from the weight and the heat.

We got a pitch there and began The Show: after about half an hour we had less than 20francs, No Problem: I spent it on wine and food. Siesta began, at least the crowds thinned out, so we headed for the park-up under Pont Neuf where we had a delicious lunch of beans, bread, cheese, and wine. And milk for Billy; he'd been drinking about a liter a day during the whole trip: I'm a Good Provider. Well... He Is.

We laid around under the bridge for a while, after tossing away the piles of shit and nappies, and tried to regain our strength, which we did. There was a van parked under the bridge that belonged to a young Englisher named Jack, who had been travelling in Spain and knew some of our friends there. We made friends with them, shared some food, and were sitting around bull-shitting when a large bus drove in. "I know you!", I said to the driver, as he said the same to me. It was Chaz, come to do some busking, just down from The Clown Farm in Mirepoix. We remembered each other from Las palmas a year earlier when he'd been camped up with us, and he'd been up to The Pad (Hadass') for lunch a couple of times.

It was Completely Great to see him; it looked like our Luck had changed, starting that morning when we got the ride from Narbonne. Now, here we were with Friends again. Chaz had the good news that Tim and Molly were expecting us at the farm and were Glad that we were coming. We Were Saved.

We drank a bottle of wine to celebrate, and Chaz allowed as that we could stash our stuff in his bus for safety while we went busking. Great! Finally, after five days, we could walk around without having to worry about Ladrones. And without the 300lbs of shit. Perfect. It was like having a new life.

We went out busking around 5:30, I think, and I think we made about 50francs, which we mostly spent to celebrate, On food and wine. And then it was back to camp for a small party, to celebrate.

Chaz had a new electronic gimmick that he'd put together at Belrepayre, and he wanted to try it out on a Terrace (tables and chairs on the sidewalk in front of a cafe), so Billy and I went with him because we'd never seen his act: it was Hilarious, in my opinion, though I don't know if he would consider that a compliment. He sang while he operated the gimmick, which sounded like a band accompanying him. It had wires, lights, whistles, buttons, a keyboard, and levers sticking allover it. The Terrace loved it and he made about 20francs in one ten minute show at a cafe right near the bridge, even though it was nearing midnight. He is obviously a Pro.

The next morning was Saturday and Billy and I had planned to busk all day because we wanted to arrive at Tim's with some wine, chocolate, and Cash.

There was one problem, though: we'd stashed most of our stuff in Chaz' bus, and after I'd gone-to-sleep/passed-out, Chaz had told Billy not to wake him up before 11 in the morning. So, I woke up around nine, ready to go busking. No Way: the shit was in the bus. I yelled You Dumb Shit at Billy while we sat around til eleven. Chaz got up, and we were out on the street by noon.

Our Plan at this point was to hitch-hike to Mirepoix the next day, after busking all day Saturday, and Sunday morning at the Cathedral Market; we figured we'd make boucoups bucks.

When we arrived at the pedestrian street it was Fucked: they had hooked up loudspeakers about every fifty feet and were playing loud soft-rock for the French shoppers. In spite of the Muzack, we tried some busking anyway: not too successful: about five franks in ten minutes. Fuck! We tried over across the Big Main Street in the plaza, and did no better. Oh me, Oh my.

Fuck it, let's not busk!", I said to Billy, pissed off because our Great plan for making lots of money was turning into Fantasy. Fuck! Well, we decided that maybe a beer would make me feel better, which it did.

We decided to try our luck at a terrace; it was nearing one oclock and we had no francs to show for all our plans. Fuck. Well, the terrace was great! We got 30francs for about a seven minute show. A Good, Funny Little Show. We were encouraged, though there were no 10franc pieces: No Puppets, No Diabolo, but we had Arrived in French Show Business. our First French Terrace.

A little while later we did another terrace: another 20francs: Fine! Billy got a pastry and I got a beer. Then we tried busking again on the Rue Peatones: Nothing, 3francs. Chaz had told us about a place called placa Wilson, so we asked directions, in our way, and finally found it around three oclock. We busked another terrace there: another seven minutes, another 30francs.

We were pretty tired by this time so we sat over on the lawn in the middle of the plaza Wilson and along came Chaz, so we watched him do his act; great: 40francs per terrace. At this point we had about 120francs: not bad for a couple of Bobos. we got up the nerve and decided to busk another terrace, which we did. We were improving our 'Terrace Act' as we went along: Billy would bop me on the head with a club when I got stuck on one refrain, shit like that.

Just as we had finished the third terrace, and Billy was passing the hat, I heard, "Jack! It's Jack!", and I looked around and, stopped about five feet from me was a very small yellow car with Three Clowns In It!! I immediately recognize:! the one hanging out of the back window as ROY, who I hadn't seen since Sitges a year before! Incredible!

To the Amusement of the Terrace-ites, we loaded up all our shit and crammed into the car and sped away. Once in the car I realized that the

Driver-in-Whiteface was Tim! Absolutely Fucking Incredible! Cosmick! The Other Very Weird Clown was a dutch guy named Thea, who I'd heard of but never met. They'd come to Toulouse on the spur-of-the-moment from The Farm to do a little busking, and had been driving crazily stoned around town for about half an hour, lost, trying to find the park-up under Pont Neuf, which is the biggest bridge over the river, and which we later drove over four times trying to find.

I knew the way for sure, but with five insane clowns in a car trying to figure out how to get somewhere, with all of them goofing off and yelling, it's impossible. We drove around in circles for about half an hour, stopping every few minutes at intersections to let everyone out to run around the car hooting and yelling and falling down. They drove off without me once, laughing, and I had to chase them down in traffic. Finally, Tim let me tell him Exactly how to get to the park-up, which we did.

We had a bottle of wine to celebrate and spent the next hour getting busking stuff out of the car and Preparing to Go Busking. What Clowns! It was Really Great to see them! We were Double-Saved!

They hadn't worked out any kind of Act, but were in Very High Spirits as we 'practiced' juggling and diabolo. They finally headed out to busk, and Billy and I followed along to eat our lunch and watch. We ran into Chaz on the way, which took another half hour of goofing off.

When we got to the plaza, they each took out their instrument: Roy on Sax, Theo on Trombone, and Tim on Guitar. They set out the hat and prepared to start the 'Show', which Never Happened: for about an hour they kept trying to start playing but the trombone would fall apart, they would get tangled up in the guitar strap, they were a constantly moving and shouting mass of musical instruments and clowns: they never played a note. I went over once to try to straighten things out but ended up hopelessly tangled up too.

Billy and I left them tangled up and falling down, and went over to plaza Wilson again to make some more money, which we did. We returned to Tim, Theo, and Roy; Billy did some Diabolo with them for a while and they did a skit called 'Busy Bee' which involves a bucket of water, while I drank beer and laughed. They were Absolutely Fucking Hilarious for about two hours and had made 20francs total. The French just didn't get it. My stomach hurt.

MIREPOIX

We all got in the car, bought a couple of bidets of wine, and headed up into the mountains to The Farm near Mirepoix, the Paradise Clown Retreat in the pyrenese Foothills, where we stayed for the next few weeks, relaxing, practicing juggling, drinking, smoking, eating amazingly well from the garden, and Generally Having A Good Time. we formed a band called 'The Armageddon Boogie Band', which practiced every night: Tim played guitar, Theo played piano and sang, Clem played whistle, Roy played Sax, I played drums and sang lead. So High, So High, From Here You Can See Andorra Forever; we forgot to turn on the tape recorder. The cow ate my plastic bean-bags.

We went busking again three weeks later when we ran out of wine, hash, and food. This was the beginning of 'Tznot Circus'.

PART SIX

MONTJUICH

Bored, Scared, and Ugly

Parked on Montjuich in the bus.

I'm bored, scared, disappointed in myself (and others), frustrated, confused, afraid, sad, nervous, slightly insane at best, lonely, and my fake tooth is falling out again and I don't have enough money to buy super-glue to glue it back in, so I'm about to become ugly also.

If this 'love-affair' with Hannah doesn't work out somehow, I'm not sure if I'll be able to recover; I've really gotten in deep this time. On one of her trips she may even Stay in England. Maybe that would be OK: It would be a Resolution, at least. A painful one, though.

I have formed myself emotionally over the years into this pattern, this Type of person: if I don't fuck a lot, I drink. And if I drink too much I can't come. I know it sounds ridiculous, but it seems that this is what I've done; and Now I can't figure a way out of it. Fucking is good for me, drinking doesn't seem to be. The Problem Is: Hannah is the best lover I've ever had, and vice-versa, and we both know it.

"Why don't you wind up your book by doing sane philosophizing?", Hannah suggested last night, after our usual argument about her-not-paying-enough-attention-to-me (which is true).

Then she said, "If you want me to fall out of love with you, you're going about it in the right way.", as I was having an emotional breakdown and weeping on her pillow.

"You're losing respect for me!", I accused her as I wept and slobbered, begging her to suck me off just one more time, even though I couldn't come last night because I'd drunk too much at Billy's Birthday Party. She declined (almost a first), saying it would be better in the morning, and that she'd suck me off if I made tea in the morning; which I did, which she did.

She gives me plenty of advice: "Get your life together.", or, "I want to see you Do something.", or the ubiquitous, "I'm meant to be independent", and, "You Chased Me!" (of course I did), and on and on it goes. I've told her that there is a chance that I may fuck up completely in the next couple of years (like die?), and this was not emotional bribery, I've been thinking about it, analyzing my situation and have come to the conclusion that I'm close to the wire.

She is being sympathetick (I think) with me when I'm on the verge of tears every few days, when I get obviously depressed, but what's Really Happening? I'm not sure.

"It's probably your Karma for the girls you fucked over before.", she told me last night, paraphrasing something I'd written that she read.

"I'm not sure about that…", I moaned.

"Fucking means too much to you.", she told me the other day, about an hour after she'd come four times and I'd come twice. I guess she doesn't need it like I do.

What I'm trying to say is that I'm Falling Apart.

Portion of a Letter to Hannah in England. Hannah's 600 Orgasms

Barcelona. Oct 86

"As far as the 'blow-outs' that I have, in your opinion, (and sometimes mine) caused: Maybe in the last year and a half I have caused 10 to 20 scenes with you and/or your friends. Maybe a few more than this; I don't know. Most of it has been NOISE. I struck you on two different occasions, if I remember correctly, and Scared you a few more times, probably. I regret these incidents; I'm sorry they happened; I can't take them back. I would like you to balance these incidents against the number of orgasms you've had, the number of times we've made love (I estimate 400 days spent together in the last year and a half, average fucking/making love probably 1 1/2 times per day: 600 incidents of sexual inter-action, almost always ending on A Very positive Note). I would like you to further add to this side of the balance the number of times I helped you, made tea, dinner, fixed the truck, told you I love you, hugged you, bolstered you, flattered you, supported you, laughed with you, appreciated you, worshipped you, licked you, etc etc. I hope that you will see why I've considered my Binges, in the past, to be of minor consequence. I feel that we are At Least Even.

If you expect Perfection I doubt that you will find it, though you may. If you expect Good Sex, You've found it. If you expect peace and Happiness, I Hope, Sincerely that you do find it.

If you expect professional Acclaim, I will do whatever I can to help, including staying out of the way. (As much as possible) .

If you expect me to Forget you: there is No Chance.

I Love You.

I just had to say all that: it occurred to me a few minutes ago that there Were Many positive Items Upon Which We Might Both Reflect, in this difficult time. (For me forsure; for you, I assume).

I've cleaned out the bed, even have a 'sheet' (actually a curtain), in case you wish to visit with me down here. Down here I think we can make as much noise as we wish without disturbing very many of your old boyfriends or fucking up the Act. I certainly hope so. Maybe your Friends Dick, Katie, and Clem wouldn't mind watching the boys some night. Maybe you can stop by while you're on your errands to town. I Still Have Hope that we can Remain Lovers."

(Author's Note, January, 1992: And she came. And came again. And it went on for another year of Fucking and Fighting and Drinking and Clowning. Then I broke my leg and she left me, went back to England. I went back to California. I cried, inside and out, for two years. I still think of her daily.

Billy's Birthday Party

MY BIRTHDAY BLOWOUT

Billy's fourteenth Birthday Party was held last Saturday night at one of our recently-discovered/favorite Cheap restaurants (A three course meal, with bread, 275ptas, about $1.50) in the Gothick Barrio, the ancient Roman city, in Barcelox. All of Billy's friend were there (except for Frank, who hung himself from a tree last year; although most of the people there were Frank's Disciples, so you-can-be-sure that Frank was there in Spirit): Me (the father), Rebecca(the mother), Sally (Billy's punk sister, a Very Together Person: gives Everyone advice, especially Billy and Me), Jacques (the hunch-back uncle), Peter (the fake australian), Hannah (Billy's fake mean step-mother, my Gal), Tarn and Chawakee (her idiot clown sons, Billy's fake stepbrothers), Joe (the clown, ex-Manchester Burglar, Billy's main pal), Scott (Hadass' American boyfriend; Hadass is in Israel with an infected leg), John (the guy with the land-rover who miraculously showed up at our camp and who had grown up in Oxford with Hannah), Naomi (Had 'Roy's' baby the next day, Billy's main dope-smoking friend, Canadian, intellectual, troubled, Frank's last disciple), Tracy (Naomi's main Partner along with Billy, A Main Friend of Billy, a 'dancer' from Canada {stripper actually} with a boyfriend named Crow who claims to be from Atlantis), Sonia (English clown, one of my favorites, six months pregnant, Hannah's main friend, we travelled with her last year, used to be Roy's friend/lover), Will (English clown, father of Sonia's coming child, 1/2-brick's father, former Tibetan-Ukranian Mountain Troupe member; former wystic Manker member), 1/2-brick, (three-year-old delight, also named Sam but everyone calls him 'Halfbrick' except for me who calls him 'Halfwit'); Andres, (American friend of Jacques who got the job in the play after I left Barcelona), Phil, (Old English Hippy, Friend of Hannah's, Friend of Mine, Friend of Billy's, Hash Dealer), and finally, Angie, ("Call me Angela" she tells everyone, no one does, Argentinian, Phil's girlfriend/lover, extremely Extremely Beautiful and Dresses-the-Part, been here for years, has fights with Phil, {I know because he and I have discussions about getting old and our relative woman-problems}). I'm forgetting one or two people, but I can't remember who. Rabbit wasn't there, for some reason.

It was a Jolly Affair, to be sure. I'd made my gang of Drongoes (Joe, John, and Me) promise not to get drunk, at least before the party. Everyone else was drinking as much as they wanted; I was cutting my wine with seltzer water so as not to end up on a Rampage at Billy's party.

Almost everyone brought Billy a Gift: a 'C' Irish-penny-whistle from me, hand-puppet from Hannah, Kazoo and red clown make-up from Rebecca, Lemon Sherbet (his favorite dessert) from Sally, Hash from Phil and Angie, A monster mask, a small rubber monster, a red top-hat, and cigar boxes for juggling from Jacques, a blank book and a small blank book for writing down 'statements' (A new hobby of Billy's, an idea that I started while in Missoula, Montana with Jacques in 1980, and which Jacques has carried on with until he has about 100pages of statements, most of them Completely Weird) from Tracy and Naomi, a pair of red-and-white polka-dotted clown overalls from Sonia and Will and 1/2-brick, and a bunch of other toys.

Billy wore the monster mask and played the whistle while the joints were passed around and the wine went down and down and the waiter went crazy trying to keep track of three dishes each for fifteen people, but he did it, Amazingly. I missed a lot of what was going on because I was at one end of the long table, Billy was in the middle, and I was preoccupied with watching Peter (my old friend, often referred to as 'Sinatra') flirt with Hannah right across the table from me; and her responses, seeming to encourage him further, him inviting her down to his 'cabin on the beach' in Castadelfells, her taking down the address, me getting jealous. I saw him in the bar a little later and told him, "I don't care what you do with Hannah, but don't fucking flirt with her right in front of me, God-Damn-It!" He apologized, bought me a beer and slapped me on the back, and went back into the banquet and started flirting with both Rebecca and Hannah! I told Jacques that Peter was pissing me off; he replied, "Sinatra is in true form tonight, Jack, don't worry about it, just watch the show!" I understood, but I Am So Fucking Jealous, at times, that it left a bad taste in my soul. I got even with Hannah later that night: tied her up and spanked her, which she loved, And expected.

Billy was in Virtual Ecstasy most of the night, the Center of Attention (though earlier he'd been pretending that it was all a bore, he got into it later), and for my part I only 'erupted' once, when I felt that Clear Directions should be broadcast to the whole party about how the Bill would be paid. It came to about 7000ptas for fifteen people. About $35, including wine, softdrinks, and dessert.

John, Joe, Will, Sonia, and 1/2-brick left about twelve. I left with Hannah and her boys a little later; we had to walk back to the mountain (Montjuich) about two miles away and the boys were acting very tired, slouching on the tables, and like that. I'd've liked to stay a little longer because Jacques and I were discussing how we were going to arrange the book, how it was going to be edited; actually 'getting into it' for a change.

It was Wonderful and Touching to see my son with so many Obviously Loving Friends.

MY BIRTHDAY BLOWOUT

Yesterday was my forty-second birthday. Hannah gave me a parafin (kerosene) lamp, and a gas bottle for my stove/cooker, both of which I really needed for my bus and had little chance of procuring due to my present=eternal economick situation. Jacques gave me a monster mask. Billy gave me a cane.

Hannah and I went to the Tapas where we met Jacques, Billy, Tracy, and Peter. Peter bought us a plate of octopusses, one of which is right next to me, clinging with one of his little arms to a hook on the wall. He's dead, been cooked, you know.

Hannah and I got into an argument on the Ramblas and both walked the couple of miles home by different routes, but she came up and slept and fucked in my bus anyway because hers was being used by Orbito Eccentrico (the clown/theatre group she's living with, all of whom have trucks or busses, all of which are inoperative at the moment). She's down at her house now, taking a 'lie-down' (her term for Nap), trying to recover from my Birthday Party. We're not on the Best of Terms right now because I made her do things she didn't want to this morning. We're not on the Worst of Terms either; she Did kiss me goodbye this morning, and then I went down to her house and made a pot of coffee while she got the boys ready for school. I brought my new gas bottle and my monster mask back up here and fried some sausage and eggs, made coffee, cooked toast, and had an 'american breakfast' for a change, a welcome change. Then I sat outside for a while and talked with my friends Alfie and Joe and tried to negotiate a Peace between them.

I asked Joe, who was sitting in my bus, "Why were you screaming that you were going to kill Alfie last night?"

"Because he fookin' lead-butted me, Jack, Look at me nose, look at me 'ead!", he told me, Showing me the bruises

I asked Alfie, who was outside, "Why did you head-butt Joe last night, Alfie?"

"Because 'e tried to boot me, dint 'e", Alfie replied.

"Joe, Alfie says you tried to kick him last night and that's why he head-butted you.", I told Joe.

"I kicked 'im after 'e lead-butted me, Jack!", Joe insisted.

"Well, fuck it!", I said, "You're Both Crazy anyway."

"Ah, well, I don't remember much anyway . ", Alfie admitted.

"Nor do I, Jack, know-what-I-mean?", Joe also admitted.

"Well, you guys should make up.", I told them.

They made up and we all began cutting vegetables for the huge stew Alfie was cooking on the campfire, while 1/2brick played with a diabolo and Will and Sonia sanded on their truck Lydia.

1/2-Brick and Second-Hand Cars

Dec 15, 86. Badalona, in the bus

Billy's here to practice for the 'gig' we have next Thursday. It's evening; the stove I made the other day out of a barrel I brought from the junk-yard is working perfectly now; now that I've punched a bunch of ventilator holes near the bottom to give it a better 'draw'. We just had a meal of brown rice with Garlick with 1/2-brick while Will and Sonia went shopping. They got back and 1/2-brick went back over to their van, Lydia. (My bus has a name too: El Monstro II) .

Knock, knock, knock, at the door of the bus. (We knew it was 1/2- brick).
"Who's there?", I yelled.
"Second Hand Car!", he yelled back.
"Who?", I yelled.
"Second Hand Car!!", he repeated.
"OK, wait a minute.", I said, nodding to Billy to let him in. He came in.
I said, "What's Happening?"
"Do you have second hand cars?", he asked.
"Yes.", I said, "What kind do you want, we have a red one?"
"No!", he said, "It must be fold-able!"
"The only foldable one we have is yellow; is that all right… ?", I asked.
"No!…. I'll have the orange one!", he ordered. I told him to go get the money from Will and came back and buy the car.
"Are you writing down all the cars, are you?", he asked.
"Not the second-hand ones, though.", I told him, as he left.

Well, he's back in here again, and he's trying to explain the whole 'Second Hand Car' episode to me, but it doesn't make perfect sense: 1/2-brick is not-quite-yet four years old. And, he's Will's son.

He came by a few minutes later and asked me if I had a car for sale that had 'Tea-cups and Candle-wax'; Will was putting him up to this: Will told him 'T-cuts and wax', an English phrase meaning polished and waxed. Ah, well 1/2-brick is having fun buy-and-selling things these days; he sold me fourteen liters of petrol today for 300ptas but I only paid him 11 because he can't really count. A Fair Deal All Around.

So, I heard Will telling 1/2-brick to get a car with an overhead cam and I thought he was going to come over here and ask for it; so I got a can of tomatoe sauce and was preparing to give it to him with instructions to hold it on his head. He didn't come here: he went outside and pretended to have done the job. I went over to their truck with the can on my head; ridiculous but it made Will and Sonia laugh, a little.

"Do you have any paraffin (kerosene) for your lamp?", Will asked me.
"Yes. ", I said.
"Good, then I can use if for washing up (the dishes) .", he said.
"What? The Paraffin!", I asked.
"No! The lamp, you idiot!", he told me.
Knock, knock, knock…. 1/2-brick again.
"Yah, who is it, Second Hand Cars??", I asked/yelled.
"No! It's me, Halfbrick!", he answered.
"Ah,", I said, "What do you want?"
"I want to come in and clean your place up!!", he yelled.
"What The Fuck Is This???", I asked.

He came in and took out some of the stuff he'd left here earlier; making the place a little bit cleaner, I suppose. Billy and I joined them in Lydia and we drank a bottle of wine and smoked some joints and watched 1/2-brick run his 'restaurant'. Everything costs "nineteen-eight". He's leaving for England soon: It'll break all our hearts to see him go.

Billy was out here for about three days; we practiced juggling during the day, ate food, and I drank wine. We went into Badalona and busked up same food and drink on Tuesday in a couple of hours. I got pretty drunk every night he was here and made it difficult for him to sleep because I either wanted to lecture him about World War Two, or pigs, or Whatever, or Give him Fatherly Advice about women or drugs or Whatever. On Tuesday night I got so drunk I went into one of my hour(or more)-long Yelling Trances. "Nonsense about Germany", Billy told me. "Absolute Rubbish", Hannah has called it. (this morning during a conversation about whether I was going to be invited to the Clown-Clan's Christmas Party or not, and the fears people were having because they were worried that I might go into a Yelling Trance.) .

Well, after a while, Will (I hear) came over here and asked me to be quiet. I didn't. He came back a while later and picked up a wine bottle outside (he was also probably drunk: we'd all sat in Lydia for a couple of hours goofing around and watching/playing with 1/2-brick and drinking wine and making musick) and broke it and stood at the door of my bus telling me to shut-the-fuck-up (however the English say That) and I suppose it very nearly turned into an ugly situation, but I think I just went to bed instead.

Christmas Picnic in Badalona

December 30, 1986

Badalona-in-the-sun-beside-the-bus.

    We had a pick-nick yesterday, and a party, complete with Charades and beer and wine. In attendance were: Me, Hannah, Will, Sonia, Clem, Katie, Dick, Joe, Alfie, Billy, Rebecca, Sally, and Johnnie and Lizabeth stopped by for a few hours in the afternoon.

    Will, Sonia, and I were in High Spirits since about ten in the morning when we began preparing the feast. All of our clown friends were finally going to visit us up here in the mountains, in the parking lot behind the bar, where we've been camped/parked for about three months.

The Food: (I Love Food!)

Salad: (I made the salad) Tomatoes, onions, garlick, vinegar, olive oil, olives, garlick, etc...
    Potatoe Salad: (by Sonia) (I burnt the hardboiled eggs, though) Potatoes, Mayonesa, Onions, Eggs.
    Salami on a plate.
    Cheese (three kinds, Hannah brought same)
    Pears
    Apples
    Two oranges
    some Lemons
    Pretzels (straight, not curved)
    Sunflower Seeds
    Corn nuts (Maiz Frito)
    Sardines
    An Avocado (Alfie)
    Beer (me)
    Wine (White: Alfie, Will)
    Cafe Con Leche
    Bananas (Billy and Rebecca)
    More Cheese (Billy)
    Chocolate (four kinds: Orbito Eccentrico)
    A Pineapple

Meat (beef cooked by Hannah; I didn't get any because by the time it was served I was too far gone to figure out what a 'plate' was and Hannah told me this morning: "Well, I Certainly wasn't going to Serve You!". "I know", I replied, "It's not your Way!1I Damned Women's Lib!

Rice (by me, served with the meat: I didn't get any of it either) . Wine (Red: Alfie walked to town and bought it) .

Beer (at the bar, where Will, Alfie, Joe and I hung out for about an hour, listening to Alfie hoot and sing obscene songs.)

Escudillers Bread (Whole Wheat, the best, bought by Joe and me) .

Milk

Pear Juice

Peach Juice

Beer

And a concoction of Olive Oil, Pummelled Garlick, pepper, salt and cumin, for dipping bread into (by me).

We spread the feast out on a couple of picnick tables on the sunny side of the bus; we were ready about noon. Alfie and Joe appeared at about 12:30 and we sat around and listened to Alfie tell stories for an hour or so. Then Johnnie and Lizabeth arrived and we did some juggling. Billy, Rebecca and Sally arrived about 1:30. It took them about four hours to get here by bus, metro, and bus, from their house near Park Guell in Barcelona. We began an Impromptu Juggling Workshop: clubs, rings, balls; we were beginning to have fun; more juggling, a bunch of hooting and yelling. I wasn't at all drunk, but Will was getting there rapidly: I was only on beer, he had wine. He took me aside to 'watch the sundown' and we sat on the little hill above here and he told me not to get drunk and fuck up the party. "Shit, Will, you're not my big brother, and you're already half~pissed and I'm Completely Sober, I've only had two liters of beer all day", I told him. We chatted like that for a few minutes and rejoined the PicNic. I stayed off the wine til much later at the bar with Alfie, who was determined to Have A Good Fucking Time, to be sure.

So, Hannah's just left, heading back into Barcelona to meet the rest of Orbito Eccentricko at plaza Espana. They're trying to get a gig or having a meeting with Circus Mundial or something important like that. Clem left this morning, Will and Sonia went into Barcelona busking this. morning.

Joe and Alfie and Hannah and I sat around here for a couple of hours drinking coffee. Well, Joe and Alfie actually stood Around, they don't sit well, I think. Joe was telling Alfie and me what we did last night: evidently we were waltzing around the campfire, singing, knocking over chairs, trying to poke Joe's eyes out (like the Three Stooges do; Joe knows the Defense), and generally Carrying On, in our Accustomed Manner; I've never gotten drunk with Alfie before: he goes right over the Top. This morning his 'gear', the assortment of carts, satchels, suitcases, and bags that he carries with him were scattered allover the camp, along with overturned chairs, bottles, plates, forks, food etc: it looked like there may have been a war. Alfie was curled up in a pile of blankets and clothes, on the ground: it was Very Cold last night. I slept with Hannah and she was only mad with me this morning until I repaired the curtain in her bus that I'd torn down last night because she wouldn't fuck me because I was too drunk. I don't remember much about it. I only remember Alfie pulling bills out of his shoe and buying bottle after bottle of wine and swilling it down: "Fuck it! Let's get drunk! Let's get pissed! Yuk! Yuk! Yuk! I could buy this whole fucking bar if they don't want to serve me!", and like that; though there was no reason to be upset actually, because the owner and his friends kept to the other end of the bar from where we were holding court. I remember leaving the bar, I remember Hannah telling me that I could have same meat and rice if I got a plate. I didn't know what a plate was, let alone know where to find one. I didn't know how to ask anyone what a plate was either. Gone. Evidently 'the others' all went to their respective busses and trucks and left me, Joe, and Alfie to our own noisesome devices. Everybody had a good time, I'm told. There was even a liter and a half of red wine left over this morning. Alfie figures that it must have been under the table or we'd've drunken it. I agree.

Before we went to the bar, we played some weird camp-fire-type games: (Billy, Rebecca, and Sally left around sundown), and had a hearty English Time of It, I think. I was somewhat out of it because the main game was one in which you try to guess what Person (Historick or otherwise) you are. You have a cigarette paper on your forehead with a name on it; you can't see it, everyone else in the game can. Well, a lot of the names were famous English People (TV stars, politicians, kings, etc) who I'd never heard of. And by the time I became Franco, I was too drunk to remember what I'd learned on my last turn. Same with will.

A Good Party, and, today a good, wholesome, non-perverted Fuck with Hannah, in my bed, in my bus, with Its heater I made, and the new blankets tacked up on the ceiling: Good Fun, Good Fuck: I came twice, she came about six times, once while I got up for a couple of minutes to get us a glass of wine and some smokes. She wasn't going to stop; but finally decided that she'd better, or go crazy. Amazing Woman! She's 'loaned' me her butane heater, that we bought in Ireland last year. Her boys are due back from Bermuda/Oxford/England in about a week, and they'll all be leaving in the van; Where, they don't know yet. I'm scheduled to meet her tomorrow, New Year's Eve Day, at Can Peret during siesta; we're all going to be in town busking tomorrow.

Got to go buy some smokes at the bar, and then scout around the hills back of here for a possible park-up in case Moving Day comes· sooner than we expect. Just a Feeling, I don't really know how the 'Jefe' here feels about us: Alfie was pretty loud last night, so was I, so was Will; Joe was almost sober for some reason.

Three Word Play

"STICK IT IN!"...HANNAH, THAT FIRST NIGHT

One day, right after I began this 'love-affair' with Hannah, when I was still a street-writer and she was a rich clown (by my-then-standards), I was walking down a gothick street in the afterglow of a few days of Complete Lust, when a play (three word play) came to me. It began with her, at that time, usual phrase of:

"Stick it in!
In Which Hole?
Whichever you please?
How about this?
Not so hard!
Is this OK?
Yah, just right.
You turn over.
Not just yet.
You'll Like It!
It hurt before?
Not this time.
Are you sure?
Don't worry, baby.

Fuck my fanny! (a word here: 'Fanny' in England is a cunt. In America a fanny is a bum; initially this led to a bit of confusion)

Are you sure?
God! Please! Yes!
Where's the vaseline?
Use Olive Oil. (We're in Spain)
It's already juicy.
STICK IT IN!
Hold your horses.
please please please!
Suck this now!
I already did.

It's gone soft.
Can't you fuck?
Not right now.
Does this help?
Keep it up.
Jush lie thish?
That's perfect, Baby!
Slurple slurp slurp.
All, ah, ah...
Slobber, Burple, sluck.
Better and Better.
schurzlle, Brobble, slucpshp...
I'm Gonna Come!
Not Just Yet!
You better stop!
STICK IT IN!! (YAYYY!!!)
Where's the rope?

(pant) Hanging over there.
Gimme your arms.
Don't do that!
You'll love it!
Just Fuck Me!
Could be fun!
Don't Hurt Me!
Didn't mean to.
STICK IT IN!! (YAYYY!!!)
OK, How's this?
Really Lovely, Baby.
Raise your ass.
Like this, Sweetie?
Yah, just perfect.
Nanny, Nanny, Nanny!
You Fucking Whore!
Nanny, Nanny, Nanny!
You Incredible Cunt!
Nanny, Annny, Annnny!
Here I Come!
I'm Coming Now!
Nanny, Nanny, Nanny!

Nanny, Nanny, Nanny!

I'm Coming, Bitch!

FUCK-ME! FUCK-ME! FUCK-ME!"

They Came Together.

(To Be Continued)

(Author's note, 1992: Well, I recited the play for her when I first wrote it and she made me promise not to put it in the book. But since she hasn't answered my letters for the last four years… …I hope She gets horny sometimes as well, remembering…)

Montjuich Again, 1987

THE TRUCK FIRE

HANNAH'S FAT LIP

THE END?

Hannah's pad on Montjuich, The last day of April, 1987

Tomorrow is May Day

Hannah's truck burned to the waterline yesterday morning. We'd just finished making Spring-Time Love when came a rapping at the door, "your truck's on Fire!", or something like that, in Spanish; we got the idea and ran out in time to see the billowing black smoke from burning puppets and costumes. Hannah began screaming and tried to get up close to save her 'children' (the puppets she's had for years, who she talked to, who had names, who she loved) just as the propane tank exploded and a ball of flame shot up about thirty feet. She was slightly fire-burned, like a sunburn. There was Obviously No Hope; All Gone: Puppets, whistles, drums, elaborate costumes, Passports (again), Orbito Eccentrico's 3D stuff (newly bought for hundreds of pounds), photo albums, tapestries, spinning wheel, and five years of memories… All Up In Smoke. Hannah calmed down after about twenty minutes and began to think about how to Begin Again.

My bus is still in Badalona, sitting on the hill overlooking Barcelona, Empty. Hannah and I went out there a couple of days ago and salvaged everything of value. The Blue Police (Badalona Version) accosted me early in the morning a week ago and hauled me down to the Brown Police Station who ran a Passport Computer Check on me, told me I'd been in Spain too long (eight months, I didn't lie), and gave me a week to get out of Badalona. They said they weren't deporting me immediately because I was a clown and they liked me and my act. It was the first night I'd spent at the truck in two weeks.

Hannah and I went to a junkyard to try to scrap my bus a few days ago, but we need a piece of paper from the Guardia Civil before the Junky will take it. I'll probably try to get Phil to help me tow it to another site, in Granollers, IF he can get his truck running, and IF the people at the commune want another out there; Sonia's is already there: She, Will, and Norbert the baby went to England about a month ago to get Norbert's foot un-clubbed.

Meanwhile, Hannah has Invited (!) me to stay with her during May so that I can 'look after' the boys while she does a gig with Orbito Eccentrico in a local club for a month, at 3AM every night, without Clem who's gone to England for medical tests to see if he has TB in his leg, without the 3D stuff which burned up with the truck yesterday.

Hannah and I have been getting along Splendidly for a month or so, except for last night when I drank too much wine and then she tried to stop me from drinking the brandy and I got mad. (she tells me). And pulled a knife?!? (She says).

So, Vivaldi on the box, It's Springtime in Barcelona. Tarn and Chawakee are home from school for siesta and are sailing their sail-cars on the hill out front. The puppy (sole survivor of Mabel's 2nd litter) is pissing on the floor near my feet, Hannah's gone to the Irish Embassy to get some forms, and Life Goes On... In a few minutes I'm going to wash off the tools we scavenged from the truck fire, then we'll have some lunch... (YAYYY!!!)...

So, a few days later:

Sometime in May, still at Hannah's; my life consists of washing the dishes, sweeping the floor, cooking dinners, drinking wine at night, and sleeping. Some Love-making thrown in. I've been trying to get ahold of Phil for over a week to try to get something done about my abandoned bus out in Badalona but haven't been able to make contact with him. The Rumour is that he'll be visiting us here in the near future. We'll see. He knows that the bathroom spigot needs repair and that I'll be asking some kind of truck-favor of him.

The weather is near-perfect. I had two soft-boiled eggs and some toast and coffee for breakfast. The insurance men are also rumoured to be paying us a visit today or tomorrow to look at the ashes of the truck. Hannah is in the bathroom cutting her hair, and sortof not speaking to me this morning because of my weird sexual habits, I suppose. I don't know.

"There's more coffee.", I told her a few minutes ago, thinking that she might like some before it got cold.

"I'm cutting my hair.", she mumbled under the Talking Heads on the box, from the bathroom.

"I can't hear you", I lied. It's like That... we'll see. I have to make some new juggling clubs today, that's my Mission...

A Few More Days Later:

The Monster took over my life last night. Hannah came back from doing her 3D show at the club at 3:30AM last night. Billy was with her, planning to spend the night here after watching the show. I'd drank a couple of liters of wine and was sitting up in a devil-trance listening to some black anarchist rocknroll. I'd spilled wine allover the floor. A bad homecoming for Hannah. Billy tried to crash out on the couch but couldn't because I was hitting Hannah in the bedroom and she ran through the living roam with a bleeding mouth. Fuck.

She's laying in bed now (3:30PM) with a swollen lip with some ice on it, and a hurt back, bruised. I'm Completely Ashamed of myselfs. This is probably the last of Barcelona Under the Influence because I've GOT to Stop Drinking before I kill myself or someone else. Over the last twenty years I've changed from being a 'Funny Drunk' to 'Obnoxious' to 'Loud and Aggressive', and finally now to 'Violent'. People have been telling me that I'm violent when I'm drunk for a few years now, but I haven't really believed them. I was wrong: My Lover is laying in bed, hurt. I've told her that if I even have one beer that I'll Leave or Kill myself so that she'll never have to deal with Me, The Monster Drunk, again. I gave my word, On My Life. That's It! Time To Do Something Else. It was fun sometimes, but it's gotten Horrible. Maybe I'll write a book about it. Maybe I'll go wash my socks in a bucket. Fuck it. (YAYYY!!!).

Three Years Later

May 7, 1987 4PM

Montjuich, Barcelox.
    I sit here and stink. Frank has been dead for a year and a half. Jacques has some grey in his beard. So would I if I wasn't shaving regularly because I'm a clown. My 'girlfriend', Hannah is lying in her bedroom trying to recover from the beating I gave her last night while I was drunk. I've Finally Decided (this time for sure) (YAYYY!!!) to stop Feeding the Monster in me who loves to get drunk and cause problems. My 14-year-old son, Billy, another clown, came home with Hannah around four last night after watching her perform with her group at a local nightclub. They do a Sinister 3D show, with a hanging, a stabbing, an evil spirit, a priest, a grave-digger, a condemned witch, etc, the Usual Clown Stuff. I've seen it once: it was a bit frightening, to be sure.
    In the last week or two same Strange and Negative events have been happening to the people in and around the show. Clem's dog, poppy, who he's had for years, got squashed by a truck. The next day a Spanish doctor diagnosed the pains in Clem's legs as possible Tuberculosis; he's flown to England for further tests, thereby Almost Ruining the Act. I was hauled in by the National police and almost expelled from the country, but they let me go because I was a clown. I had to abandon my bus in Badalona: they'd given me a week to move, but it didn't run. Hannah invited me to stay with her for a month and look after her two sons, Chawakee (12), and Tarn (10) for the month she's doing this 3D gig. The next day her van was fire-bombed here on Montjuich, and burned to the water-line, with Most of ·the 3D shit in it, all of her puppets and costumes and husking gear and five years of diaries, photos, and memories. I had to hold her back as the propane tank exploded and she was trying to get nearer to the flames to save her puppets. She was crying and screaming and sobbing for about half an hour. You'd have thought they were her children or something. She used to talk to them. Katie & Dick's bus blew a headgasket about forty miles outside of town. Katie either has a Fallopian Infection from a slipped coil (or something), or just had a miscarriage. Last night, after about a month of relative Marital (?) Bliss, I beat up Hannah. I don't know why, but she tells me that I was saying that she was insulting me.
    I'll prolly go to the club again sometime to watch their show but I'll only stay for the 'restaurant bit'; I'll forego the 3D: I'm Too Impressionable.

To paraphrase Emily Litella, 'Violins in the air' : There've been quite a few political car-bombs exploding around Barcelox lately. Angie's (Angela's) partner in the leather coat business pulled a pair of scizzors on Joe yesterday when Joe picked up a screwdriver and said, "Wull, I don't give a fook 'oo pays me, boot soomboody better fookin pay me or I'll take the fookin shelves doon that I fookin bilt!", and headed toward the shelves, after waiting for an hour and a half for Angie. It was a draw: Scizzors against Screwdriver. She arrived just in time and paid Joe the 2000ptas she'd owed him for six weeks. I heard last night from Dick&Katie that Angie told them Joe had practically destroyed the fookin place.

There's been a rash of muggings during the last month, since the Tourist Invasion began around Easter Week: cloroformings from behind being the newest trick. Stick beatings and knifings are still popular in the Gothick Barrio, though. I haven't been hanging out down there for months, so I've missed a lot of the Action, but Joe gives me a Plaza Real Report a few times a week.

I took a swing at Joe one night at Santi's because he was kibbitzing my chess game with Rabbit. I missed him, but he fell out of his chair anyway. I was sober, he wasn't. He asked me if I wanted to step outside with him. I told him to Fuck Off. He did. I won the game and bought Rabbit a beer: That's His Way… "I No Have Money." has been his Theme Song for the last few years.

I don't eat at Can (Casa) Peret any more: the head waiter beat me up in the street about a month ago because I got in an argument with the waiter Ricardo and Derek the guitar-player, and threw what money I had for the Macarrones and Wine, on one of the tables and then yelled something and slammed the door on my way out with an ugly girl-junky who was looking for a drunk to fuck and had picked me. The headwaiter/owner caught up with me down the block and punched me a few times. I went down. I got up. He knocked me down. I got up. Back down. The robbers, whores, pimps, junkies, and dealers who habitually linger in those barrio-chino streets went into ecstasy when they saw the well-known bald fag beating up the clown. The girl helped me up and we headed for Hannah's house, who was out of town; I was horny and drunk enough not to notice that the girl looked like Dracula's Sister. I stopped and sat down on a park bench to puke; she kept on going, swinging her paper bag. I saw her the next day on the Ramblas with the Famous Italian Junky.

I saw Harry the one-eyed Welsh ex-bookie wobbling out of Santi's at around noon yesterday. His picture is on all of Santi's menus, crawling out of a beer glass. He looked like the picture. He said he'd missed me the night before when he'd fallen down the three steps from the bar into the eating-cavern and I hadn't been sitting there to break his fall like I'd done for Virgil on New Years Eve when He'd performed the same act. virgil and Harry both have enough money corning in from their retirement pensions to drink the 'good wine', the shit with corks, so they can remain drinking much longer than some of the rest of us who have to settle for the cheap shit that Santi gets from the bodega in 50-liter jugs for 50ptas per liter, which makes you drunk after about a liter, and puke after another half. Virgil and Joe were also in attendance, I'm told, and virgil asked Joe to 'Step Outside' because he mistakenly thought that Joe was laughing at him. Joe declined, he tells me, because virgil is Big and Joe wasn't angry anyway.

Peter says he saw all the evening's events but was quietly keeping his distance from the ten or so Wine-crazed Englishmen in the cave. I'm glad I wasn't there.

Peter and Jacques are doing very well on the streets these days and I relate to them as Master Chalkers. Peter is now doing his chalkings on canvas treated with some kind of grit and then a fixative. Jacques is still using paper and a fixative. Peter is heavy on Madonnas while Jacques prefers Jesuses and Related Biblical Bloodiness. He says that it's his Ministry.

Hadass is still off in Switzerland or Israel with her American Boyfriend, Scott.

Crow is still lingering around in Barcelox, doing his caricatures on the Ramblas, at which he is The Master, and sometimes doing his Very Weird Original Chalkings on the street, on paper also. He no longer comes to Santi's because he got in a fight with about five of Santi's friends on New Years Eve because he insulted Fernando and then refused to apologize. They beat him up outside later, but he hurt two of them pretty bad and they fetched the police after him the next day. He's no longer friends with Billy and Joe because he refused to share his dope with them one day after they'd been sharing Theirs with him for a couple of months. Joe kicked over his money basket in retaliation. Good Ole Joe, Billy's MAIN friend…

The Swallows of Montjuich

May 11, 1987

Montjuich, Springtime.

    The Swallows have returned to Montjuich. I know, because every time I hang my head out the balcony window they nearly flap it off. They whizz past, inches away, chirping and screeching. Hannah says they're telling us that they've summered here forever and we're Just passing Through. I think some of their nests must be in the little holes under the tiles in the overhanging roof.

    Hannah is almost completely healed from last week's 'fight': the swelling has gone down, the cuts have healed, the bruises are gone, and we began kissing again yesterday and made love last night and this morning. She hadn't been able to Love or even Like me since the Fight because every time we tried to kiss it hurt her mouth and she'd remember Why. It looks like Bondage will be off limits for a while though, because it Approaches Violins. Ah, well, Equipment-Unassisted Orgasm isn't That Bad. Maybe I'll just Bite her Neck a Little, That'll probably be OK. I've tried to assure her that it's The Monster that she has to be afraid of, Not Me. And, that the monster only comes out under the influence of Some Drugs: Alcohol, Speed, and Coke. I Hope and Believe it's true.

    She's gone off to the first day of a two-week acrobat course; Tarn and Chawakee, home from school for Siesta, are playing/fighting with their Leggo in their roam; I'm smoking cigarettes, drinking strong cafeconleche, and wondering what to do with the rest of the afternoon. I may make a new puppet-board for Hannah, may make some juggling rings for all of us, may saunter down to the Bothick Garrio to see what's Happening.

    I can see the Mediterranean from the balcony behind me. I can lay in bed in Hannah's room and see the statue of Columbus (The Spanish, appropriately, call him 'Colon') pointing towards the land he discovered. I assume it was Afrika; that's the direction he's pointing. Well, I COULD see it, if there wasn't a smokey fog (smog) blanketing most of Barcelox. It's Normal: I heard that this is the smoggiest city in Europe. I hope so. It doesn't bother me: I smoke Celtas, Sin Filtro, Cortos, Machos, Hackos.

    Hannah woke me up with a cup of tea this morning after getting the boys off to school, which is supposed to be my job but I Couldn't get up with the alarm because I stayed up late reading a biography of Da-Vinci, for which She was slightly peeved with me, but she brought me the tea anyway. I had three cups of coffee with my bacon'n'eggs, and then headed into town to get some oats and honey. I stopped at Santi's on the way back and had a couple of cups of coffee. I came back here this afternoon and had another cup. I took a siesta with Hannah and then got up, sent the boys out to play, cooked same rice, and am on my third cup now…. I think I'm Speeding a bit…I have to drink all this coffee and tea stuff because I gave up wine and beer, and it gives me something to do.

When she gets back she'll probably sleep til about ten tonight then go off to do her 3D show at eleven. I'll stay here and boy-sit. It's what I was hired for, mainly. Oh, and The Fucking too, but since the 'beating' we've had to get to know each other allover again, it seems. And the dish-washing, sweeping, mopping, and prop-making. And In General: Being a Best Friend…It's a Good Job.

This morning, while returning from the Granaria, I came upon Naomi, Frank's Last Disciple, outside the Picasso Museum. She was 'busking', making Tapestries, copies of Picasso's paintings, in the alley in front of the museum, directly below her balcony, with her 6-month-old son, Arin (Aaron? Erin?) (She's Jewish, from Canada) asleep in his stroller beside her. She's been doing it for over a month; doing pretty well, too. She Was working for Angie for about a month making leather jackets or something, but she quit the other day because it wasn't a good life for AAron, and, according to Almost Everyone, Angie is difficult to work for. Angie is beautiful alright but has a reputation as an Argentinian Bitch.

Since Naomi lives only a stone's drop from the Museum, this job is Perfect for her. Somebody (a gallery owner, I think) has already offered her 60,000ptas for her first tapestry, to be paid at summer's end. She's Getting By.

The father of the Child is Roy the Clown, who Hannah, Me, Billy, The Boys, and Sonia travelled around Catalunya with a couple of years ago, and who Billy and I hung out with in France last year for a while with 'Snot Circus', and who blew up his gift-bus and went back to England to get another, and who finally wrote Naomi a letter a few months ago saying he still loved her and was happy that they had a son and would be seeing her soon etc. Hannah ran into him in London a few months ago and said he was the same: spaced. Circus Fuckoffkoff has his circus tent; they're somewhere in France right now, rumor has it. BUZZ, from the Tibetans, passed through on his way to France from the South recently and told me that Roy is rumored to have a huge 4-wheel-drive truck in England which he can't afford to run. He'll probably be showing up here sometime this spring or summer to see his new son. Naomi will be Thrilled. "That Asshole!", was all she said when I asked her what she thought of his letter, after I read it. Good Ole ROY.

My 16-year-old daughter, Sally, baby-sits for Naomi a couple of times a week and is one of her Main Friends, along with Billy and Joe. I could fall in love with Naomi, and have tentatively tried, except that she always has a pained expression on her face, and her voice has the slightest hint of a Whine, At All Times… It irritates me, though we've been friends and co-disciples for a couple of years now, and we both love Billy and Sally.

"I need to spend a day a week in bed to keep myself fat.", Hannah told me this morning as I lay in bed and she got ready to go do a show in San Andreu. She lost weight, obviously, a week or so ago when she was worrying about the 3D show and her burnt truck. She spent the day in bed yesterday and seems to have gained it back. She only has a few pounds to spare.

She has me gargling Apple Cider vinegar and water, to rinse the tooth decay out of my mouth, after I told her last night that my recent toothaches are because I'm not constantly rinsing my mouth with wine. I don't like the taste of Apple Cider Vinegar.

The Breeze is Blowing Gently

Montjuich.

It's almost sunny out, the birds are chirping, the breeze is blowing gently through the open balcony doors, and I have to stop to piss in a bottle, because of this fucking broken leg.

Back from the Hospital, Day Three at Hannah's.

June 21, 87: The Longest Day of the Year

Hannah's gone busking solo, Tarn and Chawakee are playing/fighting in the other rooms, birds are chirping, Gypsies are yelling MOOONNNYAAHHH!!! from their balconies, the breeze is gently blowing through the open balcony doors, I'm listening to the traffick noises and the rocknroll blaring from the amusement park up the hill, smoking, and continuing to purge myself thus.

She sleeps Under the covers, I sleep on top with a blanket, because of my broken leg and because she doesn't want to be Lovers any more.

She said, "I don't want to be involved with you any more That Way. It leads to you living with me: You're Strong and I'm Weak: I do whatever people want me to. I'm Tired of it. I'm tired of you being in My Space."

"Great!", I said, "I break my leg and Now you decide We're Through, Again! There's more to it than that. You can't just shut it off like that: We've Been Lovers, We've been Friends, and still are; I've been helping you, doing almost nothing else, and I know I fucked it up but it's Not All Negative. God! I hate Pleading my case, but there has been a lot of good things happened between us in the last two years."

"It's out-weighed by the Horrible Times you cause, I've had enough!", she said.

"When you needed me I was here!", I said.

"I don't want to live with you, never did, I've told you this over and over.", she said . .

"Well, my leg is broken now, and I need you to help me for a couple of weeks til I can get the small cast on, and then I'll fuck off and get a pension or live with Joe or something, but I don't want to leave til I can at least get around, I don't want to live in Somebody Else's house on my back.", I told her.

"You can stay a bit, Because There Has Been Good between us, if it wasn't for That I Wouldn't have Anything to do with you.", she told me, and the conversation went on like this for about half an hour in the morning light. We've been having the same conversation for about a year but the stakes are higher now. The End is Near?

She brought me bread, margarine, honey, tea, and coffee this morning.

Montjuich, in the Apartment, with a Broken Leg

July, 1987

A FRIGHTENING EXPERIENCE: RABBIT AND JOE ON COKE

Day 11 at Hannah's

Taking stock. Boiling eggs, which is no simple matter with this broken leg. In fact, it's almost a Major Operation taking about ten minutes and fifteen separate little tasks to accomplish, hurting my leg with each one, but I finally got them boiling, yah.

I sit here and stink: haven't had a Real bath or shower for about a month. Did manage to wash myself about five days ago, which was another Major Operation. Made coffee this morning, Another Major (Fucking Hassle) Operation: it took two days to coordinate getting the milk up here: Alfie finally bought some yesterday.

The place is a Mess because Joe, Rabbit, and an American named Bill who is working on the boat with them, came by again last night around 2:30 after Alfie and I had shared some wine and gone to bed. They came with what they had left of their cocaine and gave us a line each, my first in a couple of years. It was OK but I didn't really feel anything and it made me a little mean: I had to sit and listen to Rabbit telling us that. he loved everyone and was an artist and a poet, And Alfie doing his mad-rap and having nonsensical arguments with Bill about the Importance of Having Mags on your Chevy if you're from LA, which Bill is. Joe just sat there and grinned for a while, for a change.

Had Hannah arrived back from Valencia during the night she would have flipped out and divorced me for sure. They were a happy gang, but were driving me crazy with their drug-induced sincerity…My Friends…

Oh, they've been helping me alright: giving me same money (Joe), scrounging food from the rubbish (Alfie), and Like That, but they also make an incredible mess every night and seem unaware of things like full ashtrays, scrunge on the table and floors, empty bottles, discarded pants and shirts and shoes, pieces of paper thrown around, dirty glasses rolling on the floor etc. They stay up til about four every night singing, and arguing without listening to each other, and then flop down in chairs or on the floor and then get up at seven or eight and stumble off to work on the boat, usually leaving me here with the Incredible Mess, no water, no food, and no way to get them. If no one comes by to visit me today, one of my Major Operations will be to sweep the floor. I would also like to wash myself but there's not enough water. The water has to be fetched from the fountain down near the bar because it's been Mysteriously Off for a couple of weeks even though Hannah gave me 3000ptas to pay someone for the water bill if they came by, Whatever

IT'S PRETTY HOPELESS

It's pretty hopeless, which is not a New Feeling, really, but the Boredom is hard to take. I'm stuck up here in these rooms and the wind sometimes shuts either the front door, the bedroom door, the door from the hall into this room (the front room? the living room?), or the door into the boys' room; anyone of which cuts off the airflow through the house and I start sweating immediately until the wind blows the fucking door back open maybe and blows some more paper shit off the wall or scatters some of this book or the other allover the floor and I knock the fucking ashtray over trying to pick up the papers and hurt my leg trying to put the cigarette butts back in the ashtray and curse and my eyes start to fill with tears and I Affirm 'Fuck It!' and have another cigarette and blow my nose on my hand and wipe it on the shirt I wore yesterday because I left the crusty handkerchief way over on the table, along with my cafeconleche...

Now the living room door is shut again and I'm running out of typing paper so my next Big project will be to hobble into the bedroom and get some more. It's around two oclock and no Friends have shown up yet to help me clean something up. There's still a couple of bottles of wine left from last night though, and the two hard-boiled eggs sitting in a metal cup Way Over on the table...

Three oclock, no Friends. Glass of wine, hardboiled egg, and some of the Disgusting stew that Alfie has been making for days from the Awful Crap that he's been finding in garbage cans...Ugh! He Loves It! I ate some yesterday but could still taste the foul meat from the unfrozen little stuffed macaronis that he started it with about five days ago, not to mention the mushy eggplants that he added· yesterday... God!...

"Ah, It's Really Gettin' Good NOW!", he told me last night as I sat in here and drank wine hurriedly to avoid puking from the smell that was wafting in from the kitchen.

"Great!", I said, "I'll have some later...". He IS well-intentioned and Does help clean up the place for a bit each evening...A Friend...

ALFIE'S STAPLER

Day 13, Hannah's

Waiting in dread for Hannah to return from Valencia. Alfie is sitting at the table playing with the watches, radios, calculators, and other gadgets that he's been bringing back here from the skips, filling the place with, most of which don't quite work, "You have to hit the five very softly, then it works fine!"…or, speaking about a stapler he brought today, "Yahhh, it's just fine, know-what-I-mean, you just gotta get the whachamacallits for it…"

"Staples, Alfie…", I tell him.

"Yahhh…"

THE LITTLE THINGS

I hobbled over to the table to eat an egg and left my cigarettes on the table next to the chair here. I didn't have anything to put the eggshell in, so I used a cup full of water. My hands are dirty so I had to eat the mud on the egg after I peeled it because the eggs were in the tin cup still full of water because I forgot to dump the water when I brought the eggs in here and the shells had cracked because the fire was too high so I had to eat eggs with muddy hands… and now I'm back over here in the chair, but I left the other fucking egg Over There, on the table…and I had to piss while I was eating the egg so I had to hobble into the pissy bathroom and stepped on a fucking grape that someone dropped on the floor last night, which was frightening.

There are ants about, and the ashtray is full, but it's a Major Fucking Hassle to empty it. I re-opened the front door again while I was up. My leg hurts. I've left the bottle of wine back over on the table after leaving it over here when I went over there to eat the muddy egg…The tape has run out on the stereo but I don't want to bend over to start it again… there are still glasses sitting everywhere from last night, most with a cigarette butt or two therein.

The door to the boys' room just banged shut again. The floor needs sweeping and mopping, the rubbish needs hauling, water needs to be fetched, my body and hair need washing, the bed needs sweeping and airing, the bedroom needs sweeping, the dishes need washing, the 'stew' needs being-disposed-of-somehow-without-hurting-Alfie's-feelings, the letter to my sister needs photocopying and mailing, some bread and some beer need fetching, the boys' room needs picking-up, the balcony where Alfie is stashing his Finds needs sorting, the table needs wiping, the empty wine bottles need being dis-posed-of or taken back for deposits, my twenty-two grey teeth need brushing, the stick that I stirred the shit and piss and paper that were plugging up the toilet yesterday with, needs being-disposed-of.

Nobody's stopped by today; it's the Little Things that are getting to me.

THE LIZARD IN MY CAST

5:15, afternoon, Day 11

Really sweating now; I just swept the living room: swept most of the scum and ants into a pile under the table: from this distance the pile appears to be moving; there are five different sizes of ants crawling around on it. I haven't noticed so many before today: word must have got around last night that Rabbit was visiting and there was some high protein drool to be had at the clowns' pad.

Try sweeping sometime with one hand while standing on one leg with the wind blowing the dust around but if you close the door you immediately break out in a dripping sweat, and your broken leg hurts and there are chairs everywhere because Alfie keeps bringing them home but you've Got to Do It because you're getting nauseous from looking at five different kinds of ants crawling around carrying things home and crowding all around the squashed grapes and spilled wine. Try it.

But? Do I feel Better Now? Yes. Something Accomplished. Something done. Something to cross off the List. A Dent in the pile. A Scratch in the Fender. The First Straw.

The fucking door just blew shut again and the wine bottle is back over on the table... the milk is probably going sour, the cookies are going stale, and there are volcanick noises coming from the Alfie-stew. I have salt, but the tomato Hannah left me is all mushy.

The flies seem to enjoy my aroma.

I hope some of the bigger ants don't crawl into my cast and bite me, like I thought a lizard was doing yesterday because I'd seen half of a lizard on the floor in the morning, half of it smashed up like by accident by a foot or a chair and it must have fallen off the shelf above me where Tarn put it the other day after he found it in the street and thought it was dead, which it wasn't, because the half I saw on the floor was moving its gills (?) around and flexing its little hands and I picked it up and realized what it was and said ugh and threw it in a corner because my leg was hurting and I didn't feel like sweeping right then and a few hours later something was moving around in my cast right under my toes where I can't reach and I hopped up and screamed from fright and pain and tried to get the fucking thing out but it slithered further in under my toes so I tried to get it out with a broom but failed and then decided to kill it by squirming my foot around, which worked. But it was a leaf the whole time, blown there by the wind, which I found out later when I asked Billy to pull the dead lizard out of my cast.

HARD-HEARTED HANNAH

Day 14, Hannah's. Two weeks of this shit

Two in the morning and I can't sleep even though I've been sipping wine all day... Fucking leg still throbs when I try to sleep and I keep thinking about Hannah and what's Happened between us recently, and for the last two years: still trying to figure out what the fuck's happened.

Still Dreading her return, still pissed off at her for Getting Serious about Breaking Off with me, Still can't get all those amazing fucks and sucks out of my mind: How could it be happening/ending like this????

My Emotional Network is Intertwined with Her's and yet she's treating me like a second cousin. She's doing it Consciously...On Purpose, with her eyes, Wide Open. Maybe she's Right: maybe she Never Really Did Love Me As Much As I Love Her, etc... Maybe She's Right...and this makes me think She's a Cold-Hearted Bitch.

I can lay here and Imagine conversation after theoretical conversation with her, but when it Really comes Time To Talk, we are barely able, we end up arguing ...it Fucking Hurts to think about what's going on...And Now that I've been drinking again I suppose that there's Not A Chance that we can end it on a Positive Note...

"Look, I'm Leaving, I'll go stay at Rabbit's in a few days", I Imagine saying to her, "But It Really Hurts Me that you're treating me this way."

"Look, Jack", she might say, "I Always told you that I wanted to be independent, and Now I've had enough..."

"Yah, but we Were In Love, We Were Lovers, That's Real, and This is Fucked! This is Not Real to me, This isn't the way it's supposed to happen."...

"You get drunk."

"I always have", I might say, "I certainly meant You no harm". "Well, I don't want to live with it, or you"...

Alfie's Hernia

Day 22, Montjuich, Hannah's with a broken leg

Yah, Orbito Eccentrico got back yesterday. Hannah and I had a 'talk' about the present situation; I'm still here, though she doesn't Really want me to be. We have a 'good-night Kiss', and that's about it… She's busy cleaning and fixing up the house, even though she's probably heading for England in a month or so. I think I'm supposed to be trying to find another friend who will put me up/put up with me for the next few weeks; in the meantime I'm just laying here playing it day by day.

Somebody has given Joe an apartment to baby-sit for a month, but he's not sure if it's OK that I stay there because American Jeff may want to stay there with his wife from the states who's coming for a week or so to see if he's having an affair, which he is.

Joe and Billy stopped by here today, to make up after the fight they had at the pitch the other day; to smoke a few joints, play some chess, teach me a new tune, and then Off Busking…

Joe is extremely proud of himself because Liz, Harry's daughter, is writing him torrid love-letters, has bought a house in Newcastle, and wants him to come live there, and is visiting back here again in a month or so.

"Jack, she says, 'You can't imagine what it's like wanking off every night thinking of you'!", he bragged to me, reading from her letter.

"I'm very happy for you, Joe.", I told him, thinking about sleeping next to Hannah every night and Basically Not Touching Her… I'm happy for him. Hannah figures Liz loves him because of his Stability. I told him I thought it was his Sense of Humour.

Tony and Nuria, who Hannah'd never met before, showed up a little after Joe and Billy left, and brought some more dope with them. We smoked a few more joints, had coffee and juice, and 'rapped' (anachronistic term?) for a while. Well, that's what we did: rapped. Hannah and Nuria got on fine and exchanged addresses or something. Tony and I talked about our brains, senses, and Rajneesh for a while til we were joined by Alfie who told us stories about his skid-row experiences in New York and L.A.; for some reason he thought we needed to know which missions served the best food.

Tony and Nuria had to head out for the Tapas for dinner, Hannah went back to scraping the kitchen wall, while Alfie tried to commiserate with me by telling me one of his London Hospital Stories.

"Yah", he said, "I had a whatchacallit, a hernia, an' I'm sittin' in a wheelchair in this poxy hospital, an' I'm sittin' in with all the old geezers an' they're dyin' like flies, two died last night, innit, an' I'm sittin' out on the whatchacallit, porch, innit, an' I get a fuckin' sunburn in the chair, an' this priest comes in the door an' sayin' You're All Sinners and You Shouldn't Sin, an' here's these geezers layin' there dyin' an' the priest is tellin' 'em don't Sin! Corrr! I says, "Fuck Offff!", to the priest an' he says "You Can't Talk to me That Way, I'm the priest here", an' I tells him, "Fuck Offf, You Hypocrite Bastard!!", an' he leaves. The next day, innit, the doctor tells me I can't get the hernia cured for two years an' they kick me out of the hospital, so I go to the Labour Exchange an' they say they have a job for me an' I tell'em I can't take it cuz of my hernia, innit, an' he says "You Went To The Hospital?", an' I tell him they say two years. They send me back over to the Hospital an' I give'em a piece of paper an' I go in for the operation an' It's The Same Doctor an' he says "I Hate You Jumpers" (line-jumpers) an' I tell' him "I Ain't Jumpin', They Sent Me Over Here!". I'm surprised he din't cut me wrong or sumfin…"

DAY 25, HANNAH'S. Saturday in July

Yes, Beautiful Spain, Beautiful Barcelona, sunny and smoggy, and I'm Still sitting on the bed sweating. I'm still here; she doesn't Really want me to be, and I sortof don't either. Joe's living in some apartment "With Long Distance Phone, Shower, In' Everything!", but I haven't seen him for a few days so I don't know if I can live there or not. Hannah is probably going to stay in Barcelox, in this pad, unless she can't shake me, unless I won't Leave and Let Her Be … I'm supposed to find a pad and a Life of my own and "I'll Visit You" she said, when I suggested that I could came over here once a week to fuck.

It built up and built up until we Finally made love the other night: she admitted that it was as Hard for her as it was for me. She cried, I don't know why, starting it allover again; Now I'd want to Stay with her etc etc, I don't know. Anyway, she's gone busking to Sitges with the boys and I'm making 3D glasses…

The Last Thing I Wrote in Barcelona

(A LETTER TO JACQUES IN ITALY)

OVERLOOKING THE PICASSO MUSEUM WITH A BROKEN LEG

HOTEL CALIFORNIA, LOW RAPES

The End.

"July 31, 1987

Naomi's Apartment, Barra de Ferro.

Dear Jacques:
    I sit here and stink. I've just hobbled, with my weird Spanish Polio-Victim canes, down to the bodega near the Mercado across Calle Princessa and then back here to Naomi's. I got my breakfast: a bottle of Xibeca, one of the world's truly great pisses...
    When I look out the balcony window I can almost see you, Hunchbacked in a foul-weather coat lingering at your palette... It Is Synchronous, to say the least, that Mouski got this place, AND that I will be living here for more than a month. She's gone to Canada and left the place with Joe, on the condition that I don't stay here. I moved in yesterday. I have No Idea why Naomouski told Joe that she didn't want me here...I've never Fucked-Up any of her Deals, that I know of...Maybe it's my house-sitting Reputation??? Ah, Well, Joe and I have agreed that we'll be Good and when she gets back there'll have been no harm done. Right?
    I spent the last 6 weeks laying on my back up at Hannah's, being sortof the unwanted guest and ex-lover, though we did Make Up a few times and Made out about 5, but I was bad at It because I couldn't move around as is my want...We've Officially stopped being Boy-and-Girl-Friends as of last night when I came over here. She's been gone more than half the time since I got back from the hospital anyway...she's been doing shows in Valencia, Zaragoza, Gerona, etc...and I've been staying at her house with sometimes Joe and always Alfie-the-scrounger who has been feeding us amazingly well sometimes with the shit he finds in the skips: one day he brought back a kilo of frozen pork-chops, one day 7 kilos of warm chicken with sauce...always vegetables...etc... one-day 12 cans of beer...a bottle of gin...He's still over

at Hannah's for a few days more, til she gets back again, taking care of Mabel-the-dog while she's in heat...(Mabel, not Hannah)... Hannah's promised to visit and fuck me when she gets back, now that we're not Obligated to each other in any way, now that we lead independent lives. I can (she hopes) become One Of Her Lovers. I don't know: she's getting older, is skinny, has a natural clown nose, and small tits: I seem to be one of the few people who thinks that she is Beautiful. It's prolly because I've fucked her hundreds of times and half of them were The Best, etc.... I'll try it Her Way for a while: let both of us try to find a Better Lover...Anyway, there's A Change Happening for me right now. I have to have some kind of Non-Hannah life together by the time Mousky gets back.

    I have a new cast on my leg. now, got it last week, only from the knee down to the foot. The first one came up to my groin and I couldn't move very well with it. Now, I can almost walk except that my knee hurts because I spent 7 weeks without moving it and it's sore from moving now. I move around incredibly slow. I've only been out of Hannah's about 5 times in 6 weeks, twice to go to the hospital with Sally to get x-rays and prognostications. Now, I'll be able to go out some: like to the Liquor Store and to Santi's...I've been living on money that Joe and Hannah (and sometimes Billy, Sally, and Alfie) give me. I'm planning to busk (play the whistle only) in front of the Picasso tomorrow: there are thousands of tourists shorting in and out of there now...

    I have to have this cast on for probably 3 months more, then I think, (unless I get a new girl with money) that I'll head south for the winter cuz I've never seen the south of Spain. Maybe Joe and/or Billy will go with me??

    Hannah may go to England. She may get another truck. She may stay where she is. She may move to the country near here. If she moves then Joe and I have dibs on the house...I don't know...

The Book(?) :

I've edited (?) the first 500pages twice... I've only managed to delete about a fourth or fifth of it, though: I tend to think most of it is Acceptable... The rest of it is still up in your office, although Billy promised 6 weeks ago to get it for me; he hasn't had a chance yet; the time he Did call Marta she wasn't there... Efficient Kid, eh?.. In Rereading (and Re-writing) it, I've come to think that Some of it Is indeed worthy... that we Really Can make a book/story/novel out of it. (Notice: We). The Thing Is: Someone is going to have to go at it with a hatchet, I can't do it. I'm thinking of asking Jeanne (among other things) to have a Go at it. What do you think?

I just discovered that the 'stereo' doesn't have a volume switch/knob: it's a high-tech tape deck, looks powerful, modern, with Mousky 's weird little speakers plugged into the 'earphone' jack...and, No Volume Knob at all... Summertime by Joplin on now ...(is this strong beer?)...

There's hardly any food here, and no toilet paper. Joe said, as he left this morning to go busking with Billy, that he'd pick up some food and be back this afternoon...I can hardly wait, though I Have TO...I had 300ptas that Joe gave me this morning so I went out and got a cafeconlech (for 75!) and a bollabeer... If Steve and I were to have a race he would definitely win, for instance...

How did you get thru France without a visa? Did you have/get one? How? It sounds great there, for you: I can Definitely picture you tanning on the beach: you've always been a frustrated surfer anyway. The Hippy Thing was just a stage: Now you've found your true hole...

The Main Thing in my life right now is my sore knee; not even my broken leg; not even Hannah: no, I'm hoping that it takes care of itself soon. About a week ago, when I was mad at Hannah when she got back from a trip, I was clearing the table in her house, in a rage, as it were, and hobbled into the kitchen on one stick and smashed my Left Foot (the good one) against the door-jamb, breaking (I think) the little toe on That foot...Hannah figured I did it so I wouldn't have to leave...I figure it was an Accident (like the right leg)... I couldn't even hobble for about 3 days...I'm trying to be careful these days; like not fall down the six flights of stairs here, drunk. Broken toes heal themselfs and only the littlest toe is still blue.

Well, it's one oclock and the bollabeer is almost gone and I have to figure out what to do with the rest of the day. I've read about 20 books in the last couple of months, same shit, but some Excellent stuff...Read 'God Knows', by Joseph Heller (the guy who did Catch22): it's about (pretends to be written by) David (of Goliath Fame) : extremely funny...You Read It! OK?

Are you coming back to Barcelox? Are you staying there? Let me know.

So...I took a nap for about 20 minutes and then got ready to go out to get another beer when Joe and Billy arrived; they'd had a relatively suckcessfull day: 300ptas down by the market for an hour...god!...Joe brought back same food too, ("There's enough here for a week!", he told me, referring to enough food for a day), and we drank another beer. They've gone over to the Barrio Chino to spend the rest of Joe's money that he made (3200ptas/day, on the boat)... Here they come back now...,

Speaking of Joe; he has same sort of incredible grudge against you because of the time you told somebody on the boat that he was a thief, or something like that. Anyway, I've had about 5 talks, over the last six months, about this, and I've told him that you have a Weird Sense of Humor, and that You Didn't Mean to Hurt Him, and shit like that, but he doesn't seem to get it...He Doesn't Understand Your Sense of Humour.... It's Absolutely Insane...In fact, Joe says that the next time he sees you, he and his friends are going to tie you up with ropes and throw you in the canal. With Weights!! (He's done it before. In Manchester)...In Fact, while Joe and Billy and I have been talking about you, Joe has remembered some other Famous Manchester Tortures that he and his friends used to do to people they didn't like.

I just came up with a Great Idea, which we immediately implemented: We made a small sign that says on one side:

"HOTEL CALIFORNIA

-english speaked
-low rapes
-free dope (crossed out) food
-free wine
-bad jokes

JUST SCREAM ARRIBA"

and on the other side it says "NO FOREIGNERS", and Joe is dangling it, fishing, off the balcony. No one has read it yet because the flow is down... More Later...

Hung out with Joe and Billy for a while smoking joints and then took another nap and then went out on a Virtual Hunt for wine and cigarettes. Hobbled around for about an hour looking for an open Estanco, etc... Siesta!

Came back here and drank some beer with Joe and then accidentally knocked one of my canes off the balcony, nearly totalling a herd of blonde-haired tourists. One of the neighbors on the ground floor screeched at Joe for a bit in Spanish when he went down to retrieve the cane. all is well. No Bites yet with the Hotel Calif thing, though.

So...now it's approaching evening and the Question Is: What to do with the rest of the day. I've already been out twice hobbling around and that's probably enough of That for today. I realize after only one day here that I was having an OK time at Hannah's: at least when I didn't have anything to do I could go lay on her bed and at least her smell was there, even if she wasn't...I'd gotten to feeling At Home there over the last six months. I'm sure you understand...I guess I'll have to figure out some different behavior patterns...I can go for Hobbles and look at trees and birds. and girls? I'll probably have to: I don't have much faith in the tourist bait...

The View at Hannah's was Great! I just realized. Here, there's a view of the stone wall across the street. Solid. UP There, when you looked out the windows it gave you a feeling of Space and Freedom, I'm realizing. I'm having some kind of claustrophobick reaction, I think...I miss the 'colon' statue; this place is kind of dark, actually...

8 oclock, Joe is becoming a Dedicated Fisherman: he spends about half his time smoking dope and the other half dangling the sign over the balcony into the line waiting to get into the Picasso and cackling (that's how I can tell he has a bite) whenever someone reads it, or whenever he flashes on How Truly Weird the Whole Concept of Hotel California, Low Rapes, is...

We just had a couple of bites. They laughed, and then I told them that I was an out-of-work fisherman who had broken his leg and couldn't get on the boat any more. They laughed again. Joe cackled. I'm amused... They left.

I could go on for pages (and have many times) about Hannah and What She Means/Meant to me, etc.... and when I pass the paint store I think of her because she's going to paint her door soon, and shit like that... But, I wont.

I've written (obviously) 46 pages since I beat Hannah up a couple of months ago. I had intended to call it 'Barcelox, Out From Under...', as you know.... However.... Uh.... Maybe I'll make it an Appendicks to the first 'Book' (?) ... I'm wondering about this Being a Writer Deal, let me tell you.

All! Another Bite. "Y'all from aroun' Dallas?", I asked out the window after she'd finished reading the bait. "Sorry, Wrong country.", she said. Too bad. Maybe it's a stupid plan.

And, there's plenty to eat: white fake rice with sunflower oil. and same raisins. Thank ___ that I got a small supply of wine in today...

We hooked a couple, from Italy, but they got away: tourists.

THE NEXT DAY, SATURDAY

Billy is fishing for cigarettes off the balcony; he needs them for rolling joints. Joe is ineffectually trying to sew up his clown pants that he ripped a while ago while showing Billy and Me how he can now throw a ball under his leg: a new trick.

I went busking, solo, for the first time since the Fall today, in front of the picasso: did fine, about 700 in an hour and an easy half and then went to the market and bought some beer. Surprise. I had no clown apparatus on today. Simply a guy playing whistle with an (obvious) broken leg. or foot.

Anyway, it looks like I can survive the summer with this minimal act.

Janis Joplin was given to Joe as a gift by some Germans recently. We listen to it constantly. It's invaded my dreams (she has). I met a beautiful girl today but didn't have time to get to know her because the bartender wouldn't serve me. I suppose that he thought that I was some kind of gypsy…Out of beer, almost siesta time…

Well, to continue 'A Day in the Life'…

5 oclock. Siesta over etc…Joe & Billy've gone out busking again. They made less than 1000 this morning; they've been having terrible luck for a couple of weeks. We can't busk at the Normal spot, Puerta Del Angel, anymore: complaints, etc.

This 'Getting About' is Great! I've done more in the last day than I've done in the last 6 weeks, outside that is. I'm going to go down to the Picasso again and play the whistle, and try to pick up beautiful girls. Whatever. I'll probably mail this on monday. sure. I'm going to the Tapas tonight, for the first time since the Fall. I'll give you a report in the morning, if it comes.

Sunday Morning

The Tapas Report:

I left here about 5 and whistled in front of the picasso for about an hour and made about 300. Not bad for such a minimal act, I figure. I then hobbled (a Perfect description, by the way) over to Santi's where I met Tony and Rabbit sitting on one of the benches outside. Perfect, although Rabbit had already entered a Minor Drooling Stage. Tony was his usual amazing unscrutable (INscrutable?) self. Awkmedd's gang was playing dominoes in their usual spot nearly blocking the door. I had decided to only drink a 'few' beers so that I'd be sober enough to hobble home later. More about this further on. I bought a beer after saying hello and shaking hands with Santi. We hadn't seen each other for a couple of months. Barbara showed up with Teresa, who is amazingly alert, it seems. Moore showed up. It was great to Just Be There, if you know what I mean. It was just like I'd been fantasizing about laying up in my bed for the last couple of months. Ah, The Tapas, I'd think etc etc. Billy and Joe got back from busking with their hard-earned 1500 and proceeded to start rolling joints. I had another beer. Smoked another joint. Rabbit drooled. I told Tony that I was an intellectual and that I was having trouble relating to my lower-class friends. He understood. Joe was Rabbit-baiting. Rabbit was yelling 'Fuck Gott!', by which he means Flick Off, but he can't say it. Tony asked me to try to teach him. I did. He still couldn't get it. Billy was riding his unicycle around the plaza scaring dogs and children. Rabbit and Joe kept pretending to want to step on my cast and other funny/violent games that they enjoy. It was great to be hanging out with some of my main friends but at the same time it was a little disgusting to see who they were. The Next Major Appearance in the plaza was Jeanne, who I've also been fantasizing about quite a lot lately. Well, her body mostly. Anyway, she came strolling up Regomir with some nerds and I had been eyeing the girls anyway and I Completely Flashed on her Bodd, you know, and didn't notice it was Jeanne until she'd almost passed. She didn't recognize me right away either because I have a full beard now.

So, Jeanne was wearing a pink dress, you know, top and bottom, all pink, that flared out at the bottom, like what your sister wore when she went to visit your aunt when she was ten. And...Black Basketball Shoes! I was stunned, shocked, amazed, etc and was literally speechless. I could only mumble a few greetings and babbled minimally at her about my leg etc, but, I told her meaningfully 'See you SOON'. I'm hot for her. I think she's hot for me too. What could be more perfect? Tits, too! (for a change) (I hope Hannah doesn't read this) ... (Jeanne once told me that the best part of my book is the part about tits. Well, let me tell you, the best part about Jeanne yesterday was tits) (They're Huge!) (well, big anyway). Uh, where was I, Amani?

Well, Jeanne and her nerd-friends padded off (remember the shoes!) and Billy, Joe and I continued arguing about why everyone/someone was on Joe's Shitlist. He has a long shitlist. Almost everyone at some time or other is on it...

I had another beer, Tony bought me one. I had a conference with Santi and Barbara to decide beforehand how much Santi was going to over-charge me.

At one point something So Amazing was taking place in the plaza that I turned to Billy and said, "God, I wish Jacques was here to see this; he wouldn't believe it!". I'll tell you what it was, give you the punch-line first: five feet from me, in the middle of a heated argument that passes for normal conversation here, were Luis-the-dueno, yes, and Rabbit! Waving their arms and almost-yelling! Blew my mind. ...Ahmed was lingering on the fringes getting his 2cents in occasionally. It went on for about 15 minutes. I was wigging out about it. Incongruity Come To Life! It had begun a few minutes earlier when Ahmed and Luis walked into the plaza. Just seeing Luis there was amazing enough, so far. He and Ahmed went into the bar and had an argument with Ted first. Joe whispered (what an amazing paranoid: whispering in Plaza Regomir) that he knew what it was about. I took the bait, "What's it about, Joe?". "Keys!", he told me. Joe's the new Mystery Champion since Steve went to England. "Ah!", I said .. Well, after about 5 minutes with Ted, that's when Ahmed and Luis (1) came out and got in the argument with Rabbit. "It's about Ted's Keys!", Joe again whispered conspiratorially...Well, in Spanish fashion it ended happily with everyone smiling and shaking hands all around. I was still mystified even though

Joe knew what was going on because he understands body language so much better than the rest of us...

Ted came out with a coffee, it was beginning to get dark, Billy&Joe were off to get same more dope, Rabbit and Tony were sitting at the Bar watching Hollywood Squares, so I had a talk with Ted.

I asked him why he was still so nervous and up-tight, since he'd gotten all the money from the Dali Sketches why wasn't he just Cruising? He said that he didn't have any electricity in his new apartment and that he had a deadline coming up for his next novel. I told him that he should Fellowship with me because I'm A Writer Too. He seemed to deny this, which put me in an obnoxious mood. We argued for a few minutes and then I told him, "Most of my friends around here don't Really Like You!" "Who?", he asked, hurt. "Almost Everyone!", I kindly explained. I got another beer (#5) and Ted and I continued arguing/chatting for a while. Sitting on the stone bench with us but facing the street were a couple of nodding junkies. One of them had been moving his arm up and down for about 10 minutes. Ted thought he was jacking off and I thought he was getting ready to shoot up. It went on for so long that the attention of the whole plaza was drawn to it. Ted finally got up and walked around to see what the guy was doing. He was sharpening a pair of scizzors. When I heard That I Immediately Hobbled over to the wall near the bar, along with Ted and Rabbit. I didn't want to be the first to go when the guy finally got them sharp. His friend, who was also nodding, tried to assure us that the guy was Tranquilo! Sure.

It was getting dark. Joe went to the bodega and got me a liter of wine for later at home. sure. Ted left. Rabbit and I sat on the fountain, to be ready for a quick escape when Scizzor-Man made his move, and drank same of the wine. The 'gang' that was left decided to head for plaza Real. I wisely declined to go. I began the Hobble home, stopping out of necessity every half-block or so to sit on a stoop and sip de wine. I finished it before I got here.

Well, it must have taken me a couple of hours to get here; it's Slow and Hard Enough when sober, almost impossible when drunk. I have to put All my weight on the two little sticks with each step. Yah, well, somehow I got here and made it up the 4 flights of stairs fine. But: I'd left the keys in the door downstairs. Fuck it, I wasn't going to try navigating the Deadly Fucking Stairs twice more. I curled up on my hat on the doorstep and waited for Joe to let me in when he came home around 4 in the morning. Someone had snatched my watch, which had been on the keychain in the door. Joe is having trouble relating to his new Role as my Landlord (he thinks). He chastises me verbally about my failings. I'm sure he was worried about what the neighbors might think etc. He'll figure it out. He's Fine when he's a little drunk or stoned, but in the mornings he's Difficult to be around because of his obvious (to me) disapproval of my (our?) behavior...

Well, it must be nearing noon. I can hear the gringoes lining up at the picasso, so I oughta head on down there and whistle for a while...More Later, probably.

So...5 oclock Sunday afternoon...

Made about 500 in an hour and more. Bought a beer. drank it. Had some Spaghetti with Rabbit (yes, Rabbit, and Joe and smoked a joint or two) (on which Joe has spent the last of his money and some of mine which I was saving to buy rice on Monday, but which Joe can't seem to relate to because it's so far away...), took a nap/siesta, and Now Here I Am...Just made a cup of coffee etc etc...

And Now I'm thinking of heading over to Steve's old pitch and playing the whistle for a while so I can go over to Santi's and have a beer and see if Jeanne comes in with her tits. Or maybe go over and ring her bell except I forget which number she's AT, so maybe I'll stand in the street and yell "Jeeeeaaaaannneee!!!", and I'm sure she'd like THAT and what a way to get started.... (with her tits, I mean).... Whatever... I'm out of cigarettes and that settles it: OUT...

Amani Over and Out.

Tits.

More Tapas Report (the next night) :

Yah, well, I left here and busked til I had a few hundred pesetas and then busked some more in Steve's pitch, just for fun, and was heading for Santi's when I ran into Joe in Plaza St. Juame. He was on a beer run for Tony and Rabbit who were busking near the cathedral under the arch so I tried to help him find a bodega, which he didn't...I hung out with Tony and Rabbit and sung rocknroll songs for a while: Me: (lead singer): "I want a fat german girlfriend", a new song I made up on the spot and sung in my best hell's angels voice etcetc I'm sure you imagine the afternoon...Then Nuria (Tony's gal) and her son and I went down to Escudillers to get some more beer. No Problem. We came back, drank the beer and all headed over to Santi's...

Ted is no longer on my Friend's List. Around ten last night I was telling him that I didn't want him fucking Billy when he grabbed one of my crutches and tried to brain me with it. He missed. He hit my shoulder instead. I couldn't believe it. I stood there and he Would've hit me again but Joe came up and got into it. Ted ran for the bar. Home Safe. Joe got in one punch as Ted darted under the half-closed metal door...Barbara and Santi kicked Ted out and he came back out into the plaza. I went after him, hobbling of course, with my other stick, but couldn't catch him. He pulled a knife, Joe picked up the broken (!) crutch and went after Ted. He hid behind a huge Irish Queer (or something) (I missed some of this) and Joe threatened the Lot of them etc etc.... Anyway, My shoulder is swollen this morning. He was going for my head, remember. Broke the crutch, etc.

Joe and I and an Italian then went down to the bodega with Ahmed's uncle and drank a bunch of wine but didn't have any money to pay for it so a German girl (Nuria!!) did. The owner, as usual, threatened to call the police if we didn't pay. Then Joe and I hobbled home, with me falling down every few minutes because I only have one stick now. good morning.

Well, it's over a week later, a Tuesday, and I still haven't mailed this letter to you. Hannah left for France today, for a month or so, to get a new truck and to visit some friends, and to get away from Barcelona and me. I've got my Usual Broken Heart about it.

"Philosophize!", she told me as she got on her bike to ride away after we had a good-bye drink down by Santa Maria Del Mar.

"What do you mean?", I asked.

"Write about what you Think; write about why you think things are the way they are.", she explained, not the first time she's suggested this.

"Yah...", I said, "I don't usually write shit like that; I just write what's happening..."

"Well, Try It!!", she said.

"Yah..."

We both agreed that we (sometimes) think that the other is a Fine and Gentle Person. I said it first. I told her that she has broken my little heart. Again.... This time, I suppose, it is Rawther permanent of a Split. I don't expect that she'll want me to ever live with her again. I think she's looking for a new boyfriend/lifestyle. I'm doing the same.

I've been here for about two weeks, busking almost every day for about 4 hours (about 600/day, which I've spent mostly on beer), and Hannah came to visit me about 3 times, most of the time for only a few minutes because she was in her Permanent Hurry to Get Somewhere Else. But... she paid a surprise Horny Visit to me on Sunday and we fucked and sucked the afternoon away, making her late for the usual Appointment Elsewhere. It Was Wonderful, but Very Very Nasty.... She had to leave to go busking that evening and I continued drinking wine with Joe, Alfie, and a couple of Irish Friends of Joe's for a few hours and then went to sleep around 9, kind of passing out.... I woke up at 3 in the morning and took a cab over to Hannah's, making my Second Forbidded (by her) Visit in a few days, and got in a fight with her (again, we've been doing it pretty regularly, actually), raped her a couple of times, spent the night fucking her, raped her again in the morning and Then We Made Love, for what turned out to be the Last Time. She came by today to pick up a fucked-up bike that Joe sold her, stayed for a few minutes, we met a little later, had a beer, kissed a bit, I almost cried as usual and Now She's Gone....

I'm Sad, and Relieved, I suppose. My Emotional State, as you know, has been a mess for over a year over her.

My drinking has been only slightly out of hand lately, mostly spending the money on beer as it comes into the hat...sort of like the Old Palo Alto and Montana Days...know what I mean...been trying to keep from thinking about what I've been going through...

Been trying to keep off the wine by mostly drinking beer, and you know how badly that can work sometimes...Blowing Hannah's mind a couple of times by showing up by cab when I wasn't supposed to after she'd been so Friendly and Happy after I finally moved out of her place etc etc...She Really does love me, I think but has just had her mind too " blown by my Lifestyle (Drinking??)...

My leg is better. And Worse. I got a shorter cast on so that I can now hobble about some, but the fucking thing is chafing my leg and it's So Goddamned Frustrating travelling at that speed, and I still can't work with Joe and Billy because of the immobility....

I am definitely into an Aqualung impersonation...

Well, my friend: I'll try to save some money to copy and mail this to you; I may write more later.

I'm going out busking now. So are Joe and Billy. Alfie's at the beach. Hannah's gone to France. Naomi's due back in about a month. I'll have to have something together by then.

The police picked me up yesterday and took me for a passport check.

Jack"

(Author's Note, 1992: we lasted the month at Naomi's, the police came, my beard got longer, I got bugs in my head, bugs in my crotch, and bugs in my stomach, and went to the American Consulate and told them that I was a Clown With A Broken Leg and was dying there in Barcelona and was reduced to begging on the street. They loaned me $1000 for a plane ticket to California, which is where I flew to. I never saw Hannah again, though we corresponded for a year or so until she wrote and told me to quit writing because she had another Lover and didn't want to think about the Horrible Times she spent with me. I still send her cards on her birthday, and use her birthdate on my lottery tickets. She never writes.

The Last Thing I Wrote in Barcelona

I went back to Barcelona a couple of years later, busking as a clown with a puppet and was arrested for Clowning Without A License and deported within a month. That's another story.

Billy travels all around Europe working as a clown, Sally (daughter) works as a Translator and Teacher in Barcelona, Frank hung himself from a tree in Sitges, Jacques lives with his Croatian girlfriend near Barcelona and hangs out at the beach and chalks and paints, Peter lives in Germany with his girlfriend Martini, Tracy is a Psychologist in Toronto, Crow does caricatures on the Ramblas, Lori is in Lyon, Ahmed had more kids and won the Spanish Lottery and moved out of Pension Costa, Amani wents to Brazil, Rabbit was deported back to Venezuela, Pirate Steve is drunk or dead or dead drunk in England, Canadian Steve is a junky in Marseilles, Howdy Donna has a baby and lives in Barcelona, Tony and Nuria went to England, Santi and Barbara lost the Tapas and then got it back, Rebecca and Amy live and work in Oregon, Hadass still travels and chalks, Phil and Rene got married and live in Philadelphia where he is a chimney sweep, English Phil lives in the Spanish Pyrenees, Angie (Angela) makes and sells clothes in Barcelona, Whitey joined a rock band in Seattle, Ramon got another girl pregnant and went to Scotland with yet another girl, 'Fat' Sally still teaches English and hangs out in uptown Bars in Barcelona, Norma lives in New York City, Vivian and Aurora moved to London where he works for the railroad, Suzanne and Ellen and Gandalf disappeared, Clem married a Catalan Dancer and lives near Barcelona, Theo still lives in Limoux and does shows as Tznot Circus, Joe was deported but still busks as a clown in Southern France and is still crazy, Ted lives in Ireland, Naomi still lives with her son Aaron in the apartment overlooking the Picasso Museum, Alfie went to India, Harry still gets drunk at the Tapas, Will and Sonia live in London, Hannah quit clowning and lives in Bristol with her sons who go to a school for rocket scientists, And I Sit Here And Stink in Palo Alto, though not as much.)

Afterword...

"When I came to, I looked up and saw the coffin being lowered down on me and heard the words "Dust to Dust, Ashes to Ashes", and I let out a SCREAM!"   ... Frank Box, Opera Cafe, Barcelona, 1985

Barcelonario Diaro Glosario

BARCELONA GLOSSARY, SOME USEFUL WORDS AND PHRASES

SPANISH/ENGLISH	AMERICAN
ali-oli	pummelled garlic and rabbit grease
andalucian	foreigner
andaluthian	arabic dialect
anilla	girl
aragon	a spice
asensor	bar
athul	blue
autopista	machine gun
bajo	basement
bar	restaurant
barna	soccer team
barraca	bar
basque	trouble
basito	red wine
baso	red wine
bastardo	enough
batido	baby bat
beano	red wine
bebido	red wine
beinte-duro	see veinte-duro
biro	pen
bisonte	cigarette

SPANISH/ENGLISH	AMERICAN
bit	little
bodega	bar
bocadillo	fake sandwich
boca	face
boca raton	apartment complex
bomba	fried potatoe patty
botella	red wine
broma	broom
burger king	popular restaurant
buttifarra	guts
cafe con leche	coffee with milk
cafeconlech	bar with dirty old man
caixa	hole
calamari a la romana	squits to the romans
camarrone	waiter
carabella	cigarette
caraquillo	little prick
carburetor	primitive hash pipe
Catalan	a citizen of catalunya, a French dialect
Catalana	a female citizen of Catalunya
Catalonia	a province of Spain
Cataluna	un parte de Espana
Catalunya	a country presently occupied by spain
Catatonia	a state created by overindulgence in wine
caudillo	franc
can	bar

SPANISH/ENGLISH	AMERICAN
casa	bar
castillano	villager
cava	bar
cavallo	hat
centimo	1/100th of a peseta
cerveza	warn water
chico	skinny
chica	chewing gum
chocolate	hashish
cien	100 pesetas ($.60 in 1984), a dollar
cinco-duro	25peseta coin, a quarter
civil	mouse
clever	smart
cognac	brandy
colon	anus
conejo	rabbit, eduardo
conyo!	hey!
corazon	stomach
cordobes	luxury car
Cristo	Hungarian artist
corte ingles	sears roebucks
culo	cold
Dali	museum in Figueras
diabolo	toy
disco	Spanish music
ducado	cough

SPANISH/ENGLISH	AMERICAN
dulce	shower
duro	5 peseta coin, a nickel
Ebro	Spanish truck
el loco	famous painting
el monstro	neighbor
Elroy	the king
escucha	hey!
fanny	pussy
flan	putty
flore	floor
fresca	soft drink
fuera	lighter
futbol	soccer
futbol norteamericano	football
galon	dingle
Gerona	suburb of Barcelona
gitano	cigarette
granja	grungy bar
guapamole	pretty salad
guardia	mickey
hamburguesa	fake hamburger
hidalgo	liver
hospital	red
hombre	hungry man
huevo	ball
iglesia	singer

SPANISH/ENGLISH	AMERICAN
indio	ink
integral	brown
jamon	soap
jefe	chef
jose-maria	male Catalan
juarez	judge
kilo	2 Lbs, 1/2 mile
ladrone	moroccan
litro	red wine
liceu	green
listo	list
llibreteria	bread, pastry
llobregat	sewer
lomo	leather
madrid	soccer team
manera	fertilizer
mantequilla	woman's lace head-dress
maricon	busdriver
maria-jose	female catalan
mcdonalds	popular restaurant
mercado	mall
meson	bar
mil	thousand, thousand pesetas
miro	museum on Montjuich
moda	ice cream
morene	pastry, cowflop

SPANISH/ENGLISH	AMERICAN
motherfucker	disagreeable person
navidad	birthday
novelista	beggar
normal	normal
olandia	holland or ireland
opera	bar
oporto	to the left
osos	eyes
otra	red wine
oye!	hey!
palo alto	long crutch
papa	pope
peligroso	bird sanctuary
pelota	football
permiso	leave
peseta	1/100th of a cien ($.06 in 1984)
pi	bar
picasso	museum in Barcelona
piedra	foot
piel	hair
prado	Spanish painter
primero	3rd floor
private	public
problemo	foreign word
pta	abbrev. peseta
ptas	abbrev. pesetas

SPANISH/ENGLISH	AMERICAN
publico	privado
puta madre	excellent
ramblas	ditch
regular	regular
rubio	cigarette
restorante	bar
sagrada familia	big church
salchichon	guts
sangre de toro	red wine
sardana	Catalan fish
savvy	smart
segundo	4th floor
scizzors	2 scissor
shilling	1/12 guinea
smart	well dressed
sol	bad seat
sombra	good seat
spanner	wrench
sucio	swiss
tabacaleria	post office
tapas	snacks
tapes	hors duerves
Tapies	Catalan bullfighter
taxista	robber
tercero	5th floor
tornillo	ringworm

SPANISH/ENGLISH	AMERICAN
tortilla	potatoe mush
tortilla francesca	french fries
traviste	pedestrian
tren	railroad
turista	victim
Urina	Irene
urquinoana	yellow
valencia	soccer team
veinte-duro	100 pesetas
vespa	knife sharpener
vino	red wine
vino blanco	light red wine
vino de la casa	red wine
vino del casco	red wine
vino embotellado	red wine
vino negro	red wine
vino rojo	red wine
vino rosado	red wine
vino tinto	red wine
wellies	rubber boots
Zaragosa	suburb of Barcelona
zorro!	help!

APPENDIX

A Letter to Billy in Greece

Nov 8, 1991, Palo Alto
"Dear Billy-olino:

HAPPY BIRTHSDAY!

I just heard in a letter from Sally that you are in Greece and that you'll be there for a couple of months trying to make more money for India. India. Well, you better read what Frank had to say about That!

    I'm sending along some of 'Barcelona, Under the Influence'; the part that I've typed up and sortof edited already. I'm doing it on the computer at my dad's house. Some of it is funny, I suppose. Don't give it away because I'll probably copyright it and try to get it published next spring and I don't want anyone else to get a copy of it before I do.

Well, what's Happening. What's the Happs? WHAT HAVE YOU BEEN UP TO?

What kind of a clown deal are you doing these days? Have you ever used the dancing

puppet I left in Barcelox? Do you still have it?

What's your life like these days?

What's your Motocicleta like?

What's your english girl like?

What happened when you met Tim and Molly? You mentioned meeting them a year or two ago in England but never told me anything about them.

Who else did you see in England? Hannah? Sonia?

Who else did you see in France? Theo? JoJo? Hazzard?

What's Clowning like in France these days. I'm thinking of coming to France in a year or so.

Well, Billy, it's a few hours later. 3 in the morning. I just wrote "Rosa-jaws", or rather edited it. whatever.

anyway, I gottag go to sleep. fck.

I'm heading for mexico in december for a few months. I own three trucks now. one's for sale. one's my house. one's for travelling. I'm Rich! (hippy-rich, 3 trucks).

I will probably try to do same puppet jiggling in mexico. a friend of mine who lives there says he knows the local police and will get me permiso. whatever. Be sure to write more often, you fucker. Send pictures of girls.

More later. Love, Jacko. (my mail will be forwarded to mex.)"

A Letter from My Son Billy in Greece

Novermber 1991

"Dear Jacko,
I got your book/letter yesterday, its nice to hear from you and nice to read about the old days. I hope you send me more of your book. I'm impressed, mainly that you can actually work a computer....

I must admit that it is Funny what you've written but I don't know if it's because I know the people and can relate to how they are or were. Anyway, keep going with it. I'd like to see it Finished With.

Yes, I'm in Greece again but I'm not really sure why, maybe because it's winter, maybe because I can work as a peasant when I want to, maybe it's because I'm not together enough to be in India now, maybe because I haven't stayed in the same place longer than three months over the last two years. It gets a bit repetitive all these interesting things happening all the time....

Let's see.... Last winter I stopped working with Richard, in Cartagena (Spain) at Christmas and drove to Barna on my mobylette, which took 4 days, stayed in Barna a few weeks then caught the train to Dijon, France to see Natasha and her Family. When I got there I found they had no work and no money so we all piled in Bamboo's car (he's Natasha's dad), left his broken bus with a friend, and drove to England where he got on the dole, got an apartment in Thetford and tried (and is still trying) to save enough money to leave again. It was Jan. cold and miserable and Natasha and I tried to make a living clowning but my diabolo froze and shattered to pieces when it fell onto slush-covered pavement, we earned pennies, got police hassles, had to hitch-hike around in the snow to other towns, etc.

It lasted for three months, the bad times, then it got worse....

Natasha told me to buzz-Off, she didn't want to live with me anymore or even be a clown anymore, so I packed my bags and set off hitch-hiking with virtually no money in February, made enough money in London to catch the ferry to France. When I arrived in Calais I had 70francs and it was raining, 1000kms to Hitch and no plans. It was kind of depressing, but it got worse. It took me one week to get to a friend's house in the south of France, near

Avignon. For that week I nibbled stale bread and drank cheap sterilized milk, put up my tent in the rain every night, and I'd swear it was wetter inside than outside, it started to rot and stank of mildew.

In England I saw Tim and Molly but I didn't say much about them because there isn't much to say. They've settled down in a kind of snobby-hippy commune and do some sort of ecology-natural-charity work called "Green Desert" or something like that, where they get loads of money given to them which they supposedly use to plant trees in the Sudan. It's not clear but I don't think they want it too clear....

No news of Hannah or Sonja or any of that crowd. History. I saw Joe briefly in Montpellier about a year 1/2 ago, he's up to his usual.

Anyway, to continue my story since last winter: I arrived at my friend's house in the South of France, which is in a beautiful little town in the hills, rested there a week, went to Avignon, busked and caught the train to Barna. I stayed at Sally's for several months, busking, doing okay, smoking a lot and feeling disillusioned with life there, and life in general.

When spring finally came I got back on my Mobylette and drove to Provence (my same friends as earlier described), France, hung around there in June, busked a bit, then met a crazy Italian-French woman who's about 4 feet tall and bursting with energy. She had a van and was heading for Italy so we put my mobylette in and drove off.

She's a completely manic person and drives like a manic maniac in her van with dubious brakes and continuous mechanical problems. I wore my crash-helmet for the first two days then decided I shouldn't really worry too much, I learned not to be afraid of death.

We went to a blues festival in Pistola which lasted three days and was complete madness. Hundreds of Hippies had occupied the central park and put up hundreds of tents, TeePees, and unexplainable things which I think they might of slept in.

Crazed, drugged freaks bathed in the dirty, green, stagnant pond that was in the middle of the park, singing with their mouths full of green slime, fully clothed, while the police stood 10 meters away and pretended everything was normal. On the second day the punks had a riot, smashed shop windows and battled with the police, blood and tear gas everywhere; a bomb landed under my friends van as she was changing out of her costume, tear-gas filled it up and she ran out in a panic, half-clown, half hippy, but no one paid any attention as even stranger and more dramatic things were happening all around.

All in all it was a pretty good Festival.

After that me and Za-Za (that's her name) started making shows together, which lasted about a month.

We made pretty good money but decided we would make more working each alone, so I went off on my mobylette and worked on the Italian coast for a month and made a fortune. I was averaging between 100-200 dollars an evening. At the end of August I was very tired and went to rest at my friend's place in Provence where I ran into Richard, stayed and visited a week then drove back to Barna to visit Rebecca and leave my props there, I didn't want to take all my clown gear to India. Stayed in Barna two weeks, visited Rebecca, then headed off to England to catch the plane to India. It took a week to drive there and I was tired so I thought I'd visit Bamboo and family for a week of rest. A week became two became three, the ticket to India was more expensive than I thought, became a month then 1 1/2, then it was out of the question to go to India so I left, hitch-hiked across Belgium, Luxembourg, Germany, Austria, and to an address in Chookyslewvackia which a friend in England gave me. It was snowing and cold on my 4 day trip but nothing serious happened excecpt the cold and the snow.

I stayed in Chackoosloomvaccuum for 4 days and rested, it was interesting, again, then I caught the Athens Express train to.... Athens.

Across Hungary, Yugoslavia (I didn't see any soldiers or tanks, the press is lying), and arrived in Athens where the sun was shining and it was WARM. Two days to hitch across Greece to here where I am now, hanging out in the sunshine in an outdoor cafe with French and English hippies who come to pass the winter here or live here. It's so calm and tranquillo it's sometimes boring, which is nice when only interesting things have been happening for years.

I don't think I'll be able to go to India this winter, I'll probably have to make a fortune in Italy again in the summer, but I won't go to England after if I do.

I'll work July August going down Italy then work Greece in Sept. and October if necessary and catch the plane from Athens or even go overland through Iraq, visit Lebanon and Kuwait and say hello to the Afghanis.... Time will tell.

Anyway, it promises to be another interesting trip (the repetition is killing me), I am getting bored of interesting trips in Europe, I've lost interest in interesting European trips. It'll be interesting to see how long it will take me to lose interest in interesting trips in Asia.

So…. Keep in touch and I'll write you right away if something uninteresting happens.

I hope all is well in California, and I'll send a letter to Gramps and Grampsma soon.

I've fallen in love with a beautiful half algerian half french girl who is here with her boyfriend who, unfortunately is a friend of mine….

But maybe it's better I don't complicate my life by having any interesting love affairs.

You were right when you warned me about English-girl-clowns, they're a dangerous breed.

And I'll be careful which English-girl-clowns I become involved with in future. I learned my lesson.

Anyway, send me more of your book soon and say hello to everyone (whoever that is?) and keep in good shape.

Go to Mexico, fuck america.

Lots of love - Billy (Bobolino, Bordello, Garbanzo the Turd)."

A Letter from Jacques (My Editor?)

December 1991
"Thanksgiving, 1991, Blanes.

Dear Jack,
This typer is fucked (ribbon life) but I'm going to try and communicate anyway, Vale? First of all, the Thanksgiving vibe here is non-existent, like "King's Day" in SF, or Saint Jordi's day? Nada. I only knew about it because I bought the Herald Tribune and it was mentioned in an editorial. I got your new edited "book" stuff a while ago now. I went into such exstacy (sic) that I forgot to write you back immediately, I guess? But I liked it, I mean I was really happy to see the attention you are giving it & the high tech tools at your disposal for such an Under the Influence book. But a few comments after contemplating the sum total of what you are up to?

First, forget the Gigolo's Progress concept, it's irrelevant: you can write another story with that title and use Barcelona stuff, if you insist, but don't 'mix your metephors' (sic) (technical Editor jargon). You can do it when you reach vonnegut's level, but for now stay simple, approachable…. I think Frank would have cracked in half laughing if he could see this "Gigolo" alternative title? (Think about it!) (Authors note: Jacques seems to have forgotten that "Gigolo's Progress" as a title was Frank's idea.)

Second. I think the huge "raw", unedited manuscript is actually more valuable IF you ever find a publisher? The value of your computer version is simply that it becomes easier to read for normal, low-attention, low-interest people. I mean this "chapter" approach works for that type; they would never have the energy or interest to really attack the raw version. You have to suck that type in, and unfortunately they are the folks with printing presses and book stores. But your "real readers" (like Scott and Hadass, me. or even my girlfriend Zrinka) tend to get off on the original chaotic foaming-at-the-mouth manuscript. It suits the subject better, but it does need a true editor who understands the product, because obviously even that raw manuscript needs "some" editing? But don't misunderstand me either; I think you should carry on with the work your (sic) doing (Maybe you're even finished with it?). There won't be any harm in having the "two" versions; it's even possible that when you have "all" of it edited that some kind of synergy will make it just as legitimate as the original. It's worth your effort I think, and at the very least it will help you to be more selective the next time (if ever) you attempt another "book".? Anyway, Zrinka & I read all of it (the new version) and it was worth a whole night of deep analysis, remembering, me explaining stuff to her, and so on. So thanks alot. And send more of either version. I'm collecting it, I like it, I show it to certain people, AND I'm still your Editor (more or less)....

My life here has changed in same ways from what it used to be. For one thing, the effect of Zrinka is that I've become a kind of Right-wing Communist hater. I've got an eyewitness to that world now and it is really sick, really evil. All of the left wing chatter about socialism is nonsense I've decided, after hearing Zrinka's version and then reading about the shit in Russia these days. And then of course there is the war in Yugoslavia, with thousands dead, slaughtered by idiots, lies everyday broadcast as "news", and the world watches as if there is any solution short of literally attacking Serbia and stopping that Regime in it's tracks. It's amazing how the EC continues to try and act like it is just an average neighborhood war. The fact is that Croatia is under a major mindless aggression, a land-grab that by now is so far gone that of course the Croatians are going berserk as well. But who started it? This will probably be lost in the shuffle, but as a World War II buff remind me to explain the fundamentals to you one day? It's really a sad case of the world looking the other way while Hitler does his thing. Zrinka & I spend alot of time analyzing ridiculous news reports and writing Letters to the Editor about it, (Zrinka had one published in Van Guardia, so far?)

She is also involved in the Refugee Supply effort from Barcelona, in her own so far more or less useless way. But it helps her feel like she isn't a traitor. Her parents want her to come home (?), but she knows better despite the fact that her parents are HEAVY influences compared to me, We have realized that we're both personas non gratis here in Spain; at any moment I could get kicked out leaving her hopelessly unconnected, or she could get kicked out, leaving her hopelessly in the War Zone. Her status now in Europe is Refugee level, mine is invader, and in Spain it's somehow worse than almost any other country, because alot of the losers end up here and they are sick of it, I guess? It's also because they aren't sophisticated, so they don't know how to be nice to losers. It may also be because they are losers themselves and they won't admit it, but that is just a theory, don't quote me. Our only good luck in all of this is that we've met a very functional social worker who is encouraging BOTH of us to go to Girona before the 11th of Dec. and file for Residency. There is some kind of Amnesty until then. She says the longer you have been here the BETTER!!! That puts me in very good shape, whereas Zrinka just makes it (8 months). I think I'm going to try it, apparently there is nothing to lose? If it works we'll both get "Residency" for a year, subject to renewal in another year. For Zrinka it would be like a new life; for me it will be like an Old Life, renewed. I like it though because it could mean zero street paranoia during my Olympic debut, a factor that always weighs down on me these days when there are goon squads of commando National police roaming around Barrio Gothico! Really, A BRAND NEW kind of Police, you wouldn't last a minute in your old disguise, they are really heavy, dumb, and taught to recognize weirdos more than ever before!! Mes que mai!!!!!! Ole' !!!!!!

I don't even go to Barcelona any more, really! Too risky. If I do it's just to buy Art supplies and I make sure to look like Phil, really english tourist spaced type, no danger, no passport worry, etc. One more Passport for me and we'll be having lunch together in Alameda. But I don't want that NOW, do I!?? So I stay put here in the most boring beach pueblo on the Planet. I've got some commissions to do, some copies and some oil portraits. Shitty money, but better than homeless life in SF, the other alternative. Do I sound paranoid? I am Jack; there are 170 countries worth of police collaborating to make people like me and you feel like we belong elsewhere, like home! I'm going to beat them at their game, I think, but imagine THIS 4 years ago?????

What about you??? Drinking again? (Say no!) I had a free phone last month and even tried to call Dave at his Alameda number, but of course I got same kind of Machine? But I did get Dave K., Jerry F., my brother, my Mother, Austin, and many others. It was great. Send more stuff. photos will do, and letters, but I prefer the "book", either version. More UpDate later. Write anyway. Hang in there, amigo.

Jacques.

P.S. I've been reading about David Duke? Good Luck. What about that Fire?

Another Letter from Jacques (My Editor?)

February 1992
"3 Feb. 1992 Blanes.

Dear Jack,

I got "Picture This" the other day (book rate, SLOW motion!), and you were right, I love it!!! Thanks alot for thinking of me, I'm really into it, what a great way of looking at history. Rembrandt was really fucked up, I had no idea! But I'm learning from it, what to avoid, and also what to DO!! (Copies, right? Copies of MYSELF, which I'm already doing before I found out that's the way to be!!!???). I got a Christmas card from Beautiful Susan (SO) and she said something about you going to Mexico? That doesn't sound good to me, I don't see how you can possibly stay sober down there? But it's your Life.... I hope you don't pull a Neal Cassidy, but if you're reading this I guess you decided not to, even if you did GO? Speaking of "Going", my little yugoslavian (Croacian NOW!) left a few days ago after spending nearly a year here with me, Sad times for me now, but she had to go and see what Croacia is like now that it's an independent country for the first time in a thousand years!!! (Really!) I told her it would be a place with no vegetables, no soap, no happiness, Nationalistic propaganda everywhere, changed friends, possibly dead relatives, hysterical parents, soldiers, guns, bombs, mines, terrorists, no fun, no beach, no sun, nothing beautiful, everything tense, grey, cold, collapsed, poor, and depressing. She listened in awe and put off her trip for weeks and weeks, but finally I had to start to exaggerate because the normal true stuff didn't scare her anymore. Shortly after, I shut up, and she left, with a suitcase full of soap and coffee. I guess by now she is in the War Zone? I don't Know what to say about it, she had it made here? We're TOTALLY in love and happiness, we have fun every day, a few mutual friends, the weather has been perfect, warm, and I've got money from commissions? A kind of Beach idyl Bohemian perfection, but she couldn't wait to get back to a country that has lost nearly 10,000 people since June in brutal primitive Fraticide? Wow? But I'm SURE we were happy! She has exams to finish in order to get her degree from the University of Zagreb in English & Spanish and I guess I can understand that she wants her degree, although I never failed to include how "useless" a Degree from the U of Zagreb is in the "real world" of Western Europe. She left to get it anyway? She's gone now, indefinitely? The only good thing is that we have an SOS system planted through the phone of a friend in Lloret - if things are really as bad as I predict she'll bail out, which means I have to go get her with lots of money in my pockets to give her so she can pass into the "Real World" without being treated like a Palestinian beggar, which is about where "Croacia" stands at this time in the eyes of the "Real World"! I'll do it though, I really love her, she has worked out alot better than Marta because she likes me as I am, drugged, weird, etc. (lazy?). Our relation gets better each day in fact, it's amazing. (So why did she go to the War Zone, right? Good question! It's almost something for "Picture This"!!!!!).

There is alot of other weird stuff happening HERE, in fact maybe I should not be so clear on Croacia being the War Zone? Maybe it's hypocritical, since Barcelona has became a fucking police state, even before another 70,000 police agents from foreign countries arrive in April. It's a Drag, to put it bluntly. I'm afraid to go there, let alone work on the street. 8 years of illegal living could catch up to me in a minute with the wrong police and the wrong story, so I'm steering clear of the place. It's a pity, my whole act for the last three years is based on being on the street in Barcelona, NOW!!!, and I'm terrified to make an appearance? I've also been made aware that my entire obra could be illegal to sell because most of it has COBI in it and COBI is private property!!!! Isn't it funny, ironical, madness? I don't know what to do? I need professional counsel, a lawyer, someone like Rappy on my side, just to step outside my house these days. I guess I've come a long way from the days when I encouraged you to come to see how "neat" Barcelona is!!!!!!! Shit!!!!!!!

I still do work on the street though, in a little pueblo with a sunday market near Blanes where I have official permiso. Last Sunday I made 9 mil in 3 hours with my street copy (half finished) of the Columbus monument. (See photo, entitled "Marcelona, Pez que Mai"). I think it could be a big hit in Barcelona! Too bad, isn't it? Next to my "Barzoolona, mes que mai", this new painting staggers the Spanish mind, the two of them stretching linguistic limits of the average citizen. "Que significa este?" they ask? To one lady I said it was just my personal Vision of the monument and she replied, "Que vision mas particular!". It's funny, I love it, that's why I remain on the street, for stuff like that, you know? And if things don't get much worse I'll work the summer in Lloret, that should be OK since I am famous there by now and it would be a mini-scandal for the police to arrest me after all the time I've spent being totally visible and friendly and harmless and appreciated by the tourists.

I've scrapped my idea of having an "Exposition" too. Thru some minimal contacts with that world I've realized it's almost as creepy as dealing with banks; just a bunch of scoundrels who are stupid with stupid clients buying stupid "art" from stupid artists. No thanks, the Street is the only Gallery I can relate to; it's much bigger than any "Gallery" I know of, there are alot more people and not ALL of them are stupid! I'm the kind of painter who won't be "rich" till I'm dead anyway, and if I start planning on that it probably won't happen either, so it's better for now if I forget money, stay poor, and pursue the Happiness of Conceptuality and Freedom from Bastards. Amen.

Have you heard about what ETA is up to these days? There are two of them, famous terrorists, going around Barcelona shooting National Police point blank with pistols and then disappearing in stolen cars. Then a few days later they do it again. The reaction of the National Police each time is to blockade all the highways' and check EVERY car and cause massive traffic jams. It doesn't affect the terrorists at all, they just keep functioning. When it gets too hot they go to Valencia and murder police there, and then they come back to Barcelona and carry on. Madness. The Metro has been on strike for over a week, totally fucking up things even more. Cafe con leche costs 100 pesetas everywhere, pisos are about like in Palo Alto now, or more, for the same Spanish hovel. So much for the Olympic City, you're not missing ANYTHING!!!!!!

The only visitor I've had in months is my friend Frank, an American. He doesn't know you but you are famous to him nonetheless from your Legend and your book. Frank's favorite girlfriend (another American teaching English for a year in Barcelona) got slaughtered by a RENFE train while she was walking across train tracks to go to the beach with her new boyfriend. That happened last year, in a place where others have met the same fate? It barely makes the News, and RENFE continues to refuse to build a pedestrian walkway, or even put up a DANGER sign. Nothing happens, no Law suits, the train keeps rolling over people. So don't hurry back Jack, but don't get any Neal Cassidy ideas from this either. Be Brave, be sober, be alive!!! Thanks again for the book, I find it 100 percent illuminating, just as you thought I might! Send your book!!! I'll be writing mine soon, I mean I already did, but I have to arrange it so it reads like one instead of a mass of unconnected letters. I'll do it though, I've got alot of spare time since my street-painting days seem to be over. (Here anyway!). Write!! your boy, JACQUES."

A Third Letter from Jacques In Spain

February 1992
"28 Feb. 1992 Blanes.

"Especially the part about the Jack-monstro-droid gave us the creeps, needless to say that he is way out off-course and that even if his navigation systems return to Green, he is a potential blow-out all the time.... I liked him though when his crooked shuttle was on refuel in Milk, but did you know that the Ground Personel had trouble even finding his fuel tank opening as it was covered with loaned dollar bills?"

"Jack, how are you doing man?.nobody will ever know probably, no one will ever get any closer than amazement about your person, but you're great and the foremost talented writer, musician, architect, soldier, beardgrower, poet, fucker I've ever met!"
-from Rene's "Letters" 1984

Dear Jack,

Got your Mexican Lullaby today here in Blanes. Pretty amazing stuff, I knew you would descend into the abyss though as soon as I heard you had headed South. I guess you're really a "dork", not just pretending to be one? Well anyway, no preaching, I'm glad you lived through it and didn't go all the way with your Neal Cassady subliminations which as you know from my other letter (to your Alameda address?) I predicted might be on your secret agenda. I told you - Stay Put, get a hold of yourself, but you won't listen, will you? I hope this letter finds you back on Hollyoak drinking coke or whatever, but give your stomach-ache a long rest, like for the rest of your earthly existence!!!!!!
    Nance wrote me something on my birthday, I wrote her back, maybe she told you? That's also where I predicted dire straits for you, I'm surprised they let you drift off so easily down where nobody knew you have an alien living in your Liver! That family you stayed with sounds "classic" Mexican, and I agree with you that your Father deserves some family homage in his "last days" just like that Old Man in the Mexican Sagrada Familia by the sea. I hope you'll hang onto that Revelation, there may not be much more time for your pop, from the sound of it he's a bit bent on auto-destruct himself.... must run in the family, down to third and fourth generation kind of shit it seems? My parents aren't getting any younger either, but they seem bent on playing

golf until they drop! It's a little stupid but I'm sure a much healthier obsession than over-drinking and over-smoking when you need a heart operation, and if you don't think it will bore the hell out of him I don't mind if you let your Dad read this, one more voice in the crowd chastising him!!!! Or shall we say suggesting a better attitude towards what is left of his earthly frame? (That goes for you too you stupid shit!!!!!)

About your "book". What's this about titling it "Frank and Billy"? That's MY idea, in case you don't recall. No, I don't think you should call it that, "Barca, under the influence" is much more appropriate, in my opinion. You might be surprised (and jealous?) to learn that I've begun my own record of those days, from a street-painter's perspective. I've got 45 pages (single spaced) already, and I think it's going good. I'm bouncing off of the scads of xeroxed letters I've collected over the years, but more and more taking alot of liberty with it. It's alot of fun too. I plan to call it "On the Sidewalk: the Life of an American street-painter in Europe", and I guess the reference to Kerouac is obvious enough not to need explanation. I'm working through stuff by the year: at the moment I'm in early 84, with you and me and Sue in Amsterdam, remember? That's why I've found these quotes from Rene; I've got a whole manila envelope full of his letters and believe me it's really something, like re-reading notes from the first Mars Expedition, he's nuts, truely!!!!!

I will call Sally and if she really will "translate" it into the vernacular I think you might have something going here. If I can get a copy of it I'll do what I can, I mean show it around, I've got a few leads for that and you know I think your "book" is very good and deserves same exposure. I have some of your Word Processed version, but not very much, maybe 50 pages? I wrote in my other letter that I want ALL of it, and I do, but I also realize that's asking alot from you interms of paper, ink, time, postage, xerox, etc., but please, do what you can? If I actually had a FULL English & Spanish version of it, I can't see how I cauld have ANY EXCUSE in terms of my editorial duties, and.... HALF the money, really?

My darling Yugoslavian Croat left for the WarZone a month ago now. We're hot & heavy into the letter-world again, but it's not the same as "indirecto" and I can hardly wait for her to OD on living in a world where the people walk around with their arms dragging on the pavement and the TV emits nothing but fake or semi-fake War News. They live on pickles and cabbage there, and she writes that the only way for her to remain "sane" is to tune out completely when her friends are talking to her. Not quite, but almost that bad! poor girl, she must have been very evil in her past life to have been born in Zagreb, and then she meets ME? Oh well, I guess weirder things have happened?

Life around here remains in the Jokes Olympic frame of reference. ETA commandos have killed 15 people, mostly police, since 92 began, and everyday the population awaits another attack. The Nationals in Barcelona are walking around with Rambo rifles (automatic machine guns) and there is a big polemic about it since they say many of them haven't been sufficiently trained on how to actually use them? Tapies wants to erect a 50 foot "sock" in the National Catalan museum, but nobody else likes the idea. It's prime time for my "Homage to Tapies" to hit the street, and it will soon, as quickly as I can finish up with my "Marcelona, pez que mai!" picture of the columbus monument underwater. I've enclose another photo of it, in case I didn't last time? I sent so many off in January I forget? I realize now that I definitely over-estimated the Spanish/Catalan sense of humor because nobody gets it! The masses stand around wondering what it means, and correcting me, telling me it's "MES" que mai, not "PEZ" que mai? Oh, shit, what a bunch of stupids!!!!! I don't care though, I've set my course and I'll finish it, even if I'm the only one who gets off on it!!! So far I am? Idiocy incarnate, as I wrote in the other letter, you're not missing much, in case you think you might be! The finances ·are way down too, survival mode, just when I thought I would be "cashing in"? The few contacts I've had with "Galleries" have convinced me to forget it, they're like bank people, totally dumbfounded by anything original, freaked out, clinging to their idea of the "market". It's too depressing to even explain, like I say I over-estimated this place, it could be I've wasted my time if it weren't for the fact that I met Zrinka and had some good swimming moments due to the proximity of my house to the sea. I'll probably return to California next year, or go to Italy, one or the other, since Spain is lost now. I found out that the Spanish have a saying, "tirando al suelo" (Throwing on the floor), and it means your (sic) wasting your talent, that your (sic) lost! When people see me working on the "suelo" that's what 99 per cent of them think, according to the person who told me this? So? Is it any wonder nobody takes me seriously? I guess not, I only wish I had known this earlier!!!! When I hit 50 pages in my "book" I'll send a copy of it for your perusal and critique. until then do what you can to finish your's (sic) up & send it to me. I'm not into competing, our perspectives are different anyway. Frank should die at the End, otherwise there is no tragic effect, and you need THAT, since everything else is absurdly comic!!! Take my word for it. Good luck Jack. write me soon. Say hello to your family for me. Did Ali get married?

tu amigo, como siempre, love, from JACQUES.

P.S. I've got a book for you too!! I'll send it soon, on the boat. Patience!!!"

A Fourth Letter from Jacques

May 1992.

"THE PEANUT GALLERY & THE EDITOR DISCUSS "BARCELONA, UNDER THE INFLUENCE"

Hi Kids! Can I talk with you about Jack's book for awhile? (WHO ARE YOU???? YOU ARE WHO???) No, I'm Jacques, I never liked the "Who", too loud I thought. (BOOOOOOOOO! WE LIKE NOISE!!!!) Yeah, I know you do, but you have to let people have their own opinion about things like that, otherwise they won't like you. (JACK LIKES US!!!! YEA JACK!! YEA JACK THE MANIAC!!!) But seriously (BOO! WE HATE SERIOUS STUFF!!!) I want to ask you guys a few things about the "Book". Can I? (OK OK OK SERIOUS JOCK!!!) I liked it alot and I'm proud to be the Editor over-seeing everything, but still I can't help but think that there remains some problems. What do you think? (RELAX!! RELAX SERIOUS JOCK!!) That's exactly what I expected from you silly kids (SILLY!! SILLY!! YEAAAAAA!!!) and so I did my Homework (BOOOOOOOOOO!!! HOMEWORK?) and I have some Good Examples of Problems for you to think about.

First of all, what about Hadass? Do you really understand why Desert Jack is suddenly with Hannah the Clown, after all that Romance and baby-planning? (NO! BUT WHO CARES?) You little Fuckers, I'm trying to carry on an Intelligent Conversation with you (BOO!!! BOOOOOOOO!) is it possible? (NOOO!!! NOOOOOOO! WHERE'S CRAZY JACK????) Jack is in Palo Alto and he's not crazy anymore because he's not allowed to drink alcohol. You guys should be glad I'm talking to you in fact because now Jack is too sane to even remember your names! (SANE JACK? NOOOOO SERIOUS JOCKO; DON'T LIE TO US! WHERE'S JACK????) I'm NOT lying you Bastards, he had to stop drinking alcohol cause his stomach revolted, and now (YES; THAT'S JACK!! REVOLTING!!! REVOLTING!!! MAS!!! MAS!!!) he has to scrub boats and be an American again since Spain hates him (BOOO! ! !! BOOOO!).

Will you Kids get SERIOUS for a moment??? (NO, WE HATE THAT!!!!) OK then!!! I'm going to Edit every part with the Peanut Shitheads OUT of the Book, what do you think of THAT!!! (WHERE'S JACK?? WHERE'S JACK??) Ready to calm down then? (OK OK SERIOUS JOCKSTRAP!! HA HA HA HA HA HA HA HA HA HA HA HA HA) Hey, guess what? That's NOT original AT ALL!! You're just demonstrating how weak your

Brains are since I've heard it a million times in my life. (JOCK! STRAP!!! JOCK-STRAPPPPP!!! JOCKKKK-STRAPPPPP!!!) I see now what it is, you Kids are called the Peanut Gallery cause you have peanuts for brains, right? Ha, ha, ha. (YESSSSSSS!!!! YESSSSSS!!!!) Then you're not the Peanut Gallery, you're the Mustard-Seed Gang. (YEAAA! SMALLER BRAINS QUE NUNCA!!! MORE FUN; MORE JOKES SERIOUS JOCKO STRAP!!!!!) You kids are vicious, I never realized it, but then I should have known! How else could you be friends with Jack? (JACK!!! JACK!!! JACK!!!) What about Frank, Kids? Don't you think he deserves more info about when and how he died? For instance the letter I wrote to Jack telling him about it? (JACK LOST IT! HE TOLD US BUT IT'S A SECRET, OK????) Now you're co-operating, so let me ask you if you know anything about why the "book" suddenly becomes based on Hannah midway with hardly any reference to the Good Old Days in Barcelona? (NOOO!! WE WON'T TELL YOU!!! WE PROMISED CRAZY JACK!!!) Did you promise him to keep quiet about how he broke his leg? (YESSSSS!! IT WASN'T FUN; SO WE LEAVE IT OUT; LIKE HE DID!!!) Just what I thought, you and Jack have a conspiracy to act like the Patron Saints of Honesty but really you're just a small cynical club of Revisionists. (WHAT YOU GONNA DO ABOUT IT SERIOUS JOCK!?) Nothing, except remind you of my Editing powers? (REVISIONIST; TU!!! REVISIONIST; TU!!!!! TUT; TUT!) I might also remind you that fucking Howdy Doody's sister is Copywrite Violation if you insist on playing by the Rules? (BOO!!! BOOO!!!! RULES!!!!!) Don't misunderstand me Kids, I like that part, even though it was all in Jack's mind. (YES!!! YES!!!!! YESSS!!!) I even see Howdy Donna now and then in Barcelona and she is happily co-habitating with a famous painter there, she even has two babies! (HOWDY OONNA GOT FOCKED!!! HOWDY OONNA HAD PUPPET BABIES!!!!! YEEE-AAAAA!!!!) Yeah, but they aren't from Jack, so they are 3 dimensional, NOT cartoonish AT ALL!!! (CARTOONS!!! CARTOONS!!!) You know what else I don't like? (NO WHAT? SERIOUS STRAP???) Well, I know you'll laugh but I think the book has too much "sex", especially with Clowns. I mean it seems that Jack might be a pervert? (WE LIKE THAT!!!! CLOWNS!! SEX!! PERVERSION!! MAS!! MAS!!!!) Then I suppose you like it when your Hero is limping around with Imaginary Lizards in his Broken Leg? (YES!! YES!! OUR FAVORITE PART!!!) Do you like it when he lives in a house that seems like a Garbage Can? Are you really THAT Hard-Hearted? (DID YOU SAY SOMETHING ABOUT HARD-HEARTED HANNAH???) No, I didn't, I'm talking about Crazy Jack reaping what he sowed and it's NOT a JOKE!! (JOKES!!!! JOKES!!!! MAS SERIOUS STRAPPO; MAS SERIOUS JOCKO) I'm going to edit you Kids OUT of the Book, Sociopaths won't sell, in my

A Fourth Letter from Jacques

Editorial Opinion. (JUMP IN THE LAKE, SERIOUS JOCK!!! WHERE'S JACK???) I hope he's writing another book by now; I advised him in this direction. (ERECTION??? ERECTION???) NO!!! I said "direction", where are your Heads AT Kids? (WITH JACK!!! YOU'RE BORING, SERIOUS JACK STROP!!!) Then Puck you! (NOW YOU'RE TALKING!!!) In my opinion this is no way to Critique a book, I'm going to look for more intelligent Feedback. (WE LOVE FOOD!!! JUST LIKE JACK!! WHERE'S THE PAD??? WHERE'S THE ETERNAL STEW???) It was dumped down the toilet years ago by a Danish girl, don't you even know that? (SOOOOOOO!!!!) DO you know what else happened? (NO, SERIOUS JACK.) Well, it's not nice to spread around but actually Hadass was very upset with Jqack after he lost the "pad" by not paying the Rent, in fact she thinks he's a Jerk now! (JERKY JACK? YEAAA!)

    I'm going to call the Mosses de Squadro on you Idiots! You're perverted just like Jack, I should never have started this interviu. (INTERVIU??? CHOPPED LEGS??? SWOLLEN FACES??? NUDE WOMEN OBJECTS???) Yes, I know, you saw that part about me in Jack's book, but I saw the part about you encouraging Jack to attack Howdy Donna, not to mention your continuous approval of his relation with Hannah. (HANNAH?? WHAT ABOUT HANNAH????) I'll tell you what about Hannah! Let's say we call Jack's (JACK!!! JACK!!!) book "Autobiography of a Drunken Sex Pervert"? Do you like that? (WE'RE LIKE JACK!! WE DON'T GIVE A SHIT!! YEAAA SHIT!!!) How about if we call it "Confessions of a Shameless Idiot"??? (SHAME ON YOU, SERIOUS JOCKO!!!) I'm getting to you then, aren't I? (GET DOWN!!! GET DOWN!!!) No, I'm the Editor and it's not my Job to scrub the gutter. My clients do that enough already. (BOO! SCRUBBING!!! WE HATE CLEANLINESS!!! WE WANT JACK!! WE WANT MORE SHIT!!) Don't worry Kids (DON'T CALL US THAT!!!) Jack is scrubbing boats (BOOO!!!) now, but he'll find his way back to the Gutter or my name is Mud!!! (YEAAA!!! SERIOUS JOCKSTRAP ADMITS HE'S MUD!! !) Look, you sinister Puppets! Peter is coming her from Germany in two weeks and I think I'd rather discuss Jack's book with him. You Kids (DON'T CALL US THAT!!! ONLY JACK CAN DO THAT!!!) are Brain-washed from spending way too much time with Crazy Jack (WHERE'S JACK??) and Peter has been in Germany for years now, he will be mush more Objective (MUSH!! MUSH!!) Oh, fuck off then. I may edit the title into something like "The Peanut Gallery Are Somehow Worse Fuckers Than Even Amani!", but I now you don't care, right? (DON'T CARE 'BOUT NOTHIN' SERIOUS STRAPPO! !! HA HA HA HA HA HA HA HA HA HA; AND DON'T FORGET THAT ALL PLAY AND NO WORK MAKES GIGOLO JACK OUR KIND OF GUY! !! HA HA HA!! ! ! !)"

Letter from Hannah

August 1992

"Dear Jack,

Thanks for the letter, glad to hear you're doing Okay. Yes I'd like a copy of your book, I think it should be a good souvenir of Barcelona before '92.
    We're doing well here, still clowning etc. Chawakee has just finished school and is going to college in Sept. Tarn is still working with me and is a fine lad. Carl, my husband is very jealous of past boyfriends so don't try to communicate otherwise. He's great however and we're getting on fine.
    All the best, Hannah. x ."

(Author's Note: well... I guess That's That.)

The Abu-Dhabi National Anthem (Tune of 'Goodnight, Irene)

Sontines I live in the Desert,
Sontines I live in another part of the desert,
An sontines I live in another part of the desert,
An sontines I live in another part of the desert,

An sontines we taking all the tents we live in, in the desert,
An moving them to another part of the desert,
An sontines we don like it over there, in the desert,
So we moving our tents to some other place in the desert.

So when we moving to another place over in another part of the desert,
Sontines it gets too hot in that part of the desert.
So we put everything and the tents in bags and then we move everything to some completely different part of the desert.

But one time when we living in a part of the desert,
Some mens come who don live with us there in the desert,
An they digging holes in the sand allover the desert,
So we give them the places they digging holes in the desert,
An they giving us Mercedes-benzes for driving around in the desert.

So, then we moving all our tents to another part of the desert,
An driving Mercedes-benzes all around in the desert,
But getting stuck in the sand in Mercedes-benzes in the desert,
We getting camels to pulling Mercedes-benzes in the desert

So sontines we living in the desert,
An sontines we living in houses in the desert,
An sontines we driving Mercedes-benzes in the desert
An sontines we having camels pulling Mercedes-benzes back on the roads in the desert.

So, sontines we having washing machines in the desert,
An sontines we putting the washing machines next to the road in big piles in the desert,

Because sontines we don have water to where our houses are in the desert,
And sontines we driving Mercedes-benzes to the sand, in the desert.

(FINAL)
So, Sontines I live in the desert,
An sontines I live in a different part of the desert,
An sontines I driving Mercedes-benzes on the road in the desert, but the road only going to the end or the road in the desert,
So, sontines I live in the desert,
But I thinking Maybe I moving to a place where there not so much desert, sontine.

"The Very Bit of It"

"For it is to be, What is to be received,-

The very Bit of It, - indeed,
Shocking,-ugly - & vile —
But still, The Very Bit of It. —

And, whilst the cat plays,

There is, always,
Someone who sees & says
What is & what is not,
The Very Bit cannot be forgot
-Now or Never-

Times Change, from time to time
Indeed-
The Very Bit of It,
The Very Bit of It, Indeed-

So, Your mind's what's left, -
Maybe, even right
But, The Very Bit of It in Sight!

The Waste & the Haste,
For What?
Have we forgot
The loss of Brethren (breathren)
Which bringeth us all here?
Or
Are We to forget the Past
So Raw?

But Still,
Even the present IS!
The Very Bit of It,
Is still & now here
All the time,
Wouldn't You Say?

THE VERY BIT OF IT! indeed."
by Steve, the One-Legged Pirate.

Jack Nicholson is My Favorite Actor

All work and no play makes Jack a dull boy.
All work and no play makes Jack a dull boy.
All work and no play makes Jack a dull boy.
All work and no play makes Jack a dull boy.
All work and no play makes Jack a dull boy.
All work and no play makes Jack a dull boy.
All work and no play makes Jack a dull boy.
All work and no play makes Jack a dull boy.
All work and no play makes Jack a dull boy.
All work and no play makes Jack a dull boy.
All work and no play makes Jack a dull boy.
All work and no play makes Jack a dull boy.
All work and no play makes Jack a dull boy.
All work and no play makes Jack a dull boy.
All work and no play makes Jack a dull boy.
All work and no play makes Jack a dull boy.
All work and no play makes Jack a dull boy.
All work and no play makes Jack a dull boy.
All work and no play makes Jack a dull boy.
All work and no play makes Jack a dull boy.
All work and no play makes Jack a dull boy.
All work and no play makes Jack a dull boy.
All work and no play makes Jack a dull boy.
All work and no play makes Jack a dull boy.
All work and no play makes Jack a dull boy.
All work and no play makes Jack a dull boy.
All work and no play makes Jack a dull boy.
All work and no play makes Jack a dull boy.
All work and no play makes Jack a dull boy.
All work and no play makes Jack a dull boy.
All work and no play makes Jack a dull boy.
All work and no play makes Jack a dull boy.
All work and no play makes Jack a dull boy.
All work and no play makes Jack a dull boy.
All work and no play makes Jack a dull boy.
All work and no play makes Jack a dull boy.
All work and no play makes Jack a dull boy.
All work and no play makes Jack a dull boy.
All work and no play makes Jack a dull boy.
All work and no play makes Jack a dull boy.

All work and no play makes Jack a dull boy.
All work and no play makes Jack a dull boy.
All work and no play makes Jack a dull boy.
All work and no play makes Jack a dull boy.
The quick brown fox jumped over the lazy dogs back.
All work and no play makes Jack a dull dog.
All work and no play makes Jack a dull dog.
All work and no play makes Jack a dull dog.
All work and no play makes Jack a dull dog.
All work and no play makes Jack a dull dog.
All work and no play makes Jack a dull dog.
All work and no play makes Jack a bull dog
All work and no play makes Jack a bull dog.
All work and no play makes Jack a bull dog.
All work and no play makes Jack a dull bog

Arrrest Record

1953   Disturbing the Peace. My first official arrest. Our gang had broken into an old house and stolen a shotgun. (I took it). We were holed up in an abandoned water tower and were going to shoot at the rival gang when they attacked. Someone called the police.

1953   Shoplifting. Got caught outside a supermarket with a bag full of toothpaste and shaving cream to use on Halloween.

1954   Shoplifting. Ball-point pens. Had hundreds of them.

1955   Shoplifting. Sunglasses. Dozens.

1956   Burglary. (Housebreaking). Was breaking into houses on a daily basis for the next three years. Made hundreds of dollars. Booze.

1957   Theft. Stole all the money out of the coke machines at school.

1957   Shoplifting. portable Radios. Had a dozen of them.

1958   Shoplifting. pellet rifle.

1959   Joyriding. Stole Dad's car late at night.

1960   Joyriding. Same deal, different car.

1961   Weapon Possession. Had a straight-razor at school.

1964   Questioned about the windows that were shot out of cars with a bb-gun allover the SF Peninsula. Thousands of them. Larry and I did it but they couldn't prove it. (From 1962 to 1966 I was arrested only once: I was off seeing the world in the navy.)

1966   Tail-light out. Off to jail for warrants. No I.D., didn't pay fine, etc.

1966   Smuggling. Fifty pounds of grass from Mexico. Got Probation due to my War Record and two medals. (YAYY!!)

1967   Possession of Marijuana for sale. Under false name. Got off with probation because it was my first offense.

1967   Tail-light, Dope. One day in SF jail. Bailed out, changed name.

1967   Same. (from here on, all arrests were under phony names til 1980, when I got my birth-name back)

1967   Contributing to the Delinquency of a Minor. Young Girl.

1968   Disturbing the Peace. Both my hands broken in Hippy Riots in the Haight-Ashbury. It was an Accident, I was Drunk.

1968   Young Girl, again. Her mother didn't press charges. Stolen Car, Unidentified Substance. The car wasn't really stolen, I just didn't know who owned it. I chanted my way out of jail.

1968   A few more for tail-lights and possession. Phony names.

Arrrest Record

1968   Creating a Public Nuisance. Palo Alto, I was Yelling downtown.
1968   Disturbing the Peace. SF, I was yelling.
1968   Drinking Alcohol in a Car. Mendocino, I was drinking in a car.
1968   Suspicion of Armed Robbery. San Diego. Innocent. I was walking down the street and the cops stopped me because I had long hair. I was carrying a friend's credit card.
1969   Disturbing the Peace. Santa Cruz. I was yelling.
1969   Ran a Stop-sign. Warrants.
1969   Ran a Red light. San Rafael. No driver's license.
1969   No Visible Means Of Support. Flagstaff, Arizona. passing Thru.
1970   Desecration of the American Flag. Salt Lake City. passing thru, had the flag as a seat-cover in car. Panhandling for gas with a nigger friend with an ear-ring.
1970   Disturbing the Peace. Boulder, Colorado. Hippy Riot. I was printing and distributing an 'underground newspaper' called "Free Rock Concert", which was actually an anarchistic incitement to riot. The cops didn't like my act.
1970   Disturbing the Peace, Drunk Driving. Boulder, three days later. I was driving. I couldn't see. Main Street of Boulder.
1970   Public Nuisance. Chico, California. I was standing on the street.
1971   Hitch-hiking. Golden, Colorado. It's illegal there.
1971   Hitch-hiking. St. Louis. I was on the Interstate.
1971   Hitch-hiking, Disturbing the Peace. Watsonville, California.
1971   Girl. Dope. Palo Alto. Young Chick, she was Innocent.
1971   Threatening to Kill a Dog. Palo Alto. I meant it.
1971   Carrying A Dangerous Weapon. My Mouth. San Francisco.
1973   Drunk Driving. Palo Alto. True.
1975   Drunk Driving. Mt. View. True.
1975   Drunk Driving. Redwood City. True.
1975   Drunk Driving. Redwood City. True.
1975   Drunk Driving. Berkeley. True.
1976   Disturbing the Peace. Yelling.
1977   Drunk Driving. SF. True. I drank a lot in these days; family problems.
1977   Drunk Driving. SF. True. (All these were under different names)
1978   Disturbing the Peace. SF. Arguing with a cop.
1979   Delinquency of a Minor. young Girl.

1980	Sales of LSD. Santa Cruz. Serious Bust, Prison Ahead. It took two years, but I got off with probation after changing my Life.
1981	Assaulting a Police Officer. San Jose. Not True; I argued after running a stop sign.
1982	Disturbing the Peace. Palo Alto. I got in an argument with a clerk in a supermarket.
1984	Disturbing the Peace. SF. Not True; I was sleeping in Golden Gate Park. I argued with the cop when he said I couldn't sleep there. It was a hot afternoon.
1985	Drunk Driving. Cork, Ireland. Not True! Sure, I failed their little blow-up-the-baloon test, but I only had about five pints 'a Guinness. They stopped me at a fookin' road block, anyways.
1986	Suspicion of Smuggling. Anger, France. Not true. We'd just arrived from Ireland the day before. I asked the French Customs Cop, "Do you think we're smuggling hashish FROM Ireland into France? Think about it!" Nevertheless, they brought in the dope-sniffing dog who found Billy's three hash pipes and a booger of hash he'd lost in some clothes. I told Billy, "You Tell Them that's Yours; You Dumb Shit!", 'but they let us go before I had to give him up.
1987	Illegal parking, passport Violation, Badalona. They let me go because I was a clown. I had to leave my bus in Badalona.
1988	Violation of probation. Alameda. Sitting in my brother's office. Cop came in and ran a computer check on me. I had 'technically' violated my 1980 LSD probation by going to Europe. I spent two weeks in jail before I went to court and explained that I'd been in Europe clowning. He let me go.
1990	Clowning Without A Permit. Barcelona. Immigration Violation. Spent three days in a dungeon and three weeks in jail. Deported to New York, the Spanish Government paid. I told the federal judge that "it stinks, what you're doing here, and I'll leave even if you don't deport me. There's been clowning in the street here for over a thousand years." "Nevertheless, you are in violation of the law." Persona Non Gracias from Spain til 1995. Darn, I don't get to see the Olympicas.

The Menu, Meson Hadass

```
MESON HADASS
    MENU del DIA           145 ptas
    ─────────── ✡ ───────────

Primero:   ENSALADA con
              Acietunas
              Cebollas
  ¡Atmosphera Real!   tamatas        ¡Agua Libre!
              Ajo
              Acete
              Sal
              Pimiento negro

Segundo:   ESTOFADO  (con Pan Integral)
              con Huevo!
              Cebollas      Sal
              tamatas       Pimiento Roja o Verde
              Ajo           Bay Leaf
              patatas       Ajo y Garlick
              carrots
              turnips       Lentejas o Frijoles

Tercero:   Postre o dulce con cafe con lech
              (o fruta)

  Vino o cerveza cuando tenemos!        Huevo cortado a Su mesa
  Conversación Libre Siempre Aqui!!     Personal por el Jefe!

  Abierto cuando el Jefe no es enfermo.    Horas Variable.
```

Jack Vickland

Jack Vickland, from Berkeley, California in 1944 was born into a sailing family. He joined the navy at 17 and was a radioman on the SS Coral Sea off the coast of Vietnam. He was the only one with clearance to contact President Johnson for the captain of the ship. Jack was honorably discharged just in time to go to San Francisco and join the hippies. His fate was sealed and he spent the rest of his life in the pursuit of wine, women, and song. He passed away in 2019 in Dilliard, Oregon, where he was living in a trailer on the Umpqua River. He is survived by his wife and three children… and this book!

Made in the USA
San Bernardino, CA
16 August 2019